THE HOAX

Clifford Irving

CORGI BOOKS

TRANSWORLD PUBLISHERS
61–63 Uxbridge Road, London W5 5SA
A Random House Group Company
www.booksattransworld.co.uk

THE HOAX
A CORGI BOOK: 9780552154512

Originally published in Great Britain in 1977 by Allison & Busby Ltd
under the title *Project Octavio*

Corgi edition published 2007

Copyright © Clifford Irving 1972, 1976, 1981, 2007

Clifford Irving has asserted his right under the Copyright, Designs and
Patents Act 1988 to be identified as the author of this work.

A CIP catalogue record for this book
is available from the British Library.

Addresses for Random House Group Ltd companies outside the UK
can be found at: www.randomhouse.co.uk
The Random House Group Ltd Reg. No. 954009

The Random House Group Limited makes every effort to ensure that the
papers used in our books are made from trees that have been legally
sourced from well-managed and credibly certified forests. Our paper
procurement policy can be found on www.randomhouse.co.uk

Typeset in 11/13pt Palatino by
Kestrel Data, Exeter, Devon.
Printed in the UK by
CPI Cox & Wyman, Reading, RG1 8EX

2 4 6 8 10 9 7 5 3 1

Mixed Sources
Product group from well-managed
forests and other controlled sources
www.fsc.org Cert no. TT-COC-2139
© 1996 Forest Stewardship Council

Contents

Part Four

Preface to the 2006 Tie-in Edition

I wrote this book in the months prior to my imprison-ment for the crimes and adventures I've described in these pages. After so much dedicated falsehood, I relished the catharsis of truth-telling.

Now there's a movie based on the book. The pro-ducers, the screenwriter, and the director created their own version of events. They had every right to do that, but I think it's important to realize that the movie doesn't tell the story of what actually happened. It never intended to do so. I hope it's a wonderful movie and wins many awards. If my friends recommend it to me, I'll go see it.

This new edition of the book is dedicated to the memory of my good friend and co-conspirator, Richard Suskind, who departed this earth in November 1998. Dick liked to quote a Gallic philosopher who said, 'Upon arising each morning a man should eat a live chicken, so that for the rest of the day he doesn't have to swallow anything worse.'

I hope you're eating three-star cuisine wherever you are now, Dick. You deserve the best.

My good ex-wife Edith, who figures so prominently in these pages, is alive and well. Recently, on the island of Ibiza, where she still lives and thrives, she celebrated her 70th birthday by cooking a dinner party for eighty people. She had a throne built for herself. Hurray for Edith, the queen of Ibiza.

Nina van Pallandt is alive, too, and back on Ibiza. She lives on the other side of the island from Edith.

As for me, since the hoax I've written a number of books that have been published in fifteen languages. I nest on the Pacific coast of Mexico and in the mountains of Colorado, and I'm married now to Julie, a wonderful Australian woman. My sons are grown, and learning, as I did, that life is challenge and response, and all the rest is pudding.

I believe that the past is fiction, the future is fantasy, and the present for the most part is an ongoing hoax. Please visit my blog at www.cliffordirving.com. I've put some interesting observations there, with more to come.

Clifford Irving
2006

Author's Note

A great deal has been written about the Hughes hoax, including a few truths culled from documents and indictments. The bulk of it, however, has been defensive posturing and gossip masquerading as fact, as well as a plethora of tales woven from the whole cloth. 'But,' asked one critic, in his review of *Hoax* – a book-length compendium of newspaper clippings, misquotations, and muddled journalistic fantasies – 'even if Clifford Irving's own projected book tells the story more fully – who on earth is going to believe it?'

The answer to that question is simple and painful. My wife, Edith, Richard Suskind, and I have testified to the facts – under oath – before Federal and New York State grand juries. An extensive investigation has been conducted, which included the sworn but hitherto unknown testimony of other witnesses, to determine that we told the truth, the whole truth, and nothing but the truth. Robert Morvillo, Chief of the Criminal Division of the United States Attorney's Office of the Southern District of New York, has explained to me – and without mincing his words – that if the facts contained in this book are at variance with sworn testimony and the body of truth known to the prosecutors and the courts, Richard Suskind and I are open to a charge of perjury which carries a sentence of up to five years' imprisonment. We like to think, despite the Kafkaesque quality of the past months, that we are still sane. And no sane man would risk an additional five years in prison.

This book, therefore, contains the truth – however bizarre it may appear to be, and however shamed and regretful I may feel about what happened, particularly in regard to the plight of my wife and children. It bears my name as author, but it is a joint effort of myself and Richard Suskind, as was *The Autobiography of Howard Hughes*. Edith has also contributed recollections of her various journeys to Zurich.

Although he has been consistently pigeonholed and labeled by the press as 'Irving's researcher,' Dick Suskind is and was far more than that. He is an author in his own right, and many of the passages in this book which deal with shared experiences have been written by him from my point of view. We shared the responsibility for the caper and we share the credit, or lack of it, for this final revelation.

And so this book is dedicated to the many friends to whom we lied over the course of the affair and who, when the truth was known, still remained loyal and offered us their unqualified and unstinting help. They know who they are and need not be named.

Clifford Irving
East Hampton, New York
March, 1981

Part One

You may look for motive in an act, but only after the act has been committed. An effect creates not only the search for a cause, but the reality of the cause itself. I must warn you, however, that the attempt to establish relationships between acts and motives, effects and causes, is one of the most time-wasting games ever invented by Man. Do you know why you kicked the cat this morning? Or gave a sou to that beggar? Or set forth for Jerusalem rather than Gomorrah?

– Jean le Malchanceux

1

Genesis in Palma

The *Juan March* stood off the docks of Palma harbor. I needed coffee. A little after eight o'clock of a December morning, not yet full daylight, a raw wind blew off the mountains that fringed the north coast of Mallorca. Shivering, I pulled up the collar of my overcoat as I joined the crowd at the rail.

I spotted Dick Suskind at once. There was no missing that huge bulk, hands jammed in his pockets, planted in front of the terminal building. The gangway was lowered and a few minutes later we were shaking hands and grinning.

'Let's grab coffee here,' Dick said, 'and give Ginette time to get Raphael off to school. Then she'll fix you a real breakfast.'

We sipped our *cafés con leche* at the counter inside the terminal. On each side of us groups of longshoremen were munching thick sandwiches of *sobreasada* and drinking glasses of red wine.

I had telephoned him yesterday from Barcelona to explain that Edith's mother had died ten days before and that with our two boys, Nedsky and Barney, we had flown to Germany for the funeral. We returned to Barcelona in a one-year-old Mercedes sedan, part of Edith's inheritance. A rich man's car – absurd for the island of Ibiza, whose dirt roads made a jeep the ideal vehicle. But it was mine now, and I was willing to learn to live with it. Edith and the kids had taken the morning plane home to Ibiza and I had put the car on the big ferry.

The *Juan March* was not due to continue its passage to Ibiza until eleven. Dick and I had seen each other seldom since he had moved from Ibiza to Mallorca. In those four years he had written and published a handful of history books; now he was halfway through a biography of Richard the Lion-Hearted for teenagers. He had run into a snag: Richard's rampant homosexuality. 'How the hell do you get around something like that? I can't talk about sodomy and buggery – my editor would turn green.' The book was taking a long time to write, and Dick was in trouble. 'I'm in hock to the grocer, the landlady, Raphael's school – you name it. So what's with you? How's Edith? How's the Danish problem?'

I ducked that last one. 'Can't complain,' I said. I was two-thirds of the way through my new novel and I had a four-book contract with my publisher, McGraw-Hill, calling for a total advance of $150,000. I knew that I would have to offer Dick some money before I went on to Ibiza. Par for the course, and no problem. We had borrowed from each other in the past, and had always – although sometimes it took a while – repaid the loans.

'It's no Mercedes,' Dick said cheerfully, opening the door of a battered gray Simca, 'but it gets me there – most of the time.' We started along the coast road toward his home on the outskirts of Palma. A horde of new hotels and apartment buildings had risen since my last visit. I remembered how it had been in 1957, when Dick and I had first met to play chess at a sidewalk cafe in Ibiza: a few scattered hotels, a dozen ancient taxis, empty and pristine beaches where you rarely wore a bathing suit. My hand encountered the stiff crinkling of

14

the *Newsweek* in my overcoat pocket. I pulled it out and opened it to the article on Howard Hughes – 'The Case of the Invisible Billionaire.'

'See this? I read it on the boat last night.'

Hughes had just escaped from his Las Vegas fiefdom to Paradise Island in the Bahamas, from the ninth floor of one hotel to the ninth floor of another. His Nevada empire looked as though it might be toppling. Dick, after a quick glance, turned his attention back to the road. 'What's with that guy?' he said. 'I read the same story in this week's *Time*. There's American decadence and lunacy in a nutshell. That's why I couldn't go back there to live, not even on a bet. The Biafrans are starving, the Pakistanis are starving, *I'm* on the edge of starvation, but some old fart with two billion dollars flies off for a vacation in the Bahamas and the press goes ape. What the hell has Howard Hughes done except discover Jane Russell's tits and build that ridiculous flying boat?'

'It's not what he's done, it's the way he lives. He's the Lone Ranger of big business. He's practically a hermit. Do you know he hasn't been interviewed for fifteen years? The people who work for him have never even met him.'

'I wouldn't be surprised if he was dead and it was all a cover-up for those guys around him to steal the whole boodle.' Laughter rumbled in Dick's chest. 'Why wasn't I born a Mormon?'

'Convert,' I suggested. 'It's never too late. But listen – I've got a wild idea.'

'Your last idea was to ride an elephant from India to Ibiza and have NBC film it and pick up the tab. Just so Edith could start a zoo and have some way to crush tin cans. You were also going to sail to Odessa in that leaky tub you call your yacht. What's the latest brilliancy?'

'Look, I'm laying this on you because you think clearly and you're one of the foremost cynics I know.' Dick chuckled, accepting the compliment. 'If you think I've flipped my lid, tell me so. Okay?'

'You flipped your lid a long time ago, when you took up with the Dane again. So tell me the idea.'

'Well, Hughes fascinates me. There's never been a real biography written about him because he's so secretive. No one can get close to him. Suppose I went to a publisher – let's say my own publisher, McGraw-Hill – and cooked up a scheme with them to pretend I'd met Hughes and he'd commissioned me to write his authorized biography. Authorized, you understand, by The Man himself.' I would do the book, I explained, based on tape-recorded interviews with Hughes – just as I had written my last book, *Fake!*, based on tape-recorded interviews with Elmyr de Hory, the art forger – except that in this case I would never meet Hughes and the interviews would be faked. A hoax, a gorgeous literary caper, in which publisher and author would collaborate.

Dick's eyes swerved to me. 'And you think McGraw-Hill would back you on a thing like that?'

'It's worth a try. They're always looking for best-sellers. Hughes would never be able to surface to deny it, or else he wouldn't bother. I'd *have* to get a publisher to back it because there's a tremendous amount of research involved. It would have to be a definitive biography with plenty of quotes from The Man himself. I bet you they'd pay a hundred grand for a book like that – which we'd damn well need. We'd have to travel all over the States, dig into records wherever Hughes has lived, interview hundreds of people who knew him, see . . .'

'Hold on a minute. *We?*'

'I'm no researcher. Besides, it's too big a job for one man.'

'Listen,' Dick said, 'I think I'd rather ride on the elephant with you. McGraw-Hill's a big outfit, not to mention the most conservative publisher in New York.

16

They'd never go for an idea like that. Put up a hundred thousand bucks for a hoax? You tell them that, man, and then duck. But don't include *me* in it.'

Dick slammed on the brakes at the end of a short, dead-end dirt road marked Calle Gamundi. His poodle gave us a noisy welcome at the iron gate and led the way down the cobbled path. 'You *have* flipped your lid,' Dick concluded. 'But never mind, mental masturbation is an occupational disease. All writers have it. You finish your novel and I'll finish *Richard the Lion-Hearted*, a study in royal medieval pederasty.'

Dick's French-born wife, dark red hair hanging loose about her shoulders, greeted me with a kiss on both cheeks. Bacon and pancakes were already sizzling in separate pans. Dick and I wandered through the house to his study. I started to say, 'How about if Hughes . . .' but Dick cut me off. He wanted to know about the housing situation in Ibiza. He and Ginette missed their old friends there, life on Mallorca was dull and expensive. 'Look around for us,' he said. 'Something big and cheap. And give me a ring. We've both got telephones now, we can keep in touch. I'm lonely. I'm fed up. I feel middle-aged.'

'So do I. It's a funny feeling.'

'"The first forty years is text,"' Dick said, quoting Schopenhauer. '"The rest is commentary."'

'But I don't feel ready to give up writing the text.' Gloomily, I promised to do my best with the house-hunting chore and then, after breakfast we climbed back into the Simca and headed for the docks. The subject of money arose and I parted with 10,000 pesetas, about $150, so that the Suskinds could eat for the first month of the new year. 'Pay me back when you can,' I said. 'I don't give a damn.'

We were still rattling down the hill to join the coast road when I was struck with a variation on the theme. 'Listen, on that Hughes thing, suppose . . .'

'Go to Odessa,' Dick said.

'No, hear me out. You're probably right, no publisher would go for the idea if they knew it was a hoax. But suppose they *didn't* know? Suppose I told McGraw-Hill I was in touch with Hughes. I mean, suppose I convince them it was true. Don't ask me how, just assume I could do it. Assume I could work out a phony private contract between me and Hughes forbidding communication between him and the publishers. Think what a great book could be done, what a great character could be created – using the known facts about the man and inventing the rest. I'd still fake the interviews. I'd still research the book and write it the same way. Only the publisher wouldn't know.'

Dick had listened attentively, slowing down to approach the crossroad of the coast highway. He reached for the stick shift, to gear down into second. 'That,' he said softly, 'is a worthy idea. That's not bad at all . . .'

'They'd put up the money for the research, an advance, and then later . . . maybe . . . when the book was done, I tell them it's a hoax. Or I don't tell them. Who knows? Either way, I keep the rest of the money intact for repayment. And either way there's a book, and it could be a dilly. I'll finish my novel by April or May . . . I could start right after that.'

'Jesus Christ,' Dick murmured. Thinking aloud, I had got through to him. He slammed the gear stick so hard that it snapped off nearly at its base, two inches off the floorboards. *'That could work . . .'*

The Simca drifted off the road and came to a bumpy halt in a patch of cactus. Dick stared dreamily at the length of stick clutched in his thick fingers. 'What a fantastic idea! You know, it *could* work! We could do it . . .'

'We?'

'You asked me to help you before.' He looked indignant. 'Didn't you?'

'Get me to the goddam boat. I've got a wife and two children waiting for me. Think about it for a few days and then I'll call you. And don't get so excited about things – next thing you'll wind up with the steering wheel in your hands.'

Dick trapped the stub of the gear stick between his thumb and forefinger and wiggled the lever into second gear. We chugged along the coast road, concentrating on traffic lights and cars and the minutes ticking away. The *marineros* were already unroping the gangway when we reached the dock. I leaped out, fumbling in my pocket for the boat ticket. Dick snatched at my sleeve.

'Listen, if Hughes is . . .'

'I'll call you,' I promised. 'And drive carefully. And don't lose any sleep over this. It's a wild idea – mental masturbation you called it. There's got to be a dozen snags in it. So think about it. I'll call you,' I repeated, and stumbled up the swaying gangway.

2

Wife and Mistress

The Old Town of Ibiza soared dramatically from the dark blue Mediterranean, a pyramid of white cubes crested by the cathedral tower. The bay sparkled under the sharp light of the winter sun. I scanned the quay searching for Edith, who had promised to meet the boat with the children. There was no sign of her. An hour later the *marineros* had finally unloaded the Mercedes and still she had not appeared. I drove home, out the San José road into the countryside, with a slightly sick feeling in my stomach. When Edith said she would do something, she did it.

The *finca* was four miles out of town, a converted 15-room peasant farmhouse festooned with bougainvillaea and held together by 300 years of whitewashing, rambling over an acre of rocky land and gardens. The monkey, Eugen, whom I had won in a poker game back in 1966 and given to Edith as a birthday present, was always the first to hear a car purr or snort up the dirt driveway. As I jumped out with a suitcase clutched in each hand and a straw Ibizenco basket hanging from my shoulder, I heard her squealing. The front door was open. The uproar alerted Nedsky and he raced out, blond hair rumpled and flowing, yelling: 'Daddy! Daddy!' Dropping a suitcase, I scooped him up in one arm. Barney was next door, I guessed, teasing the chickens of Antonia, the peasant neighbor who tended our gardens and acted as his honorary grandmother.

'Where's Mommy?' I asked.

Inside the house, crammed with antique French furniture, books, and paintings, Edith appeared from the kitchen. She wore jeans and an old corduroy shirt and her honey-colored hair fell to her shoulders. Her face was drawn, unsmiling.

'What the hell's going on?' I thumped down in an overstuffed chair with Nedsky on one knee. 'I looked for you at the boat. I got scared to death. I thought the plane crashed, or you cracked up the car, or God knows what. Home is the sailor, home from the sea. What's behind all this good cheer I'm greeted with?'

'This,' Edith said, and tossed an envelope in my lap. I could see now that she had been crying. My anger vanished. I reached out to touch her but I knew what was in the envelope before I even saw it.

'I went this morning to the bank,' Edith said, 'what I thought would be a favor to you, to pick up your mail.'

'And who told you to open it?'

'I *knew*. I don't know the handwriting, but I catched one look at that letter and I smelled it. I knew it was from her.'

'Caught,' I said, 'not "catched."' Born in Germany and educated in Switzerland, her English grammar was roguish and unpredictable; and to me, endearing. But she was in no mood for lessons today.

The envelope bore a London postmark but no return address. The scrawled note inside was unsigned. I scanned it.

Darling,
     I heard through the grapevine that you were in London last month. You bastard – I agree that we

21

agreed not to see each other, but you could have
called me at least. I'll be coming to Ibiza in January.
Do you think I could pop up to the studio and that
you could spare a minute to see me?

'That bitch,' Edith raged. 'The madonna that smiles so
sweetly and swears to my face – just last summer! – that
she doesn't know whether or not she loves you, and you
swear it's only platonic or some such bullshit. And what
she does is try to steal another woman's husband! If I see
her on the street in Ibiza,' Edith vowed, tears beginning
to film her eyes, 'I cut her face with a razor. If she comes
up to your studio, I kill her.'

I coaxed Nedsky out of the room and told him to
find Barney and Antonia and Rafaela, the maid. Then I
turned to Edith, who sat on the red leather couch, head
buried in her hands.

'Darling, listen. I *didn't* see her in London. I didn't
even call her. That's the whole point, isn't it?'

Raising her head, Edith said scornfully: 'You couldn't.
You were with me. If you'd been alone you would have
called her.'

'Never,' I lied. 'It's over. We agreed to that. She agreed
to it, too. I haven't seen her since last summer and you
know that's true. And she's not asking for anything in
her letter. For Christ's sake, read it! All she asks is can
she pop up to the studio for a minute to see me. Is that
so godawful?'

For nearly an hour the argument veered back
and forth, raking up the past, bemoaning the present,
portraying either a bleak or blood-drenched future. She
was the hurt wife who feared the other woman. I was
the man who knew the truth but dared not say it. Her
world was that of a fairytale where the prince and
princess lived happily ever after in a castle in Spain, safe
from all dragons. Her rage rose to a volcanic crescendo
when I said: 'It's a perfectly innocent letter, and if you'd

read it without being prejudiced and without hating her guts, you could see that.'

'You mean she calls you "darling" and that's innocent? What you think I am, a fool? One of your mindless sluts you lay because you're bored with your wife, your home, your children, your work, your life?'

I winced inwardly. Her words had jabbed at the periphery of a truth – not the center, but close enough to make me uneasy and want to veer away.

A vase filled with red and purple geraniums, freshly picked from the garden for my homecoming, stood on the big coffee table. Edith sprang to her feet, snatched up the vase in both hands, and smashed it on the tile floor at my feet. I had jumped up, trying to duck to safety, but it was too late. Glass flew in all directions, water drenched my trousers and shirt, and a few of the geraniums, by some law of physics that still puzzles me, landed on top of my head. With that red and purple wreath garlanding my soaked hair, and water dripping down my cheeks, I stood astonished, unable to speak. I checked for blood and embedded glass, but there were only flowers.

'You fool,' Edith said, trying to keep a straight face.

There was nothing to do after that but laugh, and then kiss and make up, which we had done so many times before.

I unpacked the car and then, later in the day after a siesta, drove up to my studio. Five miles from the house, behind the Roman walls of the Old Town of Ibiza and perched on a rock that jutted out above the sea, reached only by a narrow, winding dirt road, the studio was my sanctuary from the world. It had long been agreed between us that Edith only came there by invitation. The sun flooded in through the glass doors and there was no need to turn on the gas heater. I sat down at the desk, shoved the pages of my novel to one side, and stared out at the sea.

23

If my life had had any design for the past seven years, it had been woven chiefly of four threads: Ibiza, my work, Edith Sommer, and Nina van Pallandt.

Ibiza was home. I had first come there in 1953, settling there to work for a season because it was cheap and old and exotic and beautiful: all that Europe should be for a young American who dreamed of being a writer. *La isla blanca,* the Spaniards called it – the white island. I kept coming back. By 1970 I had written four novels there and a book about Elmyr de Hory, the art forger who was my neighbor, and for a writer the place you work well in is often the place you wind up calling home. I had good friends there, a house, a sailboat, an easy life. But more than that, for me, it was the place where everything that seemed important in my life had happened. Claire, my second wife, who had died in a California car crash when she was eight months pregnant, had been introduced to me on Ibiza. Then, in 1960, wandering along the port, I saw a girl of fragile beauty whose red hair sparkled like warm blood in the sun. Her name was Fay. We traveled around the world, we were married, we had a son, and we were divorced – which is a poor way to sum up five years, but the story has no place in this tale.

Again on Ibiza – before that divorce, in the spring of 1964 – I met Nina van Pallandt.

I was separated from Fay, who was living in the village of Santa Eulalia while I had a small apartment in the Old Town of Ibiza. Nina, Danish born, was married to Frederik van Pallandt, a bearded, good-looking Dutch baron who fancied himself an intellectual and a guru in the mysteries of the Sufi sect. I had met Frederik some months before and after fifteen minutes' conversation with him had a feeling of *déja entendu;* his speeches reminded me of the discussions we had indulged in during my sophomore philosophy courses at Cornell.

24

He and Nina sang folksongs for a living and had a strong following among the mums and dads of the English midlands. In public they were the golden couple: beautiful, talented, titled, and in love, with two beautiful, golden-haired children. In private life they were miserable – 'You and the children,' he had said to her once, 'are the stones round my neck that keep me from becoming the man I need to be' – although they kept up what pretence they could for the sake of their career.

The pretence vanished when Nina and I met. Frederik had bought a yacht and was sailing it down from England to Ibiza, where they were building a summer home. Nina and I, and two friends, were part of an expedition to dig for Phoenician relics on the north coast of the island. We toiled up a mountainside in the hot spring sun and then dug for hours, with our hands, in the cool of the cave. A few potsherds and a cracked head of the goddess Tanit were our reward, and if the goddess had visited a curse on those who ravaged her resting place, we were its victims. What words we exchanged that day I have long forgotten. When you fall in love, other voices speak to you and the words you really hear are of little consequence.

We were together for three weeks when Frederik returned unexpectedly to Ibiza. He had been seasick in the English Channel, gone ashore in France, and entrusted the yacht to its crew for the remainder of the passage to Spain.

'I can't lie to him,' Nina said, and I replied: 'Don't. Tell him the truth. I love you and I want you to go away with me.'

She came to me the next afternoon in tears. Frederik, she said, had begged her not to go, had pleaded: 'Don't take my children from me . . .'

'He wants to try again. He took me for granted. He never realized he could lose me. He swears it will be different.'

'And what do you want, Nina?'

'I don't know . . .'

A week later she was still on the rack of uncertainty, torn between her husband, her children, her career, her guilt – and a man she had known for less than a month. 'I love you, my sweet, but I can't throw it all away. I can't do it to him.'

'Then stay with him.'

'Is that what you want?'

'No. I want you with me,' and she added, sobbing, 'I can't let you go, either.'

But she was pinned to the rack and as it stretched her day by day, she grew weaker and thinner and came to me each time bearing the scars. The great blue eyes that had always smiled with such wistful pleasure were permanently filmed with tears. The lines cut deeper into her cheeks and she would rock back and forth in a chair, her mass of golden hair cupped by suddenly veined hands. It was an agony for her, and I heard her repeat Frederik's constant refrain: *'Don't take my children from me . . .'*

My own marriage to Fay had ended six months earlier and I had lost a two-year-old son. As much as compassion I had my own guilt, my own fears.

'You can't decide,' I said.

'No. Don't you see that I can't? Clifford, tell me what to do.'

We were sitting on the rocks by the sea, on a headland near the town of Ibiza. 'Go back to him,' I said. 'You have to. What you're doing now will kill you. Give it a chance. You love him, I know that. You're in love with me but maybe it will pass. Call it a summer romance that came a little out of season.'

She looked at me solemnly. 'Do you believe that?'

'No,' I said after a while. 'I don't believe it for a minute. But you're going back to him and so I've got to pretend it's true, for the sake of sanity. And so do you.'

I said goodbye to her and left her there on the rocks above the sea, the tears unchecked and streaking her cheeks and her body huddled on the stone, shaking.

The memory of Nina lay between Edith and myself from the beginning, when we met that summer while I was finishing my fourth novel, *The 38th Floor*. I still had the apartment in the Old Town and Edith owned a small *finca* in the country. She was Swiss, a painter, a lovely and ebullient 28-year-old girl who prized her independence above everything else. When I met her in July, she had two daughters and was separated from her husband, a German industrialist from the Ruhr. By December they were divorced. We let love come to us slowly, with neither pressure nor promises, and in January we began living together. The *finca* on the San José road became our home.

But the shadow of Nina was always there. I had some money for the first time in my life and Edith and I traveled through southern Spain, to Morocco, to the West Indies. She was the most giving woman I had ever known and she held back nothing, but the shadow followed me. I knew from mutual friends that Nina and Frederik's marriage had cracked within a year of our parting; the only thing holding it together was their career. And in the summer of 1966 she came to my studio at Los Molinos and the affair began again. For both of us it was an obsession that lurked below the surface of our lives, ready to spring forth at a look from the far corner of a room, the mention of a name, the sudden flicker of memory. Call it love, call it madness – it may have been both. The only difference now was the presence in my life of Edith. I wanted her, too, and I refused to turn away from a harmony and warmth that grew season by season. Call it love, call it greed – again, it may have been both. The man who is willing to define his love has proved its artifice.

In January of 1967 I went to New York for a month, and Nina flew north from a holiday in Antigua to meet me. We were together in the city for almost two weeks, and word of the rendezvous leaked back to Ibiza. When I came back in February to the *finca* on the San José road, Edith was with someone else. My clothes were packed. 'Go,' she begged.

Her hurt and my guilt were too much for me to deal with. I moved to my studio in Los Molinos. Nina was in London, still with Frederik, still unhappy, busily decorating a new apartment on the Chelsea embankment. We wrote to each other, but she was too involved to leave and I felt, instinctively, that it would be a mistake for me to go to her. Whatever was to happen would have to happen in its own time. We were all in flux and I knew somehow that to fly from one woman to another would be to follow the path of a fool. Nina, equally unsure, knew it too.

Edith left the island for a month, but when she returned I was at the airport to meet her, and I said: 'It's you I love. If you feel the same way, forgive me, and let's try again.'

Wounds of the sort that we had inflicted on each other heal slowly. Edith was uncertain and I was restless. Throughout the end of May we read the papers and listened to the radio, and in that season the Arab threats against Israel mounted to a crescendo. I talked with several Jewish friends on the island. We considered volunteering. We could drive a bus in Tel Aviv, we could do whatever was needed. It was quixotic, but our feelings were real; yet inertia triumphed and we did nothing. On June 2, 1967, I left the island on the night boat to Alicante, headed for Gibraltar where I had to change the license plates on my old Peugeot station wagon. The next afternoon, in Granada, I read that Israeli tanks had broken into the Sinai desert. The Spanish newspapers carried only the stories of Egyptian victories.

I telephoned the Israeli Embassy in Paris and was told that no flights were leaving for Tel Aviv. I went on to Gibraltar and then back up to Malaga before I made up my mind. I flew to Paris, and there I waited. Two days after the war officially ended, flights began; I booked the only seat available on an Air France jet and cabled Edith: *FLYING ISRAEL CONTACT ME KING DAVID HOTEL JERUSALEM TRUST ME LOVE YOU CLIFF.*

In Jerusalem I was able to get press credentials. When I had flown out I hadn't really known why I was going, other than out of some primitive streak of Jewishness and the driving need simply to be there. But as soon as I had gone to the Golan Heights and spoken to the soldiers, I knew there was one thing I could do: write a book. On the way back from Jericho I stopped with another correspondent at the King David Hotel. A telegram awaited me at the desk. I read: *ARRIVING ISRAEL ALITALIA FLIGHT THURSDAY NIGHT TRUST ME TOO LOVE YOU TOO EDITH.*

Her coming to Israel was an act of bravery. You had to know Edith's history to understand. Born Catholic, she had been a child in Germany during the Second World War, the youngest daughter of a Swiss clockmaker in a southern Alpine town. She had lived through the bombings, had seen her mother and father led away by the Nazis to be shot, then rescued at the last minute by a local official. War for Edith was a memory of nightmare. If she read a book with true tragedy in it she would often cry, and if she saw a movie with bloody scenes or torture she would leave the theater, trembling. The fighting in the Middle East was over, but it lingered in the aftermath in both sight and smell. She had flown out because I was there. She faced it with great simplicity. I was her man, and she would follow me.

We traveled together to the Dead Sea, Gaza, the Syrian Heights, and then down through Sinai in a convoy with Irwin Shaw, Martha Gellhorn, and Jules Dassin. We trailed the convoy in a jeep, accompanied by a myopic captain of Israeli Intelligence who carried only an old rifle. The desert was full of stragglers from the routed Egyptian Army. I drove while Edith perched uncomfortably in the back of the jeep atop a litter of supplies, busily sewing two flags. One of them was white with a red cross, the other red with a white cross. 'What the hell are you doing back there?' I asked.

Finishing her handiwork, she held it up proudly. 'One is the Red Cross flag, the other Swiss. If we meet any Egyptians, I wave both. The soldiers, the poor ones, will recognize the Red Cross flag. The officers will recognize the Swiss flag because they all have bank accounts there.'

Two things of moment happened to us in Israel. We fell in love again, and we decided to get married and have a child. I bought a thin gold wedding ring from a local jeweler and put it on Edith's hand. And then, one day in the lobby of the Dan Hotel, interviewing an Israeli pilot, I ran out of tape. I asked Edith to get a fresh reel from my suitcase upstairs. In the suitcase she found Nina's last letter to me, still unanswered.

'One thing,' Edith said, a cold but somehow frightened light in her amber-green eyes. 'You write to *her*. Tell her it's all over, and you don't want to see her again.'

I felt trapped into an act that seemed final – and where I wanted, I realized, no finality.

'Is that an ultimatum?'

'I want you to do it,' Edith said, unswerving. 'And then you give it to me to mail. *You must.*'

I sat down at the desk and wrote the letter, sealed it, and then Edith went downstairs and dropped the envelope into the mailbox.

* * *

30

By any standards, the years from 1967 on were good ones for me. They started disastrously, in December of that year, two days after we were married, when a fire in my father's New York apartment destroyed the book I was writing about the Six-Day War and the almost-finished draft of a 900-page novel. But then I wrote *Fake!*, which sold well, although not up to expectations. Like most writers, I blamed it on the publisher's failure to promote it properly. And that summer, on Ibiza, my mother suffered a stroke which left her paralyzed in a Manhattan nursing home.

But at the center of my life I felt a sense of well-being. In April 1968, Edith gave birth to a son. His given name was John-Edmond and we came to call him Nedsky. A year and a half later Barney was born. I wrote a screenplay and started a new novel. With Edith, I thought, I could live out the rest of my life and make no fundamental compromises; I could graduate from the shadowy evening of my youth to what I supposed would be a calmer middle-age, because I loved my wife, my children, my home. I could keep in check the restlessness that had dogged me for so many years. I had found an answer. Beside the wife whom I loved and who expected so much from me, I had a mistress whom I loved – and she expected very little. I had Nina.

The letter from Tel Aviv had kept us at bay for more than a year, but in the winter of 1968, on Ibiza, we met again. Our affair had never ended and we came to believe that it would probably never end. We would make no promises, we would have no hopes, but we would take from each other whatever sustenance and joy was there when the season was ripe. To both myself and Nina I said repeatedly: 'Edith must never know. Edith must never be hurt.'

And Nina would echo my words and add: 'She loves you too much, and I know you love her. You'd be a fool to leave her, because what we have together is good the

31

way it is. And I don't know where I'm going. I don't know what's going to happen to me . . .'

She and Frederik had finally separated. He had his own apartment in London. He had fathered a child by another girl. That, for Nina, had stifled whatever qualms she may have felt about declaring her independence. We saw each other when and where we could, without rocking my domestic boat, from 1968 onward. Of necessity, I lived with the assumption that Edith suspected little and knew nothing. In July, returning from my father's funeral in New York, I stayed three days with Nina in her London flat.

The only real crisis of those years came two weeks later, on Ibiza. A rapprochement had been in effect for a long time; the island was small, we had too many mutual friends not to meet from time to time at a party or at the Salinas beach. For her birthday party, Nina asked Edith and me to dinner together with a dozen other people. Throughout the evening Nina and I never danced, never touched. Once, at the candlelit dinner table in the big beamed kitchen of Nina's *finca*, we looked at each other. The look was neither brief nor long. No word was spoken. But what passed silently between us across the pine table must have had an eloquence that neither of us knew how to conceal.

Driving home, Edith said: 'I know now. And I think I've always known. You looked at her in a way you haven't looked at me since the time we first met.' Her voice was weary, almost dispassionate. 'You're still in love with her. What I beg you – don't deny it.'

And at home, in the living room, after we had talked until four o'clock in the morning, I no longer tried to deny it. I dug for the truth, but all I reached was confusion – and Edith's tears. 'Do you want to go with her?' Edith cried.

'No.'

'Then will you give her up? Will you stop seeing her?'

'I can't do that,' I said, and felt I would strangle on the words.

Two days later, on a hot July afternoon, Edith drove out the Santa Eulalia road and up the mountain to Nina's *finca*. It was the first time in more than three years that they had ever talked alone. All Edith demanded to know was what Nina wanted from me. 'Do you love Cliff?' she asked, and Nina replied: 'I don't really know . . .'

'I can't live with him, this way, with a man divided, killing him and killing me worse. If you want him,' she said brutally, 'you take him. I pack his clothes and he'll go.'

'I don't know if I want it,' Nina said. 'And I won't break up a marriage. You have two children. He loves them, and he loves you. I couldn't do it.'

'Then let him be,' Edith pleaded. 'Don't see him again. Can you at least save my life and agree to that?'

'Yes,' Nina said at length. 'I won't see him any more.'

Edith returned to the house on the San José road. She had humiliated herself, but she had won. 'And you?' she said to me. 'Do *you* agree?'

'Yes,' I said, because there was no other way.

That was where things stood in December of 1970, five months after our promises, on the day that Edith found Nina's letter waiting for me at the bank and on the same day that I returned to Ibiza from Palma where I had said to Dick Suskind: 'I've got a wild idea . . .'

3

The Ibiza Mob

Peace returned swiftly to our household. After all, it was
Christmas. In our living room we laid the new red and
gold carpet we had bought in Germany and carried
down on the rack of the Mercedes. After an hour of
sweating and tugging I fell heavily into the big purple
easy chair.

'Beautiful!' I surveyed hearth and home. 'And now I
need a drink.'

Sipping a bourbon, I remembered for the first time the
discussion that Dick and I had in Palma the morning
before. The monkey munched ferociously in her cage
and Edith settled down on the sofa to work on the
sweater she was knitting for Barney. The Christmas tree
winked and blinked in the corner, almost touching the
thousand-year-old *sevinas* beams of the roof. I put a
Mozart quintet on the record player. In half an hour
Nedsky and Barney would come barreling in from the
other side of the house where Rafaela, our Spanish
maid, tried to keep them in check until seven o'clock in
the evening. Domesticity! The beast was in his habitat, at
rest. I thrived on it; we were content. Swiss tooth and
claw only showed when the feline Dane cried softly
from the steamy depths of the jungle.

'I had a funny talk with Dick,' I said. 'Came from an

idea I got on the boat. I was reading *Newsweek* . . .' I started to sketch out the general idea and Edith glanced up from her knitting, bewildered.

'Who's Howard Hughes?' she asked.

'One of the two or three richest men in the world.'

'Then he must be a schmuck,' and she went back to knitting, having disposed of the invisible billionaire with one philosophical stroke.

I explained, as best I could – since I knew little more than what I read in the magazine – why Hughes was a man of many parts and why people were interested in him. I was vague in declaring that the book itself would be a hoax and soon I realized that Edith's attention was wavering.

'Come on,' I said, 'you always complain that I never talk to you. So now I'm talking to you. And what do you do? You knit!'

She looked up sharply. 'I don't understand whether you know this man Hughes or you don't know him, or you're going to meet him or not meet him. But whatever, my advice is you should finish your novel first, that is more important than a book about a crazy man with a billion dollars.' I must have looked slightly crestfallen, because she suddenly dropped her knitting and floated across the room to pat me on the cheek. 'Do your novel, darling. If you write this book afterwards, about the crazy man, it must be full of soul-vomit. You know? A man who tells everything! You say he builded all these airplanes and drilled for oil in Texas . . .'

'No, his father invented a drilling bit. Hughes went to Hollywood and made a movie called *Hell's Angels* – '

'Okay. But make sure the book's got plenty of soul-vomit. That's what the kitchen maids like to read.'

I fell silent, thinking of the implications, Edith had not understood the nature of the project, she provided me with a key. *Soul-vomit* was one of her favorite expressions: the uninhibited pouring forth of emotion and sentimentality, of love and hate, aspiration and frustration. Soul-vomit – in this case, the accumulated wisdom, or lack of it, of a long and hyperactive lifetime; all the quirkiness and eccentricity which a billionaire recluse could manifest and which he had dammed up inside of him for lack of a suitable audience. If we chose, he would be a mouthpiece for all the opinions which Dick and I had only occasionally voiced in our own books – because who, after all, was interested in the philosophical meanderings of a couple of journeyman writers? But Hughes? I thought of the old Jewish folk saying: 'When you're rich, you're handsome, you're intelligent, you have impeccable taste, and, my, how beautifully you sing!' Hughes was rich, and if we did the book, he would sing . . .

'That's wonderful, darling,' I said, 'that's . . .'

But Edith was no longer with me. She was slowly turning the pages of a book on Salvador Dali. And a minute later the children thundered into the room, Nedsky yelling to be hoisted to my lap and Barney heading straight for Eugen's cage, rattling the bars and cooing his adoration.

I woke next morning with a cold and a fever, and spent the day in bed dosing myself with a variety of vitamins and antibiotics. It wasn't until the third day after my return from Palma that I went to the studio, intending to work. The telephone began to ring as I was inserting the key in the lock.

It was Dick, more frustrated and anxious than I had ever heard him. 'Where the hell have you been? I've been trying to get you for two days!' I started to explain but he cut me off. 'Listen. We've got to get this thing on the road!'

'What thing?'

'The Hughes thing, schmuck!'

'I want to finish my novel first,' I said patiently.

'Forget it! You can always write a novel, but you only get one chance to do the authorized biography of Howard Hughes. If he's not dead already, he's old and sick. Suppose he kicks off before the spring? You'd piss and moan for the rest of your life.'

'Dick, I've got other troubles. Edith went to the bank for my mail . . .' He chopped me off again before I could tell the woeful tale. 'Suppose someone else comes up with the same idea? You know how often two books on the same subject are published at the same time. Hughes is in the air right now. He's there to be plucked! Anyone might do it, and if it's not us you'll kick yourself in the ass till you're black and blue. Now listen . . .' He went on and on, giving one reason after another why we should plunge immediately into the project, until finally I grew testy and said: 'I can't sit here and bullshit with you by the hour. I really want to finish this novel first, and I've been sick, and I haven't had the time to look for your goddam *finca*. Why don't you come over for a couple of days? We can talk about it and you can check out the housing situation.'

I expected him to suggest visiting in a week or two, but he said: 'Great. I'll be on tomorrow morning's plane,' and hung up before I could object.

It was a cold blustery day, with gusts of rain beating against the glass door that led to the terrace of the studio. Formentera, smallest of the Balearic Islands, hung as a gray smudge on the horizon. Yesterday, when I had spoken to Dick on the telephone, it had been so cleanly incised against the sky that I could count the houses scattered like cubes of sugar along the coast.

Dick was hunched down in the big green armchair with his hands under his oak-like thighs. The electricity had broken down, as it often did during a rainstorm, and the butane heater wasn't working because it had run out of gas.

'I still think we should wait until I've finished my novel,' I said.

'I thought we'd settled that. Anyhow,' he held up his hand to forestall my objection, 'let's leave it for now and talk about the project. First: how do we sell it, and who do we sell it to?'

'Well, *if* we do it, I guess we try McGraw-Hill.' I hesitated, bothered instantly by the thought. They had been publishing me for nine years – of course they were the logical choice. They had the money and they knew I delivered on my promises, and usually without too much delay beyond the supposed deadline. 'But I hate to go to them. They trust me. They have confidence in me.'

Dick raised his eyes ceilingward in silent supplication. 'Schmuck,' he said, a measure of pity in his voice. 'That's the name of the game.'

I smiled ruefully. 'I see the point. You're driving me nuts. Okay. In a few days, when everyone's recovered from New Year's, I'll write them a letter. I'll let it drop that I've been in touch with Hughes, that I sent him a copy of *Fake!* and he liked it. That's innocent enough, and it doesn't commit me to anything. One step at a time, yes?'

Dick nodded his approval. 'Who will you write to? Beverly?'

Beverly Loo was then subsidiary rights editor, and the only one of the old guard – from the early 1960's when I signed my first contract with McGraw-Hill – who still remained in the Trade Book Division. A round-faced Chinese-American girl born in Los Angeles, she was the daughter of a veteran Hollywood actor who had played the parts of several hundred Chinese, Japanese, and North Korean villains. Over the years we had become friends, and Beverly had once flown down from the Frankfurt Book Fair to spend a week with us in the *finca* on Ibiza, where she drove Edith crazy by breakfasting on cold baked beans and bloody marys and talking nonstop about publishing and publishers. She was single, living alone in a small but chic 57th Street apartment with her dog, who seemed to be one of the two major passions of her life. The other was the McGraw-Hill Book Company. She was a company woman wrapped up in the cocoon of the publishing world almost to the exclusion of all other pursuits. If she grumbled to me occasionally that McGraw-Hill paid her less than she was worth – because she was a woman, and company policy decreed that women received less pay for equal work – the discontent rarely lasted. The thought of leaving Mother McGraw for richer pastures at another publishing house never seemed to touch her mind. 'But if you ever *do* go,' I had said to her, 'I go, too. I can't have loyalty to a company. Only to people.'

'That's another thing that troubles me,' I said to Dick. 'She's a friend. I may be a prick about women and a few other things, but I don't stab my friends in the back. If I get Beverly involved . . .'

He snorted. 'She won't be the one making the decisions. This kind of thing will go right to the top.'

That – 'the top' – was anonymous enough to quell my first uprising of conscience. 'Okay,' I promised. 'I'll write to Beverly.'

'And then?'

'You sound like Nedsky when I tell him a bedtime story. "And then? And then, Daddy?" Then we'll have to wait. We'll see what she says. If they swallow the bait, I'll wait a month or two and then take a crack at writing a letter from Hughes to me. I can use that *Newsweek* inset as a model.'

'What do you mean?' Dick's eyes widened. 'You'll forge a letter?'

'How the hell else am I going to convince them that I'm in touch with Howard Hughes? What did he do, parachute out of the sky over Ibiza, land in our rose garden, and say, "Clifford Irving, I dub thee my biographer."?'

'Can't you just say he called you?'

'Then all I've got going for me is my word on it. McGraw-Hill trusts me and loves me, but it's not puppy love. You said it yourself – they're a big, conservative publisher. They're not going to give me a contract just because I tell them I'm talking to Howard Hughes on the telephone. Put yourself in their place. Would you believe me?'

'I might,' Dick said brightly.

'Well, that's why you're a starving writer and not the head of the McGraw-Hill Book Company. And even if you believed me, *Señor* McGraw, would you sign a six-figure contract and put up the money?'

Dick's brightness faded. He shook his head glumly.

'So the only thing to do,' I said, trying to cheer him up a little, 'is write a letter from Hughes to me.'

'But how can you do it? For Christ's sake – forgery is a *profession.*'

I could hardly argue the point. In the mid-1940's, as an art student at the High School of Music and Art in Manhattan, I had helped my father with the lettering on his comic strips, 'Willie Doodle' and 'Pottsy.' In those same years I was a Dodger fan and one September I cut school three or four times and journeyed by subway out to Brooklyn to cheer the Flock to victory in a crucial series against the Cardinals. Such absence from school required an explanatory note from a parent. On two occasions I lettered the notes in my father's familiar printing. *Please excuse my son's absence from school on Thursday. He had a cold. Yours truly, Jay Irving.* And that was the extent of my experience in the arts of forgery.

'But I can try,' I said to Dick. 'After all, what are they going to compare it to? There's only that little inset in *Newsweek.* They don't have any letters from Howard Hughes lying around the office. Hell, I could use any handwriting I wanted, just so long as it was on yellow legal paper.'

Dick was beaming again. He gave a little chuckle, like a happy Buddha. 'You may be right.'

'The only problem is I don't have any yellow legal paper.'

'*I* do,' Dick said. 'About half a pad. I'll send it to you from Palma.'

We drove back through the rain to the *finca*. Edith had set out a bowl of salad and plates of cold cuts, with a bottle of red Rioja to wash it down. Food and wine vanished, our appetites whetted by the morning's conversation. Chortling like a child with a new toy, Dick examined one facet after another of the project. Edith listened, trying her best to understand. 'The best thing we've got going for us,' Dick said for the tenth time, 'is Hughes's absolute refusal to appear in court.'

'But suppose this time he does it? What then?'

'*Ach, Mensch!*' Edith's eyes sparked. 'Then you look at him and say: "*Aber* – but you're not Howard Hughes!"'

'Sure,' Dick said. 'You say, "Help! I've been duped."'

'You mean Max duped me?' I said.

'Who's Max?' Dick asked.

'Max? Don't you know Max? Max is a con man. He's one of Howard's doubles.'

Dick's eyes shone with delight. 'He looks like Hughes, he speaks like Hughes, he knows all about Hughes. But is he Hughes?'

'*Nein!*' Edith cried, jumping to her feet and thrusting out her almost-flat chest in a heroic pose. 'He's Super-*mensch!*'

'Hold on a minute,' I said to Edith. 'You don't even know what this is all about, so you can keep out of it. And stay out – don't get involved with two lunatics.' I turned to Dick. 'And you're talking like we've decided to *do* this thing. I'm a slow thinker. I've told you nineteen times already that I want to finish the novel before I

41

even think about doing this. Why the hell are we going through these contortions?'

'Because you're getting hooked on the idea,' Dick said, grinning. 'Admit it, for Christ's sake.'

'In theory,' I admitted. 'This is all theoretical.'

But our theorizing became more intense and intricate that afternoon in the studio, when we came to discuss the problem of what to do with the theoretical money. We had already, in buccaneer fashion, brazenly assumed that I could convince McGraw-Hill I was meeting Howard Hughes, get a contract from them and an advance payment to do the research. Why? Well, why not? The world was mad, wasn't it? Didn't every sane man know that? Where the plan came a cropper was in the realization that Hughes himself would have to be paid for his cooperation in the project. A check would at some point have to be drawn payable to Howard Hughes. But who would cash it?

'Only Hughes,' I said, 'and there's the rub, *amigo*. The authenticity goes out the window if a check can't pass through one of his bank accounts.'

We hammered away at the problem while Dick paced back and forth in front of the heater and finally reached a solution. We would have to do what every other person with illegal or 'funny' money did; we would look toward Switzerland, with its hitherto unbroken code of bank secrecy. 'I don't see any other way to go,' I said. 'We've got to have an account in the name of Howard Robard Hughes, and we damn sure can't have it in the States where anyone can just pick up a phone and find out who opened it. I think Edith's got an extra passport somewhere in the house – some mixup with the Swiss Consulate in Barcelona a few years ago – and I'll see if I can change it around.'

'Who'll use it? Never mind – don't answer that. I know who.' Dick shoved a pile of books and newspapers to one side and sat down heavily on the bed.

I laughed. 'Have some passport photos made. Grow a mustache and powder your temples. Rent a wheelchair.'

'It won't work. I mean, look at me . . .' Dick's down-sweeping glance took in all six-foot-two-and-a-half inches and two hundred eighty pounds of him. 'I'm too easy to remember, mustache or no mustache. And who'll push the wheelchair? You? How about . . .' He mentioned several mutual friends on Ibiza and quickly vetoed them. 'No, we've got to keep this in the family. Do you think Edith . . . ? No, that wouldn't work, either. It has to be a man.'

I walked to the window, leaned my forehead against the icy glass, and thought for a moment. 'You're wrong,' I said slowly. 'It *wouldn't* have to be a man – not if the bank signature is *H.R.* Hughes instead of *Howard R. Hughes* . . .'

It was as if we were still playing the writer's game – constructing an outline for an absurd thriller with characters but no coherent plot. I turned. 'But first, let's see if I can find the passport. If Edith sent it back, it's goodbye Charlie. I'm not about to go buying passports on the black market, if there *is* such a thing as a black market.'

'You've got scruples?'

'Well, I hope so,' I said, 'somewhere. But I've also got sense. And goddammit, don't rush me into this!'

We spent the next few hours going over the same ground, from time to time pinpointing a new angle or analyzing a new problem. We were like miners sifting the same earth time and again to look for nuggets. At five-thirty I drove Dick to the airport.

Arriving home, I climbed the outside staircase to Edith's studio and asked her about the passport. She was on her knees, just finishing a canvas that lay on the floor, dabbing a streak of color here and there, then crawling back with her head cocked to one side to examine the effect.

'I don't remember where I put it,' she said. 'Look in the old suitcase in Nedsky's room. Maybe it's . . .' She didn't finish the sentence, but inched purposefully forward and slashed a streak of bright green across the center of the canvas, giving a little grunt of satisfaction.

The passport wasn't in the old suitcase. Neither was it in the desk, nor in the bottom of the grandfather clock, where we sometimes hid money and jewelry. I finally found it in our bedroom, under a pile of art supplies I had brought back from New York after my father's death. The extra Swiss passport was the result of a curious mix-up that had taken place in 1968, and at first neither of us could remember the precise details that accounted for its existence. 'Try,' I said to Edith. 'It's important.'

'I remember now,' she said, after a while. 'It was really very simple. My first Swiss passport was with the name Edith Rosenkranz. Then when I got divorced I got me a passport in my own name, Edith Sommer. Then I married you and got me a passport in your name, Edith Irving. But in the other passport I had that American visa, what was good for all my life. Then my father got sick in Gmünd that year. And I had given before that to the Americans my other passport, my new passport, so I could get the same visa. So I had to rush to Germany, you remember, because my father was sick? And I had no passport, what meant I couldn't go. You called the American Consulate and they said they had mailed it to me, but I didn't yet get it. So I flew to Barcelona and told this story to the Swiss Consulate, and they gave me another passport to go to Gmünd. I don't think they understood the whole business but they were very nice to me. When I got back, the other passport had arrived from the Americans. I forgot to mail it back. You see? It's simple.'

'I take your word for it,' I said.

Nedsky and Barney barged into the living room for

their evening romp in the toybox. It was not the moment to broach the subject to Edith, so I waited an hour until Rafaela had come clucking to gather them up and take them away to her part of the house for supper. Then I explained the problem to Edith: how, if we embarked on this Hughes caper, we would need someone to open a bank account in Switzerland under the name of H. R. Hughes. 'The important word is *if.*'

'Darling,' she said, 'I know you too well. There's no *if* any more. I hear you and Dick from the corner of my ear. I hear you all excited, like I've never heard you before. I know you're going to do it.'

'Well,' I admitted, 'we may see how far we can go with it. Anyway, *if* we do it, how would you like to change the color of your hair, and change your name to Helga Renate Hughes, expatriate Swiss business-woman who conducts her financial affairs only with her initials?'

I explained what I had in mind. The passport would never be used for crossing borders, because that struck me as an out-and-out crime. To open a Swiss bank account with it, however, seemed to me – in probability – an everyday, mundane matter. It was something I had read, I remembered, in a book called *The Swiss Banks*. McGraw-Hill had published it.

'I wear a wig?' Edith said playfully.

'Sure. And dark glasses and lipstick.'

'Maybe, maybe not. I think about that.'

'Yes,' I said. 'Because there's a certain amount of risk. I'm not sure what, but there's bound to be *something.*'

Edith became serious. 'I'll think.'

Two days later I asked Edith, 'Have you thought about doing it?'

'Okay. I wear the lipstick, but not too much of it.'

'I thought you might not do it. I wasn't sure it was fair to ask.'

'I help you, I don't let you down. I go to Zurich, what

I love, where there is a wonderful street to shop. *If* you do this thing,' she added laughing. Because she laughed, I know that she wanted to say something more, but couldn't. Was it: 'And would your Nina do that?'

I worked for the next week on the final drafting of the letters and the doctoring of Edith's Swiss passport. Now and then I would have a fit of literary conscience and haul the unfinished novel out of the file cabinet to plow ahead a page or two; but inevitably I was drawn back to the letters and the passport. The challenge of the job fascinated me. If I succeeded, we could go ahead with the project in April or May, when the novel hopefully would be finished. If I failed, that would end it. Whatever the outcome, the compulsion was too powerful to allow for postponement.

We spent a quiet New Year's Eve at home with a few friends and some time during the next week drove up to the studio together. 'Bring your black wig and a lipstick,' I instructed Edith. I carried my camera and a pair of ping-pong balls.

'What are they for?'

'To stuff in your cheeks.'

'What you think I am, a squirrel?'

We arrived at the moment of truth, on the balcony of my studio under a gray but glaring sky, and the disguise didn't work. The wig was fine – it was a shaggy, curly, cheap affair that Edith had bought a year or two ago in Palma. The lipstick changed Edith's appearance, too. But the ping-pong balls in her cheeks made her look as if she had a particularly virulent case of mumps, or something worse. She muttered a strangled protest.

'All right. Take them out. Puff out your cheeks a little bit.'

I clicked a dozen pictures with my Nikkormat and had them developed the next day at one of the local pharmacies. They made Edith look like a woman in her forties. Using ink eradicator, I wiped out the name, birthdate, and color of hair from the passport, then lettered in the new details with a black felt-tip pen. Changing the number was even easier, except that it had to be done on all thirty-two pages of the passport. Among my father's art supplies that I had brought back to Ibiza were several sheets of letters and numbers which could be transferred to another surface simply by rubbing them on with a rounded point. It was no trick to turn sixes and threes into eights, and fives into sixes; it was only tedious to do it thirty-two times. The old photograph, of course, bore the impressed seal of the Swiss Consulate. I puzzled over that for a while and then worked out a simple method for duplicating it. I placed the blackwigged photograph of Helga Renate Hughes over the blonde one of Edith and rubbed it hard with a gum eraser. In a few minutes the faint impression of the seal appeared on the second photograph. Trimming the enlargement down to the right size, I pasted it into the passport.

Only two details remained: the purple-inked seal of the Swiss Consulate, and the signature. I must have been either tired or over-confident when I tackled those jobs. When I had finished eliminating *Barcelona* – intending to substitute *Amsterdam* or *Stockholm* – the outline was still there and the seal looked mangled. The razor blade had dangerously thinned the paper; if I was to print the name of another city it would be bound to blur. I took a purple felt-tip pen and re-inked the word *Barcelona*. It blurred.

The signature was even more difficult. Edith had written her name in a full, flowing script and the eradicator had bleached the fine watermarked design of the paper so that the name *Edith Irving* was still visible. Caution gave way to annoyance, and annoyance to an irrational boldness. Following the written outlines of the signature, I took a thick blue felt pen and scribbled a huge *Helga R. Hughes*. You could still see the white outlines. I threw the passport into a drawer, slammed it shut, and tried to forget it.

The half-pad of lined yellow legal paper arrived three days later, airmail express, from Dick in Palma. I picked it up with the rest of my mail at the bank then drove up to the studio at Los Molinos. Most of that morning I spent fiddling with a scene in my new novel that needed some strong rewriting, but my eye kept wandering to the pad of yellow paper tossed carelessly on a canvas chair. I rummaged through a trunk wedged behind the bed and found what I was looking for: an old Esterbrook fountain pen and a bottle of Parker Quink. The black ink was crusted with age, but an inch of usable fluid remained at the top of the bottle. I cleaned the pen under the cold-water tap in the kitchen. Howard Hughes was the kind of man, I reckoned, who would use an old-fashioned fountain pen. More to the point, I hadn't used one in ten years. Any letters I had handwritten to McGraw-Hill were with a felt-tipped throwaway pen.

Talk is cheap, I realized. How do you forge a letter? A signature was one thing, and with enough practice I assumed it could be done; but a letter was a formidable problem. That tiny inset from *Newsweek,* with the last paragraph of Hughes's letter to Chester Davis and Bill Gay, was all that I had. No forger in his right mind would use it as a model. I would certainly need a magnifying glass. I spent an hour searching for it, ransacking drawers and file cabinets, and wound up in a sweat amid indescribable clutter. I went back to work on the novel and bogged down after fifteen minutes, and at five o'clock I drove home.

Edith was the orderly one. I lived in a chaotic jumble of unanswered letters, shirts and sweaters slung on the backs of chairs, bills and receipts piled on top of the bed in my studio, dozens of folders into which I slung papers with bold annotations: *TO BE FILED.* But the files were for the most part nonexistent.

'Where is that goddam magnifying glass I brought back from New York?' I demanded.

'There where you put it,' she said, unperturbed.

I was in the studio at ten o'clock the next morning. The telephone rang immediately. I knew who it was and I said, without preamble: 'Yes, I got the paper. But I can't do the letters.'

'What do you mean? You *said* you could do the letters.'

'Well, I was wrong. Listen, Dick, it's not so easy. I don't have a magnifying glass.'

'What's the matter with you?' he yelled. 'You were the one who said they wouldn't have a letter to compare it to, and now you're getting finicky. You're giving up before you've even begun. So go to work. Practice!'

'Okay, Knute Rockne. I'll get back to you tomorrow. Don't call me, I'll call you.'

I got out the yellow paper, pen, ink, and *Newsweek*. The reproduced paragraph read:

As I have said, this matter has caused me the very gravest concern, and is damaging my company and all the loyal men and women associated with me in the very deepest and far-reaching way.

My sincere regards,
Howard R. Hughes

I went over it carefully, analyzing the lower-case letters first and then the capital letters. Fortunately the paragraph contained specimens of all but six lower-case letters: *b, j, k, q, x,* and *z*. It would be hard to write a letter without a *b*, but Hughes seemed to base his handwriting on the standard form of penmanship taught when I was in grammar school, so I could keep the *b*'s to the minimum, fake them, and hope for the best. To my horror, however, I realized immediately that the sample

49

I had to work from gave me only five capital letters: A, I, M, H, and R. The major problem, therefore, was to create a correspondence using only those capital letters. I mulled that for a few minutes and then hit on the simplest solution. Hughes would be the supreme egotist. He would begin every possible sentence in his letters to me with the pronouns *I* and *My*.

I quit work only when it was long past dark. The next day I shoved the novel aside and drafted the three Hughes letters on my typewriter. I made a few changes to eliminate all unnecessary capital letters with which I was unfamiliar, then called Dick in Palma. I read the letters aloud.

'Not bad,' he said. 'But a little stiff.'

'Howard's not a writer,' I pointed out. 'That's why he needs me to do his biography.'

'And how's the work coming?'

I knew what he meant by 'the work' and I said: 'Onward and upward with the arts. I'll show it to you next week.'

Dick visited Ibiza later in January, just after I had mailed the promised teaser to Beverly Loo, and again near the end of the month. Between visits we spoke almost daily on the telephone. I read him the revised text of the letters from Howard and he suggested several additional changes. I still had more work to do on the passport signature. 'Take your time,' he cautioned me. 'Whatever you do, don't fuck it up.'

It was finished when he arrived at the end of January. First I showed him where I had changed the numbers; then the photograph. He grunted approval, and I unveiled my final effort.

'How do you like the signature?'

There was a gasp of outrage; I didn't turn to look at him. 'You must be kidding! Is that what it took you three days to do? Christ! It looks like it was made by a six-year-old kid with a felt-tipped laundry marker. She'll never be able to cross the border with that. They'll pick her up in a minute.'

'She's not going to cross the border with it,' I snapped back. 'She'll use her own passport to get into Switzerland, and just show this one at the bank. *If* we go through with this crazy caper,' I added, as usual.

'And you think they'll let her open an account? You're out of your mind. Look here . . .' his thick forefinger jabbed at the 'Helga.' 'You can see where it's been eradicated. There's "Edith" coming through, like a fucking palimpsest.'

'It doesn't matter. I've talked to a few people who have bank accounts in Switzerland. They don't give a damn about those I.D. papers. If the money's real, that's all they care about.'

Dick looked dubious. 'I sure hope you know what you're doing.'

'So do I,' I said fervently.

'So let's get to the next move. You call McGraw-Hill, right?'

I looked at the telephone. Once I placed that call, we would be on our way. There would be room to maneuver and opportunity to turn back, but the direction would be set. We would be committed, willy-nilly, for better or for worse.

'You sure you want me to do this?' I asked.

He pondered for a long while and then said: 'No, I'm not at all sure. Are you?'

'Neither am I.'

Dick laughed. 'But you're going to do it anyway.'

'Oh, sure,' I said, and I laughed, too. 'What the hell. You only live once.' I thought it over. 'It's just a telephone call. It doesn't really commit me. Right?'

'Right.'

I picked up the telephone and placed a person-to-person call to Beverly Loo in New York. Two cigarettes later, the operator informed me that Beverly was out of the office. I hung up.

'The McGraw-Hill Building's been blown up by the Weathermen. No survivors.'

'Try Random House,' Dick said doggedly.

'I don't know anyone there. I'll call back in an hour. Bev's not in. Do me a favor – go back to the house and tell Edith I'll be a little late. Let me do this alone. You make me nervous, and I'm nervous enough already.'

Dick left, and an hour later I placed the call again. Beverly's secretary put me through to her.

When I opened the front door, Edith was gathering a litter of toys from the living room floor and Dick was sprawled in the overstuffed armchair. I slumped into another chair, showing the gloomiest expression I could muster.

Dick frowned. 'You didn't reach her.'

'Beverly? I reached her.' I waved feebly at Edith. 'Darling, I need a stiff drink. Bourbon on the rocks.'

Dick's frown deepened. '*What happened?*'

'I told her the story. I told her I'd got the letters from Hughes and then he'd called me before I had a chance to write back. The moment I got to the bit about the authorized biography and meeting him in Nassau, she said, "Oh, my God, not you, too? That happens twice a year to every publisher in New York. Some writer always gets the brilliant idea that he'll pretend he's in touch with the elusive Howard Hughes and that Hughes wants an as-told-to autobiography. It's the most common con in publishing. But that *you* should try it! Cliff! You should be ashamed of yourself." And so I had to apologize. I made her promise she wouldn't tell anyone else up at McGraw-Hill.'

Dick looked ten years older, and Edith, on her hands and knees by the toybox, stared at me. 'Are you serious?' she said.

'You think I'd joke about something like that? I was so embarrassed I didn't know what to say. She called it a cheap, common stunt. That's what hurt me the most. I thought it was so original.'

'Oh, well,' Dick sighed. 'Back to *Richard the Lion-Hearted*.'

'I had to squirm out of it some way, so I told her it was really *your* idea . . .' I leveled an accusing finger at him, 'and you pushed me into it. That's what softened her up.'

'You sonofabitch,' Dick murmured. My expression of gloom had broken; he saw the sparkle in my eye. 'Come on! What did she *really* say?'

'They want it. They believe. They want it so bad I could hear them salivating four thousand miles away. They want me to drop work on the novel and get cracking on it right away. They want me to find out how much Hughes wants, see him, sign him up, and get to work. They believe everything – so far.'

'I'll have a bourbon, too,' Dick said to Edith. He leaned toward me, eyes glittering. Again he was like a child about to hear his favorite bedtime story. 'Tell me everything. Tell me all she said. I want to hear all the details.'

4

South of the Border

On February 4th my aunt telephoned from Florida to tell me that my mother had died early that morning.

I had grieved for my mother for more than three years, since the summer on Ibiza when she had suffered a stroke which had left her almost completely paralyzed, speechless, and retarded to the point where one felt there was neither sense nor justice to the human condition. Those last three years she had spent in a New York nursing home. My father's visits had sustained her and then, that past June, my father had died of a heart attack. My mother lingered eight months longer, living in that terrible mute loneliness.

I cried a few tears, offered a brief thanks to the God in whose compassion I had long since lost faith, and then left the studio and went home to tell Edith.

That same afternoon I called Dick in Palma. Throughout the past three weeks I had been in erratic communication with McGraw-Hill, keeping them informed of my mythical progress with Howard Hughes, who was still no more to me than a disembodied voice on the telephone and the author of a scrawled, almost child-like handwriting. Howard and I were getting to know each other and talking about a meeting in the spring. I had proposed that I write his authorized biography, that we meet and tape a series of interviews and that he write a preface to the work giving it his imprimatur. The consummation of the deal, I explained, hinged on our meeting. We might hate each other – after all, I drank, smoked, and fornicated, and legend had it that in his mellowing years Hughes had abjured such sins and disapproved of them in those close to him.

He had also made known to me his financial demands. He wanted a million dollars, and out of this sum he would pay me a fixed fee for my services. I had tried to explain to him that from a publisher's point of view this was impossible; and in any case, writers didn't work that way. 'Well,' Howard said, 'we'll talk about all that when we meet.' These conversations were reported to Beverly Loo, who had been horrified at the outset and then mollified when I explained: 'Howard thinks in round numbers, but I can talk him out of it.' I knew, of course, that the demands were outlandish, but I wanted McGraw-Hill to balance two concepts in their corporate mind – they were dealing with a difficult man, but I was on their side and could bring him around to reason.

'My family's holding up the funeral for me,' I explained to Dick on the telephone, 'I'm flying out tomorrow. The best connection is by way of London. I have to spend half a day there and catch the night flight. Look . . .' I took a deep breath, 'I'm a little shaken up, but it wasn't unexpected. And I can't help thinking about other things. Maybe it's a defense . . .'

'You could see McGraw-Hill while you're in New York,' Dick said quietly.

'That's what I was leading up to. I didn't want to get cracking this early, but if I'm going to New York I might as well save myself a trip later on. I'll sound them out. I'll start the ball rolling and see where it leads.'

For some reason – perhaps the muted emotional turmoil it brought in its wake – the news of my mother's death enabled me, however briefly, to see my world steadily and see it whole. The hypocrisies and rationalizations with which I had cohabited for so long were swept from my head, as if by a riptide, and what was left was a naked strand of shore with every pebble and piece of driftwood etched in almost too-sharp relief. I saw, first of all, that despite my constant cries of 'if,' I was fully committed to the hoax.

But *why*? I looked at myself. How and why could Clifford Irving, a man who projected an aura of contentment and emotional stability, allow himself to take that leap, that risk, to veer so far from the clearly-marked track of his life? He was forty years old. He had worked hard. He was an established although hardly a wildly successful writer; but he had done the best he could and he was not ashamed. He was free to write as he pleased – and more than that no writer in his right mind would ask. Married to a woman he loved, with two children he adored and another son whom he saw seldom but loved deeply, he lived where and as he pleased, with all the material comforts a man needed. Still, in his private life, with Edith and the children balanced against Nina, he risked everything. Damn the cost, he would have his cake and eat it, too.

And I saw that I had lived for too long as a man deliberately projecting an image of contentment. I was not content, and I doubted that I could ever achieve that state before I was old and unburdened of mundane desire. The objects of desire were illusion; their attainment gave only ephemeral satisfaction. The risk itself provided the sense of being alive. '*Frei lebt wer sterben kann*,' Isak Dinesen had said. Men climbed Himalayan mountain peaks 'because they were there' – and for me, the hoax 'was there.' I had formulated my own challenge, and that was motive enough. The rest was peripheral – rewards that might or might not come, but in any event would have little meaning after the challenge had been met and resolved, either in triumph or disaster. The means were the end. I could turn my back on the challenge and I knew without a doubt that I would be a wiser man for having done so. It was an aberration – in one sense, highly civilized; in another, deeply primitive. But I was driven. I had known almost from the beginning, without having the courage to admit it, that the *if* was a poor delusion to help me over the first obstacle: the realization that I would take the risk.

I dawdled for a while, putting it off as long as I could, and then I called Beverly Loo. I told her that my mother had died and that I was flying to New York. 'And Hughes called this morning,' I added. 'He said he was sorry and then he said, "Well, it's fate." He wants me to stay at a certain hotel in the city and he'll contact me there, and then I'm supposed to come down to Nassau and meet him. So the timetable's changed.'

Then I called Nina in London. 'I'm catching the Iberia morning flight. I'll probably hang around the airport until the evening. Can I buy you a cup of coffee?'

'I'll meet the plane,' she said.

She was there, in leather coat and sunglasses, looking pale and worn out by the long London winter and the effort to revive her career now that she was on her own without Frederik. 'It's so goddam slow,' she said. 'And it's a drag and it's such a phony business, and I loathe it. But someone's got to pay the bills and the kids have to go to school, and there's just nothing else I can do. I've got a new manager. You won't like him – I don't like him, either – but he's working hard for me. I'm doing television guest spots and charities and maybe cutting a record in the spring. How are you, my sweet?' She looked at her watch. 'Come back to the flat for lunch. There's time, isn't there?'

Time? There was always time. That was the dimension

one could manipulate more easily than any other. One could compress it, expand it, make an hour more beautiful or hellish than a year. It was a gray London afternoon. The apartment in Chelsea, just off the embankment of the Thames, was quiet and warm. We sat drinking coffee in Nina's kitchen and I munched chocolate biscuits from the children's tin. We talked for a while about my mother. Then I said: 'You look like you need a holiday.'

'I do,' she admitted. 'I'm exhausted.'

'I've got to fly to Nassau next week on some business, some research for a book. Why don't you come with me?'

We never planned these things. We took our moments together when they were possible, by accident and coincidence rather than by design. We had learned that to plan something meant that inevitably it wouldn't work; something always cropped up in one of our lives to cancel it. And even then, when I suggested a week in Nassau, I knew that Nina had work to do, that she was waiting for auditions and interviews.

'You know I want to,' she said, 'but I can't.'

Later in the afternoon I told her about Hughes and showed her his three letters.

'What a groove,' she said. 'Howard Hughes! Can't you stay overnight and catch a plane in the morning? I could run you out to the airport.'

I called Pan Am, canceled my reservation and booked for the morning flight to New York. That evening her new manager, John Marshall, arrived with his wife. He was a short, smartly dressed, smooth-talking Englishman with superficial charm and rampant ego. He owned a stable of horses and a country manor, wore Gucci shoes and Savile Row sporting jackets. He had no telephone and he used Nina's apartment as his office. He barged in the front door, shrieking: *'Nina Superstar!'*

After dinner he and I were alone. 'You know,' he said,

'for an American you seem like a reasonably intelligent man. My star tells me that you're rather fond of each other, and that you've invited her to Nassau for a week. I think it's a bloody good idea. My star needs a holiday, and I've given her my permission to go.'

'That's very kind of you, John.'

Later I took Nina aside and repeated the conversation. 'Does that mean you'll come?'

'If you still want me to. Oh, God,' she sighed, resting her head on my shoulder, 'I'd love it.'

The next morning she drove me to Heathrow Airport and we bought a round-trip ticket for her from London to New York. We would meet there and go on to Nassau, where if all went well in New York, I was to meet Howard Hughes.

The day after my mother's funeral, wearing a gray suit and black tie, I appeared at McGraw-Hill. I knew the 20th floor of the Trade Book Division well; twice in the past five years I had been given office space there to rewrite and polish the final drafts of books which McGraw-Hill had then published. I had been around the company longer than any of the editors currently in residence. The Trade Book Division seemed to have a quick turnover. 'Cliff's practically an employee,' Beverly Loo had once said at a cocktail party, to which I countered, 'Then why won't the company let me join their Blue Cross plan?'

'Well you're not really an employee. But you are *our* author. You've been with us longer than any other writer we've got on our list.'

'Yes, I've noticed,' I said. 'They don't seem to stick around very long.'

Five years ago I had been working in the office on the galley proofs of my novel, *The 38th Floor*, when I had been invited upstairs to a company Christmas party. I hadn't shaved that day and I wore a sweater with leather elbow patches and a pair of baggy corduroy trousers. That was the first time I met Harold McGraw, President of the McGraw-Hill Company, one of the two divisions of McGraw-Hill, Inc. Harold had approached Ed Kuhn, then Editor-in-Chief of Trade, and pointed me out. 'I thought it was company policy,' he said reproachfully, 'that all employees wore jackets and ties. That young man looks like a bum.'

'That's an author,' Ed Kuhn explained. 'He writes books for us.'

'Oh,' Harold said. 'I'd like to meet one.' And so we were introduced.

That February morning I breezed through to Beverly Loo's office, stopping to chat for a few moments with secretaries and typists I knew.

Beverly and I had seen each other the night before for a drink, and now she marched me down the hall to Albert Leventhal's spacious corner office with its view of Wall Street and the Hudson River. Albert – a vice-president and head of the Trade Book Division – was a small, dapper, nut-brown man a year away from retirement, with a reputation in the book business that was both impeccable and hard-earned. He had a quick, dry wit, but there was a permanent quiver in his voice and a cloud of worry hidden behind the pleasantness of his smile, as if he felt the world were capable of crumbling around him at any given moment.

Condolences for my mother's death were offered, and then the point was reached.

'What I don't understand,' Albert said shrewdly, 'is why a man like Howard Hughes, who's avoided publicity all his life, should suddenly want to have his biography written. And with all due respect to you as a writer, why he should choose you to work with him.'

'He had to choose somebody,' I said, sidestepping the first question. 'Whoever he chose, you could ask: "Why *him*?"'

Beverly came to my aid. 'Albert, he certainly wouldn't pick someone very well known – someone like Norman Mailer – would he? Then the book would be Mailer, not Hughes. Cliff's a perfect choice. He's a professional. He delivers. And he knows how to keep his ego in check.'

'That makes sense,' Albert halfheartedly agreed. 'Well, let's see these famous letters.'

I produced them from a battered folder and dropped them on Albert's neat desk. He and Beverly Loo read carefully.

'This much is certain,' Beverly said. 'It's no practical joke. These are from Hughes.'

Albert kept reading. 'How do you know that?' I asked Beverly.

'For one thing, he always writes on that yellow legal paper. For another, I can recognize that's his handwriting. There was a reproduction in *Life* of a long letter he wrote to somebody, firing this man Robert Maheu. I've seen it. And that's exactly the way he writes, right out to the margin.'

'Have you got that issue of *Life* here?'

'No, but I'll find it. Let me read, please.'

Albert Leventhal had finished. 'I take it all back,' he said. 'Now I understand. You only have to read this part. Beverly, pay attention. Hughes says: "I am not entirely insensitive to what journalists have written about me . . ." And then he goes on: "It would not suit me to die without having certain misconceptions cleared up and without having stated the truth about my life. The immortality you speak of does not interest me, not in this world. I believe in obligations. I regret many things in the past, but I have little feelings of shame about them."'

'That's very interesting,' Beverly noted, 'where he says, "not in this world."' I had thought so, too, when I had written it.

'But it's all very clear.' Albert tapped the pile of yellow

paper. 'And he says it with dignity and eloquence. He's a sick man and he wants the truth told.'

'That's my guess, too' I said.

I had also provided McGraw-Hill with carbon copies of the first rough drafts of my letters in reply to those of Hughes. The originals, I explained, I had handwritten – it seemed a proper gesture in view of Howard's laborious efforts with the pen and his disdaining the use of a secretary. What surprised me was that no one asked me to what address I had written, or where Hughes's letters were postmarked; if they did, I would have had to make up the answers on the spot. But in the excitement of the moment, such omissions were certainly understandable. In my first apocryphal letter, dated January 4th, I had written:

On the basis of your kind note you may think the following presumptuous of me, but I'm a writer and I can't help thinking as a writer. I am aware of your reputation for carefully guarded privacy; but that itself can cause some powerful misinterpretation of a man's life and motives for living it as he chooses without regard for mass opinion. Your life – the surface details that one gleans from hearsay and the press, however distorted – fascinates me. Obviously, the truth is more fascinating; and deserves (though rarely achieves) the last word for definitive immortality. Have you ever considered an authorized biography of yourself? I would consider it a privilege to write the book . . .

Then, after receiving the affirmative reply on January 28th I had written again:

I must tell you first of all that I couldn't be more pleased – and agreeably surprised – at your response to my suggestion. But you undoubtedly realized this. It was good to talk to you on the telephone, too; it made things more real to me, and I hope, as you said, that we will be talking again within the next few days . . .

As for publication, I would choose the McGraw-Hill Book Co. They are an outstanding, prestigious, and conservative publishing house and big enough to handle what I feel would be a major publishing event. Also, I have a well-developed relationship with them which has resulted in a long-standing mutual loyalty. I'm sure they would maintain absolute discretion while the work was in progress . . . Before committing themselves, they or any other publisher would undoubtedly want to see some form of written agreement between us which would incorporate a legal release on your part and define the cooperation, since the prime value of the book would lie in the fact that it is an authorized, definitive, and ultimately uncensored biography, rather than a piece of opportunism . . . I think, too, that a brief preface or introduction to the book by you would make the concept absolutely clear. But we can discuss this later . . .

The sun has broken through here after weeks of rain, etc.

'Fascinating.' Albert Leventhal puffed nervously at his cigarette. 'Well, I'll tell you, if you meet the man and he's willing to talk, it could be a sensational book. But if he's going to give you only two or three hours of his time and then say, "Go away and write," it's no good. And that's what could happen. He's a very unpredictable man, you know. Terrible reputation. He bought a yacht once from my father, years and years ago, and it was almost impossible to do business with him. Constantly changes his mind.'

'I can't promise,' I hedged, 'but I'll do my best.'

'What did he want from us? A million dollars?'

'I told him that was out of the question. I had to give him a few basic truths about the poverty-stricken publishing industry.'

'We'll come up with an offer,' Albert said, a little annoyed. He handed the letters back to me. 'You hang on to these. Don't lose them. Even if the whole book deal fell through, these letters are probably worth $25,000 each.'

'I should get him to write more,' I said, laughing; and Beverly and Albert laughed, too.

The woman at the reception desk in the Time-Life Building shook her head. 'We don't keep out-of-date issues of our magazines. It would help if you knew the date – we could look up the article for you.'

'It was a recent issue. That's all I know.'

'Try the A & S Bookstore – Eighth Avenue and 43rd Street.'

In the rear of that shop I found a shelf piled high with back copies of *Life*. It took a few minutes to find the January 22nd issue with its tale of Hughes's exodus from Las Vegas, a picture of Robert Maheu, and a two-page spread, nearly full size, of a letter that began: 'Dear Chester and Bill . . .' The final paragraph was what I had seen in the *Newsweek* inset and used as the model for the forgeries. I paid fifty cents for the copy of *Life* and took a taxi back to the Hotel Elysee.

The three letters were locked in my Harrods suitcase, which opened only by spinning a combination dial. I dropped down on the bed and laid them out next to the open pages of *Life*, with its reproduction of the genuine letter from Howard Hughes. I felt giddy – I needed air. I stared at them for about ten minutes, then left the hotel and walked purposefully up the street to a stationery shop on East 55th Street, where I bought three pads of yellow lined legal paper, a Parker fountain pen, a bottle of Waterman's black ink, and a date stamp.

Alone, and faced with absurdity, you rarely laugh. Sane laughter must be shared with another person, and the only person with whom I could have shared the laughter and the feeling of mild horror was Dick Suskind, who was 4,000 miles away. Alone, you just smile and shake your head in bewilderment. If that copy of *Life* had been there in Beverly Loo's office and had been placed side by side with my letters from Howard Hughes, the ball game would have ended then and there. 'They were godawful,' I said to Dick, two weeks later in Ibiza. 'You can't believe how bad they were. They were the worst forgeries ever made by man or beast. *They just didn't look the least bit alike.*'

In the Elysee in New York, I sat down at the desk and worked from noon to ten o'clock at night. I wrote until I had the letters right, using up all three pads of paper, Then I tore up the old letters, dropped them in the wastebasket, slid the new ones in the file and locked it away in the suitcase; and then content but famished, went downstairs for a cheeseburger and a chocolate malted.

'Show them to Bob,' Beverly said the next afternoon, once again in Albert Leventhal's office. I slid the new set of letters across the desk to Bob Locke, a McGraw-Hill vice-president. He passed them, as he finished each page, to Albert and Beverly, who read them for the second time. They could detect no difference from the set they had read the day before.

'He must be an extraordinary man,' Locke said. 'I wouldn't mind going with you to meet him. Where'd you say you were meeting him?'

'Nassau, I think. But I'll have to go alone.' His suggestion had jarred me, but I was emphatic.

'I suppose so. I was just thinking what a hell of an experience it's going to be.'

'I haven't the slightest idea what's going to happen,' I admitted.

Bob Locke then made the offer I was to present to Hughes. McGraw-Hill would put up $100,000 upon signing a contract – 'seed money,' as Leventhal called it – a further $100,000 on delivery and acceptance of the interviews which would form the basis for the book; and a final $300,000 on acceptance of a finished manuscript and a preface by Hughes himself.

'It seems fair to *me*,' I said. 'But it's Howard's decision, not mine.'

I left the office and went straight to Western Union. I cabled Dick: *MOTHER OFFERS FIVE HUNDRED REPEAT FIVE HUNDRED STOP BREAK OUT CHAMPAGNE STOP HEADING NASSAU DAY AFTER TOMORROW*, and signed it *LOVE HOWIE*.

Nina was due in from London the following evening at seven o'clock. I went from Western Union to Eastern Airlines. 'What flights have you got on Thursday or Friday to Nassau?'

The girl behind the counter smiled at me pityingly. 'We can't even wait-list you,' she said. 'Our Nassau flights have been booked solid two months in advance. Next,' she called, and I was suddenly out of the line and heading for the door.

The girl at Northeast Airlines punched her computer. 'It's the big weekend,' she explained. 'You know, President Nixon has changed Lincoln's birthday to a Monday.'

'He's doing *what*?'

'So there can be a long weekend in winter so people can get away.'

'And the American people will stand for that? They'll let one president fool around with another

66

president's birthday? That's sacrilegious.'

'Well, they're both Republicans,' the girl said. 'It's sort of all in the family.'

I tried all the airlines that flew to Miami with connections to Nassau or Freeport. The next afternoon, having exhausted myself dashing up and down Fifth Avenue to all the airlines and two travel agencies, and feeling the beginning of panic – how could Howard Hughes not be able to arrange air tickets to Nassau or the nearby islands? – I tried the American Express office on Park Avenue, near the hotel. 'Look, I'll go anywhere south of Georgia and north of Venezuela. But I've got to go tomorrow or Friday.'

Seven telephone calls later, the agent said: 'I can get you to Mexico City, sir. But not from there to Acapulco or any of the beach resorts.'

'How about Oaxaca? That's in the south of Mexico about three hundred miles.'

He made one more telephone call. 'Two seats open. You'll have to stay overnight in Mexico City.'

'I'll take them.'

The plan, of course, had been for me and Howard to hold all our theoretical meetings on Paradise Island. But suddenly, as a result of Nixon's high-handed tampering with Lincoln's birthday, Howard Hughes was on the move. The President's thoughtfulness was to change Howard from a hibernating hermit to a peregrinating adventurer. As yet, however, I was unaware of this. And so, I need hardly add, was Howard Hughes.

Coming off the plane at Mexico City Airport, a young photographer scampered up the boarding ladder with a Polaroid camera, clicking off shots of the disembarking passengers. Nina threw up the collar of her old leather coat, shielded her face and stepped quickly toward the terminal building. I caught up to her at the gate. 'What's the matter?'

'Oh, it would be lovely if that hit page one of the London *Sunday Express*. Edith and Frederik would adore it. That would be the end of your marriage and my divorce. That's not the kind of publicity I need.'

'Are you kidding? Marshall would love it.' Her new manager had been dinning at her for months that she was a star and had to behave like one, think like one. 'I hate to disillusion you,' I said, 'but this airport isn't the King's Road in Chelsea. If they don't know you in New York, they certainly don't know you in Mexico.' And writers, I went on to explain, lived in the happy swamp of anonymity. It was one of the pleasures of the calling to be mildly known yet unrecognizable. 'Anyway, that kid was just taking tourist photographs. So relax.' I laughed. Her eyes clouded over a moment; then she smiled, too.

'Where are we staying?' she asked, when we had cleared customs and immigration.

'I have to make a phone call to find out.' I ducked off to a public booth. I had told her that Hughes or one of his mysterious intermediaries was taking care of the arrangements. I called American Express to confirm the reservation I had made in their Park Avenue office for the El Camino Hotel. The hotel had no record of it, but they had a room.

Nina was waiting, sitting on the banged-up silver metal suitcase – it held her radio, tape recorder, one change of underwear, two old sweaters, and a pair of jeans. She wore her baggy leather coat, floppy trousers, and gigantic octagonal sunglasses, her mass of gold hair coiled and tucked primly under a black scarf. Nina Superstar! The Baroness van Pallandt, mother of three, whom one of the London newspapers had just voted among 'the ten sexiest women in the world' – which accolade she had told me she considered one of the ten greatest practical jokes ever played. To a certain extent I had to agree. Wearing no makeup, looking lost and uncertain, she hunched down on her suitcase, a gangling, almost awkward figure that could uncoil into a lovely woman only if she chose, only if she let go, abandoned the armor of the wronged wife and the frightened girl-child. The large, gray-blue eyes regarded me with concern.

'The El Camino,' I said. 'It's a little way out of town.'

'Will you have to leave there to meet him?'

'If I get a telephone call. If I don't, we fly to Oaxaca at seven o'clock in the morning.'

'Let's go out tonight,' she said, climbing into the taxi. 'Let's have a siesta and then go out on the town, hear the *mariachis*.'

'And if Hughes calls while I'm out?'

'Oh, leave a message for the bloody bastard. I want to be with you. We have so little time.' And she leaned across, suddenly smiling, and kissed me lightly on the cheek.

A moment after we jumped into the taxi a boy came running up, waving a photograph at me. I started to shake my head, then looked at it carefully. I was alone, poised at the head of the gangway on the Eastern Airlines jet, peering worriedly into the distance. 'How much?' I asked.

'*Quince pesos.*'

I slipped the photograph into my briefcase. Nina frowned in puzzlement, then laughed. 'What do you want that silly thing for?'

'A souvenir,' I said, casually.

The El Camino was a sprawling, modern, brown stucco *palacio* in the suburbs. It took five minutes for the Mexican bellhop to trundle our luggage down a maze of broad, split-level corridors to the room. The late afternoon sun still slanted strongly through the wooden shutters that gave a view of the swimming pool. The bed was huge. I closed the shutters so that only glints of golden light filtered through. When I turned, Nina's long, lithe body was just vanishing under the sheet. My shy, 38-year-old Danish maiden . . . But she had tossed the blanket to the foot of the bed. I bent by her side and plucked out the brown pins, one by one, until the fragile storm of yellow hair fluttered free and came to rest on the pillow. Her eyes were closed. The room was very quiet and cool, bars of warm sunlight streaked across the brown carpeting. Her eyes opened, blinked a few times, and she smiled gently. Then murmured, into that calm, suddenly private silence: 'Oh, God. I can't believe it . . .'

'I know,' I said.

'Are we really here?'

'Yes, but it's better not to believe it.'

I undressed and slipped in beside her. She sighed deeply and threw an arm across my chest.

I woke from time to time, shifted a little, pulled up the one blanket, aware of gathering grayness and then darkness; but each time dropped heavily into sleep again, not caring or wondering, freed from all obligations to time. The room was cool and silent, an oasis.

I felt Nina's warmth as she bent over my wrist and read the luminous dials of my watch. 'It's almost midnight,' she cried softly. 'What happened?'

'I don't care. Do you?'

'No.'

'What about your *mariachis*?'

'Don't care,' she murmured. Then she flicked on the bedside lamp and looked at me with grave worry, a hint of fear. 'Did you get a call? Do you have to go? Did Hughes . . . ?'

The darkness, the lovemaking, the long sleep, all had worn away pretense, chipped away prudence. If you lie to those you love and trust, there is only one valid reason: not to hurt them. You balance in your own mind the wound that will be opened by the truth against the wound caused by lies and deceit. You examine the implications of your cowardice, and then you choose. I had already made my choice with Edith, whom I loved and trusted. 'Sit, walk, or run, but don't wobble.' So speaks the Zen master. I tried to follow, limping a long way behind him.

'Listen,' I said to Nina, 'I want to tell you something. You may be a little shocked . . . if that's still possible. But whether or not you are, I need your word that this stays with you. That your lips are sealed.'

'That sounds so serious.'

'Well, it is. I don't need your approval, but I do need your word.'

'You have it,' she said simply. 'You don't even have to ask. I never talk.' Then she chuckled, a little sadly. 'I don't have anyone to talk to, except you . . .'

I lit a cigarette and said: 'I'm not meeting Howard Hughes here in Mexico. I wasn't supposed to meet him in Nassau. It's all a lie, a hoax. The letters are forged and I never spoke to the man in my life.' I told her the details, the plan, as much as there was a plan. She listened, blue eyes wide and cavernous with bewilderment. Then she broke into a howl of raucous, witch-like laughter. She held her ribs and her eyes glistened with tears.

'What's so funny?'

'You. You are. Oh, my God. Do you really think you can get away with it?'

'I don't really know. It's just a question of letting things take their course, giving them a little shove now and then, and . . . well, we'll see.'

'I'm flabbergasted,' she said, and crowed again with enormous glee.

'But not horrified?'

She shrugged. 'Should I be horrified? You're not planning to murder anyone.'

'No,' I said, 'I'm not. But tell me what you think. It's important to me.'

71

'I think,' Nina said, 'that you're quite, quite mad. But the world is mad, so what's the bloody difference? And I love you. And I'm starving. Do you think, at this god-forsaken hour in this hotel out in the middle of bloody nowhere, we can get food and a bottle of wine? And then do you think we could go back to sleep, and get up in the morning and go to this Oaxaca place where no one knows us and no one cares, and where we can be quite, quite mad together?'

'We can try,' I said. I called Room Service and an hour later, at one o'clock in the morning, two sleepy waiters wheeled in a table with melon and shrimp and filet mignon and a bottle of cold rosé wine, and we sat in our jeans by the side of the rumpled bed, eating and drinking and chuckling. Nina, wearing my shirt with the sleeves rolled up, leaned across the white tablecloth to kiss me.

'How lovely,' she said, 'that your nasty old billionaire friend won't be there in Oaxaca to take you away in the middle of night.'

Oaxaca had not changed since 1955, when I had spent three months there on my first trip to Mexico. That was hard to believe; I was used to seeing the once out-of-the-way places that I loved, like Ibiza, invaded first by artists, then bargain-hunting tourists, then land speculators and entrepreneurs, and finally graduating to 'in' spots that sported French boutiques, Italian restaurants, Miami Beach-style hotels, and high-rise apartment houses. But Oaxaca was still a medium-sized pink-and-blue town in a lush valley surrounded by mountain-top ruins, a trading center for a dozen Zapotec Indian villages, with a plaza where you could drink cold Carta Blanca beer in the shade of the *portales* and buy a cheap handwoven serape and handwrought gold earrings from a local Indio vendor and listen to the marimba band three evenings a week. No new hotels had sprung up, although the plumbing had been improved in the old ones.

We were high up on the hill overlooking the town, in a bungalow of the Hotel Victoria. The gardens were fragrant with mimosas, bougainvillaea, and poinsettias. That first morning we went by taxi to a market in a nearby Indian town and bought black clay pottery and ate chunks of fresh watermelon after brushing away the flies. We spent the afternoon in the bungalow. After dinner the barman in the Hotel Victoria made a fine margarita – tequila with lime over cracked ice, the lip of the glass crusted with salt. Nina, no drinker, reluctantly sampled one. After the second she draped an arm around my neck and whispered: 'Oh, I'm hooked. They're marvelous. And I'm so sloshed I can't see straight. I know you're trying to seduce me and I don't care. Can we go home, darling?'

The next morning we rented a Volkswagen and drove to Monte Albán, a 2,000-year-old ruin of a Zapotec priests' city atop a mountain crowning the three valleys of Oaxaca. It was a clear, hot winter day and the sky was azure. We clambered through the temple ruins and drank cold orange soda in the shade of a tree and bought fake relics from a small Indian boy. After lunch we shopped in the streets off the *zócalo* and then went back to the bungalow of the Hotel Victoria and to bed.

'In my declining years,' Nina said that evening in the bar, shaking her head sadly and sipping a margarita, 'I've become a sex maniac.'

'Is that a complaint?'

'My God, no. *I* think it's wonderful. But objectively speaking, it's disgusting. I mean, we're practically middle-aged – and look at us. Clifford, it's shameful. However let's not stop,' she giggled. 'Let's have another margarita and . . .' She yawned, giggled again shyly, and laid her head on my shoulder.

'Tomorrow,' I promised, 'we'll go swimming. That's a

healthy thing to do. Burns up excess energy. Cools the ardor.'

'The hotel pool looks awful.'

'We can swim in the Pacific.'

'Is it far? I haven't seen a map. I'm not even sure where we are, except that it's Mexico. Is it Mexico? Yes, Mexico.'

'About two hundred miles to Tehuantepec and Salina Cruz, but we've got the Volkswagen. It's mountain country all the way. Very primitive, very beautiful.'

'You want to drive two hundred miles to go for a swim? Has anyone ever told you that you're mad?'

'Yes. You told me the other night in Mexico City.'

On the drive down to Tehuantepec on the isthmus, the next day, we stopped first at the ruins of Mitla. After that the road twisted through scarred, forsaken mountains, one hairpin curve after another, with the thatched huts of lonely Indian villages hidden in the fastnesses of the dark valleys. The morning was hot and cloudless. 'What are you going to tell your publishers?' Nina asked. 'That you spent all this time with Howard Hughes?'

'Howard Hughes? Who's that?'

She frowned. 'Be serious. You'd better think about it. Get your story straight.'

'Preliminary talks. I wasn't with him the whole time. Just a few hours yesterday and a few hours today. Imagine my shock when I discovered he was blond, Danish, and beautiful.' I squeezed her leg just as we screeched round a curve. 'Getting to know you, Howard . . .'

'Watch the road, for God's sake.'

'All right. I'll use the facts. I'll tell them we met yesterday at Monte Albán and that today he had me flown down in a private plane to Tehuantepec. There's an airport at Juchitán. I checked the map. A Mexican pilot flew me down, a trusted Hughes aide. His name is . . . his name is Pedro. Does that sound like the name of a Mexican pilot?'

'And they'll believe that rubbish?'

'I haven't the slightest idea. But I'll keep you posted.'

'Clifford, do you really know what you're doing?'

Thirteen years ago I had crewed on a three-masted schooner sailing from southern Mexico to the French Riviera. Leaving the jungle port of Alvarado, a harbor pilot had come aboard to guide us from the mouth of the river. There were shifting sandbars in the estuary, he explained. I asked: 'If the sandbars shift, how do you know whether or not you're going to hit one?' Smiling crookedly, he had replied: '*El golpe avisa*. The blow tells you.'

'Considering the nature of my life,' I said to Nina, after relating this tale, 'and the fact that we're here, which I still find unbelievable, there's only one answer to your question. Does anyone know what they're really doing? *El golpe avisa*.'

We bought lunch in a small *cantina* near Tehuantepec and then drove across to the long, rough, sand beach at Salina Cruz. The Pacific was a bright, dark blue, but cold. We ate the tortillas and drank a bottle of white wine and walked up the length of the beach for nearly a mile, with the icy surf licking our feet. The beach was vast, deserted, and bravely we peeled down to swim. Then, shivering, we lay down together on my sweater and let the Mexican sun warm our bones. At three o'clock we left, driving back for five hours through the mountain darkness to Oaxaca. Our plane left at eight o'clock the next morning.

'It's all over,' Nina said. 'It was too quick.'

'I know. You've got to be in London to sing at the Dorchester, and I've got to be in New York to tell tales to McGraw-Hill. The good things always seem to be over too quickly. Let's go to the bar and have a margarita, for the road.'

She had once, many years ago, told me that there was good luck, bad luck, short luck, and long luck. 'And you and I,' she said then, 'have had a good short luck.' She had been right, but it had happened again, and again, and become a habit, and we were both always afraid to press that luck for fear it would turn bad. 'If we ever lived together,' she had often told me, 'it wouldn't be the same. You'd be bored. You'd go away. This way, at least, it works and it's always good, always beautiful. I know you're there and that's all I need.'

'And all you want.'

'Yes, I wouldn't dare want more. I don't believe in it. I don't believe,' she said, with flat resignation, 'that anything lasts.'

'Which means that the world is all fucked up.'

'The people in it.'

'We seem to last,' I said.

'This way. Our way. Maybe it's the only way.'

'If it's not good enough for you, you've got to tell me. And then we'll end it.'

'And you tell me, too. Promise?'

I had promised, and she had promised, and we had had this conversation once or twice a year for the past seven years. The last night, in the bar of the Hotel Victoria, we sat in a corner booth on leather cushions and listened to a guitarist and drank three margaritas each. Then we walked through the darkness to the bungalow and at eight o'clock the next morning we boarded the jet for Mexico City. From there I cabled Beverly Loo that all had gone well. We changed planes for New York, arrived at Kennedy Airport and took a taxi to the Hotel Elysee, and the next morning I went with Nina back to Kennedy. Her flight to London left at eleven o'clock.

'Don't hang around,' she said, smiling. 'You have things to do.'

'All right,' I said. 'Have a good flight. Take care.'

'You too, my sweet. And good luck.'

She vanished in the crowd toward the boarding area. We always said our goodbyes that way, without plans. It was the only way when you were playing a good short luck. I took a taxi from the airport straight to the McGraw-Hill Building. Beverly Loo and Albert Leventhal were waiting.

'It went fine,' I said. 'You got my cable? He wouldn't let me call.'

'You saw him?'

'Sure I saw him. He'll do it. He accepted the terms.' I explained how I waited first in New Orleans, then Mexico City, then Oaxaca, until finally at five o'clock on the second morning in the Hotel Victoria the telephone had rung. A voice had identified itself as Pedro. I had said, 'I don't know anyone named Pedro. Who the hell are you?'

'A friend of Octavio's.'

'Look, it's very early in the morning and I'm in no mood for games. I don't know you and I don't know your friend Octavio.'

'Ah. Patience, *señor*. Octavio is the man you have come to see.'

And so at dawn I had been picked up by Pedro in a Volkswagen, driven to Monte Albán and pointed in the direction of a parked, battered Buick. The man waiting for me in the front seat – 'he's a wreck, a thin and tired ruin' – was Howard Hughes. We had talked, we had wandered through the temples. The next morning Pedro had picked me up again and flown me in a Cessna through the mountains to Juchitán. 'He was a mad pilot. He nearly killed us. He kept dipping down into the valleys to show me the Indian villages. "Look," he said, "they live like animals! *Los indios!* This is the Stone Age!" And Hughes was waiting for me in Tehuantepec. First I went to Salina Cruz with Pedro and had a swim in the Pacific. Nearly froze my ass off. Then I met Howard in a

77

little hotel. We drank orange juice together. "Best orange juice in Mexico," he said. I gave him a draft of the contract, he made a few changes, and we shook hands – well, not literally; he never shakes hands – but we agreed. I'm seeing him next month, probably in Nassau. He's going to call me. I still have no way to contact him. Now look at this . . .'

I took from my briefcase the souvenir photograph of me at Mexico City Airport. 'I was tailed all the way down. Pedro gave this to me. One of Hughes's men took it at the airport when I got off the plane – for identification.'

'And to make sure you were alone,' Beverly pointed out. 'God, that man is clever. You must feel like you're in a James Bond movie.'

'A little,' I admitted.

The next afternoon I was brought to the 32nd floor to meet Harold McGraw, President of the Book Company. He seemed equally pleased, although cautious; and the following morning one of the McGraw-Hill lawyers, Faustin Jehle, had finished reading through the handwritten draft of the contract between Hughes and myself. 'It's all right,' Jehle said, 'except for one or two clauses. We'll show you how they should be changed. And there's one thing more. We'll want a bank-documented signature, or else he'll have to sign the contract in front of a notary.'

'I don't know if he'll do that,' I explained. 'He's being sued for $50 million in Las Vegas and all he has to do is go before a Nevada notary and sign a paper that he fired Robert Maheu and he could win the suit, but he won't do it. And you know he never showed up in court for the TWA lawsuit. That cost him $137 million plus damages. I don't know if he'll do it, Faustin.'

'Well, if he wants us to publish his book, he'll have to,' Jehle said.

I gave the news to Beverly and Albert Leventhal and made the same speech. 'I'll talk to the Legal Department,' Albert promised, 'but if that's what they say, I think that's the way it'll have to be.'

I flew back to Spain the next evening, slept like a dead man for fifteen hours in the arms of my wife, then drove off to the studio in a steady drizzling rain and called Dick in Palma. 'It's all off,' I said. 'It's finished. They want a notary to witness the signature.'

'Don't they trust you?' Dick said, aghast.

'Sure they trust me. It's Hughes they're worried about.'

'How long does it take to get a notary's license? I'll cram for the course.'

'Forget it. They won't bite. It was too good to be true. I'll call them in a week or so and tell them he turned them down, and I'll get back to my novel, and you finish *Richard the Lion-Hearted*. And we'll chalk it all up to experience.'

'I don't believe you,' Dick said, laughing. 'You're conning me again, like the time you said you called Beverly and she said, "Oh, that old Hughes-authorized biography gag again?" What really happened? Don't be funny, Cliff, because I'm too nervous. I haven't had a decent night's sleep in three weeks.'

'I'm not being funny.' I repeated the story until finally he believed me. 'We're out of business. Maybe it's for the best. We always said it was a crazy idea and there had to be a snag in it, and now we know the snag. I pissed away $2,000 on a trip to Mexico and now they want a notarized signature on the contract.'

'Can't you . . .'

'No, I can't. Forget it, Dick. I mean it. The ball game's over.'

Part Two

Free speech is the right to shout 'Theater' in a crowded fire.

– Abbie Hoffman

Part Two

5

Project Octavio

If I had previously flirted with any illusions that my mind was still not made up and that I would drift with the prevailing wind – 'if they buy the idea, fine; if they don't, the hell with it' – they had vanished by the time of my arrival back in Ibiza. I had been lighthearted with Dick on the telephone, because there seemed little choice. But in my heart there was no lazy gladness, no feeling of relief, no sense of having been saved from the brink of a possibly disastrous enterprise. After all, it was a hoax, not a crime. All I tasted was the gall of disappointment.

Getting back into the novel was hard work. I would reread chapters, block out a new version of a section yet to be written – and then drift off into thoughts of what might have been if the McGraw-Hill Legal Department had not been so adamant and intelligent in their demands. To pass the time I read through the three biographies of Howard Hughes that I had picked up in New York: Albert Gerber's *Bashful Billionaire*, John Keats's *Howard Hughes*, and Omar Garison's *Howard Hughes in Las Vegas*. The Gerber and Garison books were slop. They tried for sensationalism without benefit of fact, other than material culled from newspaper clippings and interviews with unnamed 'friends' and 'reliable sources.' The Keats book was well-written, more of an attempt at true biography; and therefore, since so little truth about Hughes was available, the dullest of the three.

After an appropriate number of days had passed, I telephoned Beverly Loo. This time I reversed the charges. 'He called,' I said, 'and I told him Jehle wants the contract notarized. It's no deal. He said exactly what he said to Senator Brewster in 1947 when they wanted him to produce Johnny Meyer at the hearings in Washington. He said, "No, I don't think I'll do that."' Beverly tried to interrupt, but I went on doggedly. 'He's got a notary in the palace guard, but it's one of the men who's not supposed to know anything about the project. And he said he'd be damned if he'd go to the local candy store in Nassau. So let's forget it. I'll write about the Mexican trip in my memoirs.'

'Listen,' Beverly said excitedly, 'I'm trying to tell you something! The lawyers made that demand without consulting anyone else. Lawyers are over-cautious. Now just forget what they said. If you can get Octavio's signature on a contract and have him sign it in your presence, that's good enough.'

'Whose decision is that?' I asked.

'Everybody's.'

'Well,' I said, 'fortunately he promised to call me back in case you changed your mind. He was a little pissed off, but I think I can calm him down.'

'We're counting on you,' Beverly stressed.

I took a deep breath and said, 'You can.'

Hanging up the telephone, I let out a war whoop of joy. Then I dialed Dick's number in Palma.

He arrived in Ibiza two days later, jubilant. I had gone over the three letters from Howard to me, comparing them once again with the letter reproduced in *Life*, and decided that my second version was passable but hardly expert. I spent those two days drafting still a third version, giving up only when I had run out of yellow legal paper. That was it, I decided, as I reproduced all the doodles and stains that appeared on the second version.

It was time for what we call a P & P session – plotting and planning.

'If Howard was able to go to Mexico,' I said enthusiastically, 'he can go anywhere. I think I'll meet him in Puerto Rico to sign the contracts.'

We basked in the strong sharp light on the terrace of the studio, sheltered from the cool wind that blew across the Mediterranean from the Sierra Nevada Mountains. Dick had stripped to the waist and was leaning against the flaking white wall with his face turned to the February sun. His massive chest rose and fell almost as though he were asleep. He was content, reprieved from *Richard the Lion-Hearted*.

'Why Puerto Rico?' he murmured.

'Well, he should stay in the south. Somewhere he can get to easily by plane, without creating a fuss. And there happens to be a direct flight from Madrid to San Juan – Colombian Airlines. Edith and I flew it in 1965 when we went out to Tobago.' It would look good, I thought, if I appeared to be going out of my way slightly for our meetings. McGraw-Hill's knowledge of international airline schedules would be limited, I reckoned; Puerto Rico would seem a reasonable choice for Hughes and a chore for me, when in fact the opposite was true.

I worked for three days on the contract. I had a sizable file of old contracts with magazines, book publishers, and film companies. A paragraph from one, a phrase from another, a few additions that would be peculiar to Howard Hughes and would serve our purpose as well, then it was done. I typed the final draft on white legal-size onionskin until I could see exactly how far down the final page the signatures should go. Then I signed

'Howard R. Hughes' on about fifty sheets in the correct place.

'Pick out the best three,' I told Dick, handing him *Life*'s reproduction of the letter to Chester Davis and Bill Gay for comparison.

'I can't tell one from another,' he confessed, then looked puzzled. 'Why do you need three?'

'One copy for me, one copy for McGraw-Hill, and one for Hughes.'

'You're getting too involved in this,' he said. 'Hughes isn't going to need a copy.'

'You're right. I need a rest.'

I took my rest on the beach of the El San Juan Hotel in Puerto Rico. On the third day I flew to New York, checked into the Algonquin Hotel, and had lunch there the next day with Beverly Loo and Robert Stewart of McGraw-Hill, and Ross Claiborne, Executive Editor of Dell Books, one of the major paperback publishing houses. Dell had reprinted my last book, *Fake!*, and Claiborne, who was young and intelligent, treated me with interest directly proportionate to the sales of the book, which had been only fair.

'I can't tell you what Cliff's working on,' Beverly said smugly, 'but it's the most fantastic project of the year.'

'The decade,' said Stewart.

Claiborne's barely concealed boredom evidenced the fact that he had heard such talk before. 'Sounds interesting,' he murmured.

Beverly remained undaunted. 'When the time comes,' she promised, 'you'll pay through the nose.'

That afternoon and all the next day I held conferences with the McGraw-Hill editors and executives. It was explained to me that in the interest of secrecy Hughes had been assigned a code name, Octavio – in honor of his pseudonym during our Mexican meeting – and that the book itself would be called 'Project Octavio.' 'That's what they did at *Life* when they were working on the

Khrushchev memoirs,' Beverly said. 'That was called "Project Jones." And we'd like to bring *Life* into this for first serial rights. They're the only ones who can handle it properly. And also, probably, the only ones who'll pay the price we want.'

'How much?'

'The highest they've ever gone for anything is $200,000. I want to top that.'

'But can they keep their mouths shut?'

'On Project Jones there were only three people up there who knew about it until just before publication. And they have very good files, you know – the best. That might help you in your research.'

'You mean a file on Howard Hughes?'

'Well, they've *got* to have one, with all the articles they've done on him in the past forty years.'

'I wouldn't mind seeing those files. They could save me a hell of a lot of work.'

'Let me handle it,' Beverly cautioned. 'Let's not seem anxious.'

A discreet lunch was arranged at Barbetta's between Beverly, myself, and Ralph Graves, Executive Editor of *Life*. I liked Ralph immediately: a man in his late forties, with a deep voice and blue eyes whose keenness was curiously softened by his glasses. The meeting I judged to be crucial. McGraw-Hill was one thing, *Life* was another. If there was skepticism and challenge, it would come from Time, Inc.; they had resources to investigate not only the eventual book but the tales I might spin during the period of creation. Tread gently, I cautioned myself. But after our third Tanqueray martini, Beverly said: 'Tell Ralph about the first meeting in Mexico.' I launched into the now-familiar mountaintop scene and the wild plane ride to Tehuantepec. Graves nodded.

'And now tell Ralph about Puerto Rico and the bananas.'

I felt like a child being asked to play a Bach fugue at a

grownups' party. I would rather have been in bed reading a comic book, but I had to play. The banana story had come to me on the plane from San Juan to New York, based on an experience that Edith and I had had in Puerto Rico in 1965. During an eight-hour layover before we flew on to Trinidad, we had rented a car and driven up to the tropical rain forest.

I had been met at San Juan Airport, I related to Beverly and Graves, by the Puerto Rican equivalent of Pedro. This one's name was Jorge. He had taken the contracts from me for delivery to Hughes, whom he knew as Mr Frazier, a name I chose because of the impending bout with Muhammad Ali, and then checked me into the El San Juan Hotel near the airport. 'Stay in your room,' he had said. 'Mr Frazier might call at any time.' Remembering the long wait in Oaxaca, I had replied: 'Look, I may want to go out on the beach and take a swim.'

'In that case,' Jorge replied, 'we'll have you paged as Mr Kelly.'

'Suppose there's another Kelly in the hotel?'

'Oh, no,' Jorge explained, 'this hotel is filled with Jewish people from New York.'

Jorge – I continued – had called at four o'clock the following morning and instructed me to come down to the lobby. He had led me to a parked car on a side street. There was Howard in the front seat, wearing a shaggy black wig. (If Edith could do it, I figured, why not Howard?) 'Cost me $9.95 in Woolworth's,' he said. 'You don't know the risk I take in meeting you this way. They're always after me.' We had driven then, with me at the wheel, to the tropical rain forest, arriving at dawn. Howard had told me where to stop, and a few minutes later a peasant woman emerged from the thick grove of trees, bearing a basket of bananas on her head. Howard instructed me to buy a dozen.

'He ate six of them,' I told Ralph Graves. 'He said they didn't travel well. Very fat, short, sweet bananas. He told me that the bananas you bought in the States were made of plastic. I said I thought the Puerto Rican bananas were the best I'd ever eaten, and then he got very friendly. He likes a man who appreciates a good banana. We went over the contract and he had hardly any changes to suggest. The next night we met again and we signed it in the car.'

'Show him the notes,' Beverly instructed.

On the plane from San Juan to New York, I had filled half a spiral notebook with my recollections of conversations between Howard and me. I read them to Graves. Howard had offered his opinions on women, bananas, the loneliness of old age, the Eastern Establishment, friendship, credit cards, and Mormons. He favored bananas over Mormons, which I thought was a good move, since his palace guard consisted almost entirely of Mormons and they were the ones, in the end, who might well try to undo my good work.

Ralph Graves had listened with careful, quiet attention, but whether his nods meant belief or doubt was difficult to say. He was polite, but there was no amazement, no commitment. I rattled on about Howard's secret experiences in Ethiopia. 'He was a bush pilot out there. Went out without anyone in the company knowing about it. TWA had a contract to organize Ethiopian Airlines . . .'

'And Hemingway . . .' Beverly prompted.

'Yes, he knew Hemingway,' I said. 'Had a long relationship with him, which isn't generally known. Knew him in Cuba, I think.'

Graves said: 'We know Mary pretty well. We can ask her about that.'

'Mary?'

'Mary Hemingway. His wife.'

'I wonder if Howard ever met her,' I mused aloud, and made a mental note to make sure he hadn't.

'Let's see the letters,' Graves said.

I produced them, and Graves adjusted his reading glasses and went through them carefully. He came to the last letter, in which Hughes set forth his reasons for wanting the book written. The second page of that letter seemed to catch his attention. He studied it with intense concentration. 'Look,' he said, offering me the page.

'What's the matter?'

'The way he writes the letter *I*. You see here? How he's gone over it twice, scratched it with his fountain pen where he didn't get it right the first time?'

'I never noticed that.'

'That's a habit of his,' Graves explained. 'I've seen it before in his other letters, the ones in our file. Very characteristic. So is the phraseology.' He extended his hand to me, smiling. 'I think you deserve congratulations. You've succeeded where professional journalists have failed for the last fifteen years.'

'I'll take the congratulations when the book is done,' I said modestly, and then with a good measure of truth, 'until then I don't know what I'll come up with. But thanks.'

The two scratched *I*'s in my letter from Hughes had been an accident of the pen that I had let stand because they had a look of naturalness. In the genuine letter I had used as the model – and the one of which *Life* had a copy – Hughes made no such characteristic error. Graves's mistaken memory surprised and gratified me. It was only later, thinking about it under more private circumstances, that I felt I understood. Like the others, he was all-too-human. He wanted to believe. 'They'll help us all the way,' I had said to Dick before I left Ibiza. 'Whenever we stumble, they'll pick us up. Don't think of them as the enemy. They'll turn out to be our best allies . . .'

'Good luck,' Graves said solemnly. 'If we can do anything for you, just let me know.'

*　　*　　*

The last meeting took place in the office of John Cooke, a McGraw-Hill vice-president and the head of the Legal Department. He was a big, imposing, white-haired man. 'This was signed in your presence?' Cooke asked, indicating my contract with Hughes.

'In a parked car on a side street in San Juan.' I laughed, and both Cooke and Faustin Jehle shook their heads slowly in gentle wonder.

'What's this Rosemont business?' Jehle wanted to know. The contract contained a clause which noted that it superceded 'any previous similar agreement made between H. R. Hughes and any other person, company, or corporation, including but not limited to Rosemont Enterprises, Inc.' Rosemont, I had learned from the Gerber biography of Hughes, was the corporation to which Howard had apparently given the rights to his life story. Rosemont had twice sued to prevent publication of biographies about Hughes; both suits had failed, but I had decided it was wiser to bolt the barn door before the horse knew he had been penned.

'Hughes just told me to write that into the agreement,' I explained. 'He said it was to protect me and you. Since then I've done some research,' and I informed the lawyers about the Rosemont suits.

'Christ, that's no good,' Cooke said. 'He can't just say the contract supercedes any other contracts if the others are still valid. He'll have to warrant that he's got the rights. And whatever happens, he ought to indemnify us against suit from Rosemont. Can you get him to sign an amendment to that effect?'

'I'll try,' I said.

Cooke leaned back in his leather swivel chair, chuckling. 'What a hell of a guy. The richest man in this country, and he takes $400,000 of the advances and leaves you with $100,000, and you've got to pay all your expenses. How'd you let him talk you into a deal like that?'

'You've missed the point, John. After the advance is earned out, Hughes doesn't share. All the royalties are mine. In the long run I'm liable to make more money out of the book than he will. It's a gamble, but I'm willing to take it.'

It was later explained to me by Beverly Loo that management had been more concerned than Dick and I had realized or than anyone was willing to reveal to me, about the bona fides of my relationship with Hughes. In the early stages of the hoax, two things had served to convince them. The first was my willingness to take the financial risk; and work, in terms of percentages, for relatively little money. Irving is gambling, they reasoned, that he'll get enough material from Hughes to make a big first-rate book. If he doesn't get the material, he won't make money. So he'll make damn sure he gets it.

It was good thinking, and they were right: I would make sure I got it.

'The second thing that convinced them,' Beverly told me, 'were those first two telephone calls you made to me from Ibiza. You paid for them yourself. When Harold McGraw heard that you didn't reverse the charges, he said: "Cliff is obviously taking this very seriously." He was impressed.'

'Are you kidding me?' I asked.

'No, it's true.'

'*That* impressed him? That I paid for the telephone calls from Spain to New York?'

'Well, of course. You know that most writers usually call collect. In fact, *you* usually call collect.'

'I'm impressed, too.' But I didn't say with what.

Cooke finally handed the contracts back to me. 'Who drew these up?' he asked.

'Hughes and I did.'

'He didn't have an attorney?'

'Not that I know of, unless he was hiding in the bushes. But they look pretty good to me.'

Cooke chuckled. 'Well, they've got some cockeyed language in them, but they'll stand up in court. A lawyer would have done a better job, but sometimes when two simple people write a contract the intent is clear and it's even harder to challenge. They'll do.'

'Thanks, John.' Laughing, I stood up to leave his office. 'That's one of the compliments I'll treasure till I die – that you lump Howard Hughes and me together as "two simple people." I'll let him know that's how you feel about him.'

Back on Ibiza, I gave Dick a blow-by-blow account of the trip. The McGraw-Hill contract would be in the mail to me, signed by Harold McGraw himself, by the end of the month. 'And it's firm. I've got a contract to write the authorized biography of Howard Hughes. It's no pipe-dream any more. It's real.'

'I won't believe it till I see it,' Dick murmured.

'You'll see it. But it's time to go to work, buddy. So far it's been fun and games and tall tales, but now we've got to get down to it. There's a life out there waiting to be researched and created. And we won't do it sitting on our asses here on Ibiza.'

We spent a long day poring over the three Hughes biographies and the other material I had picked up in New York, working out an itinerary for our projected research trip. The initial idea was to accomplish everything in one month of nonstop digging and travel, then do the taped interviews with the mythical Hughes, then follow up with a second research trip whose primary purpose would be interviews of Howard's ex-friends and business associates. The breaking of secrecy was what we most feared, and the interviews could be dangerous in that respect; therefore they had to wait until the last possible moment and then be incorporated into the text of the final draft of the book.

'What happens if we get caught?' Dick asked. 'Suppose this thing blows wide open before we're finished?'

'The money will be there,' I said. 'Hell, it's no Federal case. We haven't stolen anything. I've lied, that's all. I'll have to take the consequences. So what can they do to me? They can't stop me from writing other books. Someone will publish them. As long as they get their money back, the worst thing they can do is yell. And I have a feeling they won't yell too loud, because they might look pretty foolish.'

The beauty of it, as we had conceived the scheme then in its embryonic stage – and even later, when we were fully launched into a year of plotting and labor, refining, improvising, sweating, tacking and trimming sail in rough waters – was that no one would be hurt. There was no caper that seemed to parallel what we were about to do. Rob Fort Knox? Steal the crown jewels from the Tower of London? We had no criminal ambitions and such derring-do, while it may have made for the stuff of Hollywood caper films we had seen and marveled at, was beyond the scope of my imagination, much less our intention. Implicit in theft was the possibility of violence. Dick and I were not violent men. During the 1948 War of Independence he had been a volunteer with the Israeli Army. He had been stranded in Rome, unable to pay his hotel bill. An Italian dubbing company hired him once to scream in English. The Israelis agreed to pay the hotel bill if Dick would sail to Haifa and fight. But once there, his trained baritone outweighed his temporary bravado; he wound up singing for the troops on the road to Jerusalem. I had been a volunteer in Israel as well, in 1956. I had joined a border kibbutz and one night, on guard duty, fired my only shot of the campaign at what I thought were marauding *fedayeen*. I hit a tin bell hanging from the neck of a wandering goat, woke up everybody in the kibbutz, and the next day was confined to trench-digging.

We weren't stealing anything, I had said to Dick. For whatever we received, we would be giving fair value. Not that it would be what I represented it to be – the authorized biography of Howard Hughes – but it would be a book. 'An important book,' I added. 'And *a good* book.'

With that summing up, we decided to stand pat and call a halt to our P & P session. By the second week of April, I decided, we would have digested all the accumulated material, listed our tasks and objectives for the first research trip, and then be ready to go. The next day, at the Iberia office on the main *paseo*, I bought our air tickets.

6

All Right So Far!

Dick and I flew from Ibiza to New York on April 13th with Edith due to follow in a week's time. For her it was to be a holiday, the first we had had together for three years. Dick and I stayed in what had been my parents' apartment at 92nd Street and West End Avenue in Manhattan – a gloomy, seven-room place which had not been lived in, and seldom cleaned, since my father's death almost a year ago. It was cluttered with the detritus of three lifetimes: my mother's, my father's, and mine. And over every surface in the apartment was the spoor of the New York beast: a patina of black, greasy, gritty dust.

Dick and I spent most of the week in the New York Public Library and the second-hand bookstores on Fourth Avenue, digging into Hughes and related subjects such as aircraft design and the early days of Hollywood. The second day in New York I went to McGraw-Hill; they had already received my two signed copies of the contract with them which called for an 'Untitled Biography of H (*Señor* Octavio),' and I dutifully signed an additional letter, to be kept in the Legal Department's safe, identifying the mysterious *Señor* Octavio as Howard R. Hughes.

'It's like a cartoon I once saw in *The New Yorker*,' I told

Dick. 'A guy's falling from the top of the Empire State Building and as he passes the fiftieth floor on his way to the pavement, someone leans out of a window and calls, "How's it going, fella?" The guy grins and yells back, "All right so far!" That's us. But I've said it a dozen times. If things get too hot, or even if they don't you can always go to them and tell them it's a hoax. The money will be there and then we've got an unauthorized biography or a novel.'

'What do you think they'd do to you?'

'If I told them it was a ripoff?' I thought for a while. 'I don't know. They'd either throw me right out on my ass and sue for their money, which they wouldn't have to do because I'd have the check in my hand; or, if they had the guts, they'd laugh like hell.'

That evening I had been invited to a cocktail party in honor of Germaine Greer; McGraw-Hill had just published her bestseller, *The Female Eunuch*. A British television crew was on hand to film the festivities. I arrived, grabbed a drink, ducked the hot lights and the clusters of women's libbers who had come to pay homage to Germaine, and then spotted a strange-looking figure in the corner. An old Indian, dressed in a war bonnet and full technicolor redskin regalia, sat on a sofa drinking a glass of ginger ale. I was with Beverly Loo and I said: 'Who's *that*?'

'Oh, you've got to meet him, Cliff. That's Chief Red Fox. He's a 101-year-old Sioux Indian chief. We've just published his memoirs.'

I sat at the feet of the old man for nearly an hour, swapping tales of the frontier until he clapped me on the shoulder at one point and said, 'Hey, you don't have to call me "Chief." Call me Red Fox.'

He was an extraordinary man, with a seamed, bumpy face, lively and full of himself. 'I'm on the Johnny Carson Show tonight. Second time in three months. That's rare, you know, but I kind of liven it up for him . . . Read my book yet? You should. It's terrific.' He explained to me that as a child he had been camped a few miles away from the Battle of Little Big Horn and had heard the shooting. Now he did public relations work for a meat packing company and occasionally performed war dances at supermarket openings in the southwest. Without his feathers and buckskins he could have passed for an old retired shopkeeper sitting on the stoop of a Brooklyn tenement, rattling on about his youth.

I caught Beverly Loo by the door. 'Marvelous old man,' I said. 'But you know, Bev, I have a whole library at home about the Old West in the 19th century. If Red Fox is a 101-year-old Sioux Indian chief, then you're the Empress Loo of the Ming Dynasty.'

Beverly looked alarmed. 'What are you trying to say?'

'Come on, Bev. This is me. I'm practically a McGraw-Hill employee. We can level with each other. This guy's just not for real.'

Her alarm changed to indignation. 'What basis do you have for saying that? Are you serious?'

I saw that *she* was serious, so I laughed. 'No, I'm just putting you on. Relax. See you in the office tomorrow.'

Dick was still awake when I got home. 'You know,' I said, 'I have a funny feeling that if I ever told them I wasn't really meeting Howard Hughes, they *wouldn't* laugh.'

'That's my feeling, too. I just didn't want to disillusion you. What brought you round to reality?'

I told him about my meeting with Chief Red Fox and my remarks to Beverly Loo.

'*Were* you serious?' he asked. 'Did you think he was a phony?'

'Maybe, maybe not. Am I an expert?'

'Well,' he said, grinning, 'it takes one to know one.'

* * *

The following day Beverly and I had lunch. She was unusually silent and preoccupied. We arrived back at her office and I asked: 'What's troubling you?'

'It's this man Suskind, this writer you've hired to do the research. Does he know about your meeting Octavio?'

'No. I've got a problem there. I haven't told him.'

'Where is Suskind now?'

'Right here in New York, staying with me.'

'How well do you know him? Are you very close friends?'

I wondered what she was driving at. 'Not really,' I said uneasily. 'I've known him a long time, that's all. We're old chess partners. What's this all about?'

'He's a writer,' Beverly announced. She brushed a strand of straight black hair away from her eye. 'Writers steal. Writers talk. And writers are the most jealous people in the world. We're keeping this on a top-secret basis up here, because if it leaks out to the press Octavio will wash his hands of the whole deal. What I'm getting at is I don't see any need for this man Suskind to know you're meeting with Octavio.'

'Dick's a good guy,' I said, relieved. 'And I'm glad you brought this up. This is something that's been bugging me. I hate to lie to him. I want to tell him.'

Robert Stewart, my editor, poked his head in the door, gave a nervous half-smile, half-grimace, and joined us. 'Absolutely not,' Beverly said. 'I forbid it. God, you're naive. Robert agrees with me, too. You think because you're not greedy and you can keep a secret that everybody else is that way, too. Let me tell you, they're not. If Suskind found out you were meeting with Hughes, I mean Octavio, and this was an authorized biography, he'd know what kind of money was involved in it for you. I don't know how much you're paying him, but he'd be bound to feel it wasn't enough.'

'Not Dick. He's not greedy.'

'But we don't want you to tell him,' she said darkly.

That evening, in the kitchen of my father's apartment where Dick was eating yogurt and I was knocking off a box of Mallomars, I explained the situation to him. 'Sorry, old buddy, but you're not to know. You're a writer. You steal, you gab, and you're jealous.'

'How the hell could you keep a straight face? You're a born con man,' Dick said admiringly.

'And up yours, too.'

The next day Dick came to McGraw-Hill to meet me for lunch. I took him into Robert Stewart's office and Dick suggested that McGraw-Hill might be interested in looking at his unfinished manuscript on the exploration and conquest of West Africa. 'Sure,' Stewart said, absent-mindedly, and then turned his attention to me. 'When do you leave?' he asked.

'As soon as Edith arrives. We go to Washington, then Nassau. Dick's heading out to Houston and Las Vegas.'

'Will you meet Hughes in Nassau this time?'

My eyes flicked to Dick and I cleared my throat uncomfortably. 'Robert . . . '

'Does he know Edith's coming with you? Won't he object to that? From what you've told me, I don't think he's the sort of man who'll take very kindly to surprises.'

I didn't answer. I shut my eyes a moment, then opened them. Dick was looking coldly at Stewart; then he turned to me, a frowning Goliath. 'You sonofabitch,' he rumbled, 'is *that* what this is all about?'

'He didn't know,' I reminded Stewart. 'You and Beverly made me promise not to tell him. Yesterday, Robert, right over there in Beverly's office.'

Stewart coughed, turned pink, muttered something and began to shuffle the papers on his desk. 'You and I had better go have a private talk,' I said quietly to Dick. 'I have some explaining to do.'

While I tried to quell my laughter outside in the

hallway, Dick leaned against the wall, a contented smile on his face. 'I did pretty good in there, don't you think?'

'Terrific,' I said. 'You're a full-fledged member of the club now. When we go back in, sulk a little at first, but for Christ's sake don't look aggrieved. It'll make Beverly and Robert too nervous.'

The check was ready only on Thursday morning, a scant six hours before I was to meet Edith at Kennedy Airport and take off for Washington. It was a McGraw-Hill check payable to me for $97,500 and drawn on Bankers Trust. The total amount for the first part of the advance, 'the seed money,' was $100,000, but I had been short of cash in New York during my March trip and the publisher's treasury had parted with $2,500. Dick and I took the check to the Chase Manhattan Bank, where I had my own checking account. They informed me that it would take three days to clear. 'That's no good,' I explained. 'I have to be in Washington tonight, and I need the check broken down into cashier's checks before I leave.'

'Go to Bankers Trust,' Chase Manhattan suggested. 'It's their check.'

Dick and I jumped into a taxi. 'Let me see that thing,' he said. He held it carefully, as though it were made of glass, and seemed to study every word and digit. 'Jesus Christ,' he murmured, 'have you ever seen a check that big?'

'Paper,' I said. 'This is *money*. This is ninety-seven . . . thousand . . . five . . . hundred . . . dollars. You've got to imagine it in one-dollar bills, 97,500 of them spread out on a carpet or stuffed into a suitcase. Some guys would kill for that kind of money.'

'For less.'

It was money, more money than I had ever seen, but money wasn't the name of the game. It was a necessity, a means, a reward, but it was not the reason I had flown to Mexico and Puerto Rico or lied to Beverly Loo and

Harold McGraw, and it was not the reason I was setting out that night for Washington and Nassau to meet a man who wasn't there.

But Bankers Trust shared Dick's attitude rather than mine. I was escorted immediately across a broad blue carpet to an officer of the bank sitting behind a mahogany desk. Dick stood by the door, arms folded across his chest, elephantine and expressionless. Of course, I thought, they'll assume he's my bodyguard. And God knows who they'll assume *I* am. A *capo*, probably, traveling with his hit man. I wore a gray suit and my most sincere tie, but somehow I couldn't make myself feel like a man who should be flashing a check for $97,500. The Bankers Trust officer seemed to agree. I argued with him for twenty minutes that I wanted the check broken down into bank checks, one to H. R. Hughes for $50,000 and the other to Clifford Irving for the remainder. No, that was impossible. I would have to deposit the check to my account elsewhere and wait for it to clear.

'Look, I've got a plane to catch. Let's do this the easy way. Give me the cash. I'll *buy* the bank checks.'

The banker flushed a little. 'Mr Irving, we haven't got that kind of cash on hand.'

'You mean you can't cover your own check?' I asked, stunned.

'Mr Irving, you don't seem to realize . . . this is a large check. This is a lot of money. We can't . . .'

'Call Harold McGraw,' I demanded. 'If that check's not broken down the way I want it broken down, and I can't get on that plane tonight, that whole green building may topple.'

The banker asked me to wait. He telephoned to McGraw-Hill. A few minutes later he returned and said that the bank would honor my instructions, and he apologized for having kept me waiting. In the street, with the two checks tucked away in my briefcase, I turned to Dick. A new reality had invaded me. 'You were right,' I admitted. 'It *is* money.'

'I told you so. You've met Howard Hughes just twice and already you've lost your sense of proportion. But what do we do with it?'

'Invest,' I said. 'Buy a share of American business. I'll take you over to Merrill Lynch and introduce you to my broker.'

'I'm not too sure I want a share in American business,' Dick said. 'The people who run it don't seem very bright. The banks can't even cash their own checks.'

That afternoon, with the courage of his convictions, and using some of the $10,000 I gave him, he opened a brokerage account at Merrill Lynch and bought three hundred shares of Fuji Photo.

It was cherry blossom time and the hotels in Washington were filled. The only vacancy American Express could find for us was in a deluxe motel in Alexandria, Virginia. Edith was delighted. 'I've never been in Virginia.'

We rented a car at the airport and the next day, a Sunday, drove down through the countryside to the restored colonial town of Williamsburg, which Edith instantly dubbed as '18th century Disneyland.' The following day, after deciding that work had to be done in Washington, we found a small, cheap, pleasant hotel there called the Harrington.

I spent the morning at the Civil Aeronautics Board, doggedly plowing through thick volumes of dockets containing motions and countermotions relative to TWA and Northeast Airlines, both of which had been reportedly mismanaged to the point of ruin by Howard Hughes. I left with almost two hours of tape and a feeling of total confusion. If I were ever going to understand what I had read and taped, I would have to take a crash course in legal jargon and the intricacies of bureaucratic red tape.

That same day I telephoned the Pentagon. Before leaving New York I had had an interesting discussion with Martin Ackerman, a friend and my lawyer in a libel action against my last book. Marty was one of the few people outside McGraw-Hill, *Life,* and the island of Ibiza who knew about my meetings with Hughes. I had shown him Howard's letters – of course, he had no idea they were part of a hoax. From the outset he was enthusiastic and helpful. More than a lawyer, he was a businessman and a millionaire. He understood big money and the kinkiness of the men who had battled to make it. 'I don't think Hughes will ever give you any real figures on his income and his holdings,' he had said to me, 'and that's something you really should have. Try the Pentagon,' he suggested. 'There's got to be an office that handles defense contracting, and they may have a breakdown on Hughes Tool and Hughes Aircraft. If you can get the information, you may not understand it – but I could make sense of it for you.'

I was eager to learn and grateful for his help. 'What do I ask for?'

'Don't tell them you're looking for information on Hughes himself. Give them some story that you're doing a study on contractual relations between the Department of Defense and three or four big corporate contractors.'

When I called the Pentagon I was put through to a man named Otto Pinilus, who had something to do – I never quite found out what – with payments for defense contracts. He sounded interested in my problems and bored with his own, whatever they might be. He invited me to his office that same afternoon.

The Pentagon was to me, as it must be to most Americans, a forbidding concept. I assumed it would be bristling with grim-faced Marines with machine guns demanding identification at every twist and turn of its labyrinthine corridors. I also assumed, as a matter of course, that I would get lost. I was right in one respect only: I got lost.

When I entered the building, I was prepared to be fingerprinted, searched, asked for identification and references. I told the girl at the desk I wanted to see Mr Pinilus and she handed me a map of the building, marked it with arrows and an X, and said: 'First left, then the escalator up one flight, then left, then right. It's on the inner ring. Follow this map.'

I walked past her. I was inside the Pentagon, and within thirty seconds, following her directions and clutching my map, I was lost. I can't remember whether I went right when I should have gone left or up when I should have gone down, but I soon found myself in a spacious corridor, alone, outside a door that I could have sworn was marked *JOINT CHIEFS OF STAFF*. I looked up and down, needing that Marine now to guide and extricate me; but the door opened and three men stepped out, talking. They were generals and there were more stars piled on their shoulders than on the Christmas tree at Rockefeller Plaza, and more campaign ribbons on their chests than in any hock shop. If I had been a member of Smersh or the Chinese equivalent, I could have eliminated some heavy brass with one burst – and no one as yet had even asked my name.

'Excuse me, sir,' I cornered the nearest general, 'I'm lost. I'm looking for a Mr Pinilus. Here's where he lives,' and I proffered my map.

'Down one flight,' the general said politely, 'then turn right and proceed to the inner ring. Then ask again. And good luck.'

I thanked him, followed his directions and found Mr Pinilus. He was a pleasant, balding man in his early fifties, and he seemed glad to see someone, even me, come into his office. I explained my problem. I was doing a study on payments to aircraft manufacturers. I wasn't quite sure if what I was saying made any sense;

I was trying to remember the phrases Marty Ackerman had used and I don't believe that Mr Pinilus made much sense out of it, either; but he was nevertheless eager to help. 'I thought it would be better,' I said, 'if I limited the study to four companies – Lockheed, Boeing, Northrop, and Hughes. It's pretty easy to get information on the first three, but I'm having a hell of a time finding out anything about Hughes Aircraft or Hughes Tool. I suppose that's because they're privately owned. But they just don't want to talk to me.'

'The Hughes people don't like to talk to anybody,' Otto Pinilus said, with a mixture of sadness and annoyance. 'They don't even like to talk to *me*. They're the most difficult people in the country to do business with.'

'Have you got anything I can take a look at?' I asked hopefully.

'Not much of it's classified,' he said. 'You can see almost everything we've got.' He began piling record books and confidential reports on the desk in front of me. One report contained a breakdown on the entire operation of Hughes Aircraft and Hughes Tool: their government contracts, their facilities and personnel, descriptions of the specific military projects the companies had completed or in which they were still involved, and a further report detailing the government's analysis of Hughes's capabilities, problems, and future prospects in the space and aircraft fields. The latter reports Mr Pinilus' secretary very kindly Xeroxed for me, and they were all I would ever need to create a portrait of the Hughes industrial complex which would find its place in Howard's future intimate discussions with me.

'These reports aren't really secret,' Otto Pinilus explained to me. 'They're available on a limited subscription basis, although it's very expensive and not too many people know about it. But we use them all the time.'

'Who published them?' I asked.

He checked and showed me the name of the service. 'It's a subsidiary of McGraw-Hill,' he said.

I had also stopped that first day in the Library of Congress. The taxi had to drop me a few blocks away, since the area around the Capitol building was thronged with police and roaming groups of bearded and mustachioed young men wearing unzipped Army field jackets and khaki shirts rolled up to the elbows. They were Vietnam veterans protesting against the war. A mild and pleasant spring sun beamed down on the green lawns and impressive white government buildings, but a feeling of unease and caution filled the air. You could see the affront to authority in the persons of men who had risked their lives and killed to uphold that authority, and now repudiated it, making both the police and the government officials nervous.

It was my first time in the Library of Congress: a beautiful building, with magnificently muraled ceilings and that hush of concentration in the air one finds wherever the keys to knowledge are stored. I had brought my tape recorder with me, and I spent the first part of the afternoon browsing through volumes of Standard & Poors, gathering more dreary information on the Hughes industrial empire. Then, idly flipping index cards in the library catalog, I made a lucky hit. Someone had written a brief thesis on TWA's role in the development of Ethiopian Airlines. I asked for the book and retired into an alcove near the stacks, where I read quietly into the tape recorder for two hours. Ethiopia in the early 1950's came alive for me. I saw Howard battling the downdrafts in the canyons along the Blue Nile, landing his DC-3 at deserted strips on spiny ridges. I saw him taking off from the infamous dogleg runway at Danakil. I saw him as both pilot and passenger in aircraft jammed with sheiks, peasants, rank goat hides, live chickens, and screaming children. That he had never been to Ethiopia seemed of no importance. The trip would change his life, bring him face to face with himself in his quest for identity. If he ever read what I would write, he would wish he *had* gone.

I wanted one more book: the transcript of the 1947 Senate hearings when Hughes had been accused of failing to deliver on his wartime military contracts and of currying favor with visiting Air Corps personnel in Southern California. I had already discovered that the volume I needed – Volume 40 of the Senate sub-committee's twelve-year-history – was mysteriously unavailable. An hour later, deep in the bowels of the library, in the annex reached by a tunnel cut under the buildings, I found the book in the stacks. There were three full sets of the 42 volumes, but only two copies of Volume 40. That volume alone ran more than 1800 pages. Hughes himself had testified for several days, filling more than 300 pages with questions and answers. Hunched on a stool in that airless cellar, I began quietly dictating into the tape recorder. In twenty minutes the library closed, and I quit. I slid the volume back into place on the shelf and found my way upstairs to the exit from the annex. The guard stopped me. He was a young, ruddy-faced man with an easy smile.

'Sorry, sir. Have to search your briefcase.'

Edith was waiting for me back at the hotel. She had spent the day at the Washington Zoo and had become friendly with the keeper in charge of the white-cheeked gibbons. He had promised to let her into the cage with him one day during feeding time. 'When all this is over,' she said enthusiastically, 'I want two white-cheeked gibbons. And a South American toad. And maybe a flamingo or two.'

Her lack of interest in the problems I faced in digging up material on Howard Hughes had not waned. 'You know,' I said, 'Hughes's testimony in that Senate hearing . . . '

'How would you feel about the white-cheeked gibbons? They have lovely faces and arms that come down to the floor, like this.' She demonstrated, as best she could, the gait of the white-cheeked gibbon.

'The gibbons are okay. The testimony is great, and the best thing is that it gives me a key to Hughes's speech patterns. Mind you, it was in front of a Senate sub-committee, so he's a little stiff, but . . . '

'The South American toads sing when a full moon comes out, you know.'

'The gibbons are okay. Forget the toads. Who the hell wants a toad croaking all night when you're trying to sleep?'

'*You* don't wake up even when a jet flies over the house. I want a toad. And they don't croak – they *sing*.'

'I'll never be able to tape all that testimony,' I muttered. 'But it's all good stuff. And there's some great material in the Appendix – a report on the crash of the F-11, the whole bit.'

'Oh, darling, I'm so sick of hearing about Howard Hughes. Will you have to talk about him all the time in Nassau, too?'

'I'll try to shut up.'

'Let me tell you about the flamingos. They just need a little pond to float around in, and the toad could live in there, too . . . '

The next morning was flawless, warmer, with a sky that reminded us instantly of Ibiza. We drove through Georgetown and then to the Lincoln Memorial, which I had remembered as the most impressive of Washington's sights. It had moved me when I had first been there in 1960, and I wanted Edith to see it. Climbing the steep flight of steps, we wandered round Abraham's temple, read the Gettysburg Address, then strolled back toward the car along the perimeter of a softball field.

Two teams of teenagers were playing – no uniforms, just a pick-up game, with cheering and shouting and a few girls watching from behind the batting cage. Edith and I found a patch of soft grass and sat with our backs against the trunk of a tree, while I explained the rules of baseball. One of the batters slapped a foul down the third base line. The ball came to rest in Edith's lap. Delightedly, she picked it up and flung it back toward the playing field. She was happy in Washington. And when she was happy, I was, too.

That afternoon I spent sequestered in my corner among the stacks of the annex to the Library of Congress. I dictated wearily into the tape recorder, but by the end of the day I had done some simple arithmetic: It would take me five more days to tape all the testimony I wanted, and even that omitted the time and drudgery necessary to transcribe the tapes. Each time I had gone in and out of the annex, I realized, the same young guard had been there in front of the revolving door. He knew me now. He no longer bothered to search my briefcase, just said, 'How's it going?' to which I would reply, 'All right so far.'

Volume 40 was a thick book, three inches I reckoned, impossible to slide into my thin leather briefcase – but not impossible to stick in my waistband. I *had* to have the material. In five more days of taping, which meant at least two or three more visits to the zoo for Edith, I might be committed to two white-cheeked gibbons, a pondful of South American toads, a brace of flamingos, a sloth, a chimpanzee, and a herd of wildebeest. Edith was restless, dreaming of Bahamian beaches and long siestas with the shutters drawn against the Caribbean sun. My back hurt and the sound of my voice droning Howard Hughes's testimony was putting me to sleep. I loosened my belt and stuffed Volume 40 into my waistband in the small of my back. It was uncomfortable, but the book stayed put: a hard, uncompromising bulge.

With my jacket buttoned, I doubted that it could be seen. Once I was out of the stacks, past the attendants, I would have no problem with the guard – a casual wave and I would be gone. They've got another copy here, I thought, and I can always mail this one back to them anonymously when I'm finished with it.

I tucked my briefcase under one arm and walked slowly down the corridor toward the staircase. I felt as if the book was bulging behind me like a carton of beer. Grasping my belt buckle with my free hand, I pulled it tight. The library attendants were bent to their desks or busy replacing books in the stacks. This was *Topkapi*. This was Alec Guinness, head of the Lavender Hill Mob – me, swiping the crown jewels of Afghanistan, or a ton of gold from the heavily guarded vaults of the Bank of England.

'Agent 008 reporting in, sir. I have *The Book*. Doctor Yes has been foiled again . . . '

A new guard stood at the desk. I had never seen him before. He was a man in his sixties, with a veined neck and cold, watery blue eyes. Clutching my belt, I tried to smile. He didn't smile back. He wasn't my friend. He had the most unfriendly face I had ever seen. He was The Law, and he *knew*. I knew he knew. I fluttered my briefcase toward him, hesitating, not knowing whether to stop or move on. To return to the stacks was out of the question. The one thing I couldn't afford to do was turn my back to him. He indicated the briefcase.

'Let's see it.'

I spread it open on the desk and he extracted the various notes and pamphlets, then slid them back. A cold eye regarded my tape recorder, but it was obviously nothing more than that; it concealed no priceless documents such as the original Declaration of Independence. I finally worked up a smile and an innocuous remark. 'Are you open on Saturdays?'

'Hours are posted on the wall over there.' That fishy eye bored into me. 'Turn around.'

I had always known that in moments of true crisis, the worn-out cliches of the language spring full-blown to life. I knew it then, because I had the sensation of my heart rising through my chest and into my mouth. I turned, a full turn, like a man in a trance, clutching the briefcase in one hand and the tape recorder in the other. I was afraid to turn too quickly for fear the book would slip from my waistband; I was afraid to turn too slowly for fear the telltale bulge would reveal itself. That eye, I knew, would miss nothing. I have no idea how long it took me to complete that turn, but I felt Volume 40 begin to slide. Facing the guard again, he stepped toward me and raised his hands, bringing them down the sides of my jacket toward my belt. I felt my mouth go bone-dry and my lips were instantly parched.

Just as the guard's hands reached my belt and began to move around toward my back, Volume 40 slipped quietly down into the seat of my pants. A moment later and the guard's hands touched the spot where it had lain against my spine.

'Did you say,' I croaked, 'open or closed on Saturday? I didn't catch it.'

'I said take a look at the sign on the wall.' The guard turned his back. I shuffled toward the revolving door, the weight of Volume 40 in my pants. I whispered: 'Thanks, have a good day,' then shoved my way out into the street.

Waddling down the block, I turned the corner and sank down on a bench near the bus stop. My heart had dropped down from my mouth and was now skipping around my chest, looking for a resting place. Fingers trembling, I lit a cigarette. I felt Volume 40 snug under my buttocks.

Edith was in the hotel room, writing giant-sized post-cards to her daughters in Germany, when I arrived.

'What's the matter with you?' she asked when she saw my face and I fell flat on the bed.

I told her the story – I had got my voice back but it was still shaky. 'If that guy had caught me at the door I would have gone to jail. That's government property, and I stole it. Oh, wow.' I shook my head. 'You know, I don't think I'm cut out for this kind of work. If this were a caper, I'd never make it.'

I had been shot at on the Israeli-Egyptian border, I had been on a leaky schooner chased by a hurricane in the middle of the Atlantic, I had swum among barracuda, I had skidded and turned three full circles on an icy mountain road – but the words I spoke then were the truth. 'That guard . . . that book. You know, that was one of the most frightening moments of my life. If I'd been caught I would have been arrested. This whole Hughes project would have gone right down the drain.' I wiped my forehead. 'My God, I was lucky.'

'Well, you learned your lesson. You won't ever do it again.'

'Never,' I swore. 'That's the beginning and the end of my criminal career.'

Miami was next, a planned one-day stopover so that I could visit the Hughes Medical Institute. I had considered drafting a handwritten letter from Howard to the director: 'Give this man a free checkup and access to the books . . .' but in the end had settled for a typed letter on the stationery of my London publishers, William Heinemann, Ltd, introducing myself and claiming that I was embarked on a study of American medical foundations. I signed the letter in my own handwriting: A. Dwye Evans, Chairman of the Board. It seemed an innocent and plausible method of gaining entry, but the Medical Institute was tougher to penetrate than the Pentagon. The director was away and the woman who deigned to see me was as friendly as though I had come bearing a letter of introduction from the Internal Revenue Service. I browsed through the Institute's library, which contained magnificent sets of leatherbound volumes in three languages on various esoteric medical subjects. Their pristine condition, and the fact that the library had an atmosphere of permanent vacancy, made me feel that I was the first person who had ever so much as opened a book in there. No one would talk to me except the receptionist, a young girl who apparently had nothing else to do.

'Seen the boss lately?' I asked.

'Mr Hughes? We call him "the invisible man." He's never even been here.'

I left and walked down the block to where Edith waited for me in a coffee shop. She was shivering from the air-conditioning and I was beaded with sweat from the street. It was a hot, muggy April day and the sky was piled high with clouds.

'Let's get over to Nassau,' I said. 'I've had Miami.'

By seven o'clock that evening we were sitting in the bar of the Pilot House Club, across the bay from Paradise Island, sipping a second pair of rum punches. I leaned across the bamboo table and whispered in Edith's ear.

'Keep an eye peeled for a man about six-foot-three, very thin, 65 years of age. He'll probably be wearing tennis sneakers and drinking mineral water. Might have a mustache and a false beard, too. When you spot him . . . '

'If I hear any more,' Edith said, 'I scream. You can take Howard Hughes and fold him into small pieces and shove him up your ass. This is our holiday. I want lobster and a bottle of cold white wine and then we go to bed and you seduce your wife and we sleep until noon. Or I scream.'

'Don't scream,' I said. 'It's you I love. Howard's just a passing fancy.'

*   *   *

114

It was good in Nassau between us. There were siestas in the afternoons and rum punches in the evenings, and in the mornings we loafed on the beach and I even enticed Edith into the water, despite her theory that man had struggled for a million years to drag himself out of the sea and evolve into a creature of the land. 'To go back into the sea,' she maintained, 'is to throw away everything what humanity stands for.' But with surprising skill for a nonbeliever, she swam with me to the end of the pier. Beyond that she refused to go. 'Sharks,' she cried, and nothing would deter her from the belief that they lurked in the dark blue water beyond her depth. We had moved after the second night to the Montagu Beach Hotel, about a mile out of town, a huge candy-pink structure that had seen better days but was still spacious and comfortable and cool. It was also, I thought, the kind of place that Howard would visit. The Pilot House Club was crowded, with the only entrance through the bar and narrow lobby, while the Montagu Beach had a back door, service entrances, and sprawling gardens. I took a large room on the first floor. 'He couldn't climb too many steps,' I explained to Edith.

'Will they check things like that?'

'You never know.'

'Why can't you just visit him at the Britannia Beach?'

'I can see him anywhere I want. But it would be more logical if he sneaked out to see me. Otherwise I'd have to fight my way through that gang of Mormons.' This was the pattern I wanted to build: that Hughes always ventured out in the dead of night to meet me in my hotel, that he was mobile and, more to the point, that I had no idea where he was staying and therefore no means of contacting him. My first thought, to stay at the Britannia Beach Hotel myself, I had vetoed only because of the room rates: it was $50 a day and I refused to spend that kind of money to stay in what looked to me like a displaced part of Miami Beach.

By the end of the weekend we were brown and we had spent long hours in bed and Edith was happy. And so was I. The last true holiday in the sun we had taken had been five years ago, in Tobago and then Grenada.

'You see?' We were in the water in front of Montagu Beach and she was hanging on my shoulders, one eye peeled for sharks and barracuda. 'It was a good idea.'

'It was my idea,' I pointed out.

'Only because I twisted your arm. You're a funny man. You work so hard at writing and other things but you don't see that you have to work at you and me, at your marriage, what is the most important thing you've got, you claim. There you're just a lazy slob.'

'You're right. When this is over we'll take a long trip. Anywhere you like. Where would you like to go?'

'Venice,' Edith said. 'To the Hotel Dannieli, what is the most beautiful hotel on the Grand Canal. I went there with my mother and father when I was a girl, and I always thought there was a place I would want to go back to with a man I loved.'

'I've been to Venice. How about Budapest?'

'I want to go to Venice,' she said. 'But I don't want to talk now about what we're going to do when this is over. We're here now. Talk to me. Be with me.'

'I am.' We splashed around in the water while I indicated various floating pieces of driftwood and clumps of seaweed as sharks, sting rays, and piranhas, and finally, with Edith clinging to me and threatening to pull down my trunks if I kept frightening her, I gave a tug to the bottom half of her bikini and had it nearly to the thigh before she could clamp my wrists. 'No one will notice,' I whispered. 'Just don't thrash around.'

'I'll scream, you fool.'

'You're always threatening to scream.'

I kept tugging and then Edith screamed. 'Help! Rape!' A dozen heads popped up from beach chairs on the

116

sand. She grinned at me, showing big teeth. 'Now you're in trouble. I warned you.'

'You can't be accused of raping your own wife.'

'You can rape me, but not in the ocean.'

'Is that an invitation?'

Freeing herself, she began dogpaddling toward the beach. She stood up when the water was knee-high; primly adjusted her bikini, and beckoned me to follow her.

On the Monday following our arrival I began what little research needed to be accomplished in Nassau. I went to the offices of the local newspapers, the *Guardian* and *Tribune*, skimmed through their files and dictated anything pertinent into the tape recorder. A *Guardian* reporter, Connie Jo Justice, had covered Hughes's arrival for the paper and we took her twice to dinner and I gave her $100 as a retainer; she was to send me any news about the billionaire and dig into the lives of his Mormon guard. One day I had lunch with the U.S. Vice-Consul, Lew Crosson, the man who had officially welcomed Hughes to the Bahamas the previous Thanksgiving. We ate pastrami sandwiches in a tree-house in the tropical garden of an abandoned hotel. The newspapers had quoted Crosson as saying that he hadn't known who was arriving; he had just been told to go out to the airport in the middle of the night to meet 'a very important man.'

'Which wasn't true,' he admitted. 'I knew who it was. He was supposed to come out here the same time last year, in '69, but it was canceled.'

'And did you meet him?'

'I waited at the damn airport for two hours until that jet landed. It just stood at the end of the runway and no one got out except a couple of men who were too young to be Hughes. We hung around and finally I said, "Look, would it help if I turned my back?" They said it would,

117

and so I turned around, and fifteen minutes later one of them said, "Okay, you can go now." And that was it.'

'You never saw Hughes get off the plane?'

'No one did.'

'Has anyone ever seen him over at the Britannia Beach.'

'No one's ever seen him anywhere.'

'Could this be him?'

I showed him a photograph that Ralph Graves had mailed to me for identification; it had been sent to *Life* by a freelance photographer. A middle-aged man leaned out on a hotel balcony with what looked like a closed-circuit TV camera attached to the wall beside him. The features were fuzzy but clear enough for identification. 'No,' Crosson said. 'I know that man. He's one of the Resorts International people.'

I cabled Ralph Graves that evening: *NEGATIVE OCTAVIO STOP POSITIVE IDENTIFICATION ONE OF HIS ASSOCIATES AND PERHAPS OCCASIONAL DOUBLE REGARDS EDITH,* and sent a follow-up letter to the effect that someone close to Hughes had made the identification and then Howard himself had confirmed it.

The next afternoon I decided it was time to visit Paradise Island, not exactly to beard the lion in his den – since I never came up with a single piece of evidence to indicate that he was caged there – but simply to have a look at the place. 'Come along,' I said to Edith, and we took a taxi across the bridge, paid the $2 toll, skirted the Britannia Beach Hotel and then paid an additional fee for entry to the beach. It was a fine curving strand backed by a forest of palms and casuarina trees. We wandered hand in hand until we came to some shabby wooden buildings set back among the palms.

'That's where Howard *really* lives,' I said.

It turned out to be a yoga colony, run by a Swami Devananda whose headquarters were in Montreal. The buildings were rickety, and the beds, glimpsed through rusted window-screens, were unmade. A few people began to gather for the afternoon exercises: some girls, a handful of middle-aged men and women, a croupier from the casino, and a white-haired old man. 'Howard in disguise,' I explained to Edith.

'Stop kibbitzing and go exercise with them,' she said. 'It will do you good. You're getting fat.'

'All right. What about you?'

'Me? Are you crazy, *Mensch*? I'm a decadent European lady. I watch. You're the one who's *sportif*.'

The group had laid out mats on a large cement court. I spread a hotel towel, and after ten minutes I was soaked in sweat, breathing hard.

'Headstands,' the instructress called. I watched carefully, tucked my head into the crutch of my arms on the towel, arched my back, walked toward my head, lifted my legs, and crashed to the concrete with a terrible thump.

'Let me help you,' the instructress said, and stood behind me. I wavered in the air a second and then toppled, cracking my knee on the concrete. From the shade of a palm tree I heard Edith's laughter. The rest of the group, including the old man, arched beautifully, feet pointed quivering toward the sun.

Back in the hotel I came out of the shower to find Edith on the floor between the bed and the window, head sunk into a pillow and feet braced against the wall. Her face was the color of a tomato. 'Go away,' she gasped.

'I didn't have a wall to lean on.'

'You didn't think of it. I have to cheat. I'm an old lady.'

'Good luck,' I said, and lay down on the bed with the copy of the 1947 Senate hearings I had swiped from the library. Three mornings later I was nearly to the end of the 1800-page volume and Edith was in the center of the room, perfectly arched and upside down, standing

119

on her head, smiling crookedly up at me. She flipped over at last, puffing. 'I did it! It makes you feel wonderful. Come, I help you.'

I squatted between the bed and the window. She lifted my legs and I braced them against the wall; she let go, and I fell, socking my shin against the frame of the bed. When I finished cursing I said: 'There's no room there for me to fall.'

'Lean against the door,' she advised.

Wearing only my underpants, I did as Edith instructed. Head on pillow, tucked well into arms. Swing legs up. Brace against door. View of Edith upside down. Ready to try . . .

At that point I heard the sound of a key turning, and before I could move or shout a warning, the door swung open to admit the Bahamian maid, carrying a mop and fresh linens. She saw a man upside down, toppling toward her, and she shrieked three times in a row. I fell, scissoring her head between my legs, taking her with me in a jumble of dropped mop and flying linen to the corridor floor. In the midst of my apologies and attempts to calm the howling maid, I was aware of Edith in the room behind me, having her own brand of hysterics.

Later that day I called Dick at the Towers Hotel in Houston. 'It's going pretty well here,' I said. 'Not too much hard information, but I'm soaking up atmosphere and Edith's getting a few laughs. There's a yoga colony on Paradise Island and I think we can make Octavio a member of it. We'll have him trying to stand on his head by the door and one of the Mormon Mafia opens it and he falls out and—'

'What the hell are you doing down there?' Dick interrupted. 'Are you drunk or smoking pot, or what?'

'I fell out of a door,' I said. 'It's a long story.'

'Well, stop falling out of doors and get to work,' he growled, and proceeded to tell about his trip.

120

I had left him in the apartment in New York, where the only room in an approximate state of cleanliness was the kitchen. I had propped a note for him on the kitchen table, against the sugar bowl. 'Don't let dirty dishes accumulate in the sink. They bring roaches.' And I signed it: 'Your Jewish mother, Cliff.'

'That note made me feel better,' Dick told me on the telephone. 'You have no idea how depressed I was after you left.' This was his first visit to the United States in over five years, and every time he walked down the street, read a newspaper, or turned on the television, it occurred to him that he had finally succeeded in expatriating himself: like me, he was less at home in New York, his native city, than he was in Ibiza or London or Paris.

Work was the anodyne. In the public library, Dick plowed through every volume of *The Reader's Guide to Periodical Literature*, beginning with the volume that covered 1905, the year of Howard's birth. He Xeroxed almost all the articles about the Hughes family and then went to *The New York Times Index* and repeated the process. After I called from Washington and told him about TWA and Ethiopian Airlines, he ordered photocopies of half a dozen contour maps of Ethiopia.

There were two portable typewriters in the apartment, a Royal and an old Remington Noiseless. We had already decided we would need a machine on which Hughes's mystical manservant, Pedro, would type the first part of the transcript. 'We can't use the Royal,' I had told Dick. 'I used it to type the outline of *The 38th Floor*. McGraw-Hill's got that on file.' Dick took the Remington to a typewriter repair shop in the neighborhood and told them to clean it and put it in shape. He finished his work two days later, and the next afternoon checked into The Sands in Las Vegas.

'The first thing I did,' he told me on the telephone,

'was drop about sixty bucks in the slot machines. "Schmuck," I said to myself, "if you're going to lose money gambling, do it with style, not like some little old lady from Des Moines" – so I dropped three hundred playing blackjack and another five hundred shooting crap. I had visions of becoming another skeleton in the family closet, like my uncle, Cold-Deck Charlie.' Cold-Deck Charlie had made a living as a professional card cheat on the transatlantic liners. He had died with 150 suits in his closet and $11.60 in his pockets.

'Listen,' I said, 'this call is costing a young fortune. Tell me what you did in the way of research.'

What he had done was Xerox all the Hughes material in the morgue of *The Las Vegas Sun*, get a list of properties bought by Howard Hughes and some of his front men, and have lunch with a Mr Henry Vermilion of the Atomic Energy Commission. In Houston, then, he spent three fruitful days in the public library going over microfilm copies of *The Houston Post* and *The Houston Chronicle* dating back to the early 1900's. He went slowly, making notes of the manners and mores of the period, writing down the names of department stores, prices of clothing, tools, automobiles, and houses. He also checked out the two or three decent bookstores in Houston and had shipped about twenty books to Ibiza. 'I saw a coffee table volume about the Eighth Air Force, but it's expensive. Fifteen bucks. What do you think?'

'Get it.' We had already decided that Howard was going to be a secret hero in World War II, flying reconnaissance missions over France on a top-priority pass from President Roosevelt. This was, of course, unknown to the general public, as was the fact that prior to his 1938 round-the-world flight, Air Corps General Hap Arnold had commissioned Howard to penetrate German air space and photograph the military build-up on the Polish border. It was unknown to Howard, too, but we thought he would appreciate the heroics if he were properly shy about their significance when it came time to tell me the tale.

Dick had one unlooked-for stroke of luck in Houston. He decided to hire a cab for the day and the driver, a one-legged, sixty-year-old former croupier, revealed himself as a true source of folklore about the wildcatters and highrollers who had made Texas synonymous with big money. He drove Dick to Yoakum Boulevard, where the Hughes family had lived for many years. Howard's childhood home had been torn down, replaced by the St Thomas School, a red-brick building with white columns. Dick told the cabdriver he was doing a magazine article on Hughes, and the driver began talking about Hughes Sr., whom he claimed to have known personally. He mentioned Jakie Friedman's gambling place on Main Street, too. 'All the wildcatters used to gamble there,' Dick reported. 'Big Howard was one of the highrollers – dropped a lot of money. But the Rangers closed Jakie down and drove him out of town. Guess where he went?'

'I give up.'

'Vegas. He's *the* Jakie Friedman, the guy who built the Frontier Hotel, which our boy bought when he moved there in '66.'

'Good, good. See if you can come up with more juicy tidbits like that.'

'Okay,' I heard Dick yawn, 'that's all for now, bubby. You're leaving for Ibiza soon, right?'

'Tomorrow.'

'I'll call you when I'm home. Stay away from the casino.'

That night Edith and I visited friends whose ketch was berthed in Nassau harbor, listened to two strolling Bahamian troubadors sing bawdy songs, and the next day we boarded the plane for London, with connections to Ibiza. Beverly Loo was in London on business and I

123

called from the airport to her room at the Ritz. 'How did it go?' she asked anxiously.

'Fine. It was a little tough at the beginning, but he started to open up toward the end. It's going to be a great book – if I can stand the pace.'

7

Helga Takes a Trip

Edith laughed easily. She wore a dark skirt, black boots, conservative brown silk blouse, black raincoat, and a diamond ring sparkled on her left hand. 'I don't think I've ever seen you so dressed up,' Beverly Loo said on the way to Ibiza airport.

'If I wear what usually I wear,' Edith explained, 'they stop me at customs, the same what they do to all the hippies. And I go to see my daughter in Frankfurt, too. I want people to know I'm her mother, not her sister.'

Beverly had flown down from London and stayed with us at the *finca* for three days. It had worried me slightly, since I was fresh from the trip to Nassau and expected a salvo of questions about Hughes and the time I had spent with him, questions to which I had not yet prepared solid answers. But Beverly was either uninterested or being discreet; it was hard to tell which. I told her one or two tales of Edith having to leave our hotel room at odd hours so that Howard would not be embarrassed by her presence, and then I clammed up. I had already booked Edith's ticket, Ibiza-Frankfurt-Düsseldorf-Ibiza, on the assumption that Beverly would stay on the island for nearly a week.

Then Beverly suddenly decided to see Madrid. 'I'll fly

with you as far as Barcelona,' she announced to Edith. And there was nothing to be done about it.

. . . and I always hate to fly, always, so my fright gives me wet hands and wet feet, and I was uncomfortably flying to Barcelona, with Beverly Loo sitting next to me chattering, with the sun red like a blood-orange and carrying the old-new Swiss passport, the passport of Helga Renate Hughes with my black-wigged photograph with the cheeks puffed out. The passport felt like a big stone, or, no, like a big bomb in the bottom of my handbag. I thought it would go bang when I left Barcelona or when I landed in Frankfurt and passed through customs and immigration. I thought – I had a fantasy: they would see the ends of my nerves sticking out of my skin, and I thought it was not worth it. What I was doing was so foolish and crazy, what I was doing . . . except maybe it would keep Cliff away from Baroness von Slut; he would be busy with his book about this crazy rich man and would have no time to see her and might even stop thinking about her. I could kill her! No, I knew I couldn't . . . but I could knock all her teeth out – except maybe that might make her sing better . . .

Beverly said goodbye and I rushed off for my next plane, and suffered through the second horrible flight. I cursed Howard Hughes. All this because of him! 'Why can't he fly to Zurich to deposit his own checks?' I had yelled at Cliff, who just laughed.

I took a cab from the airport to the train station in Frankfurt and bought a ticket to Zurich. It was hot in Germany, much hotter than Ibiza, and I was sweating not only on my hands and feet but all over my body. I could smell myself.

I got into an empty compartment, but soon a young American couple came in and sat down facing me. They wanted to be friendly, like most Americans traveling in Europe, and talk. I smiled and nodded but didn't talk back. I was afraid. I was traveling on my own passport as Edith Irving – maybe a little more blonde than natural, which is any woman's privilege – but Cliff had told me to stay in Zurich on the Helga Hughes passport and of course I had to look like this

126

crazy Helga. Before we reached Zurich I would have to put on my black wig and glasses in the toilet compartment of the train, and so I didn't want to become friendly with the friendly Americans and tell them some things about myself and have them maybe ask to stay at the same hotel with me and, yes, wouldn't it be lovely to see Zurich together? No!

But they talked and talked even though I said nothing. They were from Ohio, I think, or Indiana, and this was their first trip to Europe, and wasn't it wonderful, so old and full of culture and cathedrals. I excused myself.

I took my bag and went to the toilet just before we reached Zurich. I put on the wig and the eyeglasses and waited by the door of the platform a few cars further down. From the station I took a cab to the Hotel Baur au Lac – I knew it from my childhood because I had stayed there with my parents. And then it began, those coincidences that came again and again on all my trips. Call it magic or happenings, but it was terrible. They had no rooms free in the Baur au Lac and the man at the desk said he would call another hotel. It's not so easy to find rooms in Zurich – all those people rushing in and out of the city with suitcases full of funny money to put in and take out of the banks. And so I waited and a minute later there they were: the friendly American couple from the train, looking at me with their mouths open like fish. Here was the blonde woman they had shared a compartment with for six hours; here she was in a black wig and glasses. And I thought, oh, God, if they should hear my name, if the clerk should say, 'All right, Frau Hughes, we've found you a room,' it would somehow not be good.

So I quickly grabbed my bag and dashed from the Baur au Lac into another taxi and went to the Hotel Glarnischof near the Paradeplatz, the big square in Zurich. The Glarnischof had a room. I felt funny in my wig and spectacles and the heavy makeup to make me look older, but no one else seemed to think I looked funny, or maybe it's because the Swiss are so very polite and used to asking as few questions as possible. Whatever, Frau Hughes – or Hoogus, as the Swiss pronounced it –

127

went and ate a good but indigestible dinner and took two ten-milligram Valiums because it had been such a frightening day.

I slept well until the morning, then put on all that horrible makeup again and went outside to look for a bank. Cliff hadn't told me which bank to choose, so I picked the first one I saw, naturally one of the biggest: the Swiss Credit Bank, right there on the Paradeplatz, the main square. It was a big place, a big old building. It looked so safe and secure. That was good, I thought, and I went in, wet hands and wet feet and all.

I was amazed how easy it was. I thought I would have to have a long, serious talk with the director of the bank to open an account, but there were two pleasant girls at the information desk who said, 'Oh, no! You just fill out these papers.' When I had filled them out, I handed them to a man at a desk and gave him a thousand Swiss francs, which was what I had to do, they explained, as a Swiss citizen, to open an account. He made out a receipt on which he wrote Frau Helga Hughes, but in speaking he pronounced it yukus which means 'joke' in Schweizerdeutsch.

And so I waited and then a little man with a Hitlerian mustache brought me a checkbook made out in the name of Frau Helga R. Hughes, with the name on all the checks. Cliff had warned me that this might happen and that it could ruin everything, so I said: 'No, that's no good. I have a business in Paris and New York and my business runs in the name of H. R. Hughes – women have a hard time in business, you know – and so I must have the bank account only under the first initials and then the last name, Hughes. I use this account only for business,' I told him, 'and I don't want to mix it up with my personal account. I get mixed up very easily' – which was certainly the truth.

He said, 'Come back in an hour, please,' and I did. He gave me a new checkbook and new receipts, all made out to H. R. Hughes. I asked if I could now deposit the $50,000 check I had shown them, the one Cliff had given to me, and he said, smiling, 'Certainly, Frau Yukus.'

128

Then I had a terrible fright. I thought I would faint. The teller at the window said: 'Frau Hughes, you must sign the check on the back. You must endorse it.'

What could I do? I said, 'All right, just a minute,' and carried the check to one of those stands in the middle of the marble floor, and I took out the Hughes passport and copied the signature as best I could, but my hand was shaking and I knew they didn't look the same at all. But when I brought it back to the teller she took the check and didn't compare the signature with anything.

And in this way started my business relationship to this man Howard Hughes, Cliff's good friend.

The train didn't leave for Frankfurt until 11:30 in the morning, so I walked down the Bahnhofstrasse. I bought some sweaters for the children and some marzipan for Cliff, a big block of Lübecker chocolate-covered marzipan that would last him maybe two days and give him a bellyache, which he deserved for the bellyaches he had given me while I was in Zurich.

The ride back to Frankfurt was far more pleasant than the ride coming into Switzerland. I had tucked the Helga Hughes passport under a scarf in the bottom of my handbag so that I wouldn't take it out by mistake and show it instead of the Irving passport. The thought came to me then, for the first time, that I should really have another passport to travel on so I could fly straight from Spain to Switzerland and not have to go this roundabout way, and be so long away from my little boys . . . But the ride back was so beautiful that I stopped thinking after a while. It was the beginning of May, and all through the Valley of the Rhine the flieder – the lilacs – were blooming, and all the other flowers and trees, whose names I didn't know, were in blossom, too. I had forgotten how lovely it is during springtime in the Valley of the Rhine. In Ibiza you have no real spring, just almond blossoms in February, like balls of vanilla and strawberry cotton in the valleys toward San Jose; and then everything is burned and dry and you are in summer. But it's never this explosion of nature from winter darkness into spring, and the softness of the valley, and the glory of the flowers. I had a tiny cry because it reminded me of childhood and things which are forever past, and of my parents who had died; of their garden in the spring . . . and maybe, too, it was the feeling of relief and of release from terror, now that I was on the way back and the first trip was almost over.

In Frankfurt I rented a Hertz car and drove to my daughter's school, about forty-five minutes' drive from Frankfurt. I met Nicole – fifteen years old and looking so much like me that it's incredible – and we talked and met her friends, and then it was evening and we went all together and went to a very good restaurant. All Nicole's friends were between fifteen and eighteen, some without shoes, all with long hair, and when I went to park the car the parking attendant rushed up and said, 'This is only for guests of the restaurant.'

So I looked very haughty and said, 'That's fine, my good man, because we are guests of the restaurant.' He smiled a frozen smile, and Nicole's friends all laughed at him, and we went in and had a beautiful dinner with elegant but somehow very fast service, because I think they wanted us to hurry and leave. But we had such wonderful conversation, these children and me, and we stayed on and on after coffee. I liked their ideas so much, and none of us wanted to leave.

I stayed at a hotel in the town nearby and saw Nicole again in the morning, and then I drove to the airport and flew to Dusseldorf. My ex-husband Dieter was there to meet me, and my other daughter, Katja, and Dieter's wife. They all hugged and kissed me and we drove to Wuppertal, to Dieter's big house there, what I remembered so well because we had built it together after we were married. It's always good when you meet good friends, and they were my best friends in the world. People always think it strange when you say, 'My best friends are my ex-husband and his wife,' which I can't ever understand, because if you loved a man enough to marry him and have children with him, it would be even stranger afterwards if

you didn't feel some deep affection for him. And Hanne,
who married him, was really now one of my daughters' two
mothers, and I loved her like a sister. We talked and we
laughed, although I let them do most of the talking because I
couldn't tell them what I had been doing, or that I had been to
Zurich, or the crazy thing that Cliff was trying to do. But
Dieter and Hanne had just been to Nepal and visited the Dalai
Lama, and they told me about it and it was like old times
again, all of us friends together.

Hanne's son by her first marriage, Marcus, was now living
with them, and this made my daughter Katja happy. And
besides, there were Dieter and Hanne's two young children,
six and four, and the old dog, Karl, who still wagged his tail
and recognized me with his white, nearly-blind eyes, and it
was all marvelous and made me happy.

And now I must tell you something I did – something I
can't believe I did, but I know I did it. It happened when
I opened a drawer to take out the telephone book so that I
could call the airport about my plane back to Ibiza. I opened the
desk drawer and there was Hanne's kennkarte, *her German*
identity card, lying next to the book. I picked it up and put it
in my handbag. I'll travel with it, *I thought,* because Hanne
doesn't need it – she always travels with her passport.
And, *I thought,* now I can travel directly from Ibiza to
Zurich, if I have to go again, and not be gone so long
from Nedsky and Barney. *I thought all these things, but I*
was almost sick to my stomach with self-disgust, because I had
taken my dear friend's identity card. But some devil had hold
of me and I slid the card in my handbag, and my heart was
banging away in my chest, and I left the room thinking: Well,
it's too late. I've done it now.

On the day that Edith left I returned home early from
the studio. I wanted to spend some time with Nedsky
and Barney. At eight o'clock, after I had read to the kids
from a Dr Seuss book, I drove into town and had dinner
alone in the Indochinese restaurant, then meandered

along to La Tierra, the most popular bar-cum-meeting-place in Ibiza. At about eleven o'clock, just as I asked for my bill, Nina walked in. She was wearing her big leather coat and carrying her tin suitcase. She had flown down from London and taken a taxi straight from the airport to town.

The friends I was sitting with were her friends, too, and she joined us. After an hour she began to look gray and tired and she said, 'I'm exhausted.' Quietly, she asked me: 'Can you drive me home?'

On the way out to her house, in the mountains beyond the village of Santa Eulalia, I said: 'No one will ever believe we didn't plan this. No one will believe that you didn't know Edith was going to Germany today and no one will believe I didn't know you were coming.'

'Who cares what people believe?' she said. 'This is always the way it happens to us. It only proves that if you don't make plans, things work out.'

She was to be on Ibiza for a week, with faithful little John Marshall scampering down after her in three or four days. She had contracted to cut a solo album for Pye Records, a London company, and Marshall wanted photographs of her against the background of the Mediterranean landscape. 'And the roof needs repairing down here, and I just needed a rest.'

I left her at the *finca* and drove home. We were both busy the next day, I with work that had to be done on my boat, and Nina with her roof, but we had arranged to meet the morning after. 'I'm dying to go to the beach,' she said. 'If the weather's decent, let's try Figueral.'

The weather was cloudy, but occasionally the sun burned through and held possession of the sky for ten or fifteen minutes at a time. Figueral, a beach on the north-eastern coast of the island, was a rarely frequented spot we had known from that time many years ago when we had been together so briefly. No one we knew would be there to see us at this time of the year. I had told her I would bring my camera and click off a role of film. 'Maybe I'll get a shot you can use for the record jacket.'

'You won't get a photo credit for it, my sweet,' she said.

'I don't want one, thanks.'

But the day was too gray and Nina threw herself into the cold water a few minutes after we had trekked down the mountain to the beach, so that she was hardly glamorous enough for a cover photograph. I used the telefoto lens a few times for closeups, but her hair was wet and bedraggled. With the beach deserted, she had taken off her bikini top. I shot half a dozen photographs of her like that, laughing, with a bottle of red wine held aloft in one hand.

'Where will you get those developed?' she asked, a little worried.

'In the States, the next time I go. No one knows you there.'

'Send me copies. There might be one we could crop and use.'

She was in a strange mood, restless, and oddly depressed, then suddenly buoyant again. It came out after a while. She was unhappy with the record she had cut and a promised television series had fallen through. 'And I've done something I should never have done,' she said finally. 'I've loaned a lot of money. It was the biggest mistake I ever made in my life.'

'If you need money to cover the loan,' I said, 'I may have some after the summer.'

'The Hughes thing?'

I nodded.

'We'll see,' she said. 'I don't want to borrow from you. I hate to borrow money. How is that all going?'

I brought her up to date, omitting only the fact that Edith at that moment was in Zurich, marching into what I later learned was the Swiss Credit Bank as Helga

133

Renate Hughes. The real work, I explained, had yet to begin. Nina frowned.

'Do you really trust Dick that much?' she asked.

'I have to,' I said. 'Hell, of course I trust him. Why shouldn't I trust him?'

She shrugged. 'I don't know. People talk too much. They're so careless.'

'I'm trusting you,' I said, smiling.

'You couldn't get a word out of me on anything, even if you used a crowbar, if I didn't want to talk.'

I had told several friends on the island that I was meeting with Hughes and working on his authorized biography. There was no simpler way I could figure out to explain my prolonged absences, and the last thing I wanted was too much speculation. I had of course sworn them all to secrecy. Two of them, however, had already told the story to Nina, who had professed a blend of astonishment and lack of interest. 'I kept such a straight face you wouldn't believe it. And I keep thinking: *if they really knew*.'

'No one will ever know. Maybe when I'm old and gray I'll write my memoirs and tell the whole truth.'

'And no one will believe you,' she said, going off into a peal of laughter.

We saw each other once after that day, eating a quiet dinner at an out-of-the-way restaurant; and then John Marshall arrived to move into the *finca* and take photographs for the album jacket. And then, on the following day, I drove out to the airport to meet Edith.

Coincidence my foot, coincidence any other part of my anatomy you'd care to name – that the Danish Poison just happened to arrive in Ibiza on the day I left for Germany, and just happened to meet Cliff in La Tierra, and just happened to return to London the day after I came back to Ibiza . . .

I took a Valium every morning and every evening, and then

it was two weeks later, time to go collect the money, and I took two Valiums to start the day.

It was May 27th, two weeks after my first trip, when Beverly went with me to Barcelona. I flew as myself to Palma, then from Palma to Zurich as black-haired Hanne Rosenkranz. Dick met me at the Palma airport with the ticket. I don't know why, but I had put on a knitted wool dress and knee-high boots and I was sweating terribly; and then, sitting in Dick's new Citroën in the parking lot, I put on the wig and the makeup and the glasses, and it was even worse.

We went to a cafe on the Borne, one of the large shady places where the drinks are expensive and the waiters have stone faces. We didn't talk about Howard Hughes or about why I was going to Zurich. There were too many Americans and English sitting at nearby tables. We talked about the weather, about friends; we commented on the people we saw; and then it was time to go and I felt calmer and more relaxed, even though I was carrying three *identity documents: my own passport, the Hughes passport, and Hanne's* kennkarte. *I put the two passports in a zipper compartment of my handbag, so that I could not take them out by mistake; and I put the* kennkarte *in my wallet, which was also in my handbag. But then I thought:* Suppose some damned thief steals the wallet? Or suppose the handbag flops open and the wallet falls out and I lose it? *And I began immediately to get nervous again, and my hands and feet to sweat. I wrapped the* kennkarte *in my handkerchief, so that my sweat would not make the ink run, and I clutched it in my wet hand all the way to Barcelona and then from Barcelona to Zurich. I felt foolish and I murmured to myself:* You are the weak link. You don't know how to do these things. You'll make a mistake and the Swiss will find out you are really Edith Irving and that will be the end – the end of the book, and of Cliff and Nedsky and Barney and Dick and Ginette and Raphael . . .

By the time I got through Swiss immigration I felt ten years older, a feeble old woman whose heart would burst with fear, so hard it was thumping. And even, *I went on,* if nothing happens this time, what about the other trips you must make? You must never again carry three identity documents, but only one, Hanne's *kennkarte.*

It was 4:30 when I got to Zurich. The Credit Suisse was still open, and I dashed in and asked the teller if the check had cleared. It had, she said, and I told her I would be back in the morning, and left the bank walking a few feet off the ground. I slept that night in the Gotthard Hotel, and the next morning, remembering what Cliff had told me, I drew out all but the minimum balance. It was paid to me without question; no one ever asked to see my passport. And then I crossed the Paradeplatz and rented a safe-deposit box, and put into it all the Hughes papers – the passport and the bank documents. Finally, with 5,000 Swiss francs, I opened an account in the Swiss Bank Corporation in the name of Hanne Rosenkranz. Everything was so swiftly done that I had more than two hours to wait for my plane back to Palma.

So I sat on a bench by the river in the spring sunshine, sweating . . .

Dick flew to Ibiza the day after Edith's return. I handed him $10,000 in various currencies – Swiss, German, and American – and said: 'What are you going to do with it?'

'Well, let's see . . .' He mused thoughtfully. 'We've just bought that little Citroën, but Ginette could use a second car. What do you think's better, a Ferrari or an Alfa-Romeo?'

'Not even in jest, my friend,' I said. 'That money sits tight, because we may decide one day to give it back. And if we go the full nine innings on this caper, there damn well better be no conspicuous consumption.'

'Where are you putting your part of it?'

'It's tacked to a big wooden beam in the house. You can't see it unless you climb a ladder and crawl on top of the wardrobe. I nearly broke my neck getting it up there.'

'I'll put it in the refrigerator,' Dick said brightly. 'In the crisper, under the lettuce.'

But money was not the subject that had made me summon him to Ibiza. I had finally collated all the research material we had picked up on our April-May trip. I had read through everything, filed it, and then read through it a second time. What I felt, on completion, was a sense of unease and disappointment. We had accumulated enough statistics for an abridged World Almanac and enough facts to form the basis for a biography; but not enough for the definitive, free-swinging biography that I had dreamed of. There were too many gaps in Howard's childhood (we knew almost nothing about his first wife and his mother) and the Hollywood sections would have to be shaped from newspaper clippings and our imaginations. Dick argued that our imaginations would more than do the job, but I disagreed. 'Look,' I said, 'I've read the stuff twice through. I've never seen any of the movies Hughes made. I still can't figure out the TWA shenanigans. We're weak, and we're just weak on colorful material. What happened to him after his marriage broke up in 1930? Who did he live with? That's what we've got to know.'

'That's exactly what we can make up.'

'And have it checked? No.'

We argued the point and finally Dick conceded it. Then he revealed the truth, as he always did in the end. 'I just don't want to leave Ginette and Raphael again,' he admitted. 'That last trip was hell for me. You were with Edith. I was alone, and I hated it.'

'Dick,' I said, 'the book's the thing. We've got to do it right or the whole thing's a farce, and we can't do it right if we don't make one more trip.'

'Where to?'

'Los Angeles. We'll go by way of Houston and fill in the holes, and we'll stop off in New York first. I want

137

to take a crack at *Time-Life*'s files. Come on,' I urged. 'Remember, the pay is good.'

'This trip's going to cost us five thousand bucks before we're through.'

'That's what the money's for,' I reminded him.

Dick thought it over a while, then nodded emphatically. 'You're right. When do we go?'

'Next week. The first of June. And that's it, that's the last trip. We'll get lucky on this one,' I added. 'The harder you work, the luckier you get.'

8

Bonanza

I had written to Ralph Graves at *Life* in early May, while Beverly was on Ibiza, giving a progress report and adding: 'It's occurred to me that *Time-Life-Fortune* may have some good research files on Octavio and they might be of great help to me and save me some dreary leg-work. If this is so, and if they're available to my eye, would you let me know?'

Ralph had replied in a letter dated May 18th, saying: 'I don't see why I can't get you a look at the files, but it would have to be here in the office. I can't let them out of the building.' He then wrote:

You know anything about a man named Dietrich? He is supposed to be a long-time intimate of Octavio and is said to be coming out with a tell-everything book this fall. That's absolutely the extent of my knowledge, but I'll let you know if I learn any more.

The existence of the Dietrich book troubled me, but I wrote back that Hughes and Dietrich had parted company in 1956 or 1957 and therefore it was impossible for Dietrich to 'tell everything'; only Howard could do that. When I arrived in New York, Ralph Graves told me that *Life* had been offered a look at the Dietrich manuscript but had declined. Why should they bother? They had –or were going to have – the real thing.

On the telephone in New York, I explained why the Time, Inc. files might be of use to me. 'That whole business with TWA,' I told Ralph, 'is something I don't really understand. Octavio keeps getting pissed off at me when I don't have the background information. If I can fill myself in on that, I won't make such a horse's ass of myself when I see him.'

It was no problem, and Graves agreed to set it up for the following morning. Unfortunately, he wouldn't be able to be there personally – it was closing day for the magazine – but Dave Maness, the Assistant Managing Editor, would take care of me. He also apologized in advance for the fact that the files might be in haphazard chronological order. 'You may have to rummage through the whole damn thing to find what you want.'

'Is there a lot?'

'Yes, I'm afraid there's an awful lot.'

'Well, I'll plow through it. Do you mind if I bring Dick Suskind? That's the man who's helping me – my researcher.'

Graves hesitated, then said: 'I don't think so. The problem is that these are confidential files. They're not supposed to be made available to anyone who isn't a Time, Inc. staffer. *You* shouldn't even be seeing them, but I think this case warrants making an exception.'

'In other words, you don't want me to tell anyone I'm seeing them.'

'That's right,' he said, relieved. 'We won't mention it, and we'd appreciate it if you didn't either. In fact, I'm afraid I have to make that a condition.'

'Say no more, Ralph. Can I Xerox anything I need?'

'No good. We don't have really private Xerox facilities. You'd have to give the material to secretaries and the word would spread.'

'Maybe I'll bring my camera. I'll be there at ten o'clock tomorrow morning.'

At nine o'clock the following morning I went to Willough-by-Peerless on West 48th Street, one of the best camera equipment shops in New York. I had my Nikkormat in its bulky brown carrying case, complete with telefoto and wide-angle lenses. I explained the assignment to the assistant behind the counter: I had to photograph a number of documents and newspaper clippings; I could only use available light and I had no idea what that might be like. At his suggestion, I bought four rolls each of Tri-X, Plus-X, and Panatonic-X, and four close-up lens attachments that screwed on to the regular Nikkormat f 1.4 lens.

'You've got a tripod, of course,' the clerk said.

'Do I need a tripod?'

He frowned. 'If you were thinking of hand-holding the camera, forget it. You can't possibly get any decent definition.'

'I've got steady hands.'

'You'd better use a tripod.'

'I'll come back and get one,' I said, 'later.'

Whatever the risk, however brash I might be, I knew I could never walk into the office of *Time-Life*, camera in one hand and tripod in the other, and blithely ask to see the files on Howard Hughes. There were limits to audacity, and I had learned them that April day on the steps of the Library of Congress. I would attempt to photograph whatever of Time, Inc.'s files seemed useful, but I wasn't going in there with a tripod that screamed the full scope of my intentions.

I walked through the warm June morning, from 48th Street to the Time-Life Building near Rockefeller Center and took the elevator to the 29th floor.

Dave Maness appeared; then his secretary dropped a pair of keys in my hand. 'We're putting you in a separate room,' Maness explained with great solemnity. 'These are the only keys to it. If you want to, lock the door when you're inside. The files are on the desk. Just don't take them out of the room.'

'Have you been through them?'

'I haven't had time,' he apologized. 'I just took a quick look. There's one great letter from a pilot who wrote to us after the 1947 Senate hearings and told us all about his experiences flying with Hughes. He may be a crackpot, but it's a damned funny letter. Also, there were one or two things we had to remove from the file because they're confidential – there was a telephone conversation between Hughes and a *Time* executive which was really the property of that man, and it said some things we really don't feel should be revealed.'

'Oh, if it's confidential, I wouldn't want to see it.'

'What the hell is that you're carrying?'

'A camera.'

'A Minox?'

'No, a Nikkormat.' I unzipped the case and showed it to him and the secretary. 'My wife gave it to me for Christmas.'

'Can you take photographs of documents with that kind of camera?'

'I'll try,' I said. 'But without a tripod, it's difficult.'

He unlocked a door and let me into a small room. A dozen bulging manila folders were piled on the desk. 'Have fun,' Maness said, and left me alone with the files.

A good strong north light filled that little room on the 29th floor. It was one of those bright clear Manhattan days that give one the illusion that the air swirling through megalopolis is breathable and that the ecologists are winning the battle. I made some notes to this effect even before I began work, and much later, in the final draft of the *Autobiography*, I had Howard say: 'New York is the Cairo of America,' which perfectly expressed my own feelings.

The files were in better order than Graves had realized, although the indexing was occasionally haphazard. They were arranged chronologically, beginning with Hughes's neophyte days in Hollywood during the late 1920's, moving through his air exploits and business ventures to the debacle in Las Vegas. But they contained more than news clips from *Time, Life, Fortune,* and *The New York Times.* I skimmed through until I pulled out a sheaf of yellowed pages: the handwritten notes of the *Time* magazine correspondent who had interviewed Hughes at Floyd Bennett Field immediately following his landing after the flight around the world in 1938. There were impressions, sidelights, details, quotes from both Hughes and his four-man crew. I screwed the plus-4 magnifying lens to the camera, placed the sheets of paper side by side on the window ledge, clamped the camera to my eye, fiddled for a minute or two with the light meter, levered my head up and down until I had what I thought was a clear focus on the pages, and began clicking away.

In an hour I had pages strewn all over the desk and my heart was pounding. It was a treasure trove. The files were filled with interviews that had never been printed, with quotes from politicians and Hughes associates, most of them marked 'Not for attribution.' There was Robert McNamara, then Secretary of Defense, discussing with a *Time* correspondent the troubles at Hughes Aircraft in 1953 and referring to Hughes as 'that idiot.' Tex Thornton, head of Litton Industries, had reported to McNamara that Hughes believed management's dissatisfaction with the operation of the aircraft company was a communist plot. The *Time* reporter noted that 'this really kills McNamara.' There was Noah Dietrich, relating to the bureau chief of *Time*'s Los Angeles office a tale of Ava Gardner walloping Hughes over the head with a copper ashtray. Again: General Harold George, administrative head of Hughes Aircraft, detailing how Hughes would borrow dimes from him to make telephone calls. 'He was the cheapest sonofabitch I've ever known,' George concluded. Floyd Odium, the man from whom Hughes had bought RKO, told tales of Howard's assignations with both women and business-men. And always: 'Not for attribution.' The stories had never found their way into print. I finished the first roll of Panatonic-X and jammed a second roll into the camera. My knees were weak from the constant bending to get what I hoped was the perfect focus and my head already ached from the strain of peering through the lens.

I worked from ten o'clock in the morning until nearly five o'clock in the afternoon. No lunch break. I had a candy bar with me and twice I walked out into the corridor to the water fountain. Dave Maness marched in early in the afternoon. I was too weary to hide the camera. It stood on the desk next to six or seven empty film packs. 'How's it going?' he said. 'The girl says you haven't had lunch.'

'Yeah, I want to get through this in one day. I don't want to bother you again tomorrow.'

'Find anything to help you?'

I shrugged. 'It's pretty much the same old stuff.'

'Look for that letter from the pilot. That'll give you a laugh.'

Maness left and I took up where I had left off. I had come across a batch of analyses from *Time* and *Fortune* staffers, digging behind the scenes on the $205,000 loan to Donald Nixon, the Vice-President's brother, and also detailing Hughes's possible manipulations regard-ing TWA. One memo listed the favors the government seemed to have done for Hughes Tool, Hughes Aircraft, and TWA following the Nixon loan. I found the ten-page typed letter from the pilot, a man named Frank Williams, who told in insufferable detail the story of a flight he had taken with Hughes from Los Angeles to Amarillo, and accused Howard of being one of the worst pilots he had ever flown with. I photographed all ten pages. I found lists of Hughes's girlfriends with background analyses and a breakdown of the romantic possibilities and rumors. My knees were shaking and it was difficult to stand; the focus seemed more blurred with every picture I snapped. When I was done, I had taken twelve rolls of film, more than 400 exposures of possibly 300 documents. I stacked the files carefully, staggered out of the office, and handed the keys to the secretary. Dave Maness appeared again to say goodbye.

'I read the letter from the pilot,' I said. 'It's funny as hell. Aside from that,' I added glumly, 'there wasn't much.'

'I'm sorry,' he said. He looked genuinely disappointed.

I took a taxi back to the apartment on West End Avenue and found Dick in the kitchen, sitting at the table in front of a row of newly-acquired bottles of organic vitamins, drinking a No-Cal, and reading a detective novel. I dumped the boxes of exposed film on the table.

'Well?'

'We hit the jackpot,' I said. 'Listen to this – and look at these!' I gave him details and that big, ingenuous smile spread across his face. I felt proud and happy, as if I'd given my best friend a present he'd dreamed of all his life. 'Gee,' Dick kept saying, 'that's fantastic . . .'

'The only thing is,' I said eventually, to dampen both his euphoria and my own, 'the guy at Willoughby's told me to use a tripod, but I hand-held. I don't know if we're going to be able to read the damn stuff.'

Two more days in New York, during which I blackened my hands rummaging through piles of second-hand aviation and movie magazines, and Dick Xeroxed old newspaper clips in the public library; then down to Houston. In the taxi from the Houston airport to the

Towers Hotel, we noticed that, unlike New York taxis, no protective shield of bulletproof plastic separated the driver from the customers. 'We'll have Howard comment on that,' I said.

The next morning I went to *The Houston Post*, said I was a free-lance writer from Richmond, Virginia, and obtained immediate access to their files on Hughes. Dick was in the Texas Room of the public library, combing the city directories and microfilms of old newspapers for anything he might have missed on his first trip. I joined him there later and photographed the pages of a pictorial volume commemorating Hughes's arrival in Houston after his around-the-world flight. Later, I cropped several of the photographs and told the people at McGraw-Hill and *Life* that they had been given to me by Howard.

We wasted several hours in the Texas Medical Center complex in Houston, because we had read in an old clip from the *Chronicle* that Hughes had donated $125 million to build a separate unit. The director quickly disabused us of that idea. 'Not a bean,' he said. 'That man is about as far from a philanthropist as you can get.'

After a short visit the following morning to the County Records Office – where we dug up the details on Hughes's marriage to his first wife, Ella Rice, we packed and caught an early afternoon flight to Los Angeles.

We flew Continental Airlines, a smooth flight with amiable stewardesses, plenty of leg room, and good food. I was in a buoyant mood. 'This is a damn good airline,' I said. 'Let's buy stock in it for our portfolio.'

'Look it up in the *Trendline*,' Dick suggested.

Trendline – a publication that offered bar charts of leading stocks – showed Continental as suffering substantial losses over the past two years, and the stock seemed to be headed nowhere but down, at least for the foreseeable future. 'You see,' Dick said, with all the wisdom of his two months in the market, 'effort means nothing in business. All this service we're getting and all this leg room is costing the company a small fortune. Look for airlines with lousy food and cramped seats, whose motto is "Screw the customer." They're the ones that make money. Let's put our money into one of *them.*'

We had telephoned from Houston and made reservations at the Holiday Inn on Wilshire Boulevard in Beverly Hills. This would be an obvious choice for Howard, we felt, both because of its location and its anonymity. It was relatively close to the Beverly Hills Hotel, where he had kept a bungalow for some ten or fifteen years, so he would feel on familiar ground. It had no cachet or distinction of any kind. We were also fortunate in the rooms assigned to us. Both were on the fourth floor, with one of them at the end of the corridor. 'Good,' I said. 'It's all falling into place. This is just what Howard would have told me to do. You're on one side, so no one can eavesdrop. And there's only the street on the other side. Make a note of that, Jeeves. I'll include it in my introduction to the book.'

Another reason that Hughes had chosen Los Angeles as the site for our next series of interviews was that he wanted to show me the Spruce Goose, his gigantic wooden flying boat which was secluded under armed guard in a twenty-story hangar in San Pedro. 'He's promised me a look at it,' I had told Beverly and Albert in New York; and I had added to Ralph Graves: 'Maybe I can even get a photo of him standing next to it.'

'That's just what we need,' Graves said. 'But if you can't get a shot of him with the flying boat, get a recent photo – something we could use on the cover. That's very important for us.'

'I'll do my damnedest, Ralph,' I had promised . . . and our plan was taking shape. Like all of our best plans, it was a brilliant combination of simplicity and simple-mindedness. 'I'll never get a look at the Spruce Goose,' I told Dick. 'Howard keeps postponing it and postponing it until he falls desperately ill and vanishes.'

'Yeah,' Dick said, 'that's good. It'd be too easy to check if you had or hadn't seen the plane. Besides, this may help out later, if Howard stabs you in the back and denies the authenticity of the book. You can always claim he was a dying man when he left California, and force him to make an appearance in court. He'll never do it.' Dick looked briefly worried, then shook his head and repeated: 'Never!'

We spent two days in the book shops on Hollywood Boulevard, buying old screen magazines, glossies of stars in the 1930's and 1940's with whom Howard might have had affairs, and various books that covered the period. I also interviewed a lawyer named Arthur Crowley who had sued Hughes on the charge of having placed a wiretap and bug in his office in the Taft Building on Hollywood Boulevard, and another lawyer named Moss who had represented Paul Jarrico, the screenwriter Hughes had fired from RKO during the witch-hunting days of the film industry. Again, in Hollywood as well as Houston, Howard was not a very popular man. All this, I decided, would have to be changed in the book. Howard, a violent anticommunist in the early 1950's, would now have second thoughts; he would see how he had been swept into the hysteria of the McCarthy era. He would be mellow. He would recant. 'We'll make a bigger man of him than he is,' I told Dick. 'Remember – soul-vomit.'

The second morning I walked up Wilshire Boulevard to the Beverly Hills Camera Shop and handed in the rolls of film I had snapped in the Time-Life Building and Houston, as well as the one roll of Kodacolor I had taken of Nina on the beach at Figueral. I ordered contact sheets for the black-and-whites. Back at the hotel, I found Dick slumped in an easy chair, snoring. The message was clear: we needed a break. The pace in New York and

Houston had been headlong; we were tired and getting stale. 'Let's head south to Twenty-nine Palms,' I said. 'That's where this guy Williams lives.'

'Who's Williams?'

'The pilot who wrote that long letter to *Life* saying what a lousy flier Hughes was.'

'Howard won't like this,' Dick said, yawning. 'But a break will do us good.'

Dick was in an ecological mood when we started south from Los Angeles. He slouched in his seat and grumbled about the smog, about the millions of acres of arable land smothered in freeways, bedroomvilles, used-car lots, shopping centers, and restaurants whose food was as tasteless as their decor. 'It's gotten worse since '62,' he said. 'At least then you used to see an orange grove or two.'

I remembered and for a while we reminisced about the spring and summer of 1962, when we were both living in Southern California. My second wife, Fay, and I had come there from our eight-month trip around the world, which included a stay in a Kashmiri houseboat where I finished a novel, and a trip by freighter across the Pacific. Landing in California broke, we rented a house in Venice from the then aging and endlessly pontificating self-appointed guru of the beatniks, Lawrence Lipton. He preached 'holy poverty' – for others, of course. Dick and Ginette lived farther south, in Manhattan Beach. Through a friend Dick had landed a job as a technical writer for a large aerospace company in El Segundo. Hardly able to do more than change a light bulb, he was working with a gaggle of Ph.D.'s on a study concerning the feasibility of a direct flight to the moon. A bare four months later he fled back to Ibiza, armed with a contract to write a book about the First World War. 'It'll take me a year to research and write,' I remembered him saying, 'and I'll make every bit as much as I would in two months of technical writing, but . . .' and he had shrugged helplessly, a victim of both his restlessness and his passion to be a 'real' writer.

I held on a bit longer, struggling without success to sell film scripts, television plays, to start a new novel; making ends meet by teaching creative writing at UCLA and by an occasional poker-playing foray to Gardena. What stood out sharpest in my memory of those days was the fright-filled time when my son Joshua, born three months prematurely and weighing barely two pounds at birth, was fighting to stay alive in his incubator; and the endless squabbling with Fay. I was thinking about Josh, now nearly ten and living with Fay and her new husband in England, when Dick heaved a heartfelt sigh and said: 'What do you say we forget about Twenty-nine Palms? We've got photos of Williams' letter. We don't really need to see the guy. Too much knowledge is a dangerous thing.'

'You're just a lazy bastard.'

'And you?'

'Lazier,' I admitted. 'How about Palm Springs? My Aunt Beabe lives there and I wouldn't mind seeing her. And it's closer.'

'The high-powered investigative team of Suskind and Irving makes another vital, time-saving decision.' Dick's laughter rumbled up from his chest.

It was Saturday, June 12th, long past the season, but we had to drive up and back through Palm Springs twice before we finally found a motel without a *NO VACANCY* sign in front of it. Called the Black Angus, it looked neither better nor worse than all but a handful of the stucco palaces we had passed: a gravel parking area whose shady spots were all occupied, a tub-sized pool in the sun with half a dozen heat-dazed people in and around it. 'Kind of the nondescript sort of place Howard would pick to meet you,' Dick said, after we had registered and were walking down the corridor to

150

our rooms. He yawned hugely. 'Let's take a siesta. I'll shake you up when the sun falls below the yardarm.'

After dinner we held a P & P session over the coffee. Palm Springs would be a good place, it seemed to me, for Dick to meet Howard. 'It'll be an accident,' I said. 'He'll come to my room earlier than expected and find you there.'

'Why do I have to meet him?' Dick asked.

'Don't you want to?'

'From everything we've learned about him, absolutely not.'

'You mean you're not curious what he's really like? Think what a great story you can tell to your grand-children.'

'I think you're overtired,' Dick said.

'All right, forget your grandchildren. Concentrate on McGraw-Hill. The problem is that I'm the only one who's ever seen him. The day may come when I'll need a witness.'

'I've got the picture.'

Dick looked gloomy for a while, but after a cognac he perked up and the details of the story began to take shape. Howard would find us together in the room. Dick, of course, would be too large to hide under the bed and too distinguished-looking to pass for a bellhop. After an awkward silence, I would introduce them. Howard would acknowledge his identity.

'And he'll offer me a prune,' Dick said excitedly.

'A prune? Why a prune?'

'How the hell do I know? Maybe he's constipated. He has a bag full of organic prunes in his pocket, and he can't think of anything else to say, so he pulls out the bag and says, "Have a prune." He's trying to be friendly.'

'What kind of prune did you have in mind?'

'An organic prune from the Santa Clara Valley. They're the best. Howard only eats the best. Didn't you tell me he flew all the way to Puerto Rico for bananas?

151

And then we'll talk a bit about organic foods and vitamins, while you stand around and sulk because you're totally ignorant on such important subjects, and then I'll leave.'

'Good enough. What's he look like?'

'He's very tall, very thin – looks like his photos of twenty years ago, only twenty years older, of course.' Dick laughed. 'Mustache, wrinkled face, liver spots on his hands. By the way, do we shake hands?'

'Are you crazy? You stick out your hand but then draw it back. You remember that Howard is terrified of germs. He doesn't shake hands with anyone.'

'Not even with you?'

'I'm a special person. And he's checked me out and given me a B-plus rating for cleanliness.' We then worked out Howard's system for classifying the antiseptic qualities of his friends and acquaintances. His staff kept files on everybody, and they were rated A, B, C, or D, which meant, in reverse order: Filthy, Dirty, Moderately Dirty, and Moderately Clean. The system found a final resting place in the *Autobiography* when Howard discussed his attitude toward germs and pollution.

We turned in early and next morning, after loafing around the pool until the heat became unbearable, I called my aunt, Beabe Hamilburg, and accepted an invitation for lunch at her country club with a friend. I told her about Dick and she said, 'Bring him along.'

After lunch we drove out to Beabe's friend's house. It was a quarter of a million dollars' worth of architecture on the hoof, immaculate inside and out, landscaped to a fare-thee-well, opulently furnished by a decorator with a penchant for mixed styles, and as sterile as the desert we could see through the picture window in the living room. We were shown through the house, room by room, with an indefinable air of boredom and sadness as she pointed out the goodies: the toe-controlled shelves in the bathroom so that one did not have to bend over to reach the deodorant, the master bedroom with his and hers electric blankets, the tape deck that played both sides of four-track cartridges automatically, the view of the golf course. I thought of Edith and our rambling old *finca* surrounded by cactus and almond trees, and I missed it – I was almost a foreigner in the country where I had been bred. I suddenly missed Ibiza, Edith, and the kids, yelling in the sandbox, and the monkey, and I thought of my boat sitting idle in her berth at the Club Naútico.

'Lovely,' I said, trying to infuse some enthusiasm into my voice. 'Beautiful . . .' I glanced at my watch. 'I'm afraid we've got to be going.'

'Oh, Cliff,' Beabe said, 'I just remembered. Stanley Meyer's in town, visiting his in-laws. He always asks for you. Why don't we go see him?'

Again I was drawn back into the past, into my life in California in the early 1960's. I had been poor, and whatever I submitted to the television factories had been either too good or too banal for public consumption. Stanley Meyer was a fan of my fiction, a well-wisher, and he had befriended me. He had produced *Dragnet* and he was married to the daughter of the man who had owned Universal Studios. He had brought CARE packages to us in Venice: bourbon, steaks from his own steers in the San Fernando Valley, and hickory logs which he had insisted were necessary to grill the steaks properly in the fireplace. Beabe and one or two other friends had warned me that Stanley had a tendency, in no clearly defined way, to use people; but I said, 'I don't believe it. And he'd never do that to me.'

Finally, when I was at an economic low ebb, Stanley had asked me to write an outline and a screen treatment for a proposed low-budget Western called *The Cavalry-man*. I had worked on the project for a little over a month. On the question of payment, Stanley had been

153

cautious, talking in terms of 'something above the Screenwriters Guild minimum' but always referring to 'my partner, who handles the financial end of it.' The denouement came when Stanley telephoned one day and urgently requested a release on my part for the material I had already delivered; it was something about registering the title idea. I said, 'Stanley, I haven't been paid a dime yet,' and he replied: 'There's a check in the mail to you, kid.' Overjoyed, I signed the release. A check arrived three days later for the sum of $100, with a W-2 form attached so that I would have to pay income tax on his largesse.

I related this story to Beabe and Dick, and Beabe said: 'I told you so at the time. I told you what he was like.'

'Then why should I go see him here in Palm Springs?'

'Because he likes you and always asks about you.'

'Sure. He likes me because he screwed me and I never complained.'

But Beabe pressed and I gave in; it seemed so long ago as not to matter, and I had always been fond of Stanley's wife, Dodo. A certain amount of vanity was involved in it as well. The last time I had seen Stanley I was down and out, scratching for a living in a Hollywood where writers were treated like extras until they hit the best-seller list or found the formula that gave the veneer of originality to pap. In some childish way I wanted him to see that I had graduated from that world of $100 payments for screenplay treatments.

Dick and I followed Beabe in her car and arrived at Stanley's mother-in-law's house in the midafternoon. We rang the bell and no one answered.

'That's that,' I said. 'Let's go.'

'I'll try the back door.' Beabe vanished and a few minutes later we heard voices.

Stanley had just come off the tennis courts when he greeted us in the solarium at the back of the house. He had aged and somehow looked troubled, but was as

154

affable as ever, and he bubbled friendly greetings to both Dick and me while he wiped the sweat from his forehead with a towel and tugged at a pair of split tennis shorts with the other hand. 'Great to see you,' he kept saying, and we exchanged, in a few sentences, the synopses of what each of us had done in the intervening seven years. I showed him – as I did almost everyone else I met – photographs of Edith and the children. I had a beer and then started to make the proper excuses for our departure.

'Stay, stay,' Stanley said. 'You haven't even seen the house.'

In Southern California it is obligatory to take a tour of the house if you hadn't done so before, but I begged off. 'I've had a look,' I lied. 'Beautiful house, Stanley . . .'

'Yes,' he said, with a ring of pride in his voice, 'we're only one fairway from Frank Sinatra. Just this morning Frankie drove a ball onto our land, right over there. He was playing a round with Spiro Agnew.'

'How's old Spiro these days?' I asked.

'Oh, fine! We talked for a few minutes.' He stood up, holding his split shorts together with one hand. Then he asked me what I was working on at the moment.

'I'm doing a book on the four richest men in America. Dick's helping me with the research.'

'Which four?'

'Hunt, Mellon, Getty, and Hughes,' I said. That was our cover story, cooked up with the aid of McGraw-Hill to divert the possible suspicions of the Hughes Tool Company, who were to know nothing – by Howard's dictum – of Project Octavio.

A bemused look crossed Stanley's face. 'Now, isn't that a coincidence! Isn't that something! That *you* should be working on . . .' A gleam of excitement appeared suddenly in his glass-blue eyes. 'Excuse us a moment,' he said to his wife and mother-in-law, and he beckoned Dick and me to accompany him. He took us into a small study, sat down behind a desk and motioned us to chairs facing him.

'What's all this about, Stanley?' I looked at my watch. Leaning forward, he peered at me benevolently. I had seen that look before, some years ago. Then he smiled. 'Tell me, have you ever heard of a man named Noah Dietrich?'

'Sure. He was Howard Hughes's right-hand man for thirty-two years.'

'What you don't know is that Noah's written a book about his life with Hughes.' I *did* know, of course; Ralph Graves had told me. But I said nothing. 'Noah's a friend of mine,' Stanley gushed. 'He's an old man now, past eighty, and in bad health. He wants to see this book published before he dies. The book was done by a ghost writer, a man named Jim Phelan, and the guy did a lousy job. The book is unpublishable as it is.' He put his elbows on the desk and gave me his intent, executive stare, followed by his most generous smile. 'I think you're the man to put the book in shape. Noah's asked me to help him find a writer, and I think you're the man. You know what faith I have in you. How would you like to write Noah Dietrich's autobiography?'

From the corner of my eye I saw Dick's knuckles turn white as he gripped the arms of his chair. I dared not look at him. 'Well,' I said carefully, searching for words at the same time as I tried to hold back my laughter, 'I don't know, Stanley. It's certainly tempting, but . . .'

'Tempting? It's a blue chip, the bluest of the blue! Hughes is big stuff right now. Everyone wants to know about him. I can't tell you about it, but Noah's book is loaded with dynamite. There's stuff in there about Nixon, for example . . .' He shook his head in awe. 'Could blow him right out of the White House! And don't forget, we've got an election year coming up.'

'W-e-e-e-l-l,' I drawled, trying desperately to think of some way of getting a look at the manuscript.

Stanley held up his hand. 'Don't decide anything now, Cliff. I realize it's an important decision. I'll tell you what: why don't you read the manuscript – both of you – before you say yes or no. How does that strike you?'

Dick coughed, bending over and holding himself around the ribs.

'Are you all right?' Stanley asked him. He started to get out of his chair but Dick waved him back. 'Fine, it's all right now,' he gasped. 'Just give me a moment. I must have swallowed something the wrong way.'

'A prune,' I muttered.

Stanley looked at me. 'What did you say?'

I thought for a while. 'Okay. We'll look it over and let you know. Where is it?'

'You'll have to pick it up at Four Oaks – you re-member, my place in Encino.' He picked up the telephone and dialed. 'Raymonda? This is Mr Meyer. Listen carefully. Two men will be stopping by this . . .' He cupped his palm over the speaker and looked at me. 'This evening?' I nodded casually. 'This evening,' he said into the telephone. 'I want you to go into my study and give them the large blue loose-leaf notebook that you'll find on top of the file cabinet.'

'I can't let you keep it long,' he said, hanging up the receiver. 'Noah's in a terrible rush to find a new writer. You'll have to get it back to me right away.'

'By tomorrow night at the latest,' I said.

'Should I set up a meeting between you and Dietrich?'

'No,' I decided. 'Let's play it cool. Let me read the stuff first.'

We returned to the living room, made an effort to engage in light conversation with the Meyer family, and then, when I saw that Dick was about to burst with frustration, I stood up and we said our goodbyes.

'Jesus!' Dick exclaimed as we pulled out of the drive-way. 'It's right out of *Alice in Wonderland*. Could you

157

imagine using a coincidence like this in a novel? The editor would laugh you out of his office!'

We sped northward on the freeway toward the San Fernando Valley. If it wasn't *Alice in Wonderland* it was certainly Irving and Suskind in the movies. 'If I hadn't said I was tired and the hell with chasing this guy Williams at Twenty-nine Palms . . .'

'If I hadn't called my Aunt Beabe . . .'

'If Stanley hadn't just happened to be down there for the weekend . . .'

'If we'd gone away when no one answered the doorbell and if Beabe hadn't gone around to the back . . .'

We babbled like idiots; we could find no rational explanation for what had happened. I gripped the steering wheel hard, hoping not to wake up from the dream; and Dick rattled on and on about the almost unbelievable and totally fantastic coincidence. 'And besides,' he said, 'this pays Stanley back for the shafting he gave you – pays him back in spades.'

I felt a twinge of conscience. 'He's not going to get hurt,' I said. I wasn't looking to pay him back. I wasn't looking for anything.

Dick, sprawled face down across the bed, with the last half of the Dietrich manuscript on the floor just below him, cackled like a mad chicken. 'Listen to this!' and he read off a passage in which Glenn Davis, Terry Moore's husband, knocked Howard on his ass. 'Can we use that or is it libelous?'

'That's nothing,' I said from the chair in which I was reading the other half. 'It looks as though he got a dose of clap from an actress and gave Dietrich all his clothes to burn. But Noah turned around and gave them to the Salvation Army.'

'Wait till you tell that to Howard. He'll be furious.'

We read on, breaking into exclamations of delight as one treasure after another was uncovered.

'This makes it for us,' Dick said. 'Man, we're home free. We can incorporate this stuff into the book, twist it around so that Noah comes off as the prick and Howard the good guy. Mother McGraw is lucky to get this at half a million. That's cheap, that's . . .' he broke off and looked at me, a half smile parting his lips. 'Do you think . . .'

'Forget it,' I said. 'Whatever we do, let's not get greedy. Greed would be our undoing. Think about the book and let the loot take care of itself. In the meantime, let's finish reading and then first thing tomorrow morning we get a couple of Xeroxes made.'

Dick heaved himself off the bed and picked up a Yellow Pages from the dresser. 'There ought to be a copying place near here.'

There was – just four blocks down Wilshire toward the center of the city – and we were there at nine o'clock the next morning. One entire side of the shop, I was happy to see, was occupied by a late-model multiple Xerox copier. I took the manuscript out of the blue binder and laid it on the counter. 'How long will it take to make two copies?'

The owner-operator wiped his hands on a piece of cotton waste. 'How many pages?'

'About four hundred,' I said.

'What is it, a novel?'

'That's right,' Dick said. 'The Great American Novel.'

We hovered around the counter, carefully avoiding the subject that was uppermost in our minds, while the machine did its thing. An hour later we put our two copies in Dick's old briefcase, put Stanley's copy back in its binder, and returned to the hotel. I called Stanley and made an appointment to see him at Four Oaks that evening.

'Well, is it a blue chip or isn't it?' Stanley asked, once we were seated in his spacious, Early-American living room, surrounded by Grandma Moses paintings, beer steins firmly clutched in our hands.

'I'll give it to you straight, Stanley,' I said. 'I don't like Mr Dietrich. I think he's a bitter old man. He puts the knife in Hughes every chance he gets and he always comes out lily-white. It's a niggling, malicious book, and the guy who ghosted it can't write his way out of a paper bag.'

'But the material is there. It's a winner, I'm telling you. A blue chip! I don't know what McGraw-Hill's paying you for the book you're doing, but I know you could make more on this one. Now, I'll be calling Dietrich in the morning. Should I make an appointment for you to see him?'

'Sorry, Stanley. I meant what I said. I don't like Dietrich and I don't think I would work for him. So let's forget it. But thanks for the opportunity. I mean that, too.'

After ten more minutes of debate, Stanley realized I couldn't be budged. He looked at me sorrowfully, as though I were a moron. He had offered me the biggest chance of my life and I had turned it down. Then, flushing a little, he put his hand on my shoulder.

'All right. But do me two favors, please, for old times' sake. First of all, I want you to think about it for a while. I mean, if you change your mind, the offer's still there.'

'Glad to, Stan,' I said, thinking it would be a good thing if publication of the Dietrich manuscript were delayed for a while.

'And the second . . .' Stanley bit his lip. He looked confused for a moment, then regained his habitual joviality. 'This is a bit delicate. I shouldn't have showed you this manuscript without letting Noah know about it.'

'I'll never say a word.'

'It's more than that.' He cleared his throat. 'The point is that I'm not supposed to have this copy. I had it in the house for a while and I Xeroxed it, but no one knows that I Xeroxed it. I really shouldn't have done that, and I'd be . . . I'd be a little embarrassed if that came to light.'

'Stanley . . . ' I shook my head solemnly, 'I'll never tell a soul. You can trust me.'

Five minutes later Dick and I drove away.

'Oh, my God,' Dick howled. '*He* swiped it, and we swiped it from *him*! He doesn't want us to tell anybody he's got it!'

'Right,' I murmured. 'And he'll never be able to tell anyone he gave it to me. This is crazy. What next?'

'Don't you know? Howard Hughes is waiting for us at the Holiday Inn to tell you he wants you to write his autobiography.'

'I'll believe anything now,' I said, 'anything.'

Possession of the Dietrich manuscript gave us a tremendous psychic lift. It dissipated the last of my fears that we would be unable to produce anything better than a merely mundane, acceptable transcript. The actual information it contained was of minor value; most of it had been duplicated in the *Time-Life* files and elsewhere. What was important was the characteristic tone of Howard's voice that came through to us in his informal conversations as reported by Dietrich. From Dietrich I learned that Howard's two favorite solutions to business problems were: 'Fire the sonofabitch,' and 'Use other people's money.'

Appended to the manuscript was an extraordinary document. How Noah Dietrich or James Phelan came by it we were never to find out, although we developed several theories. It was a ten-page, single-spaced memo from Frank McCulloch, former Los Angeles bureau chief of *Time* to James Shepley, the President of Time, Inc., dated October 30, 1958. At the top of the first page was written: *CONFIDENTIAL, DO NOT DITTO.* The memo itself was obviously a verbatim transcript of a tape-recorded telephone conversation between Frank

McCulloch and Howard Hughes. McCulloch's remarks were excluded, so that the transcript was essentially a Hughes monologue. Aside from the information it imparted – Hughes was begging McCulloch to use his influence to scrap a forthcoming *Fortune* article on the troubles at TWA, and in effect was offering to become an unpaid correspondent of Time, Inc. if Henry Luce would kill that article – it was the only long and informal speech of Howard Hughes that had thus far come into our hands. It gave us his conversational patterns, his expletives, his spoken syntax, manner of response, love of cliches, and mangled metaphors. I sat down one evening while we were still in California and typed a three-page list of recurring phrases and favorite exclamations.

Dick took the carbon copy. 'Study this,' I said, 'and get it stuck into your mind. When the time comes, one of us is not only going to have to know all about Howard Hughes and think like Howard Hughes, but talk like him as well. And this memo is going to be our guiding star.'

We were enraptured not only by our good fortune but by Dick's meeting Howard and being offered an organic prune. Just as the securing of Time, Inc.'s files had seemed to lead in some mysterious yet inexorable way to our discovery of the Dietrich manuscript, so Dick's unscheduled interview of Howard Hughes led me to concoct a further fantasy that had taken place in Palm Springs. The idea had dawned on me from the moment that Stanley Meyer had mentioned Vice-President Agnew's presence in the area – a guest in the house of Frank Sinatra, who had been feuding with Hughes since 1967 when Sinatra had tangled with the manager of Howard's newly-acquired Sands Hotel and taken a punch in the nose which put him flat on his back. The tale I invented was totally lunatic. The interview with

Hughes in my motel room in Palm Springs had been an all-night session. At five o'clock in the morning Howard asked me to take a look outside: 'See if there's a car waiting.' Sure enough, a battered Chevrolet had pulled up in the parking lot in the breaking dawn light. 'Come with me,' Howard instructed. I followed. Howard got into the car and beckoned me closer. 'This is Clifford Irving,' he said to the man in the back seat. 'He's a friend of mine, and if he ever needs help, you help him.'

'It's Spiro Agnew?' Dick said.

'Right.'

'But why?'

'Why not? They've got business to discuss. Howard's got Spiro in his pocket. It ties in with his plans for an SST port-of-entry in Las Vegas and in the Bahamas. That, in fact, is why he's *in* the Bahamas. Didn't I ever tell you that?'

'But what if they ever ask Agnew about it?'

I laughed. 'He'd have to deny it even if it was true. Vice-Presidents don't meet with billionaires at 5 a.m. in parked cars to talk about the weather.'

Dick was unable to dissuade me and from the Holiday Inn in Beverly Hills I called Beverly Loo and told her of the meeting. I wasn't sure whether or not she believed me, so I wrote her a letter in which I confirmed it. 'You're losing your grip,' Dick said darkly.

'Come on. The wackier it is, the more they believe it. You'll see,' I promised.

Our two fantastic strokes of luck – the *Time-Life* files and the pirated copy of the Dietrich manuscript – were followed by other, lesser, ones. Soon after our return to Los Angeles from Encino I called Bob Kirsch, the book reviewer for *The Los Angeles Times* and an old friend from hard times in the early 1960's. We picked the Kirsches up at their house, took them out to dinner, went to a discotheque, and talked until past midnight. In the course of the conversation I told Bob what I was working on – a book about four millionaires – and said I was having trouble getting material on Hughes and also couldn't seem to gain access to *The Los Angeles Times* morgue.

'No problem,' Bob said. 'I'll write a letter for you to the librarian.'

While waiting for the letter to arrive, my cousin Mike Hamilburg, Beabe's son, helped me get a print of *Hell's Angels*, Howard's first major film, and we arranged to see it at a screening room on Hollywood Boulevard. The film itself, the cost of shipping it air express from New Jersey, and the rental of the screening room came to a total of about $300. 'I hope you're not planning to see *all* his films,' Dick muttered.

'Couldn't if I wanted to. They're not available. Howard apparently bought up every print around. It was just luck that this one escaped.'

But the film more than earned its keep, for in the transcript we had Howard explain how he had personally worked to achieve some of the technical effects, and relate anecdotes about Jean Harlow, Ben Lyon, and several of the ex-World War I pilots who flew in the combat sequences. We taped the film's sound track on a cassette recorder and later, listening to the hero make a violent anti-war speech, I said: 'Howard wrote that. You didn't know that, did you?'

'I didn't until you told me.'

'There's only one problem. How does he explain all that military garbage turned out by Hughes Aircraft?'

'He doesn't explain it. He brushes it aside. That's business, the other's personal. The schizoid personality of the big American businessman. He really can't see the connection between the air-to-air missiles and the other deadly hardware turned out by his companies, and his own personal condemnation of war.'

'But he tries,' I said. 'Remember, he's a hero.'

Our third bonanza came in the library of the Academy of Motion Picture Arts and Sciences. Dick and I went there to compile a list of Hughes's old pictures, who directed them, who starred in them, where they were filmed, whatever else we could find. The Academy's files on Hughes, however, contained hundreds of clippings, some about his time as boss of RKO, others concerned with his personal and business life. There was too much to plow through in one session, so we returned the next day. When we arrived, the girl at the desk said: 'Oh, by the way, something's just come in that might be of interest to you. The private papers of Lincoln Quarberg.'

'Who's Lincoln Quarberg?' we, the Hughes experts, asked.

'I'm not sure, but obviously he had something to do with Hughes, because the file is full of memoranda to him. I don't think anyone else has seen it yet. It hasn't even been collated.'

'Let's have a look,' Dick said quickly.

Lincoln Quarberg, we soon learned, had been Hughes's chief of public relations for Caddo Productions, the company that had produced all of Howard's early films. He was also a compulsive hoarder, for his file contained personal letters, memoranda, notes, cables to and from Billie Dove, Robert E. Sherwood, and other personalities of the period. I went to the nearest camera shop, bought four rolls of Panatonic-X, and spent the rest of the day crouched over a table near a window, clicking away.

The next morning, a Wednesday, I called *The Los Angeles Times* and was told that Kirsch's letter had arrived and I was welcome to use their files. In the meantime, Dick had spoken to an aviation writer named Don Dwiggins, who had done several articles for *Cavalier* magazine when Dick was its Associate Editor. Dwiggins refused to give us any information on Hughes – 'I'm doing a book on him myself,' he explained – but he did give us the telephone number of Charlie Lajotte, who had been Hughes's flying instructor at Clover Field in Santa Monica during the 1930's. I called Lajotte, made my pitch for an interview, and we arranged to meet at the Northrop Institute of Aeronautics at 11 a.m. 'If I'm late,' Lajotte said in his dry, old man's voice, 'see Dave Hatfield down there. He can help you a lot.'

Both Hatfield and Lajotte were garrulous on the subject of the young Howard Hughes. We took them to lunch at the Proud Bird Restaurant on the edge of Los Angeles International Airport – close enough to the runway so that the windows vibrated with each take-off and landing. Lajotte and Dick hit it off well when Lajotte interjected a French phrase into his conversation and Dick responded in kind. Charlie had once lived in Paris. He was spry and alert, well into his seventies, with a varied background as a flying instructor, bush pilot, World War I pilot, and chauffeur-pilot for a wealthy young woman who had wanted to tour Africa by air.

Interviews such as this – and we had several, including one with my Aunt Beabe, who with her husband had chaperoned Howard and Mitzi Gaynor on a long Las Vegas weekend back in the 1950's – posed a knotty problem. I couldn't pretend that I had never seen Lajotte, putting his words and tales into the mouth of Howard Hughes; for Lajotte would surely read the book if it were published. There was only one solution. The transcript of the tapes eventually read:

CLIFFORD: By the way, I met an old friend of yours the other day. Charlie Lajotte.
HOWARD: Charlie – for heaven's sake! Is he still alive?

I then went on, in the transcript, to relate to Howard the anecdotes that Lajotte had related to me, and Howard obligingly confirmed and elaborated. When it came time to transform the dialogue of the transcripts into the finished *Autobiography*, I would eliminate my parroting of Lajotte's remarks – with Howard's permission and McGraw-Hill's editorial blessing – and the problem, if ever scrutinized, would lend itself to a legitimate and logical explanation.

Hatfield, too, had a lot to offer. He hadn't known Hughes personally, but the bookshelves and photograph files of the Northrop Museum, of which he was curator, held a number of interesting items, and in his rambling fashion he provided us with a score of colorful tidbits about Howard the Pilot and Howard the Aircraft Builder which later found their way into the transcript. Hatfield persuaded Dick and me to take out subscriptions to a monthly newsletter published by the Institute. 'Hughes has a subscription, you know,' he said. 'I once got an angry note from one of his employees, man named Francis Fox, when he missed an issue.'

Dick laughed. 'If it's good enough for Mr Hughes, I guess it's good enough for us.'

It was mid-afternoon when we returned to Los Angeles – too late to do any more research at the *Times*'s library, too early to quit for the day. Dick solved our problem. 'Listen,' he said, 'why don't we take some photos of Howard?'

'What the hell are you talking about?'

'Well, we know he dresses like a bum, and he goes unshaven, also like a bum. So what we have to do . . .'

'. . . is take photos of bums,' I finished.

'Exactly. And where is the best collection of bums west of the Mississippi? Right here in L.A., on Pershing Square.'

Twenty minutes later we put the car in a parking lot on South Broadway and walked through the sweltering smog to Pershing Square. My Nikkormat was hanging from my neck, a new 36-exposure roll of Plus-X just loaded.

'Remember,' Dick cautioned, 'it can't be just any old bum. He's got to be damn near a cadaver, and be sure you take him a little out of focus, a little blurry around the edges.'

I set the telefoto lens opening to *f* 11, the shutter speed at 250, and focused it at infinity, ready for action.

Our first subject was passed out under a palm tree, a black crust on his lips and an empty pint of Thunderbird lying next to his outflung hand. 'Wait,' Dick said, 'I'll get him to open his eyes.' He nudged the sleeping man with his toe and one red-veined eye opened to peer up at us. The other eye remained closed, clotted together by a yellowish gummy line. I peered at him through the view-finder but did not click the shutter.

Dick nudged me. 'Go ahead.'

'No. We'd have to give him a bath first, and we haven't the time.' The red-veined eye closed and we walked on.

We came to two old men playing checkers on a bench. One of them fitted our bill of particulars except that he was totally bald.

'You got a hat, mister?' Dick asked him.

The old man gave him a quick look from under his brows, then waved him away as one would a troublesome fly.

'Listen,' Dick persisted. 'If you've got a hat, you can make five bucks.'

At that the old man looked Dick full in the face. 'Yeah?' he said, 'which one of you?'

Dick turned to me, puzzled. 'What's he mean?'

'Forget it,' I said. 'He thinks we're propositioning him.'

'I only like *clean* old men.'

We spent another half-hour in and around the park, were propositioned by two drag queens, looked at suspiciously by one cop in a uniform and two others in mufti, and decided to leave while we were still ahead.

A new shift had come on duty at the parking

lot during our absence. Hughes's spitting image, mustachioed and wearing green coveralls and a battered fedora, sat in the shed at the exit. In return for ten dollars and a promise that we would send him a copy of the *Parking Lot Promoter's Annual* with his photograph inside, he lowered the top of his coveralls, tilted the fedora on the back of his head, and allowed me to take ten photographs, all out of focus, all with the old man's face half hidden by the shadow cast by the overhanging eave of the shed.

The next day we picked up all the films – those taken at the Academy of Motion Picture Arts and Sciences as well as those from *Time-Life,* Houston, and Ibiza. We also bought an Agfalupe, a special magnifying glass for contact prints. To our relief, the documents I had photographed in *Life*'s secret file were legible, although a few of them were slightly out of focus. We pondered over the photographs of the parking attendant for all of ten seconds, then burst out laughing at our own stupidity, tore them into shreds and threw them in the waste-basket.

That evening Dick lay sprawled on my bed and I sat at the table, shuffling through the notes and photographic material. 'I've had it,' he said feebly. 'We're not going to get anything else. Let's not push our luck till it goes dry.'

'You're homesick.'

'Yeah, I am.'

I smiled. 'Don't sound so sheepish. So am I. Okay, you catch the next plane. I've still got to check those files at the *Times.* And I've got to get the photographs blown up so that we can read them.'

We debated about that and decided the wisest thing was to have them enlarged in Europe, preferably in a camera lab where English wasn't spoken, or in London, where interest in Hughes, we thought, would be minimal. I drove Dick to the airport that evening and saw him off to London with a farewell drink at the bar. 'Next time I see you,' I said, 'we get down to the real work. So go home, get some rest, and gear up.'

He raised his glass in our favorite toast. 'Confusion to our enemies.'

'*L'chayem*,' I replied. I punched his shoulder and said: 'Take care, have a good trip. And pay the bar bill,' I called as I left.

The next morning I went down to the *Times* and spent the better part of the day in their morgue. I had thought our luck had run out, but I was wrong. The files were fat with material, much of it new to me. I Xeroxed everything that was of use and when I put the last folder back in the cabinet under H, I noticed one folder that was marked *CONFIDENTIAL*. I turned to ask the librarian if I could look at the folder, but she was gone. One of the clerks told me she would be back in about ten minutes. Those ten minutes were all I needed to Xerox the file, which contained the on-the-scene handwritten notes of the reporter who had covered the 1936 car accident in which Hughes had killed a 60-year-old pedestrian named Gabe Meyer. The reporter's version of the facts had never been printed, and was at decided variance with what *had* been printed. When the time came, I decided, Howard would tell me what had really happened.

That night I boarded an SAS jet and flew over the pole to Copenhagen. I bought Danish handknitted sweaters for Edith and the children and then telephoned to London. Nina's maid, Mary, told me that Nina was in Ibiza. 'But she left a message,' Mary said, 'that if you came through you should stay here.'

Bleary-eyed and moving like a sleepwalker, I ran around London for most of the day to various photographic shops until the 500 contact negatives had been blown up to 8 x 10 glossies. The next day I caught the early afternoon plane to Ibiza. Edith, brown and beaming, was waiting for me at the airport with the children. I gathered them in my arms and said to Edith, 'God, I'm glad to see you. What a hell of a trip.'

'It went good, darling?'

'It went . . .' I was too tired to elaborate. 'I'll tell you later, and you won't believe it.' I slid behind the wheel of the Mercedes, shifted the seat back so that my legs had some room, then leaned across to kiss her. 'We've got a book,' I repeated. 'And it's going to be great. All we have to do,' I said, grinning wearily, 'is sit down and write it.'

9

'Who's Howard Today – You or Me?'

It was the moment we had been aiming for ever since Project Octavio was launched. We sat sweating in the sun-filled studio, I in my big red swivel chair with the broken rollers, Dick in the overstuffed armchair with his back to the view of the blazing Mediterranean. But we somehow dreaded to take the leap. We were committed, we were knowledgeable, we were hungry to work; yet there was a mental frontier to be crossed that held us at bay as though it contained a killing charge of electricity. No more plotting and planning – for the moment. This was it. We were about to create Howard Hughes. The hubris inherent in our scheme – there from the beginning but hitherto held in check – struck us simultaneously, although neither of us could articulate the awareness and the consequent unease.

'Let's not get off to a false start,' I said, fidgeting and lighting another cigarette. 'Let's think a while.'

Dick nodded. 'We could knock off for the day. Get cracking early tomorrow morning.'

Practically every surface in the studio, including the handloomed Moroccan bedspread, was covered with research material. A chopped-up, annotated version of the Dietrich manuscript lay on the desk next to the tape recorder and typewriter. Three shelves of my bookcase were crammed with books we had bought on our travels, and strewn about the tile floor were four dozen blue cardboard folders stuffed with Xeroxes of newspaper and magazine articles, 8x10 photographs of the *Time-Life* files, pamphlets, travel brochures, handwritten notes, and maps. There were folders marked *TWA, EARLY FLYING EXPERIENCES, RKO, SPRUCE GOOSE, HELL'S ANGELS, SENATE HEARINGS, HUGHES AIRCRAFT, ETHIOPIA, HEMINGWAY*; there were folders marked *PERSONAL EXPERIENCES, WOMEN,* and *BUSINESS,* the pertinent years noted in red ink. The apparent disorder was deceptive.

'Do you know where everything is?' Dick asked.

I had been in charge of the filing system. 'I know where everything *should* be.'

He looked unhappily at the wall-to-wall disarray. 'I couldn't work this way. How the hell can you be so disorganized?'

'It's all in my head,' I explained, poking the nearest folders with the toe of my sandal. 'I can put my finger on everything . . . I think.'

'Well, how will we begin?'

'I don't know exactly how. I guess we should talk about it. I mean, let's have a plan.'

As far as McGraw-Hill and *Life* were concerned, I had already taped twenty-odd hours of interviews with Howard in Nassau, Los Angeles, and Palm Springs. The final long interview session, scheduled for September, had yet to take place; but Dick and I would tape and write it now, in advance. 'I hope to God you remember what you told them he told you,' Dick said, reading my mind. 'Did you make notes about what you said?'

'I never had time.'

'Do you remember everything?'

'Not really. I told them he met Hemingway, but I'm damned if I can remember when he met Hemingway. I mean I can't remember when I *told* them he'd met

Hemingway. Let's do this in an orderly fashion,' I said, efficiently producing a leftover pad of yellow lined paper. 'Let's decide on certain basic things.'

'Like what?'

'Like what kind of a man we're going to create. Who is Howard Hughes?'

'He hates germs,' Dick said. 'He has two billion dollars.'

'Thanks. What else?'

'He's lonely. He has no friends. He's cursed with all that money. People are always out to get it from him.'

'Right. So he's paranoid. He feels maligned and mis-understood. He's tired of being a technological man. He's searching for himself. That's why he's telling me the story of his life.'

'Let's go back further,' Dick said. 'He grows up in Texas.'

'How's your Texas accent? Maybe it'll help if you talk with a Texas accent. You have to feel your way into this part,' I explained, remembering something of what actor friends of mine had told me about the Stanislavsky Method. 'Think Texas. It's 1905, 1910, 1915 . . . the wide open spaces. Oil gushing from the prairie. You're born, they bring you to your mother in the maternity ward and she says, "That's not Howard!" But you grow up anyway, a son of the Old West. Blacks love watermelon and Jews have hooked noses.'

'Me?' said Dick. 'Am I going to be Howard?'

'Well, you be Howard part of the time and I'll be myself, and part of the time I'll be Howard and you be me. Let's play it by ear, whoever's in the mood. Who would you rather be, Howard or me?'

'Howard. He's got two billion dollars.'

I nodded, then laughed. 'Maybe when he reads this book – if he ever reads it – he'll be so delighted he'll make me his heir.'

'And maybe he'll be so pissed off he'll send two of the

174

Mormon Mafia here to Ibiza to kill you. Did you ever think of that?'

'I think of it all the time,' I said unhappily.

'No, don't worry.' Dick was always reassuring whenever my spirits flagged or the spectre of violence loomed in my imagination. 'He won't do that. He's never done that kind of thing before.'

'He's never had anyone write his authorized biography before, either.'

I stubbed out the cigarette, leaned over and picked up the telephone. 'I think I'll give Gerry and Laurel a ring. Find out if he's got his boat in the water yet.'

'Come on,' Dick said, sitting suddenly upright in his chair. 'Let's stop looking for excuses. Let's have a whack at it. We're as ready as we'll ever be.'

I put the phone back in the cradle. He was right: it was time to fish or cut bait, as Howard would say. I plugged the microphones into the tape recorder, setting one microphone on the desk near me and the other on the file cabinet facing Dick. 'Testing, testing, one, two, three . . .' I played it back, rewound the tape, and said, 'Okay. Who'll be Howard first, you or me?'

'Me,' Dick volunteered. 'I know the Houston material purty good, pardner.' Dick had suddenly acquired as much of a Texas accent as could be expected from a Jewish boy born in the Bronx 46 years ago.

'Are we on now?' he asked.

'We're on.'

'Well, where would you like me to begin?'

'I'd like you to begin at the beginning. Keep it in chronological order and it will help me a lot in the long run.'

'The beginning. Well, I suppose the beginning is Christmas Eve, 1905, when I was born. That was in Houston. At least I think it was in Houston. There are some people say it was in Shreveport, Louisiana.'

'Hold everything,' I said, switching off the tape

recorder. 'What the hell's this business about Shreveport? Where did you get that?'

'I don't know,' Dick said. He seemed as surprised as I was. 'It just popped up. Didn't I read it somewhere?'

'No,' I said, 'you made it up.'

'Well, let's keep it in. He's confused. He's never told his life story before. How do you know where you're born? People tell you. Do *you* believe everything people tell you?'

'Okay.' I punched the *START* button again. 'Keep popping . . . How can you not know where you were born?'

'We never talked about it. I just assume I was born in Houston, and any records I've ever seen indicate I was born in Houston. So that will just have to do.'

'Who told you you were born in Shreveport?' I grinned at Dick. Squirm out of this one, buddy.

'My grandfather, and my mother, I think. He . . . I saw him a few times before he died. He was a very old man. A veteran of the Civil War. Fought for the Confederacy. Finished as a major general, as a matter of fact. He once mentioned Shreveport. Said my father was in Shreveport looking for oil. I wound up in Shreveport once myself, in jail, but that's another story. This goes way back, you understand . . . back before . . .'

I switched off again. 'That's his great-grandfather, the major general. Howard couldn't have known him. You're some researcher.' Dick shrugged. 'Put it in a footnote . . . say he was mistaken. It'll look more natural if he makes mistakes like that now and then.'

When we stopped taping, several hours later, we had crammed both sides of one seven-inch reel and part of another. We lay back in our chairs like empty sacks – dripping sweat, exhausted – and yet filled with an elation that was to run like an electric current through our lives all that summer. We were on the road to a unique creation, a remarkable man telling a remarkable

176

life story; all the more remarkable because it was based on fact and yet we had the freedom and power to infuse fact with the drama of fiction. When one of us would falter in stride, the other would step into the role. Howard Hughes, our Howard Hughes, would blossom like a plant beamed on by twin suns, one of which would always provide life-giving sustenance. Both Dick and I were aware of this from that first day's session and it had an extraordinary effect on our spirits, carrying us through all the bad moments, all the dull stretches that usually characterize the wearying and lonely task of writing a book, where under ordinary circumstances only one fallible ego acts as creator and critic.

The tapes had to be transcribed and we could trust no one but ourselves with that job. Early the next morning Dick began the work. By the time I arrived, at ten o'clock, he had typed more than thirty pages. We took turns at the typewriter until we had transcribed everything we had taped the day before. Then we plugged in the mikes and started the next section of Howard's boyhood.

Dick's research in the Houston library proved invaluable. He had diligently ransacked old city telephone directories for the Hughes family addresses when Howard was a child. These, combined with old maps, economic surveys, and the society columns of those years, gave us a chronicle of the family fortunes. They had moved often, Dick found, as Howard Sr's luck in the oil fields waxed and waned: from the Rice Hotel to various boarding houses to private homes. Dick had also culled relevant items from *The Houston Post* and *Chronicle* of those early years: the prices of clothing, for example, at Houston's leading haberdashers; and twenty pages from a 1915 Texas guide to etiquette and correct dress. I studied Texas etiquette for an entire morning and worked it into the transcript as follows:

*   *   *

HOWARD: Oh, he [his father] dressed well, but not the way she [his mother] would have liked. He bought his clothes in New York when he could, he was always very stylish but it wasn't her idea of what a gentleman wore. It was too . . . well, too modern. I remember he wore a fob and not a watch chain and she thought that was undignified, and he wore a straw hat in April, it was hot as hell, and my mother said, 'Howard, goodness me, you know you're not supposed to wear a straw hat until the First of June!' It sounds silly, I know, but she was very serious and he, well, he didn't take it too well, that sort of attention being paid to him. He had a white flannel golfing coat and it . . . it reduced her to tears when he wore it. She'd bought him a striped coat, which she considered correct, and he refused to wear it, said it was too goddam hot.

Dick also noted down bits of curiosa. One item, taken from a *Houston Post* of 1909, supplied us with the key to a spurious explanation of Howard's germ-phobia that we felt sure would delight the soul of any amateur psychologist who read the book. It was a paragraph in which a New Orleans doctor claimed that cornbread was responsible for leprosy. We used it, and amplified on the theme to some extent:

HOWARD: . . . I remember once she caught me eating cornbread and got very upset, made me take a laxative and wanted to stick a wooden spoon down my throat to make me vomit it up.
CLIFFORD: Why did she . . .
HOWARD: She believed you got leprosy from eating cornbread. Some doctor had said that and my mother believed him and she told me, 'Never eat cornbread.' I didn't pay attention, or maybe I didn't hear her, and she caught me eating

178

cornbread and, well, she worried about me. She had a lot of theories about disease, I remember. I think it was you couldn't eat gingerbread because you got . . . some disease or other. And meat had to be cooked until it was practically shoe-leather or you could catch hoof-and-mouth disease, which drove my father crazy because he liked his beef blood-rare. Also, Buffalo Bayou overflowed one year [another unrelated item we had found in *The Houston Post*] and my mother said, 'No fish, we can't eat fish now.' I don't remember exactly what the reason was. And . . . well, no pork, no pork ever, but that was very sensible. She had a cousin who died of trichinosis.

Later, after the transcripts had been finished and submitted, the McGraw-Hill and *Life* editors felt that Howard's mother was indeed the source of the billionaire's phobias. 'The material on her is a little thin,' they said. 'Next time you see him, ask him some more questions about her.' I obliged, and added to the final manuscript the following anecdote, which came from my own personal childhood experience during a summer in Rockaway Beach, New York.

HOWARD: . . . One day Mama came around to the garage and said, 'Come outside with me.' I went out with her to the street and there on the sidewalk were three boys from the neighborhood, about my age, just standing around. She had seen them playing nearby, playing cowboys and Indians. She had collared them, brought them to the front door, and told them to wait there. She brought me outside and then she announced to these boys, 'This is my son Howard and he would like to play with you.' It was one of the most humiliating experiences of my childhood. I can remember it distinctly even now –

179

that terrible feeling of shame, that my mother had forced my presence on these boys . . . She was so overprotective that . . . well, this may strike you as comical, but she was a Texas version of a Jewish mother. If she had lived to see it, I could well imagine her saying, 'Help, help! My son Howard the Billionaire is drowning.' And she would have been right, because in later years, as I intend to tell you – from the age of thirty to nearly sixty – I *was* drowning.

'Wonderful,' the editors said, when they read that. 'He really opened up to you.'

Early in the game, before our April research trip, we had decided that at some time in his life Howard would have visited India. 'We'll make it one of the climactic experiences of his life,' I said.

Dick, with a twinkle in his eye, added, 'It will complete his disillusionment with the West.'

Both Dick and I had spent some time in India – I had visited Benares and lived in a houseboat in Kashmir; Dick had touched at Calcutta, Bombay, and Madras as a merchant seaman – we reckoned that we could draw on our own experiences to lend verisimilitude to the episode.

To supplement our memories and to add point and piquancy to the story, Dick bought books on Eastern philosophy and mysticism by Rabindranath Tagore and Maharishi, and shipped them to Ibiza. We didn't have time to read them through, but we poked about in them, selected a few key concepts and a suitable abstract vocabulary, and one day towards the end of July we decided to have a go at it.

An hour later, when we finished the taping, we played it back. Dick held his nose and pulled an imaginary chain.

'Yeah,' I said, 'like something out of *The Razor's Edge*. But let's transcribe it anyhow. Maybe it will read better than it sounds.'

The yarn we had concocted was wild enough to satisfy even the insatiable appetite of the people at McGraw-Hill for the *outré;* but it read like a dime novel. There was Howard, fifty-five years old, tormented by self-doubt, looking for 'answers,' standing on the steps of the Ganges at Benares with the stench of the burning ghats in his nostrils. He sees a couple of fakirs – one who has stood on one leg for so long that the other leg has withered; the other fakir has blinded himself by staring at the sun hour after hour with open eyes. Howard is horrified and disgusted.

'But these are not the true holy men,' Howard's guide tells him. 'You must visit my father, Ramaprasad. Unlike these sad creatures, he is a repository of the true wisdom of the East.'

And so Howard visits the white-haired patriarch, Ramaprasad (the name of a 16th-century poet we had pulled at random from a book called *Hinduism),* in a village near Benares, and is astounded and impressed by the aura of serenity that surrounds him. He sits at the old man's feet, literally and figuratively, for an indeterminate period (I said it should be two weeks; Dick insisted on a longer stay; I prevailed with the argument that if anyone at *Life* checked the chronology of those years, the longest unaccountable period would be two weeks) and learns to grapple successfully with the problems of the 'self,' to tear aside the veil that separates him from the real, the true, the whole Howard Hughes.

Howard returns to visit Ramaprasad again, about a year later, and finds him dying of cancer. He sits the death-watch, donates $500,000 – anonymously – to establish the Ramaprasad School of Eastern Studies – 'it's still there in India,' Howard says, 'but you'll have trouble finding it' – and returns once more to the United States, no longer a man divided against himself but prepared to cope with anything, including the loss of TWA and a $137-million judgment.

'That'll win the Peeyoulitzer prize, all right,' Dick said when I switched off the recorder. 'Let's drop it. The book's long enough already.'

I had a different suggestion, which was accepted. 'Let's drop the Ramaprasad crap,' I said, 'but keep the encounters with the fakirs in Benares. The local color's good. That's the kind of stuff the people at *Life* really go for. And who knows? Maybe Howard's really been to India. He'd be annoyed if we left it out.'

Sometimes Dick and I taped directly from the mass of factual material we had accumulated in the folders, amplifying constantly but occasionally playing it straight. At other times, feeling playful or adventurous, we launched out into the murky waters of Howard's philosophy: his theory of corruption in American family life, of germs, of a universe in which an atom in a man's toe might contain an entire solar system. Nothing was too outrageous. 'The wilder the story,' I explained to Dick, 'the deeper their need to believe it. And, of course, it's less checkable.'

Howard's theory about his own eccentricity was provided to us accidentally by Edith. She still knew hardly anything about Howard Hughes and cared even less, and my constant preoccupation with him had led her to ban the mention of his name in our house. However, on one occasion at the breakfast table, the ban was lifted by Edith herself. 'You know,' she said, 'you and Dick always talk about this man as if he was nuts, what is wrong. He does things his own way, what he can afford to do, what is just the way Pimpi used to live.' Pimpi was Edith's affectionate nickname for her father, who had died two years ago at the age of eighty. She proceeded to tell me some tales about her father, who was certainly an eccentric in his own right. I took mental notes and that afternoon, with Dick playing my role and feeding me the right lines, we taped the following dialogue:

HOWARD: . . . If there's a price on my head, and I can tell you there is, the man who wants to collect it won't necessarily have to put a bullet between my eyes. There are other ways he could do it. That's why I'm careful. What's the matter?

CLIFFORD: Nothing.

HOWARD: If you think I'm insane I wish you'd say so and we can put a stop to this right now.

CLIFFORD: I don't think that. I just want to find out why you feel the way you do. That's what the world wants to know and so do I.

HOWARD: I'm eccentric and I make no bones about it. Eccentricity is the sign of a superior intelligence. Now, I'm not trying to say I have a superior intelligence because the truth is I don't believe I do have. I don't. I'm only saying . . . well, I'll put it this way. People who ridicule eccentricity . . . ridiculing eccentricity is the sign of an inferior intelligence. You told me about your wife's father, how he ordered food in restaurants, two French-fried potatoes and six string beans. Now that was eccentric, and the waiters probably thought he was crazy . . . that's why they were waiters and he was a rich man. Did your wife think he was crazy?

CLIFFORD: Certainly not. In fact, she thought it was great, that he was a great man.

HOWARD: He may very well have been. My point is, and I've thought about this, and I think it's of the very deepest importance that I spell this out for you . . . my eccentricities, if you look at them carefully, are just intelligent safeguards against the

183

common dangers of life. More than that, every man would have them, every man would behave in a so-called peculiar manner, not necessarily my manner, but his own peculiar manner, if he had the courage.

CLIFFORD: And the money.

HOWARD: Yes, the money, the money to indulge your wishes and to tell other people to go to hell if they don't like it. That's it precisely. That explains in a nutshell why I'm odd, why people think I'm odd, because I am odd in that way and . . . only my oddness is my individuality, which I can afford to express whereas others can't or are too scared to do so. And so naturally the world, the mass, the ones who can't express themselves and . . . they look at someone like me, what they know of me or what they think they know of me, and they say, 'He's odd, he's nuts, he's crazy,' use whatever word you please. Well, you must, by definition, be odd and eccentric and maybe even nuts if you're rich, because you can do what you like and have what you like and structure your life to suit your most, your very deepest personal tastes, without fear of the consequences, and any man's tastes are – if he expresses them honestly – goddam peculiar. Artists are the closest to this, close to rich men like myself in this sense, because they have a highly developed sense of their own individuality and they don't mind telling the world to go take a flying fuck at a rolling doughnut, and I don't either. Because in my own way I suppose I'm an artist, too, as well as being rich. Now I want to stress this, all that I've said, because it is the truth, it is God's honest truth, and I believe it and that's what I want you to say, and I want you to quote me word for word on this, maybe brush up the grammar if it needs it, but that's what I want to say about myself. That may be

184

the most important thing I have to say about myself, to squash all those nasty stories people love to tell about me because . . . never mind why they do it. I want you to say exactly what I've said. Play the tape back for me now. [The tape was then played back.] Yes, I'm satisfied. That's what I meant and I goddam well want it right out in front, and if people don't understand that or don't like it, that's their problem, not mine. You still haven't said, does it make sense to you?

CLIFFORD: If you put it that way, it makes sense.

HOWARD: Then why do you have that look on your face?

CLIFFORD: I don't know what look I've got.

HOWARD: Do I bore you?

CLIFFORD: Absolutely not. I think it's a great statement.

HOWARD: What is it, you want to go out and smoke a cigarette, put another nail in your coffin?

CLIFFORD: Yeah, I know.

HOWARD: All right, go ahead, smoke a cigarette.

CLIFFORD: Okay, we'll take a break.

This passage was later read by Shelton Fisher, the President of McGraw-Hill, Inc. 'By God,' he said to me, 'he certainly gave you a hard time. But you stood up to him.'

'I think he makes sense.'

'So do I.' Shelton Fisher beckoned to the seven or eight other executives who sat with us then in the Board of Directors Room on the 32nd floor of the McGraw-Hill Building. 'Here's the key to this remarkable man's character, gentlemen,' he said, passing them the pages which had their genesis in Edith's breakfast table remarks. 'If you want to understand Howard Hughes, read it carefully.'

*   *   *

185

Truth may be stranger than fiction, but there are times when the reverse is true and others when the two concepts become hopelessly tangled and intertwined. Some of the material which we invented out of the whole cloth was later checked by *Time-Life*'s experienced staff of researchers. We had decided to have Howard's father, a rough-cut *bon vivant*, race around Houston in a 1920 35-horsepower Peerless.

HOWARD: He rebuilt that himself down at our garage and he used to race in it. He traveled all the way up to Dallas because some colonel up there claimed he had the fastest car in Texas, and that's all my father had to hear. He went up there and bet this man $500 he could win in his Peerless, and he did, at sixty miles an hour over the track, or wherever they raced . . .

Dave Maness, the Assistant Managing Editor of *Life*, apparently put his Houston stringer to work on the story. He called me one day to inform me that Hughes had made a mistake. The *Life* researchers had talked to a number of old-timers in the Houston area.

'He went up to Dallas, all right,' Maness said, 'and raced this colonel, but it wasn't a 1920 Peerless he owned. It was a 1902 model. Will you be able to double-check that with Hughes? We want to be as accurate as possible.'

I complimented him on the diligence and doggedness of his research staff, but shrugged off the necessity for further questioning. 'Let it go as a 1902 model. It was probably just a typing error.'

Howard, we decided, had had a humiliating and comical experience in a gym in Santa Monica. We based it on something that had happened to Dick in the Great Blackout of December 1965.

When the lights winked out all over the Northeastern United States, Dick was in the locker room of the Shelton Towers Gymnasium in midtown New York, just starting to get into his shorts and sneakers. By the time he had fumbled his way back into his street clothes, an attendant arrived with a flashlight and guided him out to the reception room, where he spent the next couple of hours trying to find out what was happening. At one point he was joined by a good-looking, freckle-faced young man he knew only as Billy. Billy's face was streaked with sweat. 'What's the matter?' Dick asked him. 'Did the showers break down, too?'

'You couldn't get me in there for a million dollars!' Billy said, and gave a bitter little laugh. He had been in the locker room when the lights went out. He continued on to the shower room, naked, but stopped at the door, appalled at the shrieking and giggling that was coming from inside the room. As he turned to go, a hand clutched at him and tried to pull him inside. He tore loose and ran. 'They were going at it like fiends in there,' Billy said. 'Jesus! Imagine if you dropped the soap. It'd be worth your life to bend over and pick it up.'

'Worth your ass, you mean.'

'Great,' I said to Dick, when he had finished. 'We'll tape it and you play Howard. We've got to make the man *real*.'

Our work routine quickly established itself. No matter what time he went to bed, Dick found himself awake at six o'clock in the morning; so that after breakfast he would drive to the studio at Los Molinos and begin transcribing the previous day's tapes.

My next-door neighbor at Los Molinos, a German homosexual named Gundel, cornered me one afternoon by a patch of cactus near the studio. 'I can't sleep,' he complained. 'I hear you and your friend talking from so early in the morning to so late in the evening.'

I apologized. 'I guess we do rattle on a lot.'

I warned Dick and suggested that he spend the morning before my arrival reading through the raw material that we were going to work with that day. But each day after that, when I arrived, he seemed poorly prepared. He finally confessed to me that he had discovered in a far corner of the bookshelves my small library of volumes on the stock market. He was spending his mornings educating himself in the folklore of bulls and bears. Since the April day I had helped Dick open an account at Merrill Lynch, the market had become an obsession with him. His brain, he told me, was a constant whirl of charts, Dow theory, and the myriad contradictory rules for buying and selling. 'I dream of head-and-shoulder formations, of pennants and inverted V's,' he told me. As the summer wore on he became both a bore and a worry to Ginette. Over breakfast he would say, gloomily, 'The advance-decline line's falling behind the industrials.' At dinner he would remark that he had 'dropped a few hundred on Texas Gulf, but I think we'll make it up on Sony.'

'Schmuck,' I said to him – the blind leading the blind – 'there are two basic rules in the stock market. The first is: cut your losses and let your profits run. The second is: never tell your wife what you're doing.'

But with all that we were rarely distracted, and we worked through a hot July into a hotter August. By early afternoon Dick was usually exhausted; he would slump into the big green easy chair, his eyelids would droop and he would start to snore gently until I shook him by the shoulder and said, 'Go.' He left me then to continue the transcribing, and walked over the hill to his apartment in Figueretes. After lunch he and Ginette would fill a basket with towels, snorkels, toys for Raphael, and pile into the car to drive to Las Salinas, the site of the ancient Punic salt flats and one of the few unspoiled beaches on the island.

Nedsky, Barney, and Josh – my oldest son, come from England for the summer – were often there, sometimes accompanied by the cheerful Australian *au pair* girl Edith had hired, sometimes by Edith herself. Dick and his family usually found a spot further along the beach near a Tahitian-style French snack bar. I would arrive around five o'clock, play for a while with the kids in the shallow water; then Dick and I would head for the deeps, beyond earshot and paternal responsibilities. Under a naked blue sky our heads protruded like bobbing corks from the glittering surface of the Mediterranean.

'Tomorrow we'll start in on RKO. Go through that file on the actresses and read that book on the witch-hunt in Hollywood.'

'What did we decide about Jane Russell? Did he screw her or not?'

'Not. She's still around.'

'Listen, I read the stuff you added about TWA and I still don't understand a word of it. If he only had to come up with $40 million, why did he let them appoint a trustee for his stock? Why didn't he . . .'

And so on through the summer, while the children gamboled in the shallows and waited for us to build sand castles. After Nina arrived, in August, she installed herself on the other side of the snack bar, wearing a white bikini and baking herself to a pancake brown in the relentless sun. Once in a while, as I meandered casually along the water's edge to where she lay on her beach towel, I would catch Dick's eye. Giving me a worried smile, he would shake his head in mock reproof.

'Watch yourself, man,' he told me. 'It's a dangerous game. You could get into a lot of trouble.' And I laughed.

'Howard should have an early homosexual experience,' I decided.

'You mean he's queer?' Dick said. 'You never told me that.'

189

'Certainly not. He's absolutely straight. But there are a lot of rumors around that he *is* queer, and we've got to scotch them. So we'll have him attacked by somebody when he's a young man, just arrived in Hollywood, and he fends them off and from then on the whole scene fills him with disgust.'

'Good idea. He's driving around in downtown Los Angeles and he gives a lift to a young sailor . . .'

'No, no. Let's pick an actor, someone well-known. Let's get some mileage out of it.'

'John Wayne.'

'Be serious,' I said. 'We need a well-known actor who was around in 1930, who's queer, and who's dead.'

'Ramon Navarro,' Dick said immediately. He had an encyclopedic memory crammed with names, dates, facts, and rumors. 'He was murdered just a few months ago in Hollywood, stabbed or beaten to death by some kid he was supposed to have picked up.'

Ramon Navarro it was, and we had Howard popping him one in the jaw in the bathroom of Mary Pickford's house during a Hollywood party, after Navarro had injudiciously made a move toward Howard's open fly. Our battle cry in moments of indecision was always: 'Libel the dead.' The dead couldn't sue for libel, and when we needed an actress to join Howard and the late Errol Flynn in a schooner lost at sea off Baja California, it was the late Ann Sheridan. When we needed someone to climb into bed with Howard, drunk, after his 1946 crash in the F-ll, it was the late Linda Darnell. In some instances we deliberately – and flagrantly – libeled the living but these were incidents of no importance which were designed as throwaways; we knew that the publisher's lawyers would strike them from the final text. They had to earn a living, too.

Toward the middle of August we were working on the Las Vegas sections, which we thought were thin. It was the most obscure period in Hughes's life and we had

190

little to go on other than reports of hotel purchases and clips detailing Howard's battle with the Atomic Energy Commission. I finally hit on the solution to the problem.

'He's not *in* Las Vegas,' I said. 'That suite on the ninth floor of the Desert Inn is just a cover-up. He's on the move, the king in disguise, traveling among the people, searching for the answers to life.' We invented trips to Mexico and Puerto Rico, most of them in company with the mythical love of Howard's declining years, a diplomat's wife whom we christened Helga – in honor of the lady who handled Howard's banking arrangements in Zurich. It was intended as a private joke, but it had unforeseen repercussions at a later date. We also concocted a bizarre tale wherein one of Howard's doubles – we had no idea that he used doubles, but learned later that it was a fact – is kidnaped in 1965 from a Las Vegas bungalow while Howard himself is off trysting in Mexico with Helga. The ransom is $1 million and Howard's lieutenants decide not to pay it. Then Howard returns from Mexico earlier than expected, the gang of kidnapers, apparently realizing their mistake, return the double for a paltry $150,000. Subsequently, Howard awakes to the realization that the double himself, whom we named Jerry, is the brains behind the whole kidnaping scheme. We finished taping the story. I switched off the machine and looked at Dick.

'You believe it?'

'I believe it,' he said. 'Thousands wouldn't, but I believe it.'

It was during this same session that we taped the odyssey of Howard's adventures with Robert Gross, the President of Lockheed. Gross was dead and therefore fair game. Dick and I had had a mutual friend who used to eat his lunch and dinner in the Grand Union supermarket in Greenwich Village, marching from one aisle to another, eating his way to the checkout counter where he would pay for a ten-cent bag of peanuts and then walk home. Our fond memory of this genial, hungry shoplifter, coupled with our knowledge, gleaned from the Dietrich manuscript, that Howard loved milk and cookies above all other delicacies, led to the following bursts of creativity.

HOWARD: . . . Okay, listen, Here's something I wanted to tell you. I was mentioning Bob Gross before. You're always asking me for personal stories and incidents from my life, and I've remembered one that I can tell you about. It's not one of the important things, hardly, but Bob Gross . . . this was with Bob Gross, when we were . . . well, Bob and I were pretty good friends, as I've said many times. He was a funny man. Choleric as hell sometimes, he'd blow up over nothing, you know I told you he threw me out of his office at Lockheed. And at the same time, funny. He had a real comic sense of things. But he was very peculiar . . . I once saved him from a terribly embarrassing incident. One time, this was in Las Vegas, we'd stopped in, it was late at night, we'd stopped in at a little place for coffee . . .

CLIFFORD: When was this?

HOWARD: In the fifties, the middle fifties. Call it 1953, it doesn't matter. And Bob stopped at the counter to pay the bill. And I was looking at a magazine rack at the time, and I remember just as he paid, as the woman took his money and turned away to the cash register, I saw something I couldn't believe my eyes. I saw Bob Gross, and mind you, this is the man who was President of Lockheed Corporation, one of America's biggest corporations, I saw him reach out and stick a candy bar in his pocket. Well, I thought I must have seen things, but no . . .

CLIFFORD: But he paid for it, didn't he?

HOWARD: He didn't pay for it, he stuck it in his pocket. He stole it. And I said to myself, 'What's going on here? What is this?' And when we got outside I couldn't contain myself, I said, 'For God's sake, Bob, what in the world are you doing stealing that candy bar?' He turned red for a minute, and then laughed and said, 'Well, every once in a while, it's a kick. It's more fun than paying for it. You ought to try it some time, Howard.' Well, we went on about this for awhile, but I was totally flabbergasted. He told me he did this, not every day by any means, but whenever the impulse moved him. And, you understand, never anything of value, not diamond watches or sable coats – a candy bar, that's all. But this is not the incident I was going to tell you. This is just the beginning of it, because a few months later, some months later, I don't remember exactly when, Bob and I were returning – I'd been out in the desert with him half the night, we were negotiating the possible sale of TWA to Lockheed, or Bob's buying a percentage of the stock of Toolco, but we couldn't come to an agreement – and this was, oh, it was about nine, ten o'clock in the morning. We were driving back to Los Angeles and we passed through a little town, one of those little crossroads towns, now you see it now you don't, you know, and they had a supermarket. I suppose it was a shopping center for people all around there. And I felt a yen, I wanted some Oreos. You know Oreos . . .

CLIFFORD: Oreos are those chocolate . . .

HOWARD: Chocolate sandwich cookies. And a container of milk. That was one of my favorite snacks. Unfortunately, it's getting harder and harder to find a decent Oreo cookie. The damn fools at Nabisco, they had a winner, they used to make it with a white filling – that's the only decent kind of filling, a pure white vanilla filling, and now all I can find is goddam chocolate filling or yellow filling. I've had men go out and scour the stores to find me some Oreos and they had to go to half a dozen stores before they found what I wanted. There are all sorts of other brands, but an Oreo is like the Cadillac of cookies – at least for me. And I like Oreos.

CLIFFORD: What other kinds of cookies do you favor?

HOWARD: Well, I like butter cookies and Toll House, if they're well-made, with good-quality chocolate, and occasionally, if my . . . I'm not supposed to eat too many sweets, I never was supposed to, but I did . . . occasionally . . . and I love Mallomars. Now that's another cookie that's practically gone out of existence. There are all sorts of substitutes on the market, gooey sweet things, marshmallow things, but a Mallomar has a special quality, very crisp when you bite it, and you can't get them. I used to stock them in all my bungalows and houses, in the refrigerator, so they wouldn't get moldy. And graham crackers, of course. I used to like graham crackers. Still do.

CLIFFORD: Anyway, you were saying about . . .

HOWARD: Yes, that's right, we were coming back through this town and I wanted a package of Oreos and a container of milk. So I stopped the car and . . . well, this was in the midst of a lot of publicity about me and TWA and I somehow didn't want to go in, so I asked Bob if he would do me a favor and go in and buy me a package of Oreos. If he couldn't get Oreos, I said, I'd take plain butter cookies or graham crackers or some such thing. And a container of milk. And Bob said he'd be delighted. So he went in and I waited, and I waited, and no Bob. I said, 'What the hell is going on here?' And finally I didn't want to drive off and leave him stranded, of course, so I got out of the car and went in – it was at least fifteen, twenty minutes later – and I went in and Bob was standing, one man had him by the elbow, and he was talking hard, talking for his life, it looked like, to another.

CLIFFORD: You mean he'd been caught stealing?

HOWARD: He'd been caught stealing. He'd stuck those damn Oreo cookies inside his windbreaker, zipped it up and stuck them right in. That's not a candy bar, you know. A package of Oreos is bulky. And the damn fool had gotten caught.

CLIFFORD: Did he try to steal the milk, too?

HOWARD: No, no, he'd paid for the milk. That must have been against his principles, to steal milk. And . . .

CLIFFORD: Did you go over and get him out?

HOWARD: Oh yes. Well, at first, I didn't know what to do. I stood there, and what could I do? Go up there and say, 'I'm Howard Hughes and you must let this man go. He's the President of Lockheed Corporation.' I didn't know whether Bob had identified himself as Robert Gross, President of Lockheed, and I didn't want to embarrass him and I didn't want to embarrass myself, you know, be hailed into court as an accessory to a theft in a supermarket of a package of cookies. That would have made page one. Can you see it? *HOWARD HUGHES AND ROBERT GROSS STEAL PACKAGE OF COOKIES FROM SUPERMARKET*. Big headlines.

CLIFFORD: He had passed the turnstiles, I take it.

HOWARD: Oh, yes, they grabbed him on the outside, near the door. They always wait, I understand, until you're outside of the store or otherwise you can sue them for false arrest. Now, the point is, he didn't want to identify himself as Robert Gross.

He wanted to pay these people off, slip them some cash and just get out of there as quickly as possible. That's what he was trying to do when I walked in the supermarket. But he didn't have enough cash with him, he had maybe ten or twenty dollars in cash, and that wasn't enough to get these hicktown people off his neck.

CLIFFORD: Didn't he have a checkbook?

HOWARD: Of course he did, in the car, in his briefcase, but how could he give them a check and sign it Robert Gross? That would have allowed them to blackmail him for the rest of his days. He needed cash, and he didn't have enough. You don't buy yourself out of a situation like that with ten dollars. So he . . . well, I don't remember whether he came up to me or I went over to him, I think he, I think they had posted a man at the door, some young guy in a T-shirt, very beefy guy, probably worked there moving cartons around, but his job at the time was to see that Bob didn't run out the door. So, Bob sidled up to me and told me what had happened and he had to have cash, had to have something substantial to pay these people off, and he asked me for it, he begged me for it. 'Please,' he said, 'Howard, I've got to have a hundred dollars.'

CLIFFORD: But you didn't carry that kind of cash.

HOWARD: Not on my person, of course not, but I did in my hat. I had my hat on the back seat of the car. The car was locked. I had locked it. I went out to the car, they let me go, they had nothing against me except that I was obviously the friend of this thief they'd caught, and I tore open the lining of my hat and found a hundred-dollar bill and brought it back in.

CLIFFORD: I thought you said you only carried thousands and singles.

HOWARD: Well, I was lucky this time, or Bob was

lucky. I had a few hundreds. If I'd had . . . if I'd only had thousands it would have cost Bob a thousand dollars to get out of that jam, because I'm damn sure they wouldn't have made change for him. They probably would have had him arrested for passing counterfeit money.

CLIFFORD: It wasn't counterfeit.

HOWARD: No, of course not, but what would they think if a thief produced a thousand-dollar bill? They'd think it was counterfeit, wouldn't they? I told you, neither of us was dressed like . . . we looked like workingmen, nothing more. Well, to cut this short, I gave Bob the hundred dollars and he gave it to the store manager or whoever the guy was, and they said okay and let him go. We went outside together and he was red in the face and sweating, I'll tell you, and he said, 'Here's your damn Oreos. Next time go in and buy them yourself.' I said, 'What are you talking about? I didn't tell you to steal them, you goddam idiot.' I made him a long speech. I said, 'You ought to know that crime doesn't pay. And you should be damn grateful I had the money to bail you out of this. I could just as easily have turned tail and run and let you go to jail. How would it look if I was associated with a shoplifter? It would ruin my reputation.' And that's true, you know. I doubt very much if Equitable Life would have loaned me $40 million if I'd been involved in a shoplifting scandal, even for a package of cookies. But of course, mostly I was just kidding Bob, and he knew it.

CLIFFORD: What did he say afterwards?

HOWARD: We laughed about it, but it was kind of a strained laugh on his part, and I often wondered afterwards if he went on with his cookie and candy stealing or if that was the sort of high point of his career.

CLIFFORD: Did he pay you back the hundred dollars?

HOWARD: The next day. Bob was very scrupulous about that.

CLIFFORD: Listen, speaking of cookies, you told me a long time ago – I was reading the transcript of the first interviews again – and I noticed you told me to remind you – you told me that Noah Dietrich had told a story about you once regarding cookies which wasn't true, but you never told me what the story was.

HOWARD: Well, first of all, you have to understand that Noah Dietrich has, since our breakup, and before, has turned into a vindictive old cocksucker who wants to take my hide off. And he's told story after story about me. Unfortunately – or rather fortunately for me – he's a very imprudent man, because a lot of these stories have gotten back to me. He's told stories about business dealings we have done where he's twisted the whole thing around, where I was the one who made the decision, he's told other people, 'I made it and Howard didn't know what the hell he was doing.' This is an example of one of the things he did. The story itself is so trivial, but I'll tell it to you. It was very simple. A long time ago. It was during the . . . we had just finished shooting *Scarface* . . . the movie. I was working with the cutting editor and we were working . . . Christ, we hadn't slept for two days, and we hadn't eaten for I don't know how long. At one point, I remember, we were really hungry. I sent out for food and this guy sent out for food, and when he finished eating he was still hungry. Now, I had sent out for milk and cookies, which was quite enough to keep me going. This man hadn't sent out for any dessert, and when I started to eat my

198

cookies, he said, 'Mr Hughes, could I please have one of your cookies?' And I gave him one . . . I hesitated, because I knew . . . well, I didn't want to start a precedent, because cookies were all I had to eat. These other people would go out and gorge themselves on hamburgers and French fries and whatnot and all I had to eat was milk and cookies. I kept them in the studio or the cutting room, or wherever I happened to be working, and they were all I had to eat. But I gave him a cookie. Now . . . well, first of all, Noah twisted this all around. He told somebody that I refused to give the man a cookie and that I made a fuss about it. That's absolutely not true. I definitely gave him a cookie.

CLIFFORD: What kind of cookies were they?

HOWARD: They were, I don't remember, I think at the time I liked plain butter cookies. But the sequel to this incident was, for weeks afterward men would come up to me on the lot, whenever I went off to a corner to drink my milk and eat my cookies, they would come up and say, 'Howard,' or 'Mr Hughes, can I please have a cookie?' Now, I couldn't very well refuse them, since I'd given this other man a cookie, so my cookie supply just vanished every day under my eyes, and I was constantly running out of cookies. And I knew then that I was right in the first place, because you give one man a cookie, you've got to give every man a cookie, and pretty soon you don't have any cookies yourself. And you're a poor man – cookiewise. You think that's funny?

CLIFFORD: I think it's hilarious.

HOWARD: Well, I can see the humor in it. But when you're hungry it's not funny when your cookies vanish. Besides, it might have been hundred-dollar bills next. I didn't want to get the reputation of being an easy touch.

CLIFFORD: Don't worry.
HOWARD: What did you say?

Noah Dietrich's unpublished manuscript – taking into account the petty envy he seemed to show for the man about whom he wrote – gave us the basic clues to Howard's business methods. Dietrich might tell of an incident in a single paragraph; as in the cookie story, we would expand that paragraph into several pages and reverse the point of view to put Howard in a more favorable light.

But the major revelations of Howard's character, and the parts we most enjoyed taping were those incidents stitched together from the multicolored fabric of our imagination, our own views of life and people, and our vision of what Howard Hughes might have been had we lived in his skin. I had already given McGraw-Hill and *Life* some skimpy details of his relationship with Ernest Hemingway. No evidence existed that the billionaire and the writer had ever met. But we felt that Howard, in his search for a life-style other than the one that had brought him nothing but lawsuits, loneliness, and misery, would at one point in his life – having already failed with Albert Schweitzer in French Equatorial Africa – set out to find a man who could combine for him the qualities of hero, mentor, and friend. One muggy afternoon I plugged the mikes into the tape recorder. Dick dropped his bulk into the easy chair, with Carlos Baker's biography of Hemingway balanced on his lap. I sat at the desk, surrounded by reference books, time charts, and recent histories of Cuba. Alternately playing Howard Hughes and Clifford Irving – sometimes to the extent of interrupting each other in mid-sentence when the other faltered, so that in the end it was often impossible to tell which phrase of Howard's was Dick's and which was mine – we related the entire relationship of Hughes and Hemingway. When it was over, we were exhausted.

'That's one of the best sections we've done,' Dick said happily. 'Let's transcribe and see how it reads.'

I pulled out the microphone cords and set the machine to *PLAY*. We listened. There was a hum and an occasional high-pitched buzz, nothing more.

Dick frowned. 'Go forward a bit.'

I pushed the *FAST FORWARD* button, then switched back to *PLAY*. The machine hummed like a dying horse-fly. 'Oh, my God,' I said. 'I must have plugged the mikes into the wrong holes.'

Dick stared at me. 'I'm going to kill you.'

'Get me the knife,' I groaned, 'I'll do it myself.'

We sat for ten minutes in a state of semi-shock, muttering to ourselves, unable to think or act. It was as if a significant moment of living literature had been created, then lost forever. I snapped out of the lethargy first and jammed the mikes into the proper holes. 'We'll do it again.'

'I couldn't face it,' Dick said hoarsely, 'Tomorrow . . .'

'No. It's like getting thrown from a horse. You've got to jump back on and ride. Let's do it right now. We'll take it from the top. Come on,' I urged, 'we can do it.'

'Are you plugged in the right way this time, you stupid sonofabitch?'

'Yes, yes, come on . . . let's go.'

Dick sighed deeply, but nodded. 'Okay. Where should I begin?'

'Just the way you did before.'

'All right.' He took a deep breath. 'Despite my terrible disappointment with Dr Schweitzer, that I never got through to the man . . . '

We finished two hours later. Worn out and wilting from the heat, we played it back. 'And that,' I said triumphantly, 'is how history is made. If you don't succeed at first, try again.'

'My God, it's good. I never thought we could do it.'

He mopped his forehead with a towel. 'Now that's what I call a day's work.'

That day's work follows: the second rambling version of Howard's fictitious thirteen-year relationship with Papa Hemingway.

HOWARD: Where should I begin?

CLIFFORD: Just the way you did before.

HOWARD: All right. Despite my terrible disappointment with Dr Schweitzer, that I never got through to the man – I mean he brushed me aside like some insignificant creature from out of the bush down there, worse than one of his darling lepers he loved so much he had to lock up the place every night so they wouldn't steal the shirt off his back – despite this, I still felt that there were men in this world, and he was one of them, in some kind of perverted way who had found – well, I hate to use the word, the secret, but . . . had found a way, or had been lucky enough or something, in some way had put their feet on the right path early in their lives and never left it. They were just following a clearly marked path through the jungle that human life resembles. And I said, this is something that was missing from my life. I knew that I had my share of achievements, but when I added up everything I had done I could see no focus. I'm talking about the early fifties . . . I could see I was not on a clear track that progressed from one stage of development to another. It was helter-skelter, it was what seized my imagination at the time, and yet when I analyzed it – and I'm not trying to say that I thought about this all the time – I could see no progression. And when you can see no progression in your own life, no clearcut advance from one goal to another, leading to major goals, then you can't see yourself, which is blindness. That sort of blindness is worse than any kind of deafness. I know. And . . . well, I had met another great man, in quotes – I had met another great man in my life. That was Ernest Hemingway. We had met briefly in Hollywood when I was making movies. I don't know what Ernest was doing at the time. Writing, I suppose. But he made a great impression on me. I felt a tremendous . . . well, the force of personality more than even the power of his work, although I had read and admired his novels very deeply. Especially the one about the guy – *The Sun Also Rises*.

CLIFFORD: Did you get along with him personally then, in Hollywood?

HOWARD: Oh, we had no chance either to get along or not get along. It was hardly more than an introduction at a party in some bungalow, some crazy place he was living. The Garden of Allah . . . A lot of writers lived there. But he impressed me, Hemingway did, and I thought I would like to see him again. And the occasion arose, just after the war, some time in . . . I think the fall of 1946, when I went out to look over Sun Valley, with the idea of buying it.

CLIFFORD: For what purpose?

HOWARD: To buy it. Oh, I see. To . . . for the purpose it's being used for now. That is, a popular and successful resort area. I flew out there. I was flying a converted B-25, I believe, at the time. I knew Ernest was there with his family and he was hunting, and so I met him. I found out where he was living. Everybody knew, and I marched right up to his door, knocked on it, and he opened it.

CLIFFORD: You had gone out to Sun Valley as Howard Hughes.

HOWARD: I never travel under the name of Howard Hughes. That's the kiss of death. They would have jacked the price up fifty per cent just on that knowledge alone. I'm speaking of Sun Valley.

CLIFFORD: What name did you use?

HOWARD: I was using George Garden.

CLIFFORD: Why George Garden?

HOWARD: Well, I knew a George Garden very briefly once. I had met him out in Ethiopia. Just casually met him . . . flew on a plane with me once. He was a young Englishman who wanted to go exploring in the Danakil part of the country. Very dangerous, a lot of really savage tribes in that neck of the woods. Couldn't get permission to go. And he went anyhow, and he was never heard of again – I checked on that when I went back the last time. Now I don't want to convey any idea that I felt any kinship of any sort with this boy, this wanderer who vanished. But the story had impressed itself on me, so I used the name. And that was the name I gave to Hemingway, to Ernest, when he opened the door. I must say I was struck by his reception. I myself . . . well, the occasion would never arise where some stranger would come up and knock on my door. First of all nobody knows where my door is. Second, if they do know, there's a guard out there, outside a guard and inside a guard, and they would . . . it would certainly never occur to me to open the door myself. But there he came out to the door looking like a tramp. Beat-up corduroy trousers and a lumberjack shirt open to the waist . . .

CLIFFORD: What were you wearing?

HOWARD: Come to think of it, I was not a hell of a lot more respectable. It was a bit chilly, I had a couple of sweaters on. Old sweaters. No, I don't really remember what I was wearing, except I wasn't dressed up, that's a certainty. I wasn't wearing a business suit. And so I introduced myself and Ernest said, 'Well, come in, come in, have a drink.' I excused myself from the drink because I don't drink, and we talked for a while, and he immediately showed an interest in who I was, why I was there. Understand, I passed myself off as George Garden, member of a real estate group in California that was interested in Sun Valley. I didn't say that I personally, even as George Garden, was going to buy it. But I suppose no matter how you dress, the smell of money doesn't leave your skin. And Ernest cottoned on very quickly to the idea that I was rich, and he was fascinated by rich people. He took a tremendous interest in my proposal for the valley and the surrounding area, asked me all sorts of very intelligent and perceptive questions about how I was going to go about it. The extraordinary thing is that I had been in his house no more than fifteen minutes, and I was sitting in an armchair and talking as freely and easily as I'd talked with any man in my whole life. Writers are . . . well, we've talked about this, and I know you disagree with me. But writers give you this feeling . . . it may be true, it may be phony . . . but they give you the feeling they're interested in you, what makes you tick. I don't mean writers like Ben Hecht, not Hollywood writers, newspaper hacks – they just want your money, or your hide. But Ernest had that quality of making you feel immediately at home. We spent a very pleasant couple of hours. He talked about his books, somewhat, in general terms. He didn't . . . I'm no expert on literature, by any means, but I do read novels, a lot of them. As I remember, we talked about practical things mostly, more than about either of us. We talked about them in a very straightforward and simple way that I wasn't used to, except with pilots. Thing is, at the time, I didn't want anything from Ernest and he didn't want anything from me. I had read a couple of his books but I really hadn't dropped in to see him as a writer. It was more . . . I guess I had in my mind a certain image of Ernest Hemingway, as a person who had gone through all sorts of adventures and rough experiences, and he'd had a rough time of it, and he'd come out of it whole, tough. Toughened, I mean. And not only did I respect him for that, I was fascinated, and I wanted to know how and why. Anyhow, we spent a couple of hours talking and I invited him to take a spin with me in the B-25 next day, which he was delighted to do. Well, we hit it off very well. This flight . . . I was doing, not a geographical survey, but just to get an over-all picture for myself of the valley area, its potential. And so I flew around, in and out, through the canyons. At first Ernest was up there in the copilot's seat and asked me a hell of a lot of questions about what I was doing, why I was doing it, and of course I had no trouble answering that – that was second nature to me, it was a routine flight for me. He told me afterward that it was one of the most lucid and cogent explanations of flying that he had ever heard. And not only that. He couldn't get over the fact that I could fly and look around and maneuver, and at the same time maintain a running conversation with him about anything in the world. That really impressed him. Then I . . . I was so involved after a while, however, with what I was looking for that I broke off the conversation and just concentrated on flying. The flight was a bit low, I suppose, and looking back on it, now – dangerous. The wingtips were not brushing, but they weren't too far from the canyon walls a couple of times, and there was a time there I was totally absorbed in what I was doing. This was no Cessna 180, this was a B-25 bomber. Ernest loved all that afterward, on the way back, he turned to me. He had a . . . I guess a touch of awe in his voice, and he said, 'George, you're a hot pilot.' I left shortly after that. We saw one another briefly the following day, and then I was off. Had to go. But it was a very pleasant encounter and Ernest wanted to write to me about something, as a matter of fact, but I knew I wouldn't answer, and I didn't want to create that sort of situation, and so I told him some story. I said, I think, we were moving offices, and as soon as I had an address I would write his publishers, something like that. It was a lot easier for me to get in touch with him than for him to get in touch with me, and it was nearly nine years before I saw him again.

CLIFFORD: You waited that long? Why?

HOWARD: It wasn't a deliberate question of waiting. I was so immersed, embroiled in affairs, I just had no chance. Sort of like a man, a drowning man . . . I'd draw my head up out of the water and I could see Ernest along the shore from time to time, but I was sucked down again before I could even call out to him. And he was off on his own affairs in Europe, Africa, Cuba. Cuba, as a matter of fact, is where I saw him next.

CLIFFORD: Let me just interrupt you a second. When you met him that first time, how did you get along with him politically?

HOWARD: We didn't talk politics at all. I've never been a political person.

CLIFFORD: You knew, of course, that he had been involved in the Spanish Civil War, on the Loyalist side.

HOWARD: I wasn't concerned with that. As I said, I've never been a political person. I've only voted twice in my life, and that was for Roosevelt – that was a long time ago. I've always made sure that I had members of both parties on my payroll so that no matter who won, Hughes didn't lose. It didn't matter who was in office. And that's as far as my political interests went. During the Spanish Civil War, that would be 1937, '38, I was involved in my flights and airplanes and I was about as apolitical as you could get. In any case, politics was not what Ernest and I discussed. Moreover, politics was never, from what I can gather, was never Ernest's major interest, either. Strictly secondary. He told me that. I've always had the feeling he went to Spain because there was a war on and he wanted to see men in action. Naturally his sympathies were with the . . . not with the fascist side, because he was that kind of man. But he had this obsession with death and how men faced it. He asked me a great many questions in later years about my accidents, how I had felt about them, and I answered to the best of my ability. He was the only man I ever knew who was more banged up physically – had more broken bones, and wounds – than I was. Or maybe we were even up. I often wondered if he ever used that stuff I told him in any of his books, or whether there's some unpublished novel of his that has quotes from me or even has some incident from my life in it, because his questions were endless, about how I felt in the various crashes, and how I felt when a plane was in trouble. He was a man obsessed with death and danger. That's why he liked that ride in the B-25 so much.

CLIFFORD: Then you saw him again, and you told him who you were.

HOWARD: Yes, I saw him again in . . . eight, nine years later, I believe, in 1954. I was in Florida, where I had planned to build my own jet aircraft factory. That fell through and sort of on the spur of the moment – I knew Ernest was in Cuba – I hopped over there to Havana. Commercial flight.

CLIFFORD: Give me the details on this. You know, don't rush this story.

HOWARD: I remember it very well. First I went to the Floridita, that bar, because I knew he spent a lot of time there, but he wasn't there. It was empty at that hour. This was early afternoon – well, daytime. So I took a taxi out to the *finca*. I didn't remember the name of the *finca*, didn't even know it was called a *finca* then. I just said to the cab driver, 'Hemingway,' and he said, 'Ah, Papa!' And I said, 'No, no, I don't want Papa. I want Hemingway.' And he said, '*Sí, sí, Papa.*' And I said, 'I want *Señor* Hemingway,' and he said, '*Sí, sí, Papa, Papa.*' Of course by then we were halfway there and it turned out to be Ernest. I guess he wasn't working. As a matter of fact, I was let in without any ceremony. The maid at the door didn't even ask me my name. And Ernest was sitting around the pool with a few other people, and I remember I walked up . . . I hadn't had time to change, I was still wearing a business suit. I had taken the tie off, stuffed it in my pocket. I walked up and Ernest was sitting there with his pot belly hanging out and peered at me over his glasses, and the first thing he said was, 'Don't stand there with the sun behind your back. I can't make you out – that makes me nervous. Move around this way.' So I obediently did as I was told, till he could see me. He looked at me with a very grim expression, like: what's this? And then suddenly his face broke into a big beautiful smile, and he said, 'Goddamit, George, it's good to see you and you're welcome.' I felt wonderful. Not just at the warmth of his welcome, but that he'd recognized me after all those years. Really glad to see me. Ernest had that quality of welcoming, which is so rare. Well, the house was full of people, apart from his family. There was his wife – at least some little woman running around that I thought was his wife. And some blonde girl who, as I recall, the wife didn't like very much. And a bunch of servants, and some kids – his own and others. And some college kids from the United States. They'd come down there and just thrust themselves upon him with their manuscripts, expecting God knows what – maybe that he'd buy them and publish them. But he did read their work, with great patience. I remember that one of them left and he came to Ernest and asked him for money, because he didn't have the fare back home, and Ernest just smiled and gave it to him. One or two hundred bucks. That's the kind of man he was.

CLIFFORD: You were still George Garden?

HOWARD: I was afraid to tell him my real name, afraid it would change things too much. And it was such a good relationship that I didn't want to run that risk. We . . . well, we sat around the house, just talked, I can't remember too well about what. Ernest wanted to know what I'd been doing all those years, and I made up a few stories – paralleled my life in a sense. The events may have been different but the general content was the same, so that I wasn't lying to him, not in any meaningful way, really.

CLIFFORD: Did you stay at his house?

HOWARD: The first day I stayed at his house, and then he insisted I go out fishing with him.

CLIFFORD: No, I mean, were you his guest?

HOWARD: No, nothing like that. I stayed at one of those big hotels in Havana. The National, I think it was. Yeah, the National. But I did spend most of the day at the *finca,* except when we went fishing. That was my second or third day there. That was a very strange experience, Clifford – I really remember it that way. Ernest had always . . . I had taken him up in my plane, and now he wanted to take me out on his fishing boat, show me his specialty. I was a sportsman in the sense that I was a good golfer and a good shot, but I never went hunting or fishing for pleasure, and I didn't really know what to expect. I was taken aback to begin with, when . . . to find . . . there was Ernest on board, about five minutes after we left the dock wearing a jock strap. Nothing else.

CLIFFORD: Who else was aboard? Any women?

HOWARD: There were a couple of Cuban helpers, that's all. One who was steering and one who was serving drinks. But Ernest knew by then that I didn't drink, so he had a bottle of milk along in the ice chest for me, and every time he would pour . . . I think he drank, I don't know, tequila or daiquiris or something, and he had a couple of thermoses full of them . . . and each time he'd take himself a belt he'd say to his barman helper, 'Get out the milk for *Señor* Jardín.' And then he would crack up laughing. That broke him up, broke him up that I drank milk. But the fishing was bad. Ernest said it was the fault of the tankers that had been torpedoed there by German subs during the war . . . the garbage that had spewed out of them had killed off most of the big game fish. And he moaned and grumbled, and then it got hot, and he said his jock strap was itching, and he peeled it off. And he said, 'Come on, George, you must be dying. You're going to get prickly heat. Take off your clothes.' Now I checked over in my mind what I remembered of Ernest's sexual habits and sex life, and I figured it was safe enough, so I peeled down to my skivvies. I've always been a little shy about being naked with other men, or women for that matter. Not for any deep reason. I don't know what it is, but many times when I used to play golf, in the locker rooms all the men would shower together and I waited till they were out of there before I would shower. Crept into a corner of the locker room when I had to change my clothes. I don't know why I had that kind of shyness. I'm sure it goes back to my childhood, being tall and awkward, but I could never put my finger on the reason. Anyway, after a while, Ernest said, 'Let's go for a swim.' I peeled down and we dove over the side. That was an extraordinary experience for me, because . . . it's hard to explain it to you. There we were, we were grown men. I was then, well, 48 years old, and Ernest was older, and there we were in the water – and Ernest started playing games. He would dive under the water and come up under me and tip me over by the ankles. And he wanted to play fish. One of us had to be a shark and the other had to be a marlin, or a swordfish, and we would fight. Yell, shout, warn each other – 'Watch out, here I come.' Splash around, like children. And it was marvelous. It was a broiling hot day and there we were, two grown, middle-aged men, splashing around right in the middle of the Gulf of Mexico. It gave me a curious view of Ernest. I saw something in him which now I know is a common element in many geniuses and great men. That is, the capacity to play, to remain in some respects childlike until they're very old. I haven't got it, sad to say – never did. It's a naturalness that men have when they're not ashamed of themselves and of what's buried inside of them. A total lack of self-consciousness. And it was a beautiful day, an absolutely beautiful day. I felt more relaxed with Ernest than I felt with men I had known all my life . . . We just took each other for granted and . . . I was terribly impressed. With myself, too. Mind you, I wasn't conscious of this at the time. A lot of it came to me in thoughts afterward, because I knew that this was not the way I usually behaved. And I was happy. And then, then I made a bad mistake. I thought we had such a good relationship growing up between us that, well, I felt ashamed of myself for deceiving Ernest by calling myself George Garden. It suddenly seemed ignoble. And so I said to him, 'You know, I shouldn't really . . . I have to tell you something. My name isn't George Garden.' And he laughed, took a gulp of his drink and said, 'Who the hell are you?' And I said, 'I'm a businessman named Howard Hughes.' I thought maybe he might not . . . but he just looked at me for a minute, finished his drink, and said, 'Goddam. Sonofabitch! I should have known, should have guessed. That's why you flew so well. I should have known it.' And I was relieved at his reaction because I thought everything was going to be okay.

CLIFFORD: He believed you immediately?

HOWARD: Yes, he believed me immediately, not that this is invariably true. There have been many occasions in my life when people have refused to believe I was Howard Hughes. Times when I was in trouble, too. I spent a night in jail once in Shreveport – remind me to tell you about that – because they wouldn't believe I was Howard Hughes. And another time they turned me away from a motel for the same reason. But Ernest believed it at once. And if he had any doubts, I reminded him of the fact that I had met him a couple of times out in Hollywood in the thirties, as Howard Hughes, and I recalled the incidents and the time and place, and that of course clinched it. But he didn't doubt me. It made sense to him right away. But it was a mistake to have told him. In subtle ways his attitude began to change almost at once. The first thing that happened is that he wanted to know all about me, that is to say, about Howard Hughes. He asked me a hell of a lot of questions and that's when we got on to our long discussions about flying, what I'd been through – and that was all right. But then he started asking me the same sort of questions that reporters had asked me for years. I had developed a habit by then of instantly ducking into my shell and being brusque, the moment these kinds of questions were posed to me. And that's what happened to me then. We went back to the house and I asked Ernest, 'Please, the one thing I beg of you is not to tell anyone else who I am, because that ruins everything for me. People treat me differently and I don't like it.' He said he understood. He wished that he could be anonymous sometimes but his face was too well known, the big beard and everything. In retrospect I don't believe him, but that's what he said then. And, well, his attitude changed . . . it's very hard to explain. He had always been fascinated by rich people and he told me that, and he began to talk about money. Now money is not a subject that I'm shy about, but I didn't want to hear about it from Ernest, and I didn't want Ernest pumping me about money, how much I had, how I got it, that stuff. And the more I talked . . . I guess, when I talk, I talk about a million dollars as most men talk about a hundred . . . Ernest became almost deferential to me. He was awed by all this. The worst thing that happened was, just before I left, he became aware that he had been deferential. Because he was a perceptive man and he was, I think, aware of his own attitudes as few men are. And once it had dawned on him that he was being deferential . . . I may even have said something to him, not meaning to insult him, but said, 'For Christ's sake, don't pull that with me, that's what I get from flunkies' – he was ashamed. And he became . . . he took it out . . .

214

he turned against me. No, that's not fair, he didn't turn against me, but he became surly and difficult and . . . well, I do remember, when I left, we had one very good moment. He threw his arms around me and he said, 'Howard, I don't care whether you're George or Howard, I'm just delighted to know you, and I want you to come back and I look forward to seeing your skinny ass again.' And so everything was okay when I left.

CLIFFORD: Did you go back? Did you see him again?

HOWARD: I waited a long time. Much too long, in fact, because we had a basically very good friendship then, and if I had continued it I think I would have been the better for it. Ernest could have been the kind of friend I always needed. Very different from me, but I don't think that would have made a . . . a barrier.

CLIFFORD: Why didn't you go back?

HOWARD: Those were the years that I got so terribly involved and embroiled . . . I was drowning, I told you, drowning in details and deals, and I was sucked down into that morass of suits and counter-suits and financing – the whole horror story of TWA.

CLIFFORD: Did you correspond with each other?

HOWARD: No. He didn't write and I never write, rarely. I did go back, though, to see him finally, in . . . well, about five years later.

CLIFFORD: Just a minute. Five years later. You mean at the time of the revolution? The Cuban revolution?

HOWARD: No. The revolution was already accomplished. Maybe it was six years. It was some-time in 1959. And this time, understand, I went deliberately to see him. I had no other business in Florida. I went straight to Cuba to see Ernest because . . . it was a time in my life when I was completely fed up . . . not so much fed up as . . . well, no, I was fed up, fed up with everything, and I had nothing but good memories of Ernest and the times we had spent together, and I deeply regretted that we had been out of touch. When I went back there it was a snap decision. I had read in the papers that Ernest was back in Cuba – that was what prompted me. And I wanted to get out. This was not meant to be a two-day visit or a three-day visit or anything like that. I went, and at that point in my life, as happened again later, I was willing to burn my bridges behind me. As I said, I felt that Ernest and I had a tremendous camaraderie, and we could really be friends, and there wasn't much more I needed in life at that point other than one close friend. A man. And so when I went back it was with the idea that I would stay as long as I wanted to. It could have been for the rest of my life. I had no time limit in mind. No minimum or maximum.

CLIFFORD: You were married to Jean Peters then. You mean to say you and Jean would have moved down to Cuba?

HOWARD: I don't know what would have happened. Things were not . . . things had started to go a little sour by then. I think if I had . . . well, mind you, this is a fantasy, because as it turned out, and I'll tell you very shortly, I only stayed two days – but had I stayed on, and I was free to do so, all I had to do was throw over my entire industrial empire, so-called. Or maybe . . . anyway, when I arrived and went out to the house, it was a terrible disappointment. It was saddening, and it threw me completely. Because everything had changed. Ernest had become an old man. And I don't mean just old physically, old in appearance – he already had a big white beard. The vitality had gone out of him and . . . well, I really don't want to say anything bad about Ernest, but some of the intellectual honesty had gone out of him, I felt. He was crotchety and difficult and the first day I was there, half our conversation had to do with Cuban cigars, because Castro had accomplished his revolution and Ernest . . . I don't remember if he smoked cigars but he gave a lot of cigars away to his American friends . . . and he was only worried that Castro was nationalizing the cigar industry and the cigars would not be of the same quality that they were before, and he said, 'Howard, why don't you buy the island and go into the cigar business?' And he pursued that theme. There I'd come to talk to Ernest about, you know, my life and my soul and a possible total change in my life, and Ernest kept talking about cigars. 'The cigars won't be the same if they're not rolled on the thighs of Cuban girls, and you can make a good deal with Castro. You can buy in for a hundred million and what does that mean to a man in your position, Howard?' And I hadn't come to discuss the thighs of Cuban girls or the quality of Cuban cigars. And so I spent, as I said, just two days there. The second day was just as bad. I never got a chance to talk to Ernest alone. He got up late and he had a lot of visitors . . . we had a pickup sort of meal out at the *finca* and there were a bunch of Cuban army officers and political figures. He introduced me as, thank God, George Garden. He did respect my wish for privacy, still. But he and these other people, these officers and politicos, just chatted away furiously in Spanish all afternoon. Every once in a while Ernest would stop and throw a line or two of translation in my direction – I don't really remember much about it except I was bored. And, well, that's it. Politics. That's all I really remember. And by the time the afternoon was over, when they left, Ernest was drunk as a skunk. Head was falling on the table. I was embarrassed for him. This was a man who'd won the Nobel Prize, was a Nobel Prize author, a fine mind, and I found it, well, not a shameful thing, but a sad, pitiable thing to see a man of this power, this nobility of spirit, demeaned in this way. And I didn't want to see any more of it. So I left.

CLIFFORD: You weren't staying at the *finca* that time, either.

HOWARD: No, at a hotel, one of the big hotels in Havana. It was empty, I had the whole floor to myself – and I hadn't rented the whole floor at the time. Matter of fact, there was a parade while I was there and Castro himself came marching down the street. I watched it from my window.

CLIFFORD: But you went back to see Ernest.

HOWARD: Yes. I went back, once. It was even worse the next day – I guess I spent three days, not two. Because naturally he wanted to know all about what I'd been doing in the past years, the inside story, but I didn't feel that the stories of the machinations at Hughes Aircraft and troubles at TWA were the things that really would have fascinated him. I gave him a brief rundown on it, and all he could do was criticize me. And harp on the fact that I was wasting my life on involvements with this kind of thing and the kind of people I had to deal with. Now, I knew this, I'd been told this. That's precisely why I had gone to Havana to see him. I was like a man who had a crippled leg, and I had gone to a doctor to see if he could cure me, and all the doctor could say was, 'Your leg is crippled, your leg is crippled.' Now I knew that. What I was looking for was the cure. And Ernest offered me no suggestions. He only harped on the fact that I was

218

too involved with these people, and I would say, 'Yes, I know that, but I want to become uninvolved, and how do I do it? And where do I go? How do I cut loose?' Oh, I may not have put it in such childish terms as that, but it was very clear that I was there for help. And instead of helping me, Ernest tried to bully me. Well, when you bully me, I just vanish. Usually I vanish physically, but sometimes I just vanish mentally and emotionally. So I crawled into my shell, and the more I did that, the more Ernest tried to pry open the cover and knock holes in me. He still had a lot of the old charm, he wasn't unpleasant enough for me to pick up and leave, walk out of his house – because every time he saw me getting really uncomfortable he'd slap me on the shoulder and say, 'Oh, Jesus, it's good to see you, Howard,' or 'George.' He called me both names. People there thought my name was George Howard.

CLIFFORD: He hadn't told anybody in all those years?

HOWARD: Not that I knew of. He'd kept his promise, I'm pretty sure of that. I think it amused him that he was the only one who knew.

CLIFFORD: Any fishing this time?

HOWARD: No fishing. Ernest was in no condition. He was worried about whether the government was going to take over his farm and he didn't even want to leave the house. And he was worried about his health. I remember the doctor came out – took his blood pressure right there at the table. But there was still some of the old Ernest left. We drove into Havana together. There was just the two of us, and the car broke down halfway. Ernest cursed and muttered and started a speech about goddam machinery, and got out to open the hood. But I could tell from the way the motor sputtered that it was just probably out of gas, so I told him, and yes, that's what it was. This was where the old Ernest popped up out of that crotchetiness. There was a car parked nearby, not far from a house or a few houses. Well, Ernest took a length of rubber tubing from the trunk. 'Indispensable, Howard,' he said, I remember. 'Never travel without it.' His gas gauge was broken. And siphoned a gallon or so of gas out of this other car, sucked it up with his mouth – you know how that's done. Made me terribly nervous. I mean, if the owner had seen it he might have – God knows what – fired a shot at us. Might have been a soldier's car. Anyhow, we got to the city all right, and filled the tank there.

CLIFFORD: How long did you say that trip was all together – three days?

HOWARD: It was a bad visit. It was a mistake. It colored the good memories of Ernest with an overlay of this unsuccessful visit. What I most deeply regret is that I hadn't known Ernest as a younger man, and that we hadn't been in touch. If I had known him during those years, let's say even from '46 to 1960, that would have changed my entire life. But events intervened and you don't always see the right course to follow, and we lost touch. I left that time and I never saw him again. I was deeply, deeply saddened when I heard of his death. Not that I object to suicide. I feel it's every man's right to put an end to his life when it's become intolerable to him. But what preceded it, the sickness and the periods of insanity, the decline of a brilliant and fine man into this wretched shell. Blew his brains out.

One July morning about eleven-thirty Dick was saying, 'All right, Howard, now tell me about . . .' when there was a knock at the door. This had happened four or five times previously, and our reaction was always the same: a moment of petrified silence, then a leap into action. 'Shit!' – and Dick jumped out of the armchair.

'Just a minute,' I called out. *'Un momento, por favor.'* I unplugged the microphones, threw the cover on the tape recorder, slid open the top drawer of the file cabinet and dropped the Dietrich manuscript into it, then placed our heap of transcribed pages on top of it. Dick was dashing around the room scooping up blue folders and turning them so that their labels were hidden from view, closing books that were open to incriminating underlined passages, and looking for anything else that might give the game away.

'Okay,' he said, straightening up, his face red from exertion. 'All clear.'

I padded barefoot across the red tiles and opened the door. It was Nina. She was wearing faded light blue slacks, a man's shirt tied in a knot at the waist, and white canvas shoes. 'Hallo, darling,' she said, offering me a sunny smile. She looked pale from the long sunless months in London, but as beautiful and desirable as ever. I put my finger to my lips and motioned with my head toward Dick, who was putting some books back on the shelf. She knew that I was working with him on the hoax; but he didn't know I had told her it was a hoax.

She sat down on the edge of the bed and the three of us talked for a while. Finally I said to Dick: 'Listen, we've got some private stuff to talk about. Why don't you knock it off for now and come back this afternoon about four.'

'Yeah,' Dick said, a mischievous glint in his eye. 'Private stuff.'

'Look,' I said to her later. 'It's the wrong time and the wrong place. Let's not push our luck. I don't ever want Edith to know, because that would be the end of everything – of you and me, and of me and her. And your

221

divorce from Frederik would go right down the drain, too. He'd have *you* the guilty one.'

'All right,' Nina said.

'After the summer I'll be traveling again to the States. We'll find a way.'

Part Three

You can't cheat an honest man.

– W. C. Fields

10

Bungalow One at the Beachcomber

Toward the end of August, late one afternoon, just as I was getting ready to pack it in and head for the Salinas to swim with the kids and wheel Nedsky through the shallow water in his new canoe, Beverly Loo telephoned from New York. Every time she called – every time the international operator said: '*Señor* Irving? The United States is calling. Please hold on' – I had a moment of dread, a feeling that *this is it*. Dick and I had played it out together so many times, our own laughter counter-pointing the imagined histrionics. '*Listen, Cliff, we've just had a telephone call from Chester Davis . . . Howard Hughes has written a letter to Harold McGraw and he claims . . . The Hughes Tool Company says . . .*'

But each time in the past when she had called and I had felt that pinprick of fear in my stomach, Beverly had dispelled it, asking how things were going, veering often to the corporate hope at McGraw-Hill that the book would metamorphose from an authorized biography to a full-fledged autobiography. So that each time, when I finally put down the receiver, the glow of renewed confidence had replaced the fear, and the theme song of Project Octavio echoed once again in my mind: '*All right so far . . .*'

By late August, then, I was blasé, worn out, but filled

with confidence and a lofty hubris. We were hard at work and the Hughes tapes were nearly done. More to the point, Howard was a man singing all the roles in a contemporary opera, and his voice moved from the banal to the profound without faltering. We were the ventriloquists, but so it is in all fiction: one day the puppet starts to sing by himself and the ventriloquist, the writer, merely listens and records and marvels. I was beginning to see the grandness of the man's life taking shape on paper. I had said to Dick often: 'You know, I have the feeling I know more about this man – and I don't just mean the facts of his life, I mean the man himself – than anyone else in the world.'

'With one possible exception,' Dick said, 'and one definite exception.'

'Okay, okay. You're the possible exception. But who's the definite exception?'

'What about Howard? Have you forgotten *him*?'

'Well, maybe. I thought you said he was chained to the wall. But why do you assume such self-knowledge on his part? You think he knows why he hates germs so much? *We* know why – because his mother told him you get leprosy from eating cornbread and because in 1929 an actress gave him the clap. I don't think *he* knows that.'

'Don't get carried away by all this,' Dick cautioned me. 'It's fiction. *We made it up.* Don't forget that. You could go crazy. You could become schizophrenic. Jesus Christ, when this is over I can see you walking into the offices of Toolco and trying to give orders to Raymond Holliday and Chester Davis.'

'That, too, may come to pass. All I have to do is write out a Will for him. He'd make me his heir. "I, Howard Hughes,"' I intoned, '"being of sound mind and body, do hereby bequeath to Clifford Irving, in appreciation of the immortality he has given me by virtue of writing my autobiography and making of me a better man than ever I had realized, do hereby bequeath all my worldly goods . . ." What do you think?'

Dick looked at me, fascinated, head cocked, brown eyes suffused with a dreamy look. His voice was soft. 'Listen, don't joke. That's not a bad idea. If we . . .'

'And you think *I'm* going crazy? Get to work. Go read about Ethiopian landing fields and find out what outfit Hughes would have been flying with out of England in 1944.'

We had thus dismissed the thought of attempting to inherit $2 billion. That, we reckoned, would not only be beyond our abilities but it would smack of greed. In fact, it would be downright criminal.

And so all was going well. It was a summer of hard work and hot sun and sweat. The accumulating pages were stacked nightly and locked in the gray filing cabinet beside my desk, the key to the cabinet hidden under a Zapotec mask on my bookshelves. And then, on that late August afternoon – Dick had left for the beach – Beverly Loo telephoned and the entire edifice began to tremble.

'Cliff?'

'Yes. How are you? What's . . .'

'You'd better pay attention. We're in trouble.'

'Trouble?'

Trouble meant only one thing. I felt that cold clutch of fear and prepared to hang up the telephone the moment Beverly got halfway through her speech about how the Hughes Tool Company had telephoned Harold McGraw and denounced 'this man Irving' as a fraud. Still, Beverly had said 'we' and not 'you.' There was hope. 'What kind of trouble?' I asked.

It came out in her usual nonstop fashion. 'I have a friend at another publisher. Never mind his name. He called me an hour ago. There's a man named Sam Post and he represents, or he's a friend of, or he's involved with, a man named Eaton – Robert Eaton. Did Octavio ever mention this man's name? He's one of Lana Turner's ex-husbands. He used to know Octavio.'

'Never heard of him.'

'Well, listen to *this*. My publishing friend called to tell me that this man Sam Post came into his office to offer him *The Autobiography of Howard Hughes* as told to Robert Eaton, and he showed him . . .'

'Beverly,' I said, masking my nervousness with nervousness, 'for God's sake, don't use that name on the telephone. I told you it could be tapped. Octavio, Octavio,' I stressed.

'Yes, you're right – Octavio. I'm sorry. Well, either your friend Octavio is up to no good and playing a double game, or someone else is up to no good. My friend has known Post for a few years and they're on a friendly basis, and that's why Post went to him – says that Octavio has tape-recorded his autobiography with this writer, Robert Eaton. And he's given written authorization to Eaton to sell it, to get it published.'

'Post has?'

'No, dammit. Octavio's given authorization to Eaton. *On lined yellow legal paper*, just like yours. Post is just the middle man. And there's an agent mixed up in this, too. I don't understand the exact details, but it's some agent named Shelly Abend.'

I tried to sound more bored than confused. 'Is anyone taking this seriously?'

'Yes,' Beverly shouted. 'That's the whole point! Do you think I'd be calling you if they weren't taking it seriously? *I'm* taking it seriously, I'll tell you that much! Do you realize what this means?'

My finger was sneaking toward the button that would break the connection. I touched the button, then drew back. I was too fascinated. I had to know. 'You'd better give me some details,' I said, 'before I offer any theories. This is a lulu.'

'I told you! Post has some sort of authorization that

Octavio's given to him or Eaton, and evidently it's good enough for this other publisher to want to see the manuscript.'

'There's a *manuscript*?'

'There's a hundred pages available now and evidently there's more coming. I don't know if the publisher has read them or not. I do know that whatever agreement there is between Eaton and Octavio is almost exactly the same as the one between you and Octavio – the same secrecy clauses, same insistence that the transcripts be read while Eaton is physically present.'

'Incredible,' I murmured.

Beverly went on, her outrage building. 'I think Octavio's double-crossing you, and us in the bargain. I think he's taken the tapes he's done with you and given a copy of them to this man Eaton. His idea is to see which of you can turn out the better book, and then that's the one he'll choose.'

I protested. 'He'd never do that to me.'

'Oh, he wouldn't do that to *you*.' She was sarcastic now. 'You're so special. Listen, your ego is getting in the way of your grip on reality. Don't you think he's tricky enough to do that kind of thing? You may think he's a great man, and you may think he's such a dear friend of yours now, but don't forget that you hardly know him; and he has the reputation of being one of the most unscrupulous businessmen in the United States. Didn't you tell me how many deals he'd reneged on in his business life?'

'All that was long ago,' I said, sharply defending the integrity of *my* Howard Hughes. 'He's changed, Beverly. No, I can't believe it. I'm sorry, but I just can't believe it. I *won't* believe it.' I heard a tremor in my voice; I was in the part. 'That would be unforgivable, unethical, and . . . disgusting.'

'Yes, it would. But it's still a possibility. There's only one other possibility,' she added, carefully.

I looked at the button on the telephone. My finger was poised. 'And what,' I asked, slowly, 'is that other possibility?'

'How well do you know Dick Suskind?'

'You've asked me this before. In what sense do you mean?'

'How much do you trust him?'

'Well, I'd say we were casual friends. Not really close. But I wouldn't have hired him to do this job if I didn't trust him.'

'You didn't trust him well enough back in April to tell him you were really meeting with Octavio.' She had evidently forgotten that I had told her I wanted to tell Dick, and both she and Robert Stewart had advised me – almost forbidden me – to do so.

'No,' I said, 'that's true. I guess I didn't.'

'I think that Dick Suskind's always resented the fact that you didn't tell him, and he realized he never would have found out if Robert hadn't let it slip that day in the office. I think, as usual, that your naïveté's gotten in the way of your common sense. Don't you see what I'm driving at?'

'No, Bev, I really don't.'

'I'll spell it out for you. Does Dick Suskind have access to the transcripts of the tapes that Octavio gave you in California?'

'He's got a copy. He needs it for reference.'

'Then the other possibility,' Beverly said triumphantly, 'is that Suskind went behind your back and sold it to these people, Post and Eaton.'

'Impossible. Never! Dick would never . . .' I hesitated. 'No, he wouldn't do that.'

'But you're not sure. I can tell from the tone of your voice.'

'Look, Bev, anything is possible – theoretically. But I don't believe Dick would do a thing like that. Ethics aside, he's loyal.'

'Money sometimes speaks louder than ethics or loyalty.'

'He just wouldn't do it,' I said. 'Besides, I've been keeping my eye on him. When could he have got in touch with these guys?'

'So you *do* accept it as a possibility. You *don 't* trust him completely, do you?'

'Yes, I do, dammit. Anyway, there's a third possibility. Don't you see it?'

'What's that?'

I hesitated. I didn't know if I could or should pronounce the word 'hoax'; it would be the opening of a can of worms – more than worms: of cobras and pit vipers – of whose existence no one, as far as I knew, had yet dreamed. I hesitated; then I heard a familiar buzz. The line had gone dead. The Spanish operator had made my decision for me. She had cut us off.

I slammed down the receiver, struggled into my bathing suit, rushed out of the studio and up the hill, jumped into the Mercedes and headed for the Salinas.

By the time I topped the sand dunes and surveyed the beach in the late afternoon sun, Edith, Nedsky, and Barney had returned to the *finca*. Under a striped umbrella, like a pink-brown hippo in the shade of an African plane tree, Dick snored contentedly, while Ginette sat by the water's edge building a sand castle with Raphael. I tapped Dick on the shoulder. Opening his eyes instantly, he blinked at the glare, then saw my expression.

'What's the matter with you?' I asked. 'You look worried.'

'Because *you* look worried. Who called?'

'Beverly.'

'Oh, my God. It's blown.'

'No, no, no. Don't worry.'

'If you could see your face, you'd worry, too. What's happened?'

Too many people lounged within earshot. Dick clambered to his feet and we walked into the shallow water. Children were playing there, so we forged deeper, until our heads and shoulders protruded above the flat surface of the sea.

'You fink,' I said. 'You've sold the transcript to Sam Post and Robert Eaton. Sam Post is your brother-in-law and Robert Eaton is your uncle by your mother's fourth marriage. And Beverly Loo knows all.'

'Post? Eaton?' Dick sputtered. 'Where have you been? Did you have an accident in the car? Did Edith hit you over the head?'

'No. Beverly called.' And I told him the story. 'You can figure out what's happened, can't you?'

'I can figure it out, but I can't believe it. There's only one explanation. One or both of those guys have come up with exactly the same idea that we did. *It's a hoax!*'

'You've got it,' I said. 'You don't think there's a chance they might have the real thing, do you?'

'You mean that this Eaton's really met Hughes, and Hughes dictated his autobiography to him? You know Hughes would *never* do that.'

'I know. And certainly not behind my back.'

'Those sons of bitches,' Dick said. 'What a rotten thing to do.'

Work ground to a halt. Dick slumped in the big green armchair and I sprawled in the red leather desk chair, spinning slowly, fingers tapping nervously on the glass top of the desk. The morning sun slanted through the glass door and we sweated and talked and tried to figure the percentages.

'There's no doubt about it,' Dick maintained doggedly. 'This guy Eaton stole our idea. It's all a horrible coincidence.'

'Good ideas are in the air. You can't expect to have a monopoly on them.'

'But the timing,' Dick groaned. 'It couldn't be worse.'

'Look on the bright side of things. They could have come up with the idea *before* we did. Why don't we join forces? Cut them in for a third if they'll shut up and go away.'

'A third of *your* share,' Dick said.

'We can't just sit here and mull about it. We've got to do something. Beverly's bound to call me back today. We've got to have a plan.'

'For Christ's sake, tell her Hughes says it's a hoax.'

'But it may *not* be a hoax. And if it is and I say so, I plant the idea in her head that a hoax is possible. If Post can turn up with a letter to Eaton and convince another publisher, then Irving could have done the same thing and convinced McGraw-Hill. I don't even want to use the word. You know Beverly. Once it gets into her head nothing will shake it out. It'll rattle around in there, and one day she'll take a good long look at the contract and the secrecy clauses and she'll realize that no one at McGraw-Hill's had any verification from Hughes that he's ever met me and they're going on my word alone, plus your crazy prune story; and they haven't seen a stitch of manuscript yet. Until they read those transcripts, we've got no weapons.'

'We've got to knock Post and Eaton out of the ball game before she gets that idea.'

'We need a diversion. A big diversion. And a plan.'

'You're the mastermind. Make a plan.'

'*De l'audace*' I said. 'My right flank is crushed, my left flank is giving way, my center is demolished. What do I do? I attack! *Chutzpah* – brass – balls – gall – audacity. *Toujours l'audace*. That was Napoleon's motto, and look how far it got him.'

'Yeah,' Dick said gloomily, 'all the way to Waterloo.'

An item had appeared in the monthly newsletter of the Northrop Aviation History Library, published and written by Dave Hatfield, whom we had interviewed in California during our June trip. It noted that Clifford Irving and Richard Suskind had visited the Northrop Institute and were preparing a biography of Howard Hughes. We remembered Hatfield's mention that Hughes had a subscription to the newsletter. Our plan had been to fly to Nassau in late August or early September, when a rough draft of the tapes had been transcribed. On Paradise Island, at the Britannia Beach Hotel or the nearby Beach Inn, we would type the final draft of the tapes and I would theoretically, at the same time, conduct the final interviews with Howard. But the mention of our names in the newsletter changed everything. 'He'll read it,' Dick maintained. 'You know how he hates any books to be written about him. We won't be safe in Nassau. They'll find out we're there, and one day when you're snoozing on the beach they'll get into your room and sneak a look at what we're doing. Then we can kiss it all goodbye.'

So we shifted the site of the meeting to Florida, on the assumption that Hughes could fly back and forth un-noticed, by helicopter, from the Britannia Beach Hotel to the Fort Lauderdale-Palm Beach area. Before we left we burned all of the tapes, the two copies of the Dietrich manuscript, and most of the *Time-Life* documents. 'We may have to kiss the whole thing goodbye anyway,' I said glumly, 'because of this Eaton autobiography. We can raise a smokescreen, but there's got to come a day when the smoke settles and the McGraw-Hill gang will *see.*'

'What are you trying to say?' Dick demanded.

'That this may be the end. We may have to pay back the money and get out.'

'Admit it's a hoax?' He looked horrified.

'Not necessarily. I've got an idea. Just give me time to work it out . . .'

'If it means giving the money back, how the hell

can we do it? We've already spent twenty grand in expenses.'

'Edith and I can cover that. The point is, we'd still be left with the material, and we can turn it into an unauthorized biography or a novel. Just shut up for a while and let me think . . .'

I set about, in my mind, writing a script of the next few weeks. It had gaps and a dozen permutations; but at least I knew the characters, and they were predictably unpredictable. At the same time I realized that what we were living, and what had happened to us in the past six months, was akin to *cinéma vérité*, a real-life movie. It was happening, and we were in the center of it, creating the action as we moved through it.

SCENE: The waiting room of the Ibiza airport. Dick glances at the battered attaché case clamped between his feet. It contains our most precious possession: a thousand pages of transcript worth a minimum of half a million dollars. He peers under the table, says: 'Where's your basket?'

I look around, puzzled. 'I must have left it at the newspaper counter.'

With a yelp of agony, Dick leaps to his feet. He dashes out the door, returns a moment later with the straw shopping basket. He is pale, his brown eyes blaze. 'You're out of your cotton-picking mind! You've got almost ten grand in cash in there, and look what else I found . . . it fell out of your leather briefcase.' He flashes a familiar object – the checkbook of H. R. Hughes at the Credit Suisse in Zurich – then shoves it out of sight into the basket. 'Have you been carrying this with you on all our trips?'

'Yeah. I just stuck it in there and forgot about it. I carry everything that might be incriminating. Suppose someone broke into my studio when I was away?'

He sighs heavily. 'Jesus, can you tie your own

shoelaces in the morning? . . . Never mind, never mind,' he goes on, as I start to protest. 'Let's get back to what we've got to do – raise a smokescreen, throw dust in their eyes.'

'All right. We've agreed that it's got to be an outstanding demonstration of *chutzpah,* something so far out that it'll knock them completely off balance.'

'I've got an idea,' Dick says. 'We know Octavio hates the Luce organisation. *Fortune* zapped him five or six times and *Life's* never been friendly to him. Dietrich says so, and we've got that McCulloch memo to prove it. So why can't we . . .'

'That's it! Listen . . .'

SCENE: Our old friend Frank Powis – tall, thin, bearded, and elegant – meets us in the bar of the Ritz Hotel in London as Dick and I are drinking our second bourbon sour and we take a cab to Rule's. The place is everything Frank claimed it to be when he picked us up at Gatwick that afternoon – a splendid example of Ye Olde Englande, except for the waiters, all of whom are Spanish. 'We have a reservation,' Frank says to the *maître d'hôtel,* and a moment later we are tucked away in a corner on the second floor, perusing menus the size of small billboards.

We order a noble meal. We chat idly of this and that. Conversation is difficult for both Dick and myself; our thoughts are elsewhere. Before the dessert arrives, Frank excuses himself. The moment he is gone, Dick says: 'Okay, so he hates Luce and he didn't know that the book had been sold to *Life.* Besides, he never read your contract with McGraw-Hill and he thinks he's being cheated, that all the subsidiary money should go to him directly. It's the Eastern Establishment after his ass, just like they were after TWA. Is that what you meant?'

'Pretty much. Beverly told me not to tell him the serial rights have been bought by *Life.* So Octavio finds out and threatens to back out of the deal. He demands the full quarter of a million *Life* is paying for first serial rights. Maybe . . .' I break off as Frank returns to the table. We sit there for another hour, have coffee and several liqueurs apiece. When Frank drops us at the Ritz, Dick and I are too tired to go on with the conversation. We say goodnight and leave a call with the desk for eight o'clock. Our plane leaves for Miami at ten.

SCENE: A BOAC jet 30,000 feet above the gray Atlantic. Dick pulls the headphones out of my ears and says: 'He's got to ask for the full million, his original demand. That'll convince Mother McGraw that they're dealing with the real, the one and only, Octavio.'

'Yeah. But they're liable to cut my throat. A contract is a contract, you know. We'll hear them screaming all the way down to Miami.'

I plug the earphones back in, click the indicator in the arm of the seat from number to number. The Rolling Stones . . . *Che gelida manina* . . . Ah, Fagin's song from *Oliver* . . . I lean back with a smile and close my eyes.

The earphones are yanked out of my ears again. Dick's face is inches from mine. He's glaring at me furiously. 'How can you listen to music at a time like this?'

SCENE: Outside Miami Airport in a rented car. The air conditioner in the car works badly. As I make a sharp right turn onto the highway, water slops out of the dashboard onto Dick's shoes. He yelps. 'Christ! This isn't a car, it's a broken-down ice-cube machine.'

I smile, thinking the problem is on his side of the car. Then I make a sharp left turn and my feet are drenched with icy water. But my mind is elsewhere.

'We'll have Howard ask for a million, but then I'll

237

haggle with him and he'll come down to $850,000. That way Mother McGraw will know I'm on her side. What do you think?'

Dick is silent, mulling it over. We whip past a sign that reads *PALM BEACH 27*.

'They won't pay it, of course,' he says at length.

'Of course not. I told you: a contract is a contract. That's not the object of this triple reverse option with the tight end in motion. The object is to convince them that *we've* got the real thing and discredit this Eaton character. McGraw-Hill will insist that Howard live up to the terms of the agreement. He will – reluctantly, and that reluctance will give us an out later, when he turns against me, *if* he turns against me.'

'You don't think they'll compromise, offer say six hundred or six fifty?'

'Not a chance. They're already paying out more up front in advance than anyone's ever been paid before in the history of book publishing. They may be crazy, but they're *not stupid*.'

Palm Beach was full of palms, dull and sensationally quiet, so we headed south toward Fort Lauderdale, eyeing an occasional motel or hotel along the way. Thunderheads studded the horizon and there were intermittent flurries of rain. It was early afternoon when we finally pulled into the parking lot of the Beach-comber Motel in Pompano Beach. In addition to the main building, a dozen or so bungalows were scattered about the grounds.

Bungalow One had two bedrooms, two bathrooms, a living room, kitchen, two color television sets, and a fair number of giant southern cockroaches. It was located on the far side of the parking lot, near an astroturf putting green and well removed from the main buildings. We could type at any hour of the day or night without worrying about disturbing our neighbors, and we would

238

later claim, if it became necessary, that Howard had chosen the villa because of its very isolation.

After lunch we found a place that leased office equipment, rented two standard Underwood typewriters, bought several reams of paper, a couple of boxes of carbon paper, and carted everything back to the Beachcomber. With Dick standing at my shoulder, making suggestions, I typed a draft of the telegram to Beverly Loo. The final draft, which we sent the next morning, read as follows:

BEST YOU BE ADVISED NOW BIG TROUBLES STOP OCTAVIO REGRETTABLY BUT UNAVOIDABLY NOW AWARE GRAVES COMPANY INVOLVEMENT STOP ALSO CLAIMS PREVIOUSLY UNAWARE DETAILS MY CONTRACT WITH MOTHER AND BELIEVED ADVANCE WAS FOR TRADE ONLY NOT SUBSIDIARY STOP THINKS MOTHER AND I CONNIVED WITHHOLDING INFORMATION STOP NO LONGER AGAINST GRAVES PARTICIPATION BUT DEMANDS AMENDED CONTRACT ALL SUBSIDIARY INCOME PAYABLE DIRECTLY TO HIM OR ALTERNATELY INCREASE TO HIS ORIGINAL ONE MILLION TOTAL ADVANCE OR DEAL OFF STOP MY SHARE STILL ONE HUNDRED STOP AM TRYING TO NEGOTIATE BUT GLOOMY OVER OUTCOME STOP CANNOT TELEPHONE LETTER FOLLOWS WITH ALL HORRIBLE DETAILS REGARDS CLIFF.

We sent another telegram on the heels of the first. It read: *SAM POST SITUATION HAS NO BEARING CONTENTS OTHER TELEGRAM STOP OCTAVIO FLATLY DENIES POST BONA FIDES IS FURIOUS SAYS OTHER PUBLISHER IS BEING HOODWINKED CLIFF*

Back in the bungalow, we went over our timetable. 'Beverly will get the telegram in an hour or so. We'll write the letter today and mail it tomorrow morning. She'll have it . . .' Dick counted on his fingers, '. . .

239

Thursday afternoon at the latest. Let her sweat it out overnight, then you call her on Friday morning.'

Meanwhile, I had rolled a sheet of paper into the typewriter and was starting the letter. Dick came and stood at my shoulder, grunting approval or disapproval and suggesting changes.

Pompano Beach, Fla.
31 August 1971

Dear Bev,

If you didn't get my cable, I attach a copy. The situation has improved sharply for Mother McGraw, but it is still a big comedown from my point of view.

Here is the background. *Read carefully.* I'll try to be coherent although it's 6 a.m. and I am worn out.

Shortly after my arrival here H. asked me about McGraw-Hill's arrangements for magazine and foreign publication. I said, as you and I agreed, that I didn't know what, if anything, had happened. He asked who might be offered magazine rights – I said, 'Oh, *Look, Life, The New York Times,* maybe one or two others.' He said, 'Okay, any of those except *Life*. I won't have the Luce people increasing their circulation at my expense.' I tried to argue but he didn't want to hear a word.

I went on for four single-spaced pages, enumerating the struggle blow by blow and round by round. I had waged a furious battle on behalf of McGraw-Hill, had wrung one concession after another from Hughes. 'I do believe that he has compromised all he's going to,' I wrote at one point. 'In his eyes he's come down from a million to 850, and he's thrown in an indemnification, the right to call it an autobiography, and what he calls "a free read" for you and *Life* . . . I've fought like a tiger down here. But he says this is rock-bottom and he does not want to hear any counteroffers . . . I blush to tell you, but at one point he also asked if McGraw-Hill would pay for the expense of his typist including paper and carbons.'

'Why did you put that in?' Dick asked.

I looked at him with a faint sneer. 'It's obvious, my good man, that you don't know Mr Hughes as well as I do.'

When I finished the letter it was past midnight. Dick would take it to the post office in the morning and send it special delivery. 'Then hang on to your hair,' he said, 'and when you call her, hold the receiver well away from your ear. Otherwise you'll end up like Uncle Howard, with a hearing aid.'

We got in three days of hard work on the Remington Noiseless portable, that we also brought along, finishing The Abominable Snowman's transcription of the first taped interviews. 'The Abominable Snowman' was our name for Hughes's faithful and only semi-literate typist. We called him that because, as I would claim to have told Howard, 'he typed with all four paws.' This first part of the transcript comprised 268 pages. To provide me with an excuse for typing the remainder of the taped interviews, we inserted such things as 'sorry; tape broke; piece missing,' at intervals throughout the opening section.

At 10:30 Friday morning, with Dick all but shoving me from behind, I went to a telephone booth next to the parking lot and placed a collect call to Beverly. We had decided to call from a booth rather than from the villa, because we wanted no one to know exactly where we were staying. 'Too risky,' Dick said. 'Suppose – just suppose – they smell something rotten in Florida and send down a private detective to keep an eye on us.' All 280 pounds of him shuddered delicately. 'Disaster! Pure disaster!'

I forgot what Dick had said about holding the receiver well away from my ear, and Beverly's opening shriek of rage left me numb and helpless. For the next thirty minutes, while passing cars and trucks spewed exhaust fumes into the booth, and while I slowly became drenched in sweat and wilted like an overcooked strand of spaghetti, Beverly had hysterics. Twice she almost broke into tears and she refused to allow me to string together more than three consecutive words – usually, 'But Beverly, I . . .' Dick kept waving for me to hang up, and at length I said, 'I'll call you later, this is hopeless,' and banged the receiver back on the hook.

'Give her the weekend to cool off,' Dick said. We trudged back to the bungalow mopping our foreheads, 'then call again on Monday.'

'But not from the booth. You could die in there. I'll call from the bungalow while you make street noises, okay?'

Dick lip-farted. 'Sure. Just let me get my exhaust in shape.'

On Monday morning I was glued to the telephone for two and a half hours, subjected to such a harangue from Beverly Loo that at several points I threatened to hang up. The worst moment was when she said she had spoken to Ralph Graves and Dave Maness, and also to Harold McGraw, and that she thought they thought I was 'taking a rakeoff from Hughes.'

My voice trembled with genuine outrage. 'Beverly, that's a vicious accusation. You don't realize what hell I'm going through down here with that ancient prick. He's taking my hide off, and when I try to argue with him, he just shuts off his hearing aid and leers at me like he's won a goddam battle. And then, to top it off, you accuse me of being a crook. I won't take it.'

'Now, just a minute, Cliff, just a minute. I said I *think* that's what *they* think, not what *I* think. I mean, I don't think you're a crook, but I think they think you might be one. So . . .'

It was as close as she came to an apology, and when I hung up the receiver, slick with sweat despite the air-conditioning, I was still furious. 'What a fucking nerve!' I said to Dick, who had stood beside the desk, making Bronx cheers, revving noises with his throat, banging a pot against the wall, and periodically yelling, 'Okay, Joe, move it over here!' in a Texas-cum-New York-cum-Florida drawl. 'That really burns me up!'

Dick looked at me with a mocking expression in his eyes. 'You know, if I didn't know better, I'd believe the book was for real. Or at least I'd believe that *you* believed it.'

'Don't knock me out of the part,' I said. 'I've got to keep a fine edge of fury for the letter I'm going to write.'

'Yes, O B'wana Stanislavsky. I hear and obey.' With a groan, he stretched, then turned and walked back to his bedroom. A moment later I heard the clack-clack of the typewriter.

Again we worked until midnight on the letter. Dick had been typing since five o'clock that morning, with only short breaks for lunch and dinner, and finally tottered off to bed, unable to keep his eyes open, while I finished the final draft. I stuffed it in an unsealed envelope and left it next to the chicken livers in the refrigerator, where I knew Dick would find it in the morning and mail it.

> Pompano Beach
> 6 September 1971

Dear Beverly and Albert,

Obviously no one at McGraw-Hill has under-stood the intent or tone of my letter of 31 August to you, so I am going to spell a few things out clearly and in the simplest possible language. I deliberately did not interlard the facts with a lot of breast-beating, and that was a mistake; you wanted histrionics. You are still not going to get them. You are going to get facts.

The most important fact is that the demands I cited in that letter are *not my demands*. I am *not* in sympathy with them, primarily because they mean money from my pocket to Octavio. They are *his* demands. I merely *reported* them, after arguing myself blue in the face with him. When I wrote 'not negotiable' I am not giving you my attitude; I am giving you *his*.

There is hardly one argument you advanced to me on the telephone that I did not advance to H., and vigorously. I told you – his customary answer is: 'Bullshit.' It is almost impossible to get through to him with anyone else's logical point of view. When he doesn't like what he hears, he doesn't listen. He doesn't have a monopoly on that.

You also can't understand how I could be on the edge of walking out of this thing when there's so much money involved. I'll tell you. I'm getting screamed at from both sides, I'm in the middle and I'm just trying to do a job of work, and I don't like the screaming. You think I'm naive because I believe some things he says. He thinks I'm naive because I believe some things McGraw-Hill says. In a sense I represent McGraw-Hill to him, and in a sense I represent him to McGraw-Hill, but I am not, and I *refuse* to be, to either of you, responsible for what the other says, does, doesn't say, or doesn't do.

My interests lie clearly in getting the auto-biography finished and published with the lowest possible advance – anyway, not in excess of the stipulated 500,000. He demands 850, having come down, in his view, from one million, which makes me sick, physically sick, because I've been working my ass off for months and not only is that fat potential paycheck being chopped to ribbons, but the whole project is in jeopardy. If neither he nor McGraw-Hill will bend it will probably end my involvement with the book, from his point of view.

Regarding your suggestion that if neither of you will give in I take the material and make an unauthorized biography and/or 'memoir' out of it, this makes no sense to me at all. From a selfish point of view, there is just no money in it for me. There are already two such biographies and another one supposedly coming up. *Life* wouldn't want that kind of book from him, for two excellent reasons. One you'll understand best, and that's what I said above, that there's no money in it – and also I would be sued up, down, and sideways by Octavio, and so would you, and please remember, he's got Two Billion dollars' worth of clout and wouldn't hesitate to use it in such a case. And the other reason, which you didn't understand on the phone last time we talked, is that it would be totally and nakedly unethical. I have no intention of violating my deepest instincts on this matter, which is to act in good faith.

As for your anger that I revealed to H. the existence and details of the *Life* contract, I am simply at a loss to understand why the truth has to be so hidden and furtive. I did not intend to tell him, for practical reasons, and I lied, and I regret it. In the long run it's *his* book, his life, and there is no reason why what's going on should be hidden from him and lied about as if there's something shady about McGraw-Hill's arrangements.

That's it for now. I have taken to heart what you said in our conversation and I will certainly do my best to make him see reason, from the point of view of logic and also my personal screwing. I just don't want you to think that so far I have played patsy and let him walk over me. We have had some real wrangles and when he says, 'I can't go on like this, I'm having heart palpitations,' there is just nothing more I can do.

I will call you after I've next spoken to him, which would be tonight or tomorrow, and let you know where things stand. Whatever the result, I will definitely be in New York sometime Sunday, go to the Elysee, and call you from there; and I am counting on the readings starting first thing Monday morning. The material will be ready, unless we do any last-minute taping over the weekend. I mean it will all be ready but for anything I don't have time to transcribe. So you will probably have heard from me before you get this letter.

Regards,
Cliff

The original plan, formulated back in June with McGraw-Hill, had been for the McGraw-Hill and *Life* contingents to fly to Ibiza in mid-September for the reading of the transcripts. Robert Stewart, Beverly Loo, Ralph Graves, and Dave Maness had enlisted for the junket, which would certainly have been the gala event of the fall publishing season – if not in New York, then certainly in Ibiza. None of the editors balked at the idea of a week in the sun and it would have saved me a dreary trip to the States. The rationale behind it, of course, was secrecy. According to the terms of my agreement with Howard, I had to be physically present during the readings. My house on the San José road would be the logical, anonymous place. I could even sneak away to the studio and do some editing while Edith or Dick minded the store. Harold McGraw evidently had grumbled a bit about what he considered an unnecessary expense, but I had pointed out that a week on Ibiza for two editors, including their air fare, was cheaper than my spending a week in New York in a hotel suite – 'at McGraw-Hill's expense,' I had added.

In a letter dated July 22nd, I wrote: 'Octavio believes, at this point, that you are coming here. He knows nothing about the *Life* gang yet; I will have to tell him that next month, in person. He thinks it's far and away the best plan and has said to me that he would never have rested easy if he thought those transcripts – "my life's blood" – were in McGraw-Hill's offices. I know this is paranoid, but he is superparanoid. As you know, I'm fairly sure that this operation will be spied on; and I won't lie to him.'

I had also written, in that same letter – following a telephone discussion with Beverly, who had been worried about another Hughes biography in the works (a chapter of which had been printed in *Look* magazine) by a man named Schemmer – that 'O's anxiety that the book be published as soon as possible has prompted him to suggest, rather forcefully, that the book take the form of a long edited interview, i.e., virtually an auto-biography in the form of a conversation, with interpolated material from me, in the third person, which would clarify and comment on his life story . . . I'm not a journalist and I don't care very much about the sensationalism of the "scoop." The only true con-sideration, of course, is which will make a better and more saleable book. I don't know the answer to that yet, although I suspect the autobiographical interview. How-ever, O's pressure is formidable and that may decide it in the end. But we can discuss all this after you have all read the material which, not exactly in-cidentally, is stupendous. Far more than I ever dreamed of getting . . .'

Now, however, in view of the contractual and

financial crises, all bets were off. No one was flying to Spain, or deciding autobiography *vs* authorized biography, before the financial situation was resolved and the Eaton book laid to rest, or before the company lawyers had given a preliminary vetting to the manuscripts. Beverly would reserve a suite for me at my favorite New York hotel, the Elysee, and the readings would take place there behind locked doors. Howard, I reported, refused to let me bring the transcript to either the McGraw-Hill or *Life* offices. I explained to Beverly that he had said: 'You'll go take a piss and they'll have two hundred pages Xeroxed before you can zip your fly.'

Between hysterical phone calls and long hours spent composing letters to McGraw-Hill, Dick and I typed, rewriting as we went, calling information and advice back and forth between Dick's bedroom, where he had installed his Underwood, and the living room, where I had installed mine. For once in my life I started the day early – not as early as Dick, whom I could hear at 5:30 every morning as he rattled around the kitchen, making his daily breakfast of a chicken-liver omelette – but nevertheless early for me: between 7:30 and 8. We worked steadily through until lunch, which we ate either in Howard Johnson's or Sambo's in Pompano Beach. Then back to the typewriters until 6:30 or 7 when, groaning and stretching, we called it a day. I wrote a letter to Edith and the kids; then we put on our trunks and did a few laps in the pool, or dunked ourselves in the pea-green Atlantic; then dressed and went out for dinner to one of the nearby steak joints. We emerged from our trancelike state only twice: once we banged golf balls around at a driving range, which exhausted us for the day and made us think twice about further athletic activity; and another time we saw a movie in Fort Lauderdale. For the rest, it was work, sleep, work, sleep, while the pile of typescript grew daily higher and we gloated silently and aloud about both the quantity and the quality.

The pace was a killing one – ten to fourteen hours a day of relentless typing – and early one morning, toward the end, when I was shaving, I suddenly noticed two streaks of blood on my cheek and jaw. I looked at my hand. I could see it trembling. Then I felt a sharp, solid pain in my chest, as if someone had given me a karate jab above the heart. Dizzied, I sat down on the closed toilet seat and called weakly: 'Dick . . .'

He was passing by, enroute to the kitchen and his beloved supply of chicken livers. Poking his head through the open bathroom door, he saw my condition. 'Are you okay?' he asked.

I tried to stay calm. 'I think I'm having a heart attack.'

'Jesus. What should I do?'

'I don't know. If I faint, call a doctor.'

'I know that,' he said worriedly. 'I meant what should I do about the manuscript?'

It was an instant cure for whatever ailed me, and a mighty surge of blood poured through my body to my brain. I reached out and held the razor menacingly over his nose. 'You sonofabitch,' I yelled. 'I could be dead in ten minutes and all you want to know is what you should do with the fucking manuscript. If I go,' I swore, 'I'll take you with me.'

'Go lie down,' he said gently, but backing off a bit. 'You need sleep. You haven't had a decent eight hours' sack time in a week. Take the morning off.'

I stumbled off to bed and slept until noon, and when I woke I felt fine again.

At last there came a night – a Thursday night about nine o'clock – when the typewriters stopped their clattering, when we stood looking at one another with dazed, bleary eyes, when we said, 'Jesus!' and 'My God!' and 'We did it!' and 'I never thought . . .'

Then we sat in the living room and slowly and

painstakingly tore the original transcript into little bits and pieces, stuffing them into brown paper bags for the cleaning woman to remove. By the time we had finished – nearly two o'clock in the morning – my hands felt as though I had been on the rockpile all day. We should have burned the pages, but euphoria had us in its velvet grasp, had borne us up, up, up, beyond worry about exposure, beyond all trifling, mundane concerns.

Only one thing still troubled me: what to do with the Remington Noiseless. I started thinking about it seriously on the evening before we left for Nassau. The idea developed bit by bit as I shaved and showered, threw my clothes into my suitcase, packed my copy of the transcripts into empty boxes of typewriter paper. I could hear Dick in his shower, cheerfully singing an aria from *La Traviata*. When he joined me in the living room, I said: 'I've got it all worked out.'

'What's that?'

'How to get rid of the Remington. We've got enough time tomorrow to rent a motor boat. We'll pick up a cardboard carton and put the typewriter in it. Then we go a couple of miles out into the Gulf Stream and dump the typewriter in fifteen or twenty fathoms of water. But,' I added cleverly, 'we bring the empty carton back with us. That way no one will know we've gotten rid of anything. If anyone should see us, they'll think that we were carrying sandwiches or beer or something like that. We'll . . .' I stopped. Dick was shaking his head and grinning.

'007,' he said, 'it's off to the funny farm for you. You've been working too hard.' He held up his hand to forestall my comment. 'Those Smersh boys are tough, I know, but . . . Schmuck, what the hell are you talking about? Tomorrow morning we'll be in Miami Airport. When it's time to leave for Nassau, one of us just puts the typewriter on the floor next to a chair or one of the departure desks – anywhere, it doesn't really matter a damn and walk away from it. Eventually it will either be turned into the lost-and-found – they'll hold it for thirty days and then auction it off – or some lucky housewife will pick it up and take it home. In any case, that's the end of it. Schmuck!'

I coughed, felt myself blush. 'Yeah, well, maybe I do need a few days off. But that's why we're going to the Bahamas.'

Except for one detail, the plan went perfectly. We walked away from the Remington with still a full thirty minutes to wait before our flight left for Nassau. From time to time, as we strolled around the hall, buying cigarettes, changing a couple of thousand Swiss francs at the bank, I would glance over my shoulder in the direction of the machine in its anonymous black case. Each time I expected to see it no longer there; each time it had not moved. Finally I said, 'I think I'll take a last look at it, see if we've forgotten something.' I walked over to the machine and, on impulse, opened the case. Pasted inside the cover was a strip of yellow plastic tape with the name and address of the typewriter repair shop on upper Broadway, only a couple of blocks from my parents' apartment on West End Avenue, where Dick had had the machine serviced the previous June. I peeled it off and carried it over to him. '007 your ass,' I said. 'I ought to paste this across your nose.'

There was something lacking in our game plan, some angle we had overlooked. It nagged at me like an aching molar throughout the flight to Nassau and during the long taxi ride from the airport to Paradise Island. I was hardly aware of the passing scene – the tropical foliage, the peeling, slatternly houses, the shady aisles of casuarina trees. My brain was a whirl of figures, of probabilities and possibilities; I flitted from Beverly Loo's mind to Harold McGraw's to Ralph Graves's, trying to foresee their response to Howard's new demands.

Dick clutched the briefcase which contained one copy of the transcript – the most valuable one, for it had been hand-corrected by Howard to add to its authenticity. 'Five years from now,' Dick had said jubilantly, 'we can sell it to the University of Texas for $100,000.'

I lowered my voice so the driver couldn't hear, and told him what was troubling me. 'Forget it for now,' he said. 'We've been working our balls off all summer. Relax and let the well fill up again. You'll find an answer.'

It was sound advice but I couldn't follow it. At odd intervals throughout the day the problem bobbed to the surface of my mind, and, like a kid jabbing a bruise to see if it still hurt, I poked and prodded at it.

As soon as we had checked into our rooms at the Beach Inn, I changed into my trunks and went out to lie on the sand. That evening, dressed in our most respectable clothing, we took a cab to the Britannia Beach Hotel. We had agreed to gamble with $250 apiece. When that was gone, we said solemnly, we'd pack it up.

Except for a few addicts at the slot machines and a handful of people at one of the roulette wheels, the pit was empty. No serious gamblers would appear until well after dinner. We had a couple of bourbon sours at the bar, reserved a table in one of the three dining rooms, then wandered down the corridor to the lobby of the hotel.

'So this is where he lives,' Dick said, looking speculatively upward.

'The sanctum sanctorum. Shall I try to get him on the phone?'

'Call him and say, "Howie, baby, how ya been? This is your autobiographer, Oiving, everybody's favorite amanuensis."' He grinned broadly. 'Jesus! It's too much!

252

Half the time I feel I'm acting in a movie and the other half I'm dreaming.'

We had a leisurely dinner, then strolled down the short flight of steps into the pit. There were two crap tables working, both sparsely occupied. I found a spot at the end of the nearest one and handed the croupier a hundred-dollar bill.

An hour later I was down to twenty dollars. Dick, who had been at the roulette wheel, moved in next to me, looking gloomy. My twenty lasted a few minutes longer, then we both stepped away from the table. 'Well,' Dick said, 'do we call it a night?'

'Listen, I've got a little extra cash in my wallet. Sort of tucked away. It's up to you. If you say no, we'll head back to the hotel. Otherwise . . .'

'I've got a thousand Swiss francs and about fifty English pounds,' Dick said. We smiled shamefacedly at each other, changed the pounds at the cashier's cage, went back to the crap table, and bought another small stack of chips. The dice came to Dick. He dropped ten dollars on the pass line and crapped out. 'Your turn,' he muttered.

'I never make money shooting,' I said, 'only betting against the dice.'

My first point was a six. Dick took the odds on the hard way, and three rolls later two threes came up. I let the ten ride, and Dick added ten more to it. 'Go, man,' he whispered. 'They're getting hot.'

I picked up the dice, rattled them a couple of times, and let fly. 'Seven – a winner,' the croupier called.

My next point was a ten. I rolled and rolled, neither making my point nor busting. A middle-aged man standing next to Dick put a small stack of twenty-five dollar chips on number ten. I picked up the dice. A five-dollar chip sailed past the corner of my eye and I heard Dick's voice say: 'Ten the hard way.' I threw the dice. Two fives. Dick looked at me with shining eyes, the collar of his shirt dark with sweat. 'They're talking to me!' he said excitedly.

The middle-aged man evidently had confidence in me also. He called 'Press' to the croupier – letting his winnings ride on the pass line and the numbers.

'Bet on eleven,' Dick's voice whispered in my ear. It was too late. The dice had already left my hand.

'Eleven – a winner,' called the croupier.

'Goddamit, listen to me!' Dick said. 'I told you that they're talking to me.'

Seven passes later, we walked away from the table with both hands full of twenty-five-dollar chips, a total of $2,100, giving us a net profit of about $1,600. The middle-aged man who had bet with me, calling 'Press' after each win, had won ten times that much. He filled both pockets of his jacket with chips, said, 'Thank you, young man, that was good shooting,' and strolled casually away, with not a hair out of place.

We drank two double cognacs apiece at the bar, then took a cab back to the Beach Inn. As we were crossing the bridge to Paradise Island, the answer came to me.

'*Press*,' I said. 'That it. We're going to press.'

Dick came into my room and watched while I dashed off, on Beach Inn stationery, two notes in Howard's cursive script. One of them gave McGraw-Hill permission to publish the book as an autobiography. The other was addressed to me. It read:

9-11-71

Clifford Irving –

In the event that no agreement is reached between you and McGraw-Hill by 9-21-71 concerning the publication of my autobiography, I authorize you to offer my autobiography for sale to another publisher on the terms to which you and I have agreed in our Letter of Agreement, and also to show them the manuscript in your possession. This authorization expires 9-30-71 at which time both copies of this manuscript are to be returned to me.

Yours truly,
Howard Hughes

'What's the point of that?' Dick said.

'Watch. You'll see.' I dug around in my leather brief-case and found the H.R. Hughes checkbook. After three attempts I was satisfied with the check I had made out to McGraw-Hill for $100,000.

'I get it,' Dick said, admiringly. 'If they refuse to up the ante, you're going to offer them the check.' His voice took on a note of alarm. 'But suppose they accept it? What's left in the account? About two hundred bucks?'

'I'll *show* them the check, not *give* it to them. Howard's note gives me nine days to find another publisher. In those nine days we can funnel a hundred grand back into the account – some of the loot you've got stashed away, some of mine, some from Edith's Merrill Lynch account – and *then* give them the check. That takes us off the hook, and we've still got a manuscript we can sell or turn into a novel. But that's only if they're dumb enough to turn down the book.'

'Not a chance,' Dick said. 'No one could be that dumb.'

11

The French Quarter

We checked into the Elysee Hotel on a Sunday evening. Beverly had reserved a suite for me – the Geisha Room – but one look at its oriental trappings convinced me it was inappropriate for the occasion. Something more austere was called for, so I changed to a suite on a lower floor. This one, though called the French Quarter, was decorated in a businesslike manner. In addition, it contained a kingsized bed, which I felt was necessary; I had a premonition of restless nights where I might need rolling room. Dick took an adjoining room with a connecting door that could only be locked from my side.

'Don't come through there to find out how things are going,' I cautioned him. 'And don't eavesdrop. Someone's liable to think it's a closet and you'd look pretty silly with Ralph Graves's jacket hanging from your ear.'

But on the second morning, Tuesday, that was almost precisely what happened. Dave Maness of *Life* opened the connecting door, looking for a place to put his coat. Dick was downstairs having breakfast, but his big yellow suitcase stood open against the opposite wall. I hauled Maness away from the door and muttered something about asking the management to lock it. 'This is a hell of a security setup,' Maness said, annoyed. 'Whoever's next door could come in here and steal the transcripts.'

Beverly had called me on Sunday night, hoping that we could have dinner and a drink and that she could have a quick look at the precious transcript. 'I'm exhausted,' I told her. 'Come for breakfast tomorrow morning, before the gang gets here.'

She arrived at 8:30 a.m., by which time I had set out the two copies of the transcript, each one packed tightly into two boxes I had obtained from the stationery store in Pompano Beach. I filled her in on recent events for the next hour, until Ralph Graves and Dave Maness arrived. The last time I had seen them, in June, they had been friendly to the point of unctuousness. This time they shook hands briefly, threw their coats down and asked to see the transcript. Their greetings were so cool that they gave me a sudden feeling of dread. I didn't understand it until three nights later, when Beverly told me: 'Your last call from Florida did it. I finally had to tell Ralph and Dave that Hughes had raised his price. I knew they'd think it was a holdup. I was afraid they'd back out.'

'A holdup?' I asked. 'You mean on Hughes's part.'

'No. A holdup by you. And I was right. Dave Maness read your letters and said, "Something's funny. I don't like the smell of it."'

'I don't understand.'

'He thought it might all be a hoax,' Beverly explained.

'A *hoax*? He said that?'

'He said it and he believed it. Don't forget, he hadn't read a word of the transcript. We only had your say-so that it was 950 pages. You said it was great material, but no one was ready to trust your judgment. Dave thought you were really pulling a fast one.'

'That's frightening,' I said, and I meant it. 'Jesus Christ! And you didn't even tell me.'

'I tried – what do you think I was hinting at when you called from Florida? You wanted me to tell Ralph and Dave and I kept saying no. But you insisted. They got furious. They said, "He may be your author but he's not ours, and it looks fishy. I can tell you, we're going to take a *very* careful look at that transcript."'

Maness sat behind the big desk in the living room, while Graves shared the adjacent love seat with a box of transcript. He and Maness took one copy. Beverly parceled out the other to Robert Stewart and Albert Leventhal, both of whom arrived shortly after ten o'clock. I ordered two pots of coffee, smoked one Gauloise after another, and tried to read a Travis McGee novel. After less than an hour I gave up and began leaning over Beverly Loo's shoulder. Before the readings began I made some mumbled introduction, to the effect that the beginning parts were on the dull side. 'Hughes was a little stiff at first. You'll see what I mean. He wasn't used to this kind of interrogation. During those first sessions . . .'

'We'll read it,' Graves said curtly.

I knew it was good stuff. We had checked it out thoroughly for errors, we had read and re-read it in Ibiza and Pompano Beach. But suddenly I was able to think of a dozen things that no intelligent and knowledgeable reader could swallow: Hughes wandering around anonymously in Ethiopia, and going south by plane and canoe to meet Doctor Schweitzer? Hughes and Hemingway? Hughes flying reconnaisance missions out of England in 1944? Moreover, no one as yet had challenged my inability to produce even a single cassette of the actual taped interviews. I had told the publishers that Howard refused to part with them, but I had given no reason other than his paranoia. In Pompano Beach, I said, when I was transcribing, the bungalow had been under 24-hour-a-day observation by trusted (but anonymous) Hughes aides.

'There's some interesting material in the appendix,' I said, trying to break their concentration and stifle my own growing panic. But the best I got was a brief nod from Leventhal.

I smoked, I poured coffee, I hopped in and out of Travis McGee's unlikely adventures, I peered frequently over Beverly's shoulder.

'You're nervous,' she said.

'Tired, tired,' I explained. 'I think I'll go inside and lie down.'

That didn't work, either. After ten minutes I was back at her shoulder. 'Let me show you something,' I said. I leafed through the second box of transcript and pulled out pages 894-905, the anecdotes about Bob Gross being caught shoplifting a package of Oreo cookies from a California supermarket and Howard's being dunned for cookies while he was shooting *Scarface*. 'Read this,' I said jovially, 'if you want a chuckle.'

Beverly read it, broke into laughter, and passed it to Leventhal and Stewart. They read and they laughed, too. 'Take a look at this, Ralph,' Leventhal said, shoving it at Graves.

'No,' Graves said, 'I'd rather read in sequence.'

But the interruption broke his concentration and I saw him flip through the appendix material. He read for ten minutes, carefully, then brought the appendix over to the desk where Maness sat, poker-faced. I was unable to sit still and I wandered from the sofa to the side of the desk, where I had slipped photographs of Edith, the kids, and our *finca* under the glass top. I saw what Graves had passed to Maness: the transcript of the 1958 Hughes–McCulloch telephone conversation. Maness read the first page, then looked up at me sharply.

'Where did you get this?'

'From Hughes. It looks to me like it's verbatim. The funny thing is, he left out all of McCulloch's remarks.'

Maness read it, line by line, all twenty pages of double-spaced manuscript. In Pompano Beach I had retyped it, changing the paragraphing and punctuation so that it would read almost precisely like the transcribed conversation McCulloch had sent to James Shepley, but appear as if it had been taped on Hughes's end rather than McCulloch's. The McCulloch version, I assumed, had been one of the private documents removed from the *Time-Life* files prior to my seeing them the previous June. Graves stood at one side of the desk, passing him the pages after reading them a second time. Maness finished his reading, ignoring me completely.

He looked up at Graves and said: 'It's good.' Graves nodded and went back to the love seat. That's it, I thought, hardly able to suppress a smile. That's the clincher. *They're hooked*.

It was almost lunchtime. Albert Leventhal had been skimming and had dipped into the appendix, too, where he fastened on the six-page memo dealing with the shaping of Jane Russell's nipples for the filming of *Macao*. It had been appended to the Dietrich manuscript, and I had worked it into Howard's tale of his stewardship at RKO. 'My God,' Leventhal said. 'You've got to read this. This is the most extraordinary thing I've ever read. This has *got* to be in the book. Hughes gave this to you?' he asked me.

'He was really proud of it,' I explained. 'He wanted to prove that he hadn't run RKO at a distance, that he was really on top of things and involved in the day-to-day direction of the studio.'

'But he's crazy,' Leventhal said. 'He keeps repeating himself over and over again.'

'He wanted to make his point absolutely clear.'

'It's the most hilarious thing I've ever read.'

'No,' said Beverly. 'The story of his shoplifting with Bob Gross is funnier.'

'And the cookies,' I interjected. 'The cookies he gave to the guy when he was making *Scarface*.'

'Let's break for lunch,' Leventhal said. 'Can we order it up here?'

260

'There's a restaurant downstairs,' Graves suggested. 'I think we should have something of an atmosphere of celebration.'

'You like the material?' I asked quietly.

'Like it?' he said. 'It's fantastic.'

The readings continued all week. Graves and Maness were by far the most diligent; they skipped nothing and by Tuesday evening had finished all 950 pages of transcript plus my 49-page appendix, which explained some of Hughes's more esoteric references and also related some of the tales he had told me when the tape was not running. Graves said: 'We're picking up our option. That's firm. It's an amazing piece of work.' He extended his hand and said, warmly and sincerely: 'Congratulations.'

I tried to be humble. 'All I did was ask the right questions.'

'I can tell you this much,' Graves went on. 'It's the most exciting and revelatory first-person story that *Life* will ever have published, at least while I've been there. And there's something else.' He turned to Beverly and Albert. 'We pride ourselves at *Life* that we can take any book, no matter how long it is, and gut it.'

'What do you mean by "gut" it?' I asked.

'We can excerpt anything in ten to twenty thousand words and get the guts, the meat, the heart, out of it. But we can't gut this book. It's impossible. There's too much material in it – it's packed. We're going to have arguments up at *Life* day and night about what to put in and what to leave out.'

On Wednesday the contingent from Dell Publishing showed up. It had taken some arm-twisting on Beverly Loo's part to get them to come. They had read more than a hundred pages of the Eaton 'autobiography' and they had been offered, through a writer named Ovid Demaris, a book by Robert Maheu which evidently contained dozens of private memos from Hughes to his erstwhile major-domo in Nevada. The Dell people included Helen Meyer, president of the company; Bud Toby, Vice-President; and Ross Claiborne, Executive Editor. Ross was the only one of the three to read the transcript from beginning to end, but Bud Toby, after going through the first two hundred pages (which Dick and I had deliberately made dull to give a sense of mounting revelation to Hughes's later ramblings), turned to Beverly and said: 'You don't have to worry about the competition.' He was referring to Eaton and Demaris. 'This is the real McCoy.'

Some time Tuesday or Wednesday, Harold McGraw himself showed up at the Elysee. He hadn't wanted to come and at the beginning could not understand why I wouldn't deliver one of the transcripts to the executive offices of McGraw-Hill. I relayed a message to him through Beverly Loo. 'I can come up with it,' I told Harold, 'and you can read it in my presence. But if I'm up there at McGraw-Hill with you, then there's no one to guard the shop at the Elysee. Hughes won't let any readings take place unless I'm physically present. That's in the contract. I'll come up, but then the editors can't read that day.'

Harold agreed to come.

The legal contingent also arrived, in the person of Faustin Jehle. Leventhal had been worried about libel, in particular the passages dealing with the Nixon 'loan' and similar favors to other politicians. Jehle read selected passages and then began skimming. 'Jesus,' he said, 'it's full of libel. He's telling a story here about the president of Lockheed stealing candy and cookies from a super-market . . .'

'Yes, but Bob Gross is dead,' I explained. 'You can't libel the dead, can you?'

'And then there's this Colonel Kuldell who stole from Hughes Tool, according to Hughes, back in the forties.'

'He's dead, too.'

'There's this story about how Ramon Navarro attacked him sexually at Mary Pickford's house. He's not dead, is he?'

'I'll have to check it out,' I said. I knew, of course, that Navarro had been murdered a few months previously in Hollywood. Jehle named a few other individuals whom Hughes had defamed or libeled. 'All dead,' I said.

Jehle nodded. 'That's a lucky break. Seems to me that most of the people we might have to worry about suing us are dead.'

I nodded agreement.

'But our main problem,' he said, 'is this man Noah Dietrich. What about him?'

'He's 83 years old. Hughes says he's dying.'

'Well, I don't wish any harm to him, but if he's dying I hope it's painless and soon, because he can give us a lot of trouble.'

I repeated this story later to Dick, who said: 'Tell them not to worry about Dietrich. When he reads the book and sees that we've swiped those stories from his own autobiography, he'll have a heart attack on the spot.'

The passages about Richard Nixon, however, weighed heavily on the corporate mind of the executives at McGraw-Hill. Harold McGraw had read the Nixon story and had evidently taken it up with some of his fellow executives. Beverly gently explained it to me: McGraw-Hill did a fair amount of business with the U.S. Government. If Mr Nixon were offended and if Mr Nixon were re-elected, that business might suffer. 'We may have to cut out that whole story of the loan.'

I was incensed, and after a talk with Ralph Graves I called Beverly at her office. 'You can't cut it,' I said. 'Howard will have a fit and I won't let you do it. It's the truth and it's got to stay. Ralph says *Life* will include it in their excerpts. You're going to look pretty gutless if they print it and McGraw-Hill doesn't.'

'They can't do that legally,' Beverly pointed out. 'They can only excerpt from our final text.'

I thought for a minute, then said: 'In that case I'll sell them the Nixon chapter as a separate article. Howard wants it printed, and there's not a damn thing in the contract that can stop me from doing it.'

Beverly called later.

'They'd like you to bring the transcripts to the 32nd floor, to the Board Room.'

'Who's "they"?'

'Everybody from Shelton Fisher on down.' Shelton Fisher was President of McGraw-Hill, Inc., the parent corporation of McGraw-Hill Book Company, of which Harold McGraw was President. 'I've never even met Shelton Fisher,' Beverly said, obviously pleased at the prospect of doing so. 'And John McGraw, Chairman of the Board, and Bob Slaughter and Joe Allen, and everybody.'

'Then I'd better wear a jacket and tie.'

'Oh, I think so,' Beverly said, alarmed. 'Definitely.'

The meeting took place on Monday morning in one of the executive conference rooms – no long table, just sofas and leather easy chairs and portraits of defunct McGraws on the walls. I had selected what I thought were key passages in the transcripts, a kind of crash course in Hughesiana. I distributed them to the various executives. Joe Allen, Executive Vice-President, read the section about Hughes's early sex life. There were tears visible in his eyes. John McGraw read the sections dealing with Hughes's financial manipulations to save TWA. 'Very complicated,' was about all the comment he was willing to offer. Finally Shelton Fisher came to the passage in which Hughes describes his theory about eccentricity. Dutifully, at Shelton's command, every man in the room read them and nodded his head: now they understood what Howard Hughes was all about. The readings continued, as in the Elysee, punctuated by chuckles, guffaws, wrinkled brows, and head-shakings of astonishment, pity, and admiration.

'I don't see that there's anything here particularly vulgar,' Shelton Fisher said. 'I don't think we have to worry about the language.' This was directed to Harold McGraw, who shrugged but accepted the dictum. Beverly Loo sat in one corner of the room, looking pleased. Fisher and one or two of the others read the Nixon passages.

'I think,' Fisher said, 'that we have an obligation, as publishers, to publish this book and not cut anything out, even if it is political.' I said nothing, but I gave Shelton Fisher full marks for that. He was a fearless publisher. He also summed up the general executive attitude toward Howard Hughes, gleaned from the two-hour reading session: 'Well, he may be crazy, but he's a hell of a man.'

Later, at the Elysee, with a certain pride, Beverly related to me a discussion that had preceded the conference. Harold McGraw had spoken to Shelton Fisher late Friday afternoon. According to Beverly, Harold had said: 'Irving is in town with the manuscript of the Octavio Project. I think it's important enough for all of us on the executive level to read some parts of it, and Irving suggests Monday morning, because Octavio is putting pressure on us for some changes in the contract. He wants the advance raised from half a million to $850,000.'

Fisher stared at him. 'What in hell is the Octavio Project? And who in hell is this Octavio person that we should pay him half a million dollars in the first place?'

'You see how well the secret was kept?' Beverly said to me. 'Even the president of the corporation didn't know.'

*   *   *

By the time everyone concerned had read the transcript, or at least important sections of it, McGraw-Hill's deadline was fast approaching. It was time to 'press,' as I had said to Dick after our hot roll with the dice in the Britannia Beach, and I showed Beverly Loo and Albert Leventhal the two letters that Howard had supposedly given me in the Beach Inn, and also the check for $100,000 drawn against his account in the Credit Suisse. 'His instructions were clear,' I said. 'If McGraw-Hill won't meet his terms, I'm to find a new publisher and pay back the entire advance.'

'He's blackmailing us,' Beverly said angrily.

'Hell, no,' I waved the check at her. 'He's willing to pay back the money.'

'We won't take it. We'll tear up that check if you give it to us.'

'I don't think you can do that,' I said quietly.

'We want that book,' Beverly shouted. 'Do you understand that? *We want that book!*'

'Then it looks like you'll have to pay for it. If you don't, what choice do I have? I've got to go to another publisher. If I can't find another publisher, and I doubt that I can in the time he's given me, I've got to go back to Nassau and return his damn transcripts. And then I'm out. He kisses me off for the lousy $50,000 I've gotten out of it – and I've already spent $30,000 in expenses – and he's got the transcripts. All he has to do is eliminate my questions and he's got the raw material for an autobiography. He gives it to another writer, and I haven't got a leg to stand on.'

'You could sue him,' Beverly snapped.

'Sure,' I sighed. 'I'll sue Howard Hughes. Wish me luck.'

'We'll sue him,' she countered. 'That's a breach of contract. We have a bona fide contract with him.'

'No, you don't,' I reminded her, sadly. 'You have a contract with me. I have a contract with Howard. You can't sue a man for breach of contract when you don't have a contract with him. Don't you see what a clever sonofabitch he is? He's got us in a bind.'

'Oh, no,' cried Beverly. 'I know the way he does business now. But that's not the way book publishers do business. Don't forget, this is a gentleman's business where everyone knows everyone else. It's a fraternity, a club. If he breaks his contract with us' – it was difficult to disabuse her of the idea that Hughes and McGraw-Hill had a contract – 'we'll spread the word so quickly that he'll never be able to get another publisher. No house will touch his goddam autobiography, I can guarantee you that. And you can tell him I said so. You may be scared of Howard Hughes, but I'm not, and neither is McGraw-Hill.'

'There's one publishing house that will touch it,' I said.

'Which one?' she challenged me.

'The publishing house that he'll buy to publish this book.'

'He wouldn't do that,' Beverly decided.

'I told him in Florida that you were pissed off and that you might fight him all the way. I told him about the publishing fraternity, too, and he said: "Bullshit. And if it's not bullshit, I'll buy a publishing house." Then he leaned back in his chair and said: "And the publishing house I buy might just be named McGraw-Hill, in which case all those so-called executives who are giving you such a hard time up there can count themselves lucky to get jobs running the elevators."'

'Oh, you can't believe that kind of talk,' Beverly said, laughing.

'With Hughes, anything is possible.'

'He'd spend a hundred million dollars to buy a publishing company just so that he'd get an extra $350,000 as an advance on his autobiography?'

'According to him it would cost a little over two

hundred million. He'd need a controlling interest in the stock – it's a publicly held company, don't forget, listed on the Big Board. He knew all the figures.' I parroted them to Beverly, having lifted them earlier from the most recent issue of Standard and Poors' *Trendline*.

Beverly protested. 'But that would be insane!'

'Have you read the transcript of the interviews?'

'Well, you know I have,' she said irritably.

'Then you know what kind of man he is. He's capable of anything.'

'How can a man with two billion dollars be so greedy?'

'He didn't get to be a billionaire by being philanthropic. And it's not just a question of money to him, it's a question of pride. He feels McGraw-Hill diddled him, and I was a party to it, consciously or unconsciously.' I overrode her burgeoning objections. 'Look, I'm not saying he's right. Basically he feels his autobiography is worth a million dollars. He's come down to 850 as a favor to me and because I bugged the hell out of him and just wore him down. It's a matter of pride. He says, "That's what I'm worth and I won't take a nickel less." He means it.'

'He's crazy,' Beverly kept repeating, and each time she said it, I replied: 'He's Howard Hughes.'

That night I reported the conversation to Dick. 'So what's going to happen?' he asked anxiously.

'They'll stick to their $500,000,' I said. 'They'll never buy the story that Hughes is going to take over McGraw-Hill or any other publisher. But our plan worked. Not a peep out of any of them about the Eaton book. They're so snarled up in their own worries that they've forgotten completely about the other thing.'

'And how the hell do you explain Howard's taking five hundred grand after all the fuss he's made about raising the ante?'

'He's a totally unpredictable man. If they know anything, they know *that*.'

The following day I had lunch at Sardi's with Beverly and Albert. Albert told me what I had expected to hear: McGraw-Hill would under no circumstances meet Hughes's demand for an additional $350,000, which would raise the total sum of the advance against royalties to $850,000. It was outrageous. McGraw-Hill had a contract with me, and I had a contract with Hughes, and McGraw-Hill would go to court on my behalf if Hughes wouldn't play ball.

'So what do I tell him when he calls?'

'Read this letter to him,' Albert said, and handed me an unsigned draft copy of McGraw-Hill's proposal. It was addressed to me at the Elysee Hotel, and read, in part:

The notes and text materials that you supplied us with, and which we have read this past week, are superb and acceptable to McGraw-Hill.

We were, however, startled and disturbed by the suggestion of Mr Hughes that we scrap our existing contracts and substitute new ones calling for an additional guarantee of $350,000. As you know, these documents, which were hammered out with blood, sweat, and tears, are in our judgment completely equitable and valid.

On the other hand, we are more than eager to make certain that Mr Hughes is happy with McGraw-Hill as his publisher. In that spirit, therefore, we are willing to amend our original contracts, increasing the advance from $500,000 to $750,000 . . .

'But not a penny more,' Albert said firmly.

*   *   *

Dick was in his room when I got back to the hotel. As soon as I slid my key in the lock, I heard him rapping insistently on the connecting door.

I unlatched it and he said: 'Well?'

I had planned to wear a long face and tell him they had refused to pay a cent more than the five hundred thousand, but the patent anxiety in his voice made me relent. 'They won't go a cent higher than . . .' I hesitated an instant, '. . . than seven-fifty. That's their last offer.'

'*Seven hundred and fifty thousand dollars?*'

'Not a penny more,' I said, grinning. 'They've upped the advance a quarter of a million. When they told me that, I nearly fell off my chair. That means, theoretically, the same $100,000 for me and the rest to Hughes.'

'I don't believe it.'

'It's true. . . I swear it.'

It was the last possibility we had considered when we swung into action with our triple reverse option play. The irony, the absurdity of it, left us glassy-eyed and incoherent for more than an hour. We had intended to create a diversion and run a play that would at best hold the line for us. Instead, we had scored a touchdown. We were richer – in theory – by $250,000. And by now I had joined Dick in the realization that it was money, even if I hadn't the slightest idea of what I would do with it all.

The rest of the plan was simple and we threw our ideas in the pot and cooked it up within half an hour. George Gordon Holmes, a new mythical intermediary between Howard and me, would call me that evening, instructing me to go to a public telephone booth and call another number, which would also be that of a public telephone booth. From that booth, using an electronic device called a Blue Box – which I had just read about in the most recent issue of *Esquire* – he would switch the call to Howard's private number in Nassau or Palm Beach. I was never to know its location and, with my habitual carelessness, I would lose the number of the public telephone booth that I had scribbled on a page of *The New York Times*. At first, Howard would refuse the offer of $750,000. Then, determined that the project had to be saved, I would offer him the additional $100,000 out of my share of the royalties.

'I don't want *your* money,' he would yell. 'I want McGraw-Hill's money! That's the most obscene offer I've ever heard.'

'Take it or leave it, Howard.'

He would take it. He would yell at the publishers, he would call me naive and a fool, he would rant that it was a plot on the part of McGraw-Hill and myself – but he would take it. The next day I would pick up the check and fly to Florida, spend the night somewhere near Miami, pretend to meet with Hughes, fly back to New York and then on to Spain.

'Okay,' Dick said, 'but for Christ's sake, be careful. You'll be carrying a check for $275,000 and if anyone can lose it, you can. Besides, they might follow you to make sure you're really delivering it. So rent a car and be certain you're not being tailed. Take plenty of twists and turns, and check your rearview mirror.'

The checks were ready the next afternoon. Albert Leventhal passed them to Ralph Webb, McGraw-Hill's treasurer, who handed them to me. One was my share: $25,000. The other check was for $275,000, made out to Howard R. Hughes. I looked at it, frowning.

'What's the matter?' Webb asked.

'Well, it's a minor point, but Hughes asked me to have all checks to him made out in the name of H. R. Hughes. I suppose it's to keep up some pretense of anonymity. We've had so damn much trouble with him lately, Ralph, that I'd hate like hell to get him into a stew over a little point. Can you make it out again – to H.R. Hughes?'

'I don't see why not,' he said, and the next day he placed the new check in my hand. Accompanied by Webb and Faustin Jehle, I went downstairs to the Chase Manhattan Bank where we rented a safe-deposit box. Into it we placed one Xerox copy of the transcript. McGraw-Hill had explained to me that if my plane crashed enroute to Spain, they would have paid out a total of $400,000 and would have no manuscript in their possession. With a grim-visaged bank guard hovering nearby, we signed an escrow agreement for the transcript: it could be removed from the bank by mutual agreement between McGraw-Hill and myself, or in the event of my death, or if one of the signing parties in any way breached the contract.

I went back to the hotel at four o'clock and waved the big check in front of Dick's nose. He stared at it for a moment and then shook his head slowly.

'A piece of paper. A lot of numbers.'

Strangely, we had come to the realization simultaneously: this check had less meaning, less reality, for us than the one we had cashed back in April. For that first check of $97,500, we had done almost nothing; for this one we had sweated and created a book and teetered on the brink of disaster for weeks. Its receipt, its physical presence, seemed anticlimactic. Almost disdainfully, I slid it into my briefcase.

12

The $1,000 Letter

Three days later I was back in Ibiza. I had flown to Miami as planned, on September 23rd, rented a car and headed for Key Biscayne. It was night, and I remembered Dick's fears that I might be followed. I checked the rearview mirror so often that I missed the turn off the highway, got lost, and by the time I reached the Sonesta Beach Hotel it was too late to do anything other than watch the eleven o'clock news and go to bed. In the morning I cabled to Beverly Loo: *ALL WELL CHECK TRANSFERRED OCTAVIO PLEASED ALTHOUGH NOT IN GOOD HEALTH SWEARS CONTINUING COOPERATION ROUGH VERSION PREFACE SIGNED MINOR PROBLEM REGARDING POSSIBLE EARLY SECRECY BREAK WILL WRITE DETAILS TO ALBERT BUT REPEAT ALL WELL LOVE CLIFF.*

The details of the cable were critical. McGraw-Hill had begun to make some noises just before I left New York to the effect that they might want to announce the book earlier than originally planned. It was a disturbing idea. I wanted the book at the printer, preferably bound and ready for the bookstores, before the world-at-large – and most particularly the Hughes organization – had even a clue. Howard's deteriorating health was also key to our defense should any problem arise after the announcement, whenever it might take place. As for his acceptance of the check, according to the newly amended terms of the contract with me – which, I had explained, we, too, had hammered out 'with blood, sweat, and tears' in Pompano Beach – once he had endorsed the check and deposited the $275,000, he was locked in. From that point on, McGraw-Hill could publish the autobiography whether or not he gave it his final approval. I had hesitated before including this clause in the addendum to Howard's contract with me. It had seemed too bold a stroke; but I had felt it would convince McGraw-Hill that Hughes, an unpredictable man at the best of times, had boxed himself in. That he would do so, of course, was ridiculous, but people see what they want to see, and no one at McGraw-Hill had seemed surprised.

The entire sequence of events, beginning with Hughes's supposed fury at *Life*'s involvement and ending with the offer to return the initial $100,000 payment, had turned the tide in the hoax. The publishers had adopted a new attitude. They no longer thought of Howard Hughes as eccentric or possibly crazy. Now they saw him as a financial fox. They were afraid of him. More to the point, they seemed to believe that I had some strange power over him. Robert Stewart, after reading the transcripts, had remarked: 'He treats you like a son.'

It was a perceptive insight. In rewriting the tapes, I had inserted remarks and full paragraphs calculated to create that precise impression. I had known of Stewart's orientation toward Freud and psychology in general. What I had failed to see was that the implied relationship would instill in McGraw-Hill an almost unlimited faith in me. If I snapped my fingers, they seemed to believe, the richest man in the United States would come to heel.

Dick flew over from Palma to Ibiza the day after my

return, and a key discussion took place. First we decided that the basic responsibility for reworking the transcript into an autobiography would be mine. Whole scenes had to be shifted in order to achieve a rough chronology, although we elected to keep certain moments of revelation in their original order, lest the narrative lose the power it gained from Howard's backtracking on some less-than-true tales he had told me in the earlier interviews. In the Nassau interviews, for example, he had refused to talk about his early sexual experiences, and he had invented a story of an orgy in Monterey, California, involving two girls and a pilot named Frank Clarke. During the California interviews, when our personal relationship had been cemented, he had told me that the story of the orgy was a lie. At the same time, with tears in his eyes, he had related a harrowing tale of a visit to his father's weekend cabin near Galveston when he was fifteen years old, his first experience with a woman – his father's mistress – and the horror of his realization that his father, drunk, had watched the entire performance from a doorway. The incident had colored his whole sex life. The contradictory revelations, of course, were as wholly fictitious as the stories they contradicted. We had been writing a novel without realizing it, and our fictioneering skill had been sufficient to dispel any doubts on the part of McGraw-Hill and *Life* as to the authenticity of the incidents.

But the drama was the thing, and I refused to sacrifice it for mere chronology's sake. To keep the whole of the work balanced in mind and then to reconstruct it was a one-man job, and I wanted to do it alone. Pride and vanity forced my decision as much as objectivity. I wanted to put my mark on the book. Dick seemed to realize it, and he gave way goodnaturedly. 'Just write the appendices,' I told him, 'and come over here every week or so to edit what I've done.'

The second problem we tackled was that of the

money. Edith would be flying to Zurich in a few days, as Hanne Rosenkranz, to deposit a check for $275,000. And then, in the winter, when the final manuscript was delivered, there would be an additional $325,000. The sums still had no reality for me, and my attitude was reflected by Dick's.

'What the hell can we *do* with it?' he said.

We faced the odd predicament that we might, jointly, be millionaires. If the book was published and royalties flowed in, there would be no doubt of it. As writers, neither of us had ever been prepared for such an eventuality; as hoaxers, it had been a peripheral consideration and we had never faced it squarely or honestly. And as money managers, we were about as experienced as first-graders confronted with adding two plus two. Moreover, we were aware that the bulk of the money had to be squirreled away, untouched, until some undecided-upon future date when we would either return it or begin to tap it.

'We'll invest,' I proclaimed. 'Pick a good portfolio of stocks and bonds, and the income from it ought to be about fifty thousand bucks a year.'

'Which would give me twelve to fifteen thousand,' Dick mused. 'Well, that's manageable. I could buy a house. Ginette's always wanted her own house. Nothing extravagant, just a nice three-bedroom place with a little swimming pool. That certainly won't attract any attention.'

The problem was that I would be left with the rest of the income: some $35,000 a year. Added to what I could ordinarily expect to earn from my novels, it gave me far more money than I could possibly spend in Ibiza, even if I traveled around the world and went twice a year to New York. I could swap my 24-foot sloop for a 32-footer, but beyond that I had no material ambitions. We had a 15-room house. We had servants. We had all we needed, and more.

'I'll tell you one thing,' Dick said presently. 'I didn't expect money to be such a constant pain in the ass. When you have *no* money, it seems to me, you worry less than when you have a *lot* of the stuff. I'm getting pretty goddam bored with worrying about whether the market's going up, down, or sideways, and as soon as I can figure out someplace to stick the loot, without all that worry, even at a lower rate of return – I'm going to do it.'

But we had the immediate problem of how to disperse the $275,000 Edith would carry to Switzerland. Dick had arrived in Ibiza bearing analyses of about a thousand American businesses which he had obtained via a three-month trial subscription to Value Line, an investment service. We drove up to the studio, laid out the heavy Value Line book, the latest issue of *Trendline,* and the Granville Market Letter, and began listing stocks and bonds for Hanne to buy.

First we had to decide whether or not we were going to pay income tax on the proceeds. The temptation was to avoid it, but we both agreed that the risk of being caught was too great. 'Christ,' Dick said, 'for that much money – that's three hundred fifty grand in taxes, man – the IRS could keep a couple of guys on our tails for years. But how do we pay it?'

I found a solution. 'After all the money is in, Howard will sign a new agreement in which he gives it all to me – in an uncharacteristic outburst of generosity. Then I pay the taxes in *my* name, and that's the end of the problem. So long as they get it, the IRS doesn't care where the money comes from. They won't report to McGraw-Hill that I've paid it, so who's to know?'

We returned to the investment problem.

'We've got to keep two things in mind,' I said. 'We want to have the money available to give back to Mother McGraw if this thing should go belly up; and if we do manage to pull it off, we don't want to risk losing the whole thing by being greedy.'

Dick agreed, and we spent the day compiling a list of stocks and bonds which we hoped would give us a balanced portfolio: so much in international AAA-rated industrial bonds with tax-free dividends; so much in blue-chip stocks such as IBM, Upjohn, and Cities Service; so much in Canadian gold mining companies; so much in slightly riskier stocks such as Texas Gulf and Carlisle; and finally, a small percentage in pure risk stocks, mostly in the electronic and mini-computer fields.

Dick had trouble going to sleep, he told me the next morning. 'I finally made it by trying to figure the interest our bonds would bring in over a three-year period, and the quarterly dividends on our stocks. As a soporific, it beats barbiturates all to hell.'

Edith's second pair of round trips to Zurich – one in late September to deposit the check for $275,000 in the Hughes account, the other, two weeks later, to transfer the cash to the Rosenkranz account – were uneventful as far as the banking and the crossing of borders were concerned. At the start of the second trip, however, she had a disconcerting encounter with a young American friend who lived in Ibiza. She had just arrived in Barcelona, put on her black wig and spectacles in the Ladies' Room, and was walking with her airline bag to the International Departures Lounge, when she came face to face with him.

He peered at her hesitantly and said, 'Edith?'

Her first impulse was to put her nose in the air and breeze past him; but she immediately abandoned it. 'Hello, Tom,' she said.

Tom took in the wig, the glasses, the thick layer of lipstick that disguised the delicate lines of her mouth. 'What's all the cloak-and-dagger about?'

Thinking fast, Edith came up with an answer. She put her fingers to her lips. 'Please, you won't tell Cliff,

278

will you? He thinks I'm in Palma to see a gynecologist.'

Like all the foreign residents in Ibiza, Tom relished a scandal. 'Who is it – anyone I know?'

'No. He's . . .' she remembered Howard's Helga, '. . . he's a South American diplomat from an embassy in Madrid. Please, don't say anything to Cliff.'

'Not a word. I promise.' He chuckled. 'It's about time you gave him some of his own back . . .'

'And so you must not let on when you see Tom,' Edith said to me, after her return from Zurich. 'Wear your horns bravely, darling, as I wore mine.'

While Edith was purportedly cuckolding me in Barcelona, I got to work on the final manuscript. I hired a middle-aged, close-mouthed Scotswoman named Bunty to help with the typing, and settled down with the pastepot and scissors to transform the transcript into a book.

In New York, in conference with Leventhal and Stewart, we had decided to retain the question-and-answer format. 'It's the soul of the book,' I had maintained. 'Converting it to a third-person narrative would rob it of all spontaneity.' What I didn't say was that it would also take an additional six months or more of hard work to do such a conversion job. Fortunately, they agreed with me.

We had abandoned the idea of faking a photograph of Howard; after the reading of the transcript at the Elysee there was no longer any need to shore up the authenticity of the relationship. However, I still felt obliged to deliver something in the way of illustrative material to Ralph Graves. '*Life*'s paying a quarter of a million dollars,' I explained to Dick, on one of his October visits to Ibiza. 'They're a picture magazine, so let's give them a break. I'll get David Walsh to do some illustrations.' David was an English painter who lived on Ibiza, an old friend and one of the finest draftsmen I knew. He had recently married a young Dutch girl and they had a newborn baby. Of late, times had been tough for him. He had three other children to support and was perennially broke, in debt, and churning out landscapes like a factory.

'We're coming out of this pretty well,' I said to Dick, 'so why not spread the joy? I can describe Howard to David, work with him a little bit, and he'll turn out a batch of oils and sketches. He's bound to get the cover of *Life*. They'll be delighted and so will David. It will solve his financial problems.'

'You've got a good heart,' Dick said.

'Yes, I do. Thank you.'

'But a pygmy brain. If Hughes won't allow a photograph because he looks so godawful, why would he give his okay to a painting?'

'Because it *will flatter* him, schmuck.'

I brought David up to the studio in late October and explained the assignment. He was impressed and excited. 'What a challenge! To paint the portrait of a man you've never met! But it's going to be bloody difficult.'

'You can do it,' I reassured him. 'I guarantee it.' I gave him all the photographs of Hughes that we had collected and lectured on Hughes's present physical appearance. 'Cheap clothing. Almost always wears a nondescript short-sleeved shirt, pale green or blue, and a tan cardigan with a button missing. White socks that usually slide down into his shoes.'

'I thought he wore sneakers,' David said.

'Don't believe everything you read. They're actually gray loafers.'

'And how does he sit when he's talking to you? Give me some physical mannerisms. Does he slouch? Cross his legs? What gestures does he make with his hands?'

'David,' I said, 'do him in various positions. I'll tell you which one looks right. And keep his left hand out of sight. It's crippled and he's very sensitive about it.'

David worked for the better part of a month, came up several times to show me preliminary sketches and check with me on such details as the bushiness of Howard's mustache, the length of his hair and the expression of his eyes. 'Would you say they were piercing or reflective?'

'Depends on his mood. Do both.'

He finally presented me with a portfolio of seven oils and two dozen black-and-white sketches. 'You've got it,' I cried. 'That's him!'

David blushed with pleasure. 'It was a bitch of a job.'

'But I knew you could do it. I had complete faith in you.'

'Does Hughes have to give his approval?'

'He will,' I said, and to back up my conviction I gave David a thousand dollars as an advance against whatever *Life* paid him for the illustrations.

My own work continued to go well and by the second week of November I thought I could see daylight at the end of the tunnel. I had over 700 pages typed and edited, Dick had finished the appendices, and I had begun a rough draft of the introduction. I had occasional conversations with McGraw-Hill and all was quiet there; they were urging me toward my self-imposed deadline of December 1st, and I said, 'I'll make it.'

Then, during the second week of November, Beverly Loo called. As usual she launched into the heart of the conversation without even bothering to say hello. The news was like a hand grenade that fell without warning in our peaceful back yard. She had just spoken to John Mack Carter, Editor of *Ladies' Home Journal*. They were going to print excerpts from the Robert Eaton book and there was a strong rumor in the trade that some other hardback publisher was contracting for the book itself. The *Journal* would announce its coup in less than two weeks.

281

'But it's a hoax,' I yelled. 'Octavio will sue the shit out of them!'

'I can't tell them that,' Beverly yelled back. 'I certainly can't tell them we've got the real book. We'd be breaking our secrecy clause with Octavio.'

'Beverly, you've got to stop them.'

'Will you listen to me? I *know* that. We've been arguing about it here all day and we've decided there's only one way. Octavio's got to give us permission to announce that *we're* publishing his real autobiography.'

'When?'

'Right away. By the end of next week.'

'He won't do that. I know he won't. And I can't even get in touch with him to tell him.'

'He's *got* to do it. And you've *got* to reach him.'

I explained the rest of it to Dick early that evening on the telephone. McGraw-Hill and *Life* took a very simple position, no matter what panic or hysteria accompanied its presentation. The existence of two Hughes autobiographies could shake the credibility of both, and there was a potential $750,000 investment in jeopardy. We were right back where we were in September, with one difference: now McGraw-Hill and *Life* knew that they alone had the real thing. The opposition had to be beaten to the punch. The contracts with Hughes, however, prohibited either McGraw-Hill or *Life* from announcing the news of the autobiography until thirty days after final payment. Any changes in that contract had to be in writing.

'In writing?' Dick's voice rose a notch. 'You mean an amendment to the contract?'

'No. I mean a letter. From Octavio to Harold McGraw. Which they want right away.'

'But you can't reach Octavio.'

'That's what I told Beverly. But he can reach me, can't he? In fact, I'm hoping to hear from him early next week.'

'Oh,' Dick said. Then, after a pause: 'How the hell can he write to Harold McGraw? He's in Nassau and you're in Spain. Have you got a trained carrier pigeon up in your studio?'

'Come over to Ibiza tomorrow,' I said. 'Catch that early morning flight. I'll explain the whole plan to you.'

Dick arrived at 8:30 a.m., Monday, and took a taxi from the airport to the *finca*. I was still sleeping. Edith made coffee for him and finally I stumbled out of the bedroom, yawning and scratching my head. Before I could even brush my teeth, Dick had hustled me into the library to harangue me. 'I don't know what you've got in mind, but it won't work. I stayed up all night thinking about it and it finally hit me on the plane. You forgot something.'

'Dick, let me have a cup of coffee first . . .'

'You forgot that if McGraw-Hill announces the book in the next week or two, before the final payment, we'll never get that last check cleared and into Hanne's account. The shit will hit the fan a week or two after the announcement, at the latest. And you won't have the book finished for another three weeks. This brilliant letter to Harold McGraw will cost us exactly $350,000.'

'No,' I said. 'It will cost us $1,000. Let me drink my coffee, will you? Then we'll go up to the studio.'

I had given Bunty an extra key to the studio and she was already at work when we arrived. She sat in her usual posture – legs crossed, one eye squinted against the rising plume of smoke from the cigarette dangling from the corner of her mouth, clicking off the pages expertly and relentlessly. She knew that Project Octavio, as we still called it in her presence, was very much hush-hush, so she wasn't surprised when I told her we had some special work to do and gave her the rest of the day off.

As soon as she had gone, I unlocked the file cabinet and took out the nine-page letter on yellow legal paper that Howard Hughes had written to Harold McGraw the day before. The first three pages were full of rantings and ravings about McGraw-Hill's incompetence; then Howard went on to Robert Eaton, denouncing him as a fraud, phony, crook, and giving McGraw-Hill permission to silence him 'using all legal means at your disposal.' And, lastly, he gave McGraw-Hill the right to announce publication immediately – provided it was done simultaneously with the final payment of $375,000.

'Now you see why we won't lose any money?' I said to Dick after he had read the letter, wearing my old pair of leather driving gloves so that he wouldn't leave fingerprints. I had worn the same gloves when I wrote the letter. 'If Mother McGraw goes along with it – and what choice does she have? – I'll be hand-delivering the check to Octavio in Florida, and I'll mail it from there.'

'But . . . Wait a minute. The letter to Harold . . .' An expression of dismay appeared on Dick's face. 'How are you going to mail it? No, wait. Don't tell me. You sonofabitch – I'm going to earn my twenty-five percent the hard way.'

'Right. You go back to Palma tonight. You leave for London in the morning. You should reach Nassau on Wednesday afternoon. Call me Thursday morning from your hotel and I'll let you know whether or not to mail the letter. I'll have spoken to Bev in the meantime.'

I tried to blot out the problems from my mind and concentrate on work. So much hinged on Dick's trip, however, that I found myself mentally accompanying him. I was with him on the first leg to London, spent the night with him alternately dozing and reading a spy thriller in the transit lounge at Heathrow; caught the ten o'clock plane to Nassau on Wednesday morning.

I called Beverly that afternoon, told her that Howard had phoned me and that I had delivered the message. He had ranted, grumbled, but finally agreed. He would write a letter to Harold McGraw giving him full authority to announce the forthcoming publication of the autobiography. 'He said there would be special conditions of some kind,' I told Beverly, 'but he refused to be specific.'

'That sounds ominous,' she said.

'He also said he'd call me again when he had mailed the letter.'

At noon on Thursday Dick phoned from the Sheraton British Colonial in Nassau.

'What's the score?'

'All systems go,' I replied, which meant he was to mail the letter immediately.

Late the next day he called me again, this time from Palma, and told me about his trip. 'Insanity,' he said. 'Twelve thousand miles and a thousand bucks to mail a letter. Who would believe it?'

'Not McGraw-Hill,' I said, 'hopefully.'

13

'McGraw-Hill Announced Today . . .'

I needed ten days more to complete the manuscript for the December 1st deadline. What concerned me most was McGraw-Hill's reaction to Howard's letter, and the timing of the announcement relative to the payment of the final check. I toyed with the idea of flying to New York earlier than scheduled, bearing an unfinished manuscript which I could finish there. I delayed my decision for the most prosaic of reasons: I had come down with a grippe that was rampaging round the island. Dick was due to leave for England any day. He was tired of Palma, he had never found a decent *finca* on Ibiza, and he had begun to think about putting his son into a good English school. Coincidentally, Nina had been looking for someone to drive her car from Ibiza to London, and Dick had agreed to do it.

'Don't tell Edith I'm coming to Ibiza to pick up the car,' Dick had said to me. 'She'll see me driving it and I'd just as soon skip any awkward explanations.'

On Sunday evening, suddenly, Eugen died. A tiny, fragile creature, she had been ailing throughout the cold early winter. She was an old monkey and she had lived a good life, but we were saddened beyond reason, and Edith cried for most of the night while I tossed restlessly with a light fever. On Monday afternoon, depressed but unable to sit around the house, I dragged myself up to the studio. For an hour or two I puttered around, and was about to give up for the day when I received two telephone calls that once again changed the course of events.

The first was from Beverly Loo, who informed me in a worried, nervous voice that the letter from Howard to Harold McGraw had not arrived in New York.

'Did he tell you he *definitely* had mailed it?'

'That's what he said, Bev.' I immediately envisioned all possibilities: the Nassau post office had swiftly relayed to the Hughes organization that they were in possession of a letter with the scrawled initials 'H.H.' on the envelope, and Intertel had intercepted it; Dick hadn't had it weighed and had put on insufficient postage, and since there was no return address the letter would never be delivered and we were out $1,000; or the letter had been lost in the mails.

'Can't you fly here earlier?' Beverly asked. 'God knows what demands the man's made, and this is the sort of thing we may have to discuss face to face.'

'I've got the flu. I feel lousy. If I feel better tomorrow, I'll come.'

The second call, following almost immediately, was preceded by the familiar voice of the local international operator: 'The United Estates calling *Señor* Cleefort Eerveen.' It was Nina.

'Where the hell are you?'

'Las Vegas,' she said, laughing. 'Christ, it's unbelievable. It's seven o'clock in the morning here and *everybody's downstairs gambling.*'

'What are *you* doing there?'

'I'm here with Marshall. Trying to drum up work. I haven't talked to a human being in a whole week and I had to call you.'

'What a bad break,' I said. 'I'm flying to New York

next week. Same continent, but three thousand miles apart. Where do you go from Vegas?'

'To Los Angeles. Somebody's given us a house. Why don't you come earlier? Fly out to California and have Thanksgiving dinner with me.'

I thought it over for about five seconds and then said: 'All right. I'm game. Why not? Give me your number in L.A., and I'll call you from New York. If I can make it, I'll be there.'

For once the Iberia flight was on time and I landed at Kennedy Airport at four o'clock Tuesday afternoon. My fever had gone but I was weak from antibiotics and my throat felt full of hot coals. I telephoned Beverly Loo from the airport. 'Come straight to McGraw-Hill,' she said.

'But I feel awful.'

'We've got Octavio's letter, and Ralph and Dave are due here from *Life* in fifteen minutes. It's a summit conference.'

'My God. What did he write?'

'Come over here and I'll show you.'

I arrived on the 20th floor at 5:30, bearing two copies of the incomplete manuscript. I had reached page 882 in the typing and had something over a hundred pages still to do. I had also brought David Walsh's paintings and sketches. I tramped into Albert Leventhal's office, sneezing and wheezing, carrying my suitcase, a huge artist's portfolio and the familiar overstuffed straw shopping basket, bulging with boxes of manuscript. After I had collapsed on the couch, I asked: 'Well, what are Howard's demands?'

Leventhal's answer was the most startling I could have received. 'None,' he said, smiling. 'He must have been kidding you. All he asked was that we lean more to the side of dignity than sensationalism when we release the news, and he wants the final payment at the same time as the announcement. We thought he really was going to ask the earth – something outrageous.'

I whistled with relief, but for different reasons than Albert and Beverly. I had imagined that the simultaneous payment would stick in everyone's throat; but they had expected so much worse that they never considered the one demand to be excessive. I was shown a typed copy of the nine-page letter. The original, they said, was in Harold McGraw's safe.

'By God, Howard sure can rattle on,' I said. 'Now you see what I have to go through.' I finished reading the letter, careful not to skim through it too quickly. 'This is fine,' I said. 'We're home free.'

Albert Leventhal had already prepared a draft of the press release. The release and the last check would be delayed about a week. I explained that plans had changed and I was meeting Hughes again in California; he would read the completed part of the manuscript and we were going to celebrate Thanksgiving together.

Albert also gave me a confidential memo, addressed to me but meant to be shown to Hughes. It confirmed McGraw-Hill's intentions to avoid sensationalism and establish a channel whereby 'O' could see and react to advertisements and publicity in advance. Albert concluded by noting that McGraw-Hill had 'established the utmost security in the plants which will set the type and manufacture the book.'

The following afternoon, after calling Nina, I boarded an American Airlines flight for Los Angeles,

At the airport I rented a car, and Nina and I drove to Beverly Hills, to a house perched high in the mountains above the city. The house had been loaned to Nina and her manager by a film producer named Paul Radin whom we had all known in Ibiza. Marshall had landed a contract for Nina at the International in Las Vegas, and now he was trying to plug his 'superstar' in Hollywood.

He had taken over the downstairs half of Radin's house. When he was not on the telephone to various record companies and producers, he was buzzing up and down the mountain and popping into bars and discotheques.

But what I realized, after a few days under the same roof with them both, was that Nina had become dependent on him to a degree I found difficult to understand. It may have been that she saw him as her last hope to revive her career. She was 39 years old; it was now or never. 'I know I've only got a few years left,' she said, 'and I've got to make money. I have to think about the kids.' Whatever the reason, when Marshall crooked his finger, Nina came to attention. She went where he told her to go, she wore what he told her to wear, and she trooped obediently to meet the people he thought could help her. She was unconsciously picking up bits and pieces of Marshall's style, which was crass opportunism. It was something I had never seen in her and it disturbed me. If I thought of Edith, who was the most straightforward woman I had ever known – and who found it almost impossible, at gut level, to compromise herself or her love for another human being – Nina came off poorly. For the first time, the image of Nina that I had always believed in – a woman searching for something of value in her life – began to tarnish and look more like fantasy than reality. When I challenged her on it, she grew tight-lipped, almost surly.

I said: 'Suppose you do have some sort of success? And you knock yourself out, and you sock your money in your Swiss bank account, and you go from city to city and nightclub to nightclub with John Marshall and his friends – where do you wind up? You'll be 45 years old and worn out, and you won't have anything to show for it except a scrapbook. You're losing the one thing you've always had. You were always you. You never played petty little games.'

'It's a world you don't understand.' Her surliness had

turned suddenly to anger. 'If you're going to make it, the only way to make it is Marshall's way. I don't like it, but I have to go along.'

'But you're the victim.'

'Not in the end,' she said. 'You'll see. And there's another thing you don't understand. There's nothing in the world that matters more to me now than my career.'

I looked at her for a long time. I could only nod and say: 'I'm sorry about that . . .'

The strain stayed with us the whole time we were together in California, easing only during the two days we drove north to Big Sur and Monterey. For a moment, then, we recaptured something of what we had had during the time in Mexico. We were alone; the pressures of 'making it' were temporarily gone. But the moment we got back to Beverly Hills she was uptight again. There were people to see, auditions, appointments. She was worried that Marshall might think she had stayed away too long. And there was a feeling in us both, tacitly acknowledged by some few words or the lack of them, that she and I were on the downhill slope. What was my restlessness but a refusal to give up a fantasy world that both entranced and enslaved me? For seven years I had been held in thrall; suddenly I felt the glimmer of an inner freedom.

Almost as soon as I arrived in Los Angeles Nina had asked me how the Hughes book was progressing. I showed her the paintings and drawings that David had done. 'I'm supposed to be showing them to Hughes now, for his approval. What do you think?'

'They're bloody marvelous,' she said. 'Do they look like him?'

'How the hell should I know? Which ones do you like best?'

She pointed out two of the oils and several of the pencil sketches. 'Fine,' I said, 'that's Howard's choice, as of now.'

'God,' Nina laughed, 'it's all so unbelievable. You mean I'm Howard Hughes?'

'Anyone can play,' I explained.

Marshall was let in on the secret, too – not that it was a hoax, but that I had been seeing Hughes and working with him on his autobiography. He was impressed, of course, although basically uninterested in the manuscript other than from a commercial point of view. He skimmed through one or two chapters and then put the book aside, evidently weary.

'Would it make a movie?' he asked.

'Sure it would. Don't you think so?'

'I know everyone here in Hollywood, you know. I might be able to help you on that. Do you have an agent?'

'Not yet, but that's very kind of you, John. When the time comes, I'll ask you for some introductions.'

On the Monday following Thanksgiving I called McGraw-Hill in New York. Hughes, I explained, had spoken to me on the telephone, heard my hacking cough and refused to meet me until I was in better health. He was sick, too, he said, which compounded the danger of infection. I had been instructed to turn over the manuscript to the intermediary, George Gordon Holmes. Holmes had flown to Los Angeles. He would deliver the manuscript to Hughes. A meeting with Howard was tentatively scheduled for next week, in Florida or Nassau. As for the press release, he had approved it and made only two minor changes.

'How are you coming with the work?'

'Slow,' I said. 'I've had a fever and I've just been hibernating in bed. I'll be back in New York tomorrow.'

I flew back Tuesday morning. Nina was to have gone on the same flight and then on to London, but at the last minute Marshall told her she would have to appear at a cocktail party in Los Angeles, and she changed her reservation to a night flight. She would have part of a day in New York on Wednesday, between planes, and I said, almost halfheartedly: 'Come up to the Elysee. I'll be out, but you can get some sleep there.'

Wednesday morning I appeared at McGraw-Hill to tell tales of my illness in California, telephone conversations with Howard Hughes, and the streetcorner meeting with George Gordon Holmes. I was now about to meet Howard again in Florida, specific location unknown. Florida was the logical choice for Howard: he had met me there before on two occasions and obviously had a house in the Palm Beach area. It was also a logical choice for me. It was a comfortable place to work, I liked the southern climes in winter, and once McGraw-Hill made their public announcement of March publication, I didn't want to be caught in Nassau by any part of the Hughes organization – especially Intertel, the private security army. The announcement had been scheduled for later in the week. The last check to H.R. Hughes – for $325,000 – would be ready on Thursday, and I would leave immediately afterward. 'Make sure you get him to sign the preface,' Leventhal reminded me. 'And if he'll do it, we'd like it handwritten. Then we can reproduce the whole thing in the book.'

'If he's well enough. You should have heard him screech on the telephone when he heard me coughing and sneezing. He was furious. He said it would literally kill him if we met.'

Beverly had joined us by then in Albert's office. 'By the way,' she said, '*Life*'s taken that letter from Octavio to Harold and given it to the handwriting expert, the same man who analyzed that letter they printed last January.'

I felt slightly sick, but I tried to be casual. 'What's that all about?'

Beverly shrugged. 'Just a preventive move in case there's any trouble after the announcement. The newspapers might kick up a little fuss. It's not a bad idea to have ammunition.'

'It's a good thing I wrote to you in early January to tell you I'd heard from Hughes. It once occurred to me that if I'd written you after January 22nd – after the *Life* article came out, I mean – you might have had some cause to be suspicious.'

'Oh, it occurred to us, too. We went over all that.' Beverly smiled.

'When will you get Kanfer's report?'

'Tomorrow morning. Why? You don't have doubts, do you?'

'No,' I said, laughing. 'These experts always give you the opinion they know you want from them. If you'd told the man you thought it was a forgery, he'd probably report that it was a forgery. This way you're guaranteed an affirmative opinion. But it's a good thing,' I added, 'that it's really from Hughes.'

When I got back to the Elysee, Nina was there. Her plane for London left at 7 p.m. 'You look worried,' she said.

'I am. McGraw-Hill's given one of the Hughes letters to a handwriting expert.'

'But then . . .' Nina looked pale. 'They're going to find out.'

'I don't know. I just don't know.' I was pacing the room, smoking one Gauloise after another. 'I could admit it's a hoax. I could pretend I don't understand. I could bring up the theory that I've been meeting an impostor. I don't know what I'll do. Of course, there's always the off-chance the man will say the letter's genuine.'

For a moment Nina seemed concerned with something other than her own problems. 'My God,' she said, 'I won't sleep tonight. Will you call me in London when you find out?'

'Yes,' I said. I was touched.

'Promise?'

I promised, and an hour later we hailed a taxi for Kennedy Airport, and there we said goodbye.

On the plane to Miami I took a McGraw-Hill envelope from my briefcase and scribbled the address of the Credit Suisse in Zurich. Using a plain sheet of yellow paper, I wrote a note to the bank asking them to clear the enclosed check as soon as possible. The plane was crowded, every seat taken, but the passengers flanking me in the coach section were buried in their respective copies of *The New York Times* and *Playboy*. If the one had taken less interest in the sports pages and the other in the centerfold, they might have sneaked a look at a check for $325,000 made out to the richest nonexistent man in the world. Using a ballpoint pen, I endorsed the check – 'deposit only to the account of H.R. Hughes' – then signed it. Letter, check, and envelope took about ten minutes to write. The handwriting had degenerated into a scrawl. Howard was getting older. He was sick; and I was tired. I sealed the envelope and shoved it into my briefcase just as the stewardess bent over me, smiling toothily, to deliver a tiny glass of fresh orange juice.

Miami Airport was familiar territory by now. I rented a car at National and headed north, veering off the superhighway first to drop the letter in a mailbox and then to rent a typewriter. Where I stayed seemed of no importance and I cut over to the coast road, Route A-1A, and pulled up in front of the first decent-sized motel removed from the bizarre strip of condominiums and other architectural litter that made up the so-called Gold Coast. Called the Newport Beach Motel, it was big, self-contained, with a restaurant, coffee shop, drugstore, newspaper stand, swimming pool, and sizable strip of beach. Still a few weeks short of high season, the suites were reasonably priced, and I rented a good one with twin terraces facing both the beach and the pool. At seven o'clock the next morning I was at work in the living room, papers stacked on all available surfaces. I could imagine the look of distaste on Dick's face if he could see it. He couldn't live with clutter and it seemed as if I couldn't live without it.

A week's work, I reckoned. The final part of Howard's life – the Las Vegas and Bahamas period; the various trips to Mexico; his last big love affair with Helga, whom Howard had requested I rename Inga – had to be edited and typed. A batch of insertions and changes had to be made in the 882 pages I had already delivered to McGraw-Hill. I had to decide on the final form of the preface and get Howard to sign it. The most difficult job was my own introduction to the book, from which *Life* would excerpt its 5,000-word article by me. That would tell the farfetched tale of our meetings, describe how the book slowly metamorphosed from authorized biography to autobiography, treat the problems involved in editing it, and offer a few of my personal impressions of the man himself. 'It's vital,' Robert Stewart had stressed, 'because that's what everyone will want to know. Will you have to show it to Hughes?'

'Only as a courtesy. The contract with him gives me the right to say whatever I please. No censorship.'

'Terrific. You've got to tell all about that plane ride in Mexico and eating bananas with him in Puerto Rico and the man with the cane who watched your bungalow in Palm Springs.'

'Pompano Beach,' I corrected him.

'And Dick's prune story. Don't leave that out.'

'It's essential,' I agreed.

I also developed a new twist for this last meeting in Florida. I would be met at the airport by George Gordon Holmes, the man who had taken the manuscript from me in Los Angeles when Howard was too sick to make the rendezvous. Holmes would herd me into his car, blindfold me, and drive me north to what I would guess to be Palm Beach. Once inside a private house, the blindfold would be removed. Howard would be in bed, thinner than ever, pale, gasping, and wheezing – an oxygen tank close by the bedside – battling stubbornly for his life. Too sick to read through the entire manuscript, he would nevertheless give it his final blessing. He would say farewell.

'I can't see you again, not for a long time. Once it's known that I've done this book with you, Clifford, they'll hound you. They'll follow you wherever you go. They'll try and track *me* down through you. I can't have that! Do you understand? I don't know how long I've got, but I want to live those days in peace. So I'm going away. *Far away.*'

Goodbye, Howard. It was good to have known you. We'll meet again, in a better world.

I worked all weekend in the air-conditioned suite, but now and then I would break into a private sweat thinking of the man at work in New York – the handwriting expert hired by *Life*. The letter he was using was the one I had written to Harold McGraw. I had scrawled it more quickly than any of the others but it was the only original Hughes letter available for comparison to whatever genuine material *Life* had in its files. I postponed the moment as long as possible, but on Monday afternoon I decided there was no longer an excuse for staying incommunicado, and I called Albert Leventhal in New York. Since I never called collect he had no idea at first where I was and, as usual, he seemed reluctant to ask. The cloak-and-dagger aspects of the whole odyssey had permeated all levels at McGraw-Hill. But this time I volunteered the information, although I added: 'Be careful of the phone. I was put in here by Octavio. Chances are there's a tap.'

'Have you seen *him*?'

'He signed the preface. But he's sick.' I sketched

swiftly the tale of the blindfolded ride to parts unknown. Albert asked if Hughes was aware that the announcement was pending and I coughed, hesitated, and replied that I wasn't sure.

'But you said you saw him. What do you mean, you're not sure?'

'Albert . . .' I tried to be delicate. 'This is for your ears only. He's . . . well, I said he was sick. I don't want to go into details on an open line. There's a lot he doesn't understand. It's hard to get through to him. Do you follow?'

'Don't say any more,' Albert replied. 'I've got it. Anyway, we're making the formal announcement tomorrow at one o'clock.' He read a few changes to me and then put Beverly on the line.

'We got that report from the handwriting expert,' she said. 'I thought you'd like to know his opinion. There's no doubt that the letter's from Octavio. He quoted the odds as a million to one.'

I snorted. 'Am I supposed to be surprised?'

'Well, I just thought you'd like to know.'

'I am, Bev. Sorry if I was snappish. I guess it makes the people up in New York rest a little easier.'

'*We* never had any doubts,' she insisted. 'But it might come in handy if there's any trouble after the announcement.'

'What trouble could there be?'

'With Octavio?' She laughed heartily. 'Don't forget, I've read his autobiography. I know the things that man is capable of. He could even deny he's ever met you.'

To that I could only reply with a sustained chuckle that clearly meant: *I doubt it, but anything is possible.* And I promised to call Beverly on Wednesday, the day after the announcement, in case there were any problems.

I wrote a brief note to Nina, to ease her mind and let her know that the crisis was past.

*   *   *

On Tuesday afternoon I stood on my balcony, idly gazing out at the rows of deck chairs that flanked the swimming pool. I had chosen the wrong kind of hotel. The room was large and cool and there was good work space, but the noise of merrymaking drifted up from the pool, even through the closed glass doors of the terrace. A steel band drummed and tinkled its rhythms in the early evening. Chubby young men from New York splashed about in the shallow water, knocking a volley-ball back and forth across a low net, yelling, 'Hey Julie, let's go!' On the deck chairs, bleached blondes and middle-aged executives sipped Cokes, oiled themselves with cocoa butter, and waited patiently for the sun to break free from a scudding cloud and resume its appointed task of making them beautiful and brown. Up there on my little island with Howard Hughes, a pile of manuscript and a waiting typewriter, I felt suddenly alone. I had been dumped here from an alien planet. But they're living their truth, I thought, and I'm living mine. If mine is founded on a grand deceit, it's no less true. Lived to the hilt, as it seemed to be at the moment, it was as real as any of the lives that were sprawled out beneath me, hidden behind those glistening skins. I felt no shame then, no contempt. I simply felt cut off.

Sitting on the far edge of the pool, a tall blonde girl of surprising loveliness was fitting her long feet into flippers and strapping a scuba tank expertly to her back. She wore an alligator-green wetsuit. I wondered about her: she didn't fit by the side of that pool any more than I did. Then an obese young man popped out of the water by her dangling legs, and she cupped her hands to call out instructions, and I understood. I went back to the typewriter, thinking about the denouement of the affair with Nina, and thinking about Edith waiting for me in Ibiza, and the work went badly.

Later in the afternoon I went down to swim. The ocean surf was high and I did laps in the pool, ending up panting for breath but with a good feeling of having extended myself. The willowy blonde in the green wet-suit was just stuffing her diving gear into a bright orange scuba bag. I was only a few feet away from her.

'You do this for fun or profit?'

She showed me her card. Her name was Anne Baxter and she was a qualified scuba instructor for the Aqua-Fun Divers. She had pleasant blue eyes and a voice that twanged softly with a southern lilt. I had always wanted to learn scuba diving and after we talked for twenty minutes I went up to my room and came back with forty dollars in cash, as advance payment for a four-lesson course to be given in the pool. We made an appointment for the next morning at nine o'clock and she wrote my name in her little blue appointment book.

'Do I call you Anne, or Annie, or Miss Baxter?'

'Whatever you like. Just please don't be late,' she said sharply, 'and don't eat a big breakfast.'

She was a very serious girl, and very professional, and she had long brown legs. Learning scuba would pass the time nicely for the rest of the week, between chapters.

The Miami Herald carried the news of the Hughes auto-biography on page one. I read it over a plate of scrambled eggs and pork sausages. The story was datelined December 7th – Pearl Harbor Day. McGraw-Hill had attacked but the Hughes Tool Company, far from quiescent and confused, as Dick and I had assumed they would be, had fired back with all their guns. 'There is no such book,' said Richard Hannah of the Carl Byoir Agency, a public relations firm employed by Hughes Tool. Donald Wilson of Time, Inc. had shot right back with: 'Oh, we're absolutely positive. Look, we're dealing with people like McGraw-Hill. And, you know, we're not exactly a movie magazine. This is Time, Inc. and McGraw-Hill talking. We've checked this thing out. We have proof.'

But Hannah and Chester Davis – Hughes's lawyer and Executive Vice-President of the Tool Company – had continued to deny and protest. Dick and I had assumed a period of confusion: *Could the old man have done it? How do we get in touch with him to find out? Or, if he were dead or incapacitated: How do we stop it? What if they demand that Hughes make a personal denial? Suppose there's a subpoena? Listen, Chester – not so fast. Maybe this can be a good thing for us* . . .

I had a hard time keeping my mind on Annie's instructions, and once, at the bottom of the pool while I was trying to adjust a weight belt and slip into the tank harness, it occurred to me that Hughes Tool or Intertel detectives might at that precise moment be slipping a passkey into my door and pouncing on the manuscript. My name and photograph had been on the front page of the local papers, right next to Howard's. It was a jolting thought, and the next minute the breathing regulator slipped from my mouth, the tank thumped solidly on the pool floor and I found myself gulping what felt like a quart of chlorinated water. I shot to the surface, sputtering.

'What's the matter with you?' Annie said crossly. 'I've told you three times to put the tank across your knees when you're sitting on the bottom. You're not listening to me, Clifford. This is a very important part of the course. Suppose that happened in fifty feet of water, in the ocean? You could *drown*.'

I felt half-drowned already, but I apologized. 'I've got a lot on my mind today. Don't you read the newspapers?'

An hour later she was in my room, sitting cross-legged on the couch, poking through the various news clips after having slipped her contact lenses into place. I came out of the bathroom, showered, scrubbed, dechlorinated, and wearing freshly pressed khakis.

'Gee,' she said, 'how did you ever get involved with a

man like that? Is he really so rich? Is he a nut or something?'

'I can take you to dinner tonight and give you a crash course in Howard Hughes. And if you're a spy for Intertel I'll make sure you self-destruct within five seconds. In the meantime I have to call New York. So be a good girl and go dive for a pearl somewhere. I'll pick you up at eight o'clock.'

What remained of the afternoon I spent on the telephone, talking alternately to Albert Leventhal, Beverly Loo, Robert Stewart, Ralph Graves, and then to Leventhal again. Confusion was clearly the order of the day, in New York as well as Florida. 'We're not upset,' Beverly kept repeating. 'We're not upset, but Albert is panicking. He put his name on the press release and his phone's rung nearly a hundred times so far today. He's never had so many telephone calls in his life. He's very nervous.'

Albert got on the wire: 'I'm not upset. I think we should call a press conference. Every newspaper and TV station wants a statement from you. Even the BBC's ready to run a crew over from London. I think you should fly up here this evening and we'll schedule it for tomorrow.'

Robert Stewart then clarified the situation. 'Everyone's in a panic except me. I think it's the best publicity we could ever get. I'm sure Hughes is just chuckling away, having fun. Everyone's in a panic except me.'

'That's because your telephone's not ringing,' I said. 'What the hell is going on? Robert, they want me to come up for a press conference, but I've got work to do and I'm on tap for Octavio, for a final meeting.'

'There are some newspaper people who don't even believe that you *exist*,' Robert explained.

Graves was next, and he was calm. 'I think this press conference is a terrible mistake. For every question you can answer, there'll be a dozen you'll have to duck. And if you tell the full story of your meetings with Hughes we won't have any article to print.'

'Ralph, I couldn't agree with you more. They'll go away more frustrated than enlightened and they'll rap me over the knuckles. But I just promised McGraw-Hill I'd fly up tonight. Will you call them, please, and make a joint decision? And then one of you please call me back and tell me what it is.'

'There's just one thing. I think we could short-circuit a lot of unnecessary controversy if you ask Octavio to issue a statement contradicting the denials of the Tool Company and the Byoir Agency. Or at least get him to tell them to shut up.'

I promised to do my best. George Gordon Holmes was supposed to contact me that evening, and I would explain the urgency of the situation.

An hour later Beverly called. 'Ralph told us he spoke to you, and we've talked it over. He's probably right. They have more experience in the public relations area than we have. We'll hold off on the press conference for a while.'

'Marvelous. What does Albert say to that?'

'He can hardly speak. He's losing his voice answering the telephone.'

'Listen, Bev, I've got to hang up. I've got a date.'

'With Octavio?'

'No, with a blonde.'

'I don't believe you. Everyone up here is in a panic, and your name's splashed over every newspaper in the country, and every reporter in the world is out hunting for you – and what's more, you're supposed to be working! You wouldn't dare go out with a blonde tonight!'

'Would you believe a brunette?'

'No, they're not your type. But I'm glad you were only joking.'

That evening at dinner with Anne Baxter I started to

303

worry in earnest. The denial had come too quickly and with far too much vigor. Arriving in New York, there would be questions followed by more questions and to some of them I might not have such ready answers as in the past. The press conference would almost certainly take place and the reporters, as Ralph Graves had intimated, would hardly be the gentlefolk I had dealt with so far. They had no vested interest in either trusting or believing me. Annie prattled on about scuba diving, blue holes, staghorn coral, and the places she dreamed of seeing, like the Great Barrier Reef and Buck Island off the coast of St Croix in the Virgins. We ate at a restaurant called The Cattleman and I chewed my way half-heartedly through a pound of rare sirloin and from time to time tried to match her exuberance, but my mind wasn't there. The check was winging its way to Zurich. It would take two weeks to clear, and during those two weeks anything could happen. They could stop the check. They could hire detectives to be at the bank when Edith walked in to cash it. They could give me a very rough time if Hughes refused to silence the Byoir Agency. The concept of *they* began to take on gigantic, threatening proportions. *They* were everywhere. *They* would be out to get me. I felt increasingly uneasy, a budding convert to paranoia. *Howard, now I understand!*

Every time we had been in trouble we had managed somehow to turn it to our advantage. Our luck had held, and when it was going good, as in Pompano Beach and Paradise Island, we had pressed it. *All right so far!* That was our motto – tongue in cheek to an extent, because in the tale the pavement is looming up to make jelly of the plummeting man; and we had no intention of ending up that way. But we were near that pavement now, and we needed to spread a net . . .

Annie and I went back to her apartment, had a drink, and then I said, 'Look, I'm no good for company tonight. I've got to get back to the Newport and work. Can you meet me at the pool tomorrow afternoon at three o'clock?'

I was at the desk of the Newport by midnight and I cabled Edith: *PROBLEMS TOOLCO HAS DENIED AUTHENTICITY OF BOOK STOP CALL ME IM-MEDIATELY LOVE CLIFF.* I went upstairs to bed, and lay in the dark listening to the waves thrash against the unseen shore and the beat of the calypso band by the swimming pool. At two o'clock in the morning the idea came to me. With the time difference it was eight o'clock in the morning in Spain. I put through a call to Dick.

'We've got troubles,' I said. 'Do you have any idea what's happening?'

'The *Tribune* hasn't arrived from Paris. Where are you? What's going on?' I gave him all I knew, which wasn't much. 'Then it's not so bad,' Dick said. 'Just hang in there and get the hell out of New York as fast as you can.'

'But it could get worse. We don't know what they've got in store for us.' I explained that I had cabled Edith to call me. 'I want her to go to the studio and get that copy of the Octavio letter, the original one to Chester and Bill. I haven't got any handwriting samples with me. I think I've got to write another letter. He's got to kick the Tool Company in the ass.'

'No,' Dick said, alarmed. 'Let it lie. Don't do anything rash. Do you want me to fly over there and meet you? You sound like you're panicking.'

'I'm not panicking. But McGraw-Hill *is*. Goddamit, you don't understand – this thing's page one news over here! It's on every TV newscast. I'm going up to New York and my head's going to be on the chopping block.'

'I'll come,' Dick decided. 'You need help.'

He was right. I needed help, I needed someone to talk to, and he was the only man in the world I could turn to because he was the only man who knew the truth. 'Let me wait for Edith's call. Then I'll get back to you.'

Again, the day was spent on the telephone. With all the publicity so far, and undoubtedly more to come, I was worried about staying at the Elysee. I carried too many papers with me, legitimate and otherwise, that might be of interest to Intertel and McGraw-Hill alike. I called Marty Ackerman in New York and explained the problem. 'Stay with us,' he volunteered. 'The house is burglarproof.'

Edith called next, and I instructed her to go to the studio, find the key to the file cabinet under the Zapotec mask and dig out the 'Dear Chester and Bill' letter. 'Never mind why, but I need it. Dick will pick it up on Saturday.' Then I got back to Dick in Palma with instructions. 'Bring the letter. We'll have a P & P session in New York and decide what to do. I'll be at Marty Ackerman's and I'll book you into the Commodore Hotel.'

'Don't say anything to Ackerman,' he warned me.

'For Christ's sake, no. Just call me from the airport when you get in on Sunday evening.'

McGraw-Hill was next on my list. I had lain awake in bed half the night preparing the scenario. 'Hughes is sick,' I told Beverly. 'How sick, I don't know, but I do know that something funny's going on. I spoke to George Gordon Holmes a few minutes ago and he's in a flap. He's the original unflappable man, but he's flapping and I can only guess the reason why. I told him I had to see the old man – that's what Holmes always calls him – and he said he'd try to arrange it, but he couldn't guarantee it. He's going to call me back.'

Beverly dropped her voice. 'Is he . . . dying?'

'I don't know. I'll call you back.'

Anne Baxter arrived at three o'clock and flopped onto the living room couch. 'The season hasn't even started and I'm exhausted.'

'So am I. How would you like to get away for the weekend?'

'Where to?'

'It's serious business, Annie. Can I trust you?'

'You can trust me,' she said eagerly.

'I've got to meet Howard Hughes somewhere. I don't know where yet. One of his men is going to tell me. Probably in the Bahamas. He isn't going for the diving. It'll be wherever he says. You go have a cup of coffee, or go home. I'll call you when I know.'

It was Lincoln's Birthday weekend all over again. I called Eastern and National and BWIA and Pan Am and Caribair. Nassau was fully booked. Flights to Puerto Rico were wait-listed. I could get to Jamaica and there were rooms at the Hilton but it would cost me an additional $150 in air fare.

Eastern called back. 'Mr Irving, we have two cancellations on the Friday flight to St Croix.'

'I'll take them. What about a hotel?'

'It won't be difficult. For you and your wife?'

'The other party is named Mr Baxter. Two singles or two doubles, I don't care.'

I called Annie at her apartment. 'It's all set. I heard from the man. It's St Croix. Do you still want to go?'

'St Croix! That's fantastic! That's where Buck Island is! That's the best diving in the Caribbean! Will we have time to dive or will you be with Hughes all the time?'

'Annie, this is an open line. Don't even mention the name. The code word is Octavio. To answer your question, yes, we'll have time to dive. Bring all the gear and meet me here tomorrow at five o'clock.'

I called Beverly Loo at McGraw-Hill. 'I heard from Holmes. He's still flapping. I don't know what the hell is really going on, but he said he thinks he can arrange a meeting. I told him whatever happened I had to be in New York on Sunday night and he said not to worry. He wouldn't guarantee I'd see Octavio but he'd do his best and he'd definitely contact me. I'm supposed to catch a flight tomorrow afternoon and then sit in some hotel and wait. Bev, I don't want this to leak, or the press will

307

be there in full force. You know what that means. Octavio won't show.'

'You can trust me,' she said.

'St Croix.'

'St Croix! That's out in the Virgin Islands, isn't it? Why out there?'

'I don't know. Maybe he likes scuba diving. Maybe that's where he really lives,' I said, finding a sudden inspiration. 'He's sick, so if he were moving for medical reasons he certainly wouldn't go to an out-of-the-way island. Maybe that's where his private doctors are. Maybe, Bev, that's home.'

'And you've got to sit around in a hotel room and wait for him to call?'

I laughed. 'I'll take that blonde along for company.'

Beverly said tartly, 'At least you've still got your sense of humor. Octavio would love *that*. Just make sure that you're here on Monday morning. You're the star of this show now and you can't stay in hiding.'

'I'll be there,' I promised. 'I won't let you down.'

After I hung up I worked until midnight, when the last part of the manuscript was done. I stacked the papers, tore up the last bit of transcript, dumped it in the wastebasket, and then went downstairs to the bar for a drink. I felt weak and I was tired to the bone. It was a weariness that struck me without warning and the second cognac had no power to dispel it. I was in Miami Beach, in the bar of the Newport Beach Motel, and I didn't know why. I was alone at a bar surrounded by voices that couldn't reach me. On Monday morning I would be in New York, and there was no emotion I could feel except a dull dread; what a soldier must feel when he goes into battle outnumbered and poorly armed, but knowing he has no choice, he has to go, has to fight, duck, hide, fight again, and find rest wherever and whenever he can.

I had a last cognac and I knew that what I wanted

more than anything, right then, was to be at home: to be back in Ibiza with Edith and my kids and my funky, funny, cluttered house; to be at the core of my life and not dangling on the periphery. I paid the bar bill and wandered through the lobby with its sparkling colors and announcements of current attractions in the disco-theque. The core was back there on Ibiza with Edith. Hers was all the love that any sane man could need or want in one life. The rest was a game. I had to play. But when the din was too loud or I was too tired to go on, I wanted to go home,

I couldn't go home, and I had to be in New York on Monday morning. And in the meantime I would fly to St Croix with long-limbed blonde Annie, who was easy to be with and with whom I might bury a ghost. And I would pretend to wait for a man who wasn't there.

14

Confusion to Our Enemies

The weather was flawless; all storms were internal. Three or four times a day Annie stopped at the front desk of the King Christian Hotel in Christiansted, on the waterfront, to ask for messages: 'Are you *positive* no one's telephoned to Mr Irving?' Each time the clerk or the manager would shake his head wearily.

'I can't understand it,' Annie said to me.

'Neither can I.'

'Let's go diving. We'll get down to fifty feet and an old grayhaired man will come creeping out from behind a clump of brain coral. Then you'll meet Howard Hughes.'

We did that, but the only grayhaired man we met was the genial diving instructor who whipped us out in his speedboat to the reef off Buck Island. We floated lazily for two hours among the tropical fish and the coral and then returned to the King Christian. Annie checked at the front desk. No one had called.

'You don't seem worried,' she said, puzzled.

'I am, I am. But there's nothing I can do. I just have to wait.'

By Sunday afternoon, to my feigned amazement, neither Howard nor George Gordon Holmes had telephoned or contacted me. I had no choice but to board Pan Am's afternoon flight to New York. Annie had decided to stay on in St Croix an extra day. The relationship was over as quickly and casually as it had begun.

'Will I see you again?'

'*Inshallah*,' I said.

'What?'

'If I ever come back to Florida. Take care, Annie. You're a good girl.'

She looked a little miffed, then realized that I meant it, and she smiled as I got into the taxi for the airport.

Marty Ackerman had one of the most elegant homes in New York, a private white-fronted house on Park Avenue near 38th Street. Its seven stories were paneled in teak, the walls covered with Picassos and Dufys and old *Saturday Evening Post* covers, its sanctity guarded by closed-circuit television and one of the most elaborate burglarproof systems in the city – to the point where if you opened the wrong window at the wrong time the alarm sounded in both the protection agency and the local police precinct house. Marty installed me in a suite on the fifth floor and said: 'Make yourself at home,' and went out to dinner with his wife, Diane.

Dick called at ten o'clock Sunday evening, a few hours after my arrival. He was already unpacked in his room at the Commodore. 'How do you feel?' I asked.

'Beat. But I've seen the papers. I think I'd better come over.'

After I had showed him through the house we settled down in the study on the fifth floor. I brought him up to date and said, 'I think Howard's got to write another letter to Harold McGraw.'

Dick shook his head violently. 'I knew you were going to go off the goddam deep end here in New York. That's why I came over.' He argued with me for the next hour, and in the end I had to admit that his points were more sane than mine. The decision of the handwriting expert had clinched McGraw-Hill's belief that they were dealing with the real man. To take any further risks made no sense. The check was already in Zurich and probably by now on its way to Chase Manhattan for clearance. Moreover, we had had one extraordinary break – perfectly in keeping with the other absurdities that marked the history of the whole affair, but no less extraordinary. Noah Dietrich, from whom we expected the most trouble and suspicion, had told *The Los Angeles Times* that in his opinion the material was genuine. 'I heard,' he said, 'there was a writer, Irving, who had been invited by Hughes to the Bahamas.' He went on, according to other reports, to reveal that I had met Howard in the Britannia Beach Hotel and interviewed him with a glass partition between us.

Dick's eyes were glazed with fatigue. It was difficult to comprehend, much less assess, the rapidity of events. 'So get the manuscript in to McGraw-Hill and then get the hell out. What do they think of it?'

'They think it's sensational.'

'Then don't make waves,' Dick counseled. 'What about me? Am I here in New York now?'

'Why not? I called you in to help me with the editing. Who knows the material better than you do?'

'One thing more,' he said, coughing delicately. 'I had a little problem with Nina's car. I mean before I left Ibiza.'

Nina's station wagon had been parked for several weeks near the tunnel that led through the Roman wall to the Old Town. The best way to avoid meeting Edith by accident, Dick figured, was to spend the day in Santa Eulalia and return in time to put the car on the ferry for Palma, and then go on to Barcelona to start the trip across France to England.

A few minutes out of Ibiza on the road to Santa Eulalia, Dick came nose to nose, as it were, with Edith in the Mercedes. She had just dropped Nedsky off at the kindergarten in the village of Jesús. 'She recognized me and the car both,' Dick told me at Marty Ackerman's, 'so I turned around and went back to find her.'

Edith sat nursing a coffee at a sidewalk table outside the Bar Alhambra, filled with paranoid suspicions that Dick and I had conspired with Nina against her. Dick told her the truth – which was that he hadn't wanted her to see him driving Nina's car – and she calmed down.

'At least I *thought* she'd calmed down,' Dick said. 'But when I went over to Ibiza yesterday to pick up this goddam letter for you, she was all in a state again. She'd just gone up to the studio to get the letter, and she handed it to me and marched off without a word.'

'She'll be all right,' I said, puzzled but not particularly troubled. 'I'll square it with her when I get back.'

On Monday morning I appeared at McGraw-Hill and handed the last 133 pages to Robert Stewart for editing. A Xerox copy was given to Faustin Jehle for legal vetting. I was prepared for a mild panic but I found everyone in a sanguine mood, more amused than annoyed by events. John Cooke of the Legal Department had fired off a sharp letter to Richard Hannah of the Byoir Agency, who handled Hughes's public relations, demanding a retraction of their various statements to the effect that McGraw-Hill and I were 'either the victims or perpetrators of a gigantic hoax,' and threatening suit in the bargain.

The letter must have caused some second thoughts at the Byoir Agency, for Richard Hannah wrote back almost immediately, saying that he did not believe that McGraw-Hill would knowingly participate in the publication of an autobiography that was not genuine. And under such circumstances, retractions or denials were unnecessary and inappropriate.

Cooke seemed pleased with this response; and if he was pleased, I was pleased. Harold McGraw, on his part, had refused to speak to Chester Davis, the Hughes lawyer, who was calling almost daily. The newspapermen were being held at bay. I was given the 29th floor conference room of the Legal Department as an office. Robert Stewart journeyed up from the 20th floor. 'The new material is marvelous,' he said, 'and you've done a great editing job.'

'What do you think about this denial?'

'I predicted it,' Robert said. 'I think Hughes is just playing a huge joke at everybody's expense. It's absolutely in character. He'll never come out of the woodwork now. He's a devil. He knows we've got the contract and the canceled checks, and I think he's just sitting back laughing like hell.'

'If he's alive,' I said gloomily, and related the story of our missed rendezvous on St Croix.

That afternoon Albert Leventhal asked if I would say a few words at a sales luncheon the following day at the Hampshire House, and I agreed – 'if I have time,' I added, 'and there are no newspapermen there.'

A few minutes later I was called to the 32nd floor for a talk with Shelton Fisher and Bob Slaughter, another executive of McGraw-Hill, Inc., the parent company. I repeated the St Croix story and then Shelton backtracked to the week in Florida and the last two meetings with Hughes.

'You were blindfolded in broad daylight?' Shelton asked, incredulous.

'That's right.'

'Where were you sitting?'

'In the front seat, right next to Holmes.'

'But suppose you'd been stopped for speeding? Or some cop had seen the blindfold? How would this man Holmes have explained it?'

It was something I hadn't thought of and I was grateful to Shelton for pointing out the flaw. 'He told me to say that I was tired, the glare was bothering me, and I wanted to sleep.'

'It's wild,' Shelton said, chuckling. 'And this happened on the day you arrived?'

I had meant to shift that event to my second day in Florida, but Shelton seemed so positive that I couldn't remember whether I had told Beverly that it had been the day of my arrival or the second day, and it seemed safer to stick to the version Shelton believed.

'Yes,' I said. 'The day I arrived.'

It was a tiny mistake, and an unnecessary one; if Beverly had contradicted me I could easily have said she had misunderstood. But at the time, that day in Shelton Fisher's office, it seemed unimportant.

'I got married here,' I said to Dick, as we stepped out of the taxi in front of the Hampshire House. It was warm and sunny, more like April than December. Central Park South was thronged with lunchtime strollers from the nearby hotels and office buildings. Some girls wore shortsleeved Indian-summer dresses, and a few of the more adventurous men walked with their jackets slung over their arms.

'Yeah,' Dick said, 'which wife?'

'The first, wise guy. You only marry the first time in a hotel – when your father-in-law's paying the bill. After that you go very unostentatiously to City Hall. I've been married in more City Halls than anyone else I know.'

The McGraw-Hill luncheon was on the second floor of the Hampshire House in a private banquet room. The bartender shoved drinks in our hands as we entered, and I was whisked away by Beverly Loo and a woman I vaguely associated with Dell Books – or was it *Women's Wear Daily*? 'Circulate,' I called over my shoulder to Dick, 'but don't get drunk.'

Dick was no drinker – although once, in Houston, celebrating at Trader Vic's our finds in the morgues of the *Post* and *Chronicle*, he downed two enormous frothy violet concoctions with unpronounceable Polynesian names and I had to guide all 280 pounds of him back to the hotel, while he cursed all things Texan and mooned for his wife and son in faraway Mallorca. There in the Hampshire House, that balmy December day, he had the same glazed look in his eyes. I knew exactly how he felt. I, too, felt as though I were walking onto a movie set. My God, I thought, looking around, what hath Irving wrought – and immediately amended it to Irvkind. What hath Irvkind wrought? I liked the ring of it, but was stupefied by the apparent enormity of the forces we had set in motion, dating back almost exactly a year to that innocent breakfast meeting in Palma de Mallorca, when I had said: 'Hey, listen, I've got a wild idea . . .'

Some 200 people were present, almost all of them McGraw-Hill employees. They ranged from executives in the Trade Book Division to salesmen from Chicago, Denver, and San Francisco. I spotted Albert Leventhal, cheerfully chatting with Ed Kuhn, a former holder of Albert's job and now running Playboy Books. There were dozens of other familiar faces – editors, department heads, peripheral figures in the Jolly Green Giant of publishing – milling about with drinks in their hands.

The walls were lined with six-foot photographic reproductions. There was Jean Harlow, showing a nice bit of cleavage; Jane Russell in a scene from *The Outlaw*, showing more; Our Man in Nassau looking determinedly handsome and wearing the helmet and goggles of a pilot of the thirties. Above all, stunning in their impact, hung several gigantic reproductions of the book's dust jacket – white with stark black lettering. There was nothing hesitant or crafty about that book jacket; it flashed forth its message with all the vigor and certainty of a newspaper headline. *THE AUTO-BIOGRAPHY OF HOWARD HUGHES: INTRODUCTION AND COMMENTARY BY CLIFFORD IRVING*. I felt an idiotic grin starting to form and took another gulp of bourbon on the rocks to kill it. All these people are taking this seriously, I reminded myself. You'd better do the same. Don't crack, and don't crack up – or you've had it.

Several months ago, after we had vanquished that first frightening challenge created by Messrs Post and Eaton – whose book was destined never to be published – Dick had said to me: 'Look is it possible that McGraw-Hill has figured it out? That they're playing the game because they know we'll all come out winners? That they really *know*?'

'That it's a hoax? My God, never. No way.'

Dick arched an eyebrow. 'Are you sure?'

'Absolutely sure – I think.'

'It's got to occur to them. How can they be so naive?'

'Because they *believe*. First they wanted to believe, and now they have to believe. They want to believe because it's such a coup for them, it's weird and wild, it's Howard Hughes and the Richest Man in the World and they're personally, vicariously, in cahoots with him. They can identify because they like Oreo cookies, too, and they can marvel because Howard pisses away $137 million without a second thought. That's the way *they'd* like to live. Can't you see what an ego trip it is? The secrecy part – the thing that protects you and me – is what they love the most. That takes them out of the humdrum into another world, the world we all dream of living in, only we really don't want to because we know it's mad. And the greatest thing for them is that this way they can live in it part time. They're participating but they're protected by an intermediary. I'm their buffer between reality and fantasy. It's a fairy tale, a dream. And the beauty part for them is that they'll make money out of it, too. Corporate profit justifies any form of lunacy. There's been no other hoax like it in modern times – it's like that crazy guy in *Catch-22*, Milo Minderbinder, who was doing business all over Europe during the war – doing business with both the Americans and the Germans – but it was okay, *because everybody had a share.* Everybody benefits. Even Howard, in this case, because he becomes a folk-hero and gets a better auto-biography than he could ever write himself.'

'Or than he deserves. What a sonofabitch he must really be. Boy, if anyone knows, *we* know.' Dick's eyes glinted mischievously. 'But I still think you may be wrong. When it's over, when you deliver the book and they hand you the last check, they'll pat you on the back and give you a big wink, and Harold McGraw will say: "Good job, kid. We knew you could pull it off. Just make sure you pay the taxes."' Dick broke up laughing, and so did I. It was a sweet vision to contemplate. But then I stopped and shook my head.

'Never. They're straight. They're the Establishment. They believe. They've got to believe or they'd never get a night's sleep.'

And now that it was over, now that The Book was in the hopper and 'Project Octavio' a success beyond any-one's hopes, we could see that I had been diabolically right: they believed. Never mind that Hughes Tool had denied, never mind that Chester Davis thundered daily threats by hand-delivered letter and over the tele-phone to Harold McGraw, John Cooke, and Marty Ackerman. Belief had metamorphosed into something that bordered on religious faith. The luncheon at the Hampshire House was a feast of thanksgiving, for faith and toil had brought forth a bountiful harvest. So joyous was the hour that even the moneychangers were admitted to the temple.

We saw this, Dick and I, and we wandered among the throng of well-wishers, hardly daring to look into each other's eyes. A feeling of solemn lunacy pervaded. It was almost no longer possible to distinguish between illusion and reality; and, if we were ultimately successful, that distinction would vanish altogether. That in itself, I thought, would be an achievement worth carrying to the grave in silence. It contained a seed of bitterness, too, for the world could be fooled and mocked too easily. What hath Irvkind wrought?

The meal was typical banquet fare: rubber chicken and fat green peas, the kind Howard despised. 'Where's your silver rake?' Dick called to me from across the table. I waved him to silence. He was referring to the tiny silver rake Howard used to comb through the peas on his plate. Those small enough to pass between the tines, he ate. The others he left.

About halfway through the main course, a couple of men placed a microphone nearby. Jesus Christ, I remembered in a panic, they expect me to make a speech. I'll screw up, I know I'll say the wrong thing. I stood up – fortunately Albert Leventhal, sitting beside me and gnawing hungrily at a drumstick, was deep in an anecdote about his last telephone conversation with Chester Davis – and walked over to Dick, who was listening with a bored expression to the ecstatic sales figures being thrown at him by the man at his left.

'You're the hero of the hour,' Dick said, grinning.

'I forgot about the speech. What'll I say? I'm half-pissed. Give me an opening line.'

Dick thought for a moment. 'Okay, after the usual introductory bullshit, say: "Chester Davis may disagree, but from what I've heard at this luncheon this book is obviously the biggest thing to come down the pike since The Bible. I can say that to you without blushing, because I'm not the author." Then finish up on the right note. Say: "In conclusion, I give you Howard's favorite toast: *L'chayem*."'

'I can't do that,' I whispered. 'They know he's not Jewish.'

'So tell them he's Jewish. The best-kept secret of modern times. They'll believe anything.'

I slid back into my seat as Albert Leventhal was

finishing his anecdote. '. . . He demanded to see the manuscript. I said I was sorry. He kept asking for more information and I said, "It's all in the press release, Mr Davis." He kept asking if I couldn't give him something more, and I said: "How about syphilis?"'

'You didn't actually say that, did you, Al?' asked the man on the other side of him, speaking over the burst of nervous laughter.

'No,' Leventhal said mournfully, 'but I wish I had.'

Immediately following the dessert – a coconut ball which I liberally doused with chocolate syrup – Leventhal stepped to a nearby podium and made a speech. Richard Hannah, he explained, PR-man for Hughes Tool, had already denounced the autobiography as a fraud, but McGraw-Hill knew that Hannah spoke in ignorance. They *knew*. They had the literary coup of the decade, if not the half-century. They knew that Howard Hughes had kept his meetings with Clifford Irving secret from even his closest associates. How did they know? Irving had told them so. 'And moreover,' Leventhal explained, 'I can now reveal to you that Mr Hughes himself has been in written communication with a top McGraw-Hill executive and has empowered us to act in his behalf should any such quasi-legal challenges arise.'

A murmur of approval rippled through the banquet room. '. . . And we who have had the privilege of reading the manuscript,' Leventhal continued, 'know that it would take a Shakespeare to invent such a work. And as much as I admire our author, Clifford Irving, he is no Shakespeare.' Everyone laughed politely, except me. I was flattered, and at the same time mildly annoyed. *Listen, Albert, knock it off. I've got a little surprise for you.* But I held my tongue and restrained a frown as Dick, from across the table, flashed two fingers at me. A casual onlooker would have taken it as a V-for-Victory sign. I knew he meant '*two* Shakespeares.' So I smiled with proper humility.

There were murmurs of further approval, and even awe, when Leventhal announced that the Book-of-the-Month Club had just agreed to pay the largest price in their history – $350,000 – as advance against royalties for the rights to the *Autobiography*. More nods and tongue-clucking followed when Leventhal said that Dell Books had bought the reprint rights for an advance of $400,000 – although this figure, as Beverly Loo loudly remarked, was a steal. 'If Hughes hadn't wanted so much money up front,' she had bitterly complained on several occasions, 'we could have waited for galleys and put the book up for bids in February. I know I could have squeezed them for six hundred thousand, maybe even as much as seven fifty . . .'

Leventhal finished with a little joke, and then introduced me. I took a deep breath and walked up to the microphone. I waited for the applause to die down and then began. I had had an inspiration, possibly resulting from the combination of bourbon and wine. 'I don't really deserve to be up here,' I said, truthfully, 'and it's a little frightening. There are a lot of people sitting in this room, people like Ed Kuhn and Beverly Loo, who knew me when I was just a novelist and a bum. Well, I had an inspiration and a few lucky breaks, that's all. And,' I said prophetically, 'when all this is over I have every intention of becoming a novelist and a bum again.'

I launched quickly into a generalized discussion of the book, dropping a few tidbits concerning my meeting with Hughes, offering as little of substance as possible; tossing out accolades, whenever I felt myself wandering into trouble, to the various members of the Trade Book Division whose serious, thoughtful faces regarded me, remembering all I had learned in my days of lecturing at UCLA and the California Palace of the Legion of Honor in San Francisco. After the luncheon, when I was mopping my brow, Ed Kuhn said to me wryly, 'Don't look so hangdog – you did great. Best speech I've heard in years. You spoke for fifteen minutes without saying a damn thing.'

At the end of the ordeal I raised my glass and said: 'And in conclusion, ladies and gentlemen, I can do no better than to offer you Howard Hughes's favorite toast – although he prefers skim milk and Poland Springs mineral water to bourbon.' *L'chayem* formed in my palate, but I held it back. There was such a thing as going too far.

'Confusion to our enemies,' I said stoutly.

I saw Dick sputter in his cup of coffee and hide his face in a napkin to keep from laughing. Basking in the warm glow of applause, I returned to my seat. Albert Leventhal leaned toward me: 'You really should have mentioned Dick Suskind, don't you think? It would be a nice gesture.'

'I certainly should have.' I stood up again, tapped a spoon against my glass for silence, and said: 'Last, but by no means least, I have to give credit where credit is due . . . as Howard would say. I'd like you all to meet my researcher, Richard Suskind, an author in his own right and a man who stood by my side all the way. And without whom, I can truthfully say, I could not have done the job I did and this would not be the book it is. Let's give Dick a hand, which he richly deserves.'

A red-faced, smiling Dick half rose in his chair, wearing the gold jockey shirt he had bought in Pompano Beach, clasped his hands above his head like a benign Primo Carnera who had just KO'ed Jack Sharkey, bowed right and left, and sat down again. There was more appreciative applause. Dick's round face split with a grin of delight. Albert Leventhal patted me on the arm and nodded. 'Good,' he said. 'That was nice.'

When Dick and I made our escape, about fifteen or twenty minutes later – 'Sorry,' I said gravely, to one and all, 'but we have to get back to the shop and work' – we took a wrong turn in the hallway and opened the door on a roomful of salesmen being addressed from another podium by Leventhal: '. . . and Irving's right. If the opening gun orders from bookshops are less than 150,000 copies, then I've got to say you men are in the wrong business. Now let's break the figures down region by region . . .' We hurriedly closed the door and walked toward the street.

'Jesus,' Dick said. 'Do you believe all this?'

I shook my head slowly. 'I'll tell you – it's hard. But they're convincing me. It's going to happen.'

We gulped the fresh, crisp air, It was noticeably colder than when we had entered the hotel, but nothing could chill our spirits. We knew that back there in the Hampshire House the machinery was inexorably in motion, the wheels were turning. The sunlit sweep of Central Park, with the hansom cabs lined up outside the Plaza, looked like a painting done by a child. Out here it was fantasy now; back in there, real.

'How many copies are they figuring to sell?' Dick prodded me.

'That's what Leventhal asked me. They had a production meeting, and I was there, and they were trying to figure it out, and he turned to me and said, "How many copies do you think we'll sell, Cliff?" I said: "415,000 the first year." He said to the production manager, "Okay, we'll do a first printing of 150,000." Now they've upped it to 200,000, and with the Book-of-the-Month Club they have to do a run of half a million. That's just the first printing, you understand.'

Dick looked puzzled. 'Why did he ask you the sales figures? What the hell do you know about that sort of thing?'

'Absolutely nothing. Whenever they need the answer to a question these days they ask me, and they take what I say as gospel. It's insane. But it's happening.'

'Why did you say 415,000?'

'I don't know. I pulled it out of a hat. It was the first

figure that popped into my head. It sounded pretty good, didn't it?'

Dick blinked as we jumped into a taxi and I gave the address of the McGraw-Hill Building. 'Jesus,' he said again. There was no blasphemy in his tone, only reverence for something beyond our control or understanding. 'You may be right,' he murmured. 'They may publish the damn thing . . .'

'Who the hell can stop it?' I said quietly.

The beginning of the answer to my question came sooner than expected – late that same afternoon. The mood of dazed euphoria continued throughout the day, which Dick and I spent working on the manuscript in the conference room on the 29th floor of the McGraw-Hill Building. Robert Stewart, the editor of the book, felt I had effaced myself too efficiently and modestly from the dialogue and he said: 'Beef up your questions. Make them more searching. They're too thin and staccato.'

'You mean go back to the original questions in the transcripts? The ones you told me to take out?'

'Well, yes,' he admitted. 'Something like that.'

McGraw-Hill's lawyers were giving the book a simultaneous reading, and they marched into our office every day with more and more suggested changes. A libelous passage about Norris Poulsen, the ex-mayor of Los Angeles, had to be excised in its entirety. The Nixon episode had to be modified slightly, as much for libel as for political considerations. Hughes's description of Lyndon Johnson's 'climbing out of the White House swimming pool with his giant-sized Texas pecker hanging out' had to be chopped. 'Johnson is a private citizen now,' Faustin Jehle explained to me. 'He could sue.'

'Would you sue if you were nearly seventy years old and someone said you had a giant-sized Texas pecker?'

Jehle conceded the point but still insisted. 'The book is

packed with good material. Taking out a few question-able remarks won't hurt it. Let's not invite trouble if we don't have to.'

I argued for every point. I was fighting for the integrity of my own work, not Howard's, and that made me stubborn to the point where Jehle often wondered why I battled with such ferocity against a possible emasculation of the text. 'Look,' he explained, 'Hughes is talking here about how much he manipulated the stock of TWA on the New York Stock Exchange so that he could exercise his option more cheaply. Now I'm sure it's true or he wouldn't have said it, but TWA could have a stockholders' suit on their hands.'

'Faustin, he'll kill me if I take that out. The man set out to tell the truth. I can't, in conscience, dilute it.'

'And what about this business where he says he paid $100,000 to the Democratic Party to get that indictment quashed?' Jehle was referring to an alleged fraud on the part of Hughes Aircraft in 1948, whereby the company had used veterans' priorities to buy surplus C-47's cheaply and then converted them to luxury aircraft for businessmen. 'His own company could get into trouble on that little hanky-panky.'

'Twenty years later?'

'It's possible. It certainly won't do their reputation any good.'

'I guess he just doesn't give a damn,' I maintained. 'The man's honest.'

'I've read the manuscript,' Jehle said. 'He's also crazy.'

'Is that the feeling you get out of it?'

'It's a conclusion that's hard to avoid. He puts a leaded glass screen in front of his TV set to cut out the gamma rays. He says that everyone and his uncle is out to kill him and the price on his head is half a million dollars. Is that the talk of a completely sane man?'

I mulled that over. 'I'll have to trim down those parts,

I don't want the reader to have that impression. I owe that much to Howard.'

Jehle stopped by my office that afternoon, too, worried about the latest hysterical letter from Chester Davis. 'Didn't you tell Beverly Loo,' he asked, 'that someone who was with you had met Hughes by accident out in California?'

Dick looked up from the end of the table, where he was correcting and revising fresh anecdotes that I had added to the manuscript in Florida. 'Me,' he said. 'He offered me a prune.'

'He did what?'

'He offered me a prune.'

'I see,' Jehle said wearily. 'Would you mind making a statement to that effect?'

'Not at all.'

Jehle brought in a secretary, and Dick dictated a brief version of the incident we had concocted during that strange weekend in Palm Springs. The secretary typed it and brought back three copies. Jehle read one, shaking his head half in amusement and half in bewilderment, then gave them to Dick to sign.

'That's not quite the way it happened,' Dick said, frowning as he scanned the page. 'I didn't ask him if the prune was organic. *He* said it was organic. And he didn't take it out of a cellophane bag. It was a brown paper bag.'

'No,' I said, 'it was a cellophane bag.' I explained to Jehle: 'We always have this argument. We never can agree. He says cellophane and I say paper.'

'The other way round,' Dick corrected me.

'Not important,' Jehle said. He took the three signed copies into his office and returned with them notarized. By then I thought he had the impression that Hughes had infected us and we were *all* slightly crazy.

'I can just see my picture in *Time*' Dick said, 'with one of their cutesy captions underneath: *Offered a Prune*. Do you think I could do a television commercial for Sunsweet? *"Howard Hughes and I prefer organic prunes. But if you can't find an organic prune in your neighborhood grocery, the next best thing is Sunsweet."* What do you think?'

'Could be,' Faustin said. He left, still shaking his head.

The rest of the afternoon passed swiftly, while we worked, until just after five o'clock when the telephone rang. It was Beverly Loo, calling from the 20th floor. 'Get down here right away,' she snapped.

I had never heard her so grim. 'What's going on?'

'Just get down here. This is urgent.'

I swallowed hard. 'Look, everyone's gone from the Legal Department and I can't leave the manuscript lying around the table. This is all top-secret stuff. You better tell me what it's all about.'

Beverly rapped and I listened. I hung up the telephone and turned to Dick, who looked apprehensive. He had already popped a gout pill into his mouth while I was waiting for Beverly to finish. 'I don't think I want to know,' he said. 'I think I'm catching the night plane for Madrid.'

'No, you're going with me. I need you. The shit is about to hit the fan.'

'Then let's duck while the ducking's good.'

'We can't,' I said hoarsely. 'We've got to brazen it out. Listen to this.'

Less than ten minutes ago Ralph Graves of *Life* had called Albert Leventhal to advise him that Chester Davis – acting as Hughes's principal spokesman – had telephoned an hour previously to Don Wilson, the Time, Inc. publicity director. Davis had claimed that Howard Hughes wanted to talk to Frank McCulloch, New York Bureau Chief of *Time*. McGulloch was the last reporter to have interviewed Hughes – some time in the late 1950's – and had evidently had intermittent telephone conversations with him since that date. According to Chester Davis, Hughes wanted to discuss seven points: six to do with the situation in Nevada, and the seventh regarding the book to be published by McGraw-Hill. Davis would place the call himself from the Time-Life Building between 5:30 and 6 p.m. Graves had told Leventhal: 'I think you'd better get over here in a hurry, and bring Irving. We've agreed to go through with it.'

Dick and I locked up the material for the night and went downstairs. Leventhal, Beverly, and Robert Stewart waited by the elevators, already wearing their coats. Before anyone could talk, I launched into the attack.

'Why the hell did Graves and Wilson agree to this? It's just Davis' way of getting a confrontation. He's no more going to call Hughes than I am. For Christ's sake, he's never even *met* Hughes in his entire life. It's a trap,' I grumbled, 'a ploy, and those guys from *Life* just stepped into it.'

It was no bluff on my part; I half believed it when I set out from the 29th floor, and by the time the elevator had reached the 20th floor I was completely convinced.

'I agree,' Beverly said angrily. 'Why are they butting into our business? It's *our* book, not theirs. We should insist that they call it off.'

'We're late,' Leventhal muttered, as he fumbled for the keys to his car in the parking lot next to the McGraw-Hill Building. Albert seemed to have developed a nervous tic since I had last seen him only a few hours before, holding forth cheerfully at the salesmen's luncheon. He grimaced repeatedly, as though false teeth were pinching his gums. Squeezed into the back seat between Dick and myself, Robert Stewart chattered on and on, as Leventhal maneuvered through traffic and nearly scraped a dozen fenders on the way to Rockefeller Plaza. 'Isn't this the most . . . I mean, really! . . . what do they think they're doing? . . . It can't be Hughes, and if it is . . . I mean, why do you think he's acting this way, Cliff?'

'He'll never get through to him,' I said. 'We'll hang around there till midnight while Davis goes through his wounded boar routine.'

I had never thought of Beverly as inscrutable. No mysteries of the East were contained in that round, open, pleasant face. Usually she was more of a talker than even Robert. Now, however, she silently glowered in the front seat next to Leventhal.

Graves, Maness, Wilson, a Time, Inc. lawyer named Jack Dowd, and one other unknown man were waiting for us in Wilson's plush executive office. I walked in casually, unshaven, my overcoat slung over my shoulder. Graves, who looked pale and solemn, said to me abruptly: 'Cliff, this is Frank McCulloch.'

A little startled, I stuck out my hand and said, 'Hello, Frank.'

'Mr Irving . . .'

McCulloch nodded and shook hands. He had a hard grip. He was a man of about fifty, tall, ruggedly built, with eyes to match his handshake and a completely shaven, knobby skull that gleamed and rippled almost as though it were made of muscle. He looked at me coldly. He didn't want to know me, and he had nothing more to say to me. I suddenly found that I had nothing to say to him, either. He spoke to the others: he was from the south or southwest, I judged, with a swift, rasping voice that grated like a file on metal. He was tough, and he was the enemy. Until now the enemies had been gentle, sympathetic, believing, and the weapons I needed were almost too easy to come by. But McCulloch didn't believe, and I had no weapon. Under that hard stare I felt weak and vulnerable, an amateur in the ring with a professional. Don Wilson was busily attaching a tape recorder to the telephone.

'You're going to tape the conversation,' I said, to no one in particular.

'Absolutely,' Graves replied.

'Good idea,' I said.

'If the goddam thing works,' McCulloch growled.

'I want to hear it afterwards,' I said to Graves, 'if Davis really makes the call.' I managed to draw Dick aside for a moment and whispered, 'Listen. If there's anyone on the other end of that line, no matter who it is, I'm going to yell that it's not Hughes. If the voice is strong, I'll say Hughes's voice is weaker, and if it's weak, I'll say Hughes's voice is stronger. Take your cues from me if you get a chance. Just back me up.'

Dick nodded. 'What if they want you to talk to him?'

'I'll ask for the code word and when he can't give it I'll say, "Good try, but you're a goddam phony," and then I'll hang up.'

'Get ready to fight your way out of the room,' Dick counseled. 'I'll block for you.'

Davis and two lawyers from his Wall Street office were due to arrive in five minutes. The presence of a gang was deemed undesirable, as was a confrontation between Davis and myself. Graves, Maness, Stewart, Leventhal, Beverly, Dick, and I were herded down the hall to another office, where we dispossessed its puzzled owner and sat down to wait. I was behind the desk, doodling on a pad of paper, when I realized to my horror that it was a pad of yellow lined legal paper and I was unconsciously – for my mind was in the office next door with McCulloch and Wilson – writing the signature of Howard R. Hughes. No one was looking at me; they were silent, with Dick slumped on the couch next to Beverly and Albert. I tore off the sheet of paper, folded it carefully, and put it in my back pocket. After a few minutes I went to the door, opened it and poked my head out. I saw three men, one of them ruddy-faced, gesticulating and talking in a loud voice, marching toward me from the bank of elevators. I ducked back in and swiftly shut the door.

'There's Davis,' I said jauntily. 'With his Praetorian guard.'

The jauntiness deserted me ten minutes later. Ralph Graves had stepped out of the room. He came back a minute later to say that he hadn't gone in to Wilson's office, but that he had stood outside the door for a moment and heard Frank McCulloch's voice. 'He was on the telephone,' Graves said ominously. 'They're talking. The call's gone through.'

'McCulloch hasn't seen Hughes since 1957,' I said. 'How could he possibly recognize the voice?'

'He spoke to him six years ago,' Ralph said, looking straight at me.

Twenty more minutes passed. The tension inside me built to a point where I thought I would either burst or faint. Dick, on the couch, looked like a gray mammoth, gutshot, and about to sag to his death. I had told everyone present that we had a dinner date with the Ackermans, which was true, and that we were already late. I stood up suddenly and said: 'This is a farce. I'm damned if I'll wait. You're taping it, so I'll come round tomorrow and listen, and I'll tell you if it was Hughes or not.' Dick got quickly to his feet.

The coolness and aplomb must have been impressive, because no one objected to our leaving. They would have kept me there by brute force if they could have peered past my poker face to the terror within. 'Call me from the restaurant,' Graves said. 'I'll tell you what happened.'

The door closed behind us and Dick clutched my arm, eyeballs rolling in their sockets like Zero Mostel. 'Walk swiftly, don't run, to the nearest exit.'

We tried the glass doors leading to the bank of elevators and found them locked. It was long past closing time for the building. 'How the hell do we get out of here?' Dick asked, an edge of panic in his voice. We found the emergency staircase. It was locked.

'Oh, my God,' he groaned. 'We're trapped in the Time-Life Building.'

'Go back in there and ask Graves for the key.'

'You go back. I'd rather jump.'

We heard a clanking sound coming from the far end of the hall and half ran, half walked in that direction. A janitor stood by the freight elevator, swishing a mop in a pail. We stepped past him into the elevator and he said, 'Sorry, no passengers.' I explained that the door to the main elevators was locked. He shrugged and clanked his bucket. 'Listen,' I said sharply, 'we've got to get out of here right now. We're on a special assignment. Plane to catch . . . Washington.'

'Brazil,' I heard Dick mutter.

The janitor took us to the ground floor. We ducked out of the building, into the rain and icy wind, and hailed a taxi. I pulled my collar up around my face while Dick slumped in the corner of the seat, looking like a man in shock.

'Are you okay?'

'Yeah, I think so – just.' He shook his head slowly. 'You know . . . you know what it is that's so stunning? They're real. All those people we wrote about – they're real, they *exist*. They walk around in clothes. They're flesh and blood. They speak. All these months I've been thinking they were people we created, characters in a novel. But that was the real Chester Davis, that loud-mouthed bastard you saw in the hallway. And that baldheaded guy with eyes like marbles was Frank McCulloch. I mean really Frank McCulloch. *The* Frank McCulloch, not *our* Frank McCulloch.'

It had hit me, too, but I had not been able to articulate it. 'Yeah,' I said, 'and one thing more. Try to swallow this one. That was Howard Hughes on the other end of the line.'

'Howard Hughes?' Dick said weakly. 'The billionaire?'

*   *   *

332

Marty and Diane Ackerman were waiting for us in the restaurant. Marty listened to my tale, saying little. I looked at my watch. 'I promised to call Graves,' I explained.

Beverly Loo answered on the second ring. 'It's all over,' she said, and her voice had a hollow ring. 'Frank McCulloch wants to talk to you.'

McCulloch got on the line and said, without preamble: 'I have to tell you, first of all, that to the best of my knowledge that was Hughes I spoke to. The voice is unmistakeable, as I assume you know.'

I ducked that one. 'Where was he?'

'Davis placed the call on his credit card. To Paradise Island, he claimed.'

'And what did Howard have to say?'

'Among other things, that he'd never met anyone named Clifford Irving in his whole life, that he'd never even heard of Clifford Irving until a few days ago, and that he'd never met your father. He also said that he had information that checks that were supposedly going to him were being cashed outside this country, and he was going to find out all the facts, and that he was going to prosecute you to the full extent of the law.'

'I can't believe it,' I said. 'It couldn't have been him.'

'It was him,' McCulloch repeated. 'I asked him two trap questions, and he got them both right. It was him, and he says he never met you.'

'I'll tell you if it was him, after I've heard the tape,' I said bravely.

'There was no tape. Hughes wouldn't allow it. There's a meeting tomorrow morning at ten o'clock at McGraw-Hill. We'll all be there, and Leventhal says he'll expect you to be there, too.'

'Sure,' I promised. 'So long, Frank.'

'So long, Cliff,' he said quietly.

He hung up. Beverly Loo reported to me later that he turned to the small gang of McGraw-Hill and *Time-Life* people who were listening to his end of the conversation.

'He's scared shitless,' he said to them. 'And off the top of my head, I have to tell you – I think your man's a phony.'

15

Confusion to Our Allies

Marty Ackerman refused to let me go alone to McGraw-Hill the following morning. 'You're going to need help,' he said. 'They'll take you over the coals if you're on your own, but if you've got an attorney with you they'll have to be careful.'

'You're going to get awfully involved, Marty.'

He shrugged. 'I'll give you all the help I can.'

The meeting took place in one of the executive conference rooms. Clustered about the huge board room table were two members of the McGraw-Hill legal staff, Harold McGraw, Albert Leventhal, Time, Inc.'s lawyer, Ralph Graves, Frank McCulloch, Marty, and myself. McCulloch looked red-eyed and tired. He had been up half the night, he explained, reading the first third of the autobiography. He took command of the interrogation.

'I've got the best damn file on Howard Hughes that exists,' he said. 'It's in my cellar and I've been collecting it for the last twenty years.' He addressed himself to the McGraw-Hill contingent. 'I'll have to tell you this – most of what I read in the manuscript checks out against the facts. But those facts are available to anyone who would take a lot of time and trouble to research them.'

Everyone stirred uncomfortably. I said nothing.

'However,' McCulloch rasped, 'there's one thing that

manuscript contains that Cliff couldn't have gotten from any pile of newspaper clippings. That's the authentic voice of Howard Hughes. I know that voice. I know the way the man speaks, his turns of phrase, his idioms, his quirks. It's unique, it can't be duplicated. If I were placed before a court of law, I'd have to say that to the best of my knowledge and belief that material could only have come directly to Cliff from Howard.'

Everyone seemed to relax. Then McCulloch focused on me. 'I don't want you to be insulted, but I have to ask you a few questions. I just want to get the story straight about your meetings.'

'Fire away,' I said.

He asked me questions and I talked for the better part of an hour, going over the now all-too-familiar tale of the Mexican meeting, the Puerto Rican meeting, the tape-recording sessions in Nassau, Beverly Hills, and Pompano Beach. Every time I described one of Howard's foibles and kinks, or quoted some earthy bit of dialogue, McCulloch chuckled with appreciation. He was with me, I believed, and I had a lock on this hand of the poker game; but still I decided to uncover my hidden ace.

'He talked about you once, Frank. He once had a long conversation with you, I think it was back in 1957 or '58, when he wanted to call off an article that *Fortune* was supposed to run on him. He must have taped it, because he had a transcript of what he said. He talked about some *Fortune* writer named Murphy who wanted to bury an axe in his skull.' I snapped my fingers, as if the thought had only then occurred to me. 'And I remember one of the last things he said to you in that phone call, because it struck me as so peculiar. He said, "Whatever happens, Frank, you and I will still be friends, right?"'

'Goddamit,' McCulloch said slowly. 'That's just about exactly what he said.' He turned to the men in the room, nodding his head. 'Well, I'm satisfied that Cliff's met him. I never told anyone else about that conversation.

336

He had to get it from me or Howard, and I never spoke to Cliff in my life until last night.'

I sat back in my chair, astonished. I knew that the transcript of the conversation I had just quoted had been sent to the president of Time, Inc. in a confidential memo, and that memo had made its way through unknown means to Noah Dietrich. I also guessed that it had been yanked from the *Time-Life* files before Dave Maness had let me photograph them; and I knew that Maness, in the Elysee, had read my re-punctuated version of it and said to Ralph Graves: 'It's good.' But Graves, now in the conference room, said nothing. Could he have known that McCulloch was wrong?

'There's just one thing,' I went on, looking McCulloch hard in the eye and trying to rake in the whole pile of chips at one time. 'Are you *positive* it was Hughes you spoke to last night?'

'It was a bad connection,' Frank said stoutly, 'but if I went before that same court of law, I'd have to say that to the best of my knowledge and belief it was Howard Hughes on the telephone.'

'You couldn't have been fooled?'

'It's within the realm of possibility,' he admitted.

I started to laugh. 'Frank, if you got before that court of law and swore that you'd spoken to Hughes and he'd denied ever meeting me, and then you swore that you thought the manuscript was from Howard and that you were sure I'd met him – hell, they'd commit you to the loony bin.'

'No.' McCulloch spoke with renewed confidence. 'Because it's entirely consistent with the personality of Howard Hughes to do just that – to dictate his auto-biography and then deny it.' For the first time he grinned at me, 'Jesus, Cliff, you know the man. Am I right or wrong?'

There was nothing to do but shrug and admit that he had a point.

One final point was made that rocked me almost as much as Frank McCulloch's statement that he had never told anyone else about his 1958 conversation with Howard Hughes. The question arose as to what would be Chester Davis' next move following yesterday's telephoned denial by Hughes. Davis would announce it to the press, we decided. How would McGraw-Hill retaliate?

'We've got the ammunition,' Jehle said. 'We've got Cliff's contracts with Hughes, the letters to Cliff, the letter to Harold, the letter authorizing us to publish, Hughes's comments all over the transcript, and the expert's statement that the odds are a million to one against anyone else but Hughes having written that material. Not to mention the text of the book, which speaks for itself and could only have come from Hughes.' In the event of a court battle, however, McGraw-Hill was loathe to make the bulk of the material available to public record and adamant against any disclosure of the manuscript itself, which was precisely what Davis and his law firm were clamoring for. 'And of course,' Jehle added, 'we've got the final proof in the form of the canceled check for $275,000.'

Jack Dowd, Time, Inc.'s lawyer, asked a question that surprised me, since I had assumed that he and everyone at the conference already knew the answer.

'Where did Hughes cash that check?'

'The Swiss Credit Bank in Zurich,' Jehle said.

'A numbered account?'

'No. We have a photostat of a check for $100,000 that he drew on the account when he was trying to pay us back. He has his name printed on the check.'

'And,' Albert Leventhal said to Dowd, 'that $275,000 check – that's McGraw-Hill's check to Hughes – has a bank-documented signature. Documented, in fact, by *two* banks – the Swiss Credit Bank in Zurich and Chase Manhattan here in New York.'

Dowd and everyone else nodded, satisfied. I ducked my head and began shuffling papers back into my briefcase. I knew that Leventhal was wrong. I had seen a photostat of the back of the check. The Swiss Credit Bank had affixed their stamp under the forged signature of H.R. Hughes; it said: *Pay to the order of any Bank, Banker or Trust Company: Prior endorsements guaranteed* – which meant simply that they guaranteed the endorsement to be that of the holder of the account. Chase Manhattan's stamp, placed on the back of the check after its receipt for clearance by the Swiss Credit Bank, read: *Endorsements guaranteed.* What that referred to, of course, was the fact that the Swiss Credit Bank had offered a prior endorsement; it was no guarantee or documentation of any kind on the part of Chase Manhattan, who had no way of knowing not only whether or not the signature was genuine, and no knowledge whatsoever that the account belonged to Howard Robard Hughes.

It was an easy mistake to make and Leventhal, who was anxious to wrap up the meeting, certainly had no intention of trying to mislead the *Time-Life* contingent. A publisher and editor could hardly be expected to have an expert's knowledge of bankers' jargon. On that note of welcome misinterpretation, accepted without question by everyone present, the meeting broke up. I hustled back to my office on the 29th floor and called Dick at the Commodore.

'Are we alive?'

'Alive and well,' I said. 'Cancel your reservation to Brazil and get the hell over here. We've got work to do.'

That weekend I drove with Marty and Diane Ackerman to their house in Lakeville, Connecticut. The hullabaloo all week long had made it almost impossible to edit the manuscript at McGraw-Hill; and over the weekend, in Marty's study, I accomplished more than I had been able to do in the five preceding days. Friday morning, just before I left the city, Ralph Graves called me. He was surprised I hadn't been in touch with Frank McCulloch since Wednesday's meeting. 'Frank's a little hurt,' he said. 'I know he'd like to talk to you some more. Why don't you call him?'

I smelled the setup immediately, but I called Frank from Connecticut on Saturday and made a Monday afternoon appointment with him at McGraw-Hill. Casually, he mentioned that he had 'a few more' questions to ask.

On Monday morning I told Faustin Jehle of the impending conversation. 'No good,' Jehle said, 'unless I'm there. And I want it taped. McCulloch's a *Time* reporter and it's got to be off-the-record, all of it. I'm going to stipulate that the conversation is an attorney's work-product, which means that everything that's said is confidential. It belongs to McGraw-Hill, and only McGraw-Hill can quote from it.'

When McCulloch arrived that afternoon I explained that I had wanted a private conversation but the legal boys had found out and turned thumbs down. 'You get mixed up with lawyers,' Frank said gloomily, 'and that's the end of you. Well, what the hell. We'll talk anyway.'

Jehle started the tape recorder and Frank and I talked for more than an hour. Again we went over the story of my meetings with Hughes. I had enough instinct to dwell on certain details that I had failed to mention on the Wednesday board meeting, to omit others and to be suitably vague when the occasion called for it; the man with too perfect a memory, I reckoned, has got to be suspect.

'What does the old man look like now?' Frank asked.

'Old, what else? Thin, tired. One eye droops a bit. I think the left one.' That was out of the whole cloth, but since Frank hadn't seen Hughes since 1957, it seemed a safe bet.

340

Frank nodded. 'What about his face? You notice any disfigurement?'

I remembered that Dietrich had described a broken left cheekbone – the result of a plane crash – which had never been properly rectified by surgery. 'The left side of his face,' I gambled, 'is all banged up. As if the bone's sunk in and . . .'

'And it looks frozen,' McCulloch jumped in excitedly. 'Right? As if it was half-paralyzed.'

'Well,' I said, 'you *could* say that, but . . .' I left it hanging.

'Anything else?'

'His hand,' I shrugged. 'Hell, he had that when you knew him.'

'And his voice? What's that like?'

In the *Time-Life* files that I had read in June, I had come across a memo from McCulloch which had said: *'To confirm: his voice has a reedy, nasal quality.'*

'Nasal,' I said. 'Thin and tired.'

'But grating, too, like something's stuck in the back of his throat.'

'Sometimes,' I said cautiously.

'And does he still have that habit of rubbing his nose when he talks?' Frank demonstrated the gesture.

'You know,' I said, 'there are friends I've known for twenty years, and if you asked me about habits like that I wouldn't be able to give you answers. I'll tell you one habit he's got, though. He calls everyone he's ever known a sonofabitch and then he yells, "They stole me blind."'

'Yeah,' Frank said, 'he's earthy. He's really earthy. By God, you've met the man. There's no doubt about it.'

On Wednesday, Dick left New York for Palma. The roundtable conversations were still taking place at McGraw-Hill, but the editing job was done and I decided that the less they saw of Dick the better. 'Keep a low profile,' I said, 'or they're liable to wake up one day and wonder why you're always around during the crises.'

That afternoon Faustin Jehle and Ralph Webb, McGraw-Hill's treasurer, dropped by my office. In view of the troubles created by Hughes Tool and the Byoir Agency, it had been decided to remove the Xerox copy of the transcript from its safe-deposit box in the vaults of Chase Manhattan. It would be placed in McGraw-Hill's safe, to be on call when needed. Since I was the joint signatory to the escrow agreement, once I left for Spain it would be difficult on short notice to pry it loose from Chase Manhattan. Webb and I went downstairs together, presented our key to the guard on duty, and I handed over the transcript. The meeting gave me the opportunity to ask a question that had been worrying me all week. I was thinking of Edith's next trip to Zurich.

'What are we doing about that last check, Ralph? I mean the one to Hughes for $325,000.'

'What should we do about it?' Webb asked, puzzled.

'Any inquiries to Zurich? Did it pass through that same account?' I knew I sounded anxious; but in view of the present emergency, I reasoned, that would be understandable.

'We couldn't get the time of day from a Swiss bank. Anyway,' Webb said, 'I had word on it just this morning. It's already cleared and deposited.'

'Good,' I said. 'Maybe he'll stop bitching us now.'

That same day, one of the McGraw-Hill editors threw this one at me. 'You couldn't back out now if you wanted to. If you recanted, denied you'd ever met Hughes, the whole world would know you'd been paid off by the Tool Company. I can tell you,' he added, laughing, 'McGraw-Hill would crucify you. And we'd publish anyway.'

'Don't worry,' I said.

'No, that's not what worries us. I was only kidding.'

What worried them was the expectation, as Shelton Fisher put it, that 'the bomb was going to be dropped any day.' The bomb was Chester Davis' presumed revelation to the press that Hughes had spoken to McCulloch, denying Irving and the autobiography with one shot. Both Fisher and James Shepley, the President of Time, Inc., carried a press release in the pockets of their suit jackets, in battle readiness for the counter-attack.

But nothing happened. We reached the judgment that Davis was waiting for McCulloch himself to make the announcement. In lieu of that, he obviously expected *Life* and McGraw-Hill to back off a step – in the least, to let him read the manuscript. 'There's something in that manuscript,' I said to anyone who would listen, 'that scares the shit out of him. I don't know what it is, though, and I don't think he knows, either.' I pro-pounded a theory that Davis feared Hughes, in his ramblings to me, had backed up Robert Maheu in his Nevada controversy with Davis. 'Which isn't true,' I said, 'but the poor bastard has no way of knowing it.'

When it became obvious that the publishers were moving forward rather than backward, the Davis forces proposed a second telephone call. The first one had been off the record; this one, between McCulloch and Hughes, would be for the record.

McCulloch telephoned to me. 'I set two conditions. One, that you be there. And two, that it be taped this time. Otherwise I won't go through with it unless I'm ordered to.'

'Good, Frank. We can't let them shove us around any more.'

On December 17th McGraw-Hill and *Life* decided to shore up their defenses even further, and I was informed that they were engaging the services of Osborn, Osborn and Osborn, reputedly the finest handwriting analysts in the country, whose principal business was the examination of questioned documents. They were the blue-chip company in the field. Russell Osborn immediately flew to Nevada to secure documents submitted by the Hughes Tool Company – purportedly in the handwriting of Howard Hughes – with which to compare the letters and signatures in McGraw-Hill's possession.

After the earlier report, I had no worries. Whatever the reputation of the Osborns, I had developed a blind belief that the letters could pass any kind of inspection. A week later the Osborns confirmed: the letters had been written by Howard Hughes. 'The evidence,' said Paul Osborn, 'that all of the writing submitted was done by one individual is, in our opinion, irresistible, unanswerable, and overwhelming.' This was later restated in a sworn affidavit submitted by the Osborns in the Rosemont suit, whose purpose was to halt publication of the *Autobiography*. The Osborns' affidavit went on: 'The genuine handwriting of Howard R. Hughes is unusual not only in the distinctiveness of its developed forms and habits, but also in the great number of genuine variations thereof, all of which are a product of the great speed, freedom, and carelessness of his writing and all of which constitute his basic writing identity. This combination of speed in execution and distinctiveness and unusual variation in developed forms and habits, which are revealed in the specimen writings, determine the parameters of the monumental task which would face anyone attempting to imitate the genuine writing of Howard R. Hughes. Any attempt to imitate accurately the distinctive forms and habits of the writer of the specimen signatures and continuous writing, including the unusual number of genuine variations thereof, would be, for all practical purposes, in our opinion practically impossible. To put it another way, in our experience and in our opinion, it would be beyond human ability to do so.'

The report and the affidavit went on, in fascinating detail, to discuss 'hook-backs to the left in the letter *r* . . . variations in *w*'s . . . distinctive *p*'s and *P*'s . . .' until I was dizzy with the minutiae of proof that Howard was Howard was Howard was Howard. Much later, I showed the report to Dick.

'Beyond human ability,' I murmured. I was quietly impressed, then jubilant. 'Do you think I missed my profession?'

'Well, if we get caught now,' Dick said, 'you can always write yourself weekend passes out of Alcatraz.'

'They've closed Alcatraz.'

'For you they'll reopen it.'

'Thanks.' And my jubilance lost its fine edge.

Marty Ackerman had been to see Chester Davis, subjecting himself to two hours of ranting and raving. He had told Davis that the book upheld his position against Robert Maheu, the challenger for the Nevada empire, and therefore Davis had nothing to fear. 'But the man literally foams at the mouth,' Marty reported. 'He talks, he never listens.'

I hammered away at my theme. 'He's never met Hughes in his life, by his own sworn admission. The man at the other end of the line has got to be an impostor.'

Marty, if he had ever had any doubts, now professed total belief. Reading the transcript of the tapes the previous weekend in Connecticut, he had said to me: 'If the man you met wasn't Howard Hughes, it had to be John Paul Getty. I'm telling you, this guy's a pistol! There aren't six men in the United States who have that kind of business acumen. You don't know much about business – you don't realize how brilliant he is. I've got five million bucks, and I know my way around, but this guy's in another league. Brilliant,' Marty murmured. 'I fly a plane, too,' he added, 'and I can tell you, when your man talks about flying he knows what he's talking about. It was Hughes you met, no question about it.'

I thanked him silently for his praise of my business knowledge, which was that of a man who had barely passed an elementary freshman course in economics at Cornell more than twenty years before. Most of the business discussions in the *Autobiography* were culled from *Fortune* articles and juiced up with a combination of imagination (what would *I* have done if I had been Howard?) and doubletalk. I marveled once more at the nature of gullibility. And yet Marty Ackerman was no starry-eyed publisher. He had his five million dollars, a Park Avenue town house, a 23-room country cottage, and a collection of French Impressionist paintings. He had owned a conglomerate, a private jet, a bank, and – briefly – Curtis Publishing and the ill-fated *Saturday Evening Post*. He was a warm-hearted man, hardnosed in business but generous, loyal, and hospitable to his friends. He had befriended me from the moment I told him I was working with Howard Hughes on the billionaire's autobiography; he had come to my aid, with no strings attached, the moment the Hughes Tool Company had declared war.

How could I say to him: 'Listen, Marty, that great business brain in the transcripts is *me* and you know goddam well I don't know a debenture from a convertible bond. If I'm so brilliant, how come I'm not running General Motors or IBM?' I couldn't say it. It would not only make Marty an accessory after the fact; but worse, a fool. I was too grateful for his loyalty to do that.

'So you think Davis is trying the big con?' he asked me.

'You mean setting up an impostor in Nassau? I don't know. Maybe he really believes it's Hughes he's talking to. Anything is possible.'

'My God,' Marty murmured. 'One thing you have to give the man credit for – he's got balls! But he's so *stupid* – how does he think he'll get away with it?'

'"Vilify! Vilify!"' I quoted, digging into my reserve of aphorisms: this one from some French revolutionary. '"Some of it will stick."'

It was my last day in New York, December 22nd. I was flying out from Kennedy that evening at seven o'clock on the Iberia jet to Madrid, and then home to Ibiza for Christmas, carrying a load of 39 oil paintings and *gouaches* left over from Edith's exhibition in a Madison Avenue gallery two years ago. Things had gone well, we had weathered the worst storm of all in the Hughes-McCulloch telephone call, and I was feeling ebullient, bold. Leave on a note of confidence, I decided.

That morning, in my office on the 29th floor at McGraw-Hill, I ripped out a letter to Shelton Fisher, the President of McGraw-Hill, Inc. I had a slight feeling of uneasiness that once I was no longer on the scene, the troops might weaken under pressure. They would never raise the white flag of surrender, but if even one flank took a pounding they would be on the telephone to me in Ibiza asking me to come back and buck up the defenses. I wanted more than anything to go home and stay home with Edith and the kids. But: *toujours l'audace.* I wrote, in part:

Dear Shelton:

Apropos of our roundtable conversation last night in your office, I feel I should go on record to you with my feelings.

I strongly believe that under no circumstances should the proposed telephone conversation between Frank McCulloch and Chester Davis' 'Mr Hughes' be allowed to take place. In my opinion there is absolutely nothing to be gained by it from *Life*'s, McGraw-Hill's, or my point of view. Since Mr

Davis is organizing the proposed telephone call and he calls the autobiography a fraud, we pretty much know in advance what the man on the other end of the line is going to say, and it cannot be of any benefit to any of us. It puts us in the submissive, reactive role, and it means we are playing the game by the rules set down by the opposition. In my opinion, Mr Davis is a street-fighter. He's swinging blindly, throwing random punches in the hope that he'll connect with something, anything, and there's no reason for us to obligingly stick out our chins. If we play any games it should be by our rules or mutually-agreed rules.

In addition, I would also propose that Mr Davis and I sit down together and take a lie-detector test where each of us prepares ten written questions which are asked alternately to each other. My only condition is that the questions *must* be answered and that if one of us responds with 'no comment' or 'I can't or won't answer that,' the ball game's over. The only possible negative result that I can foresee resulting from such a confrontation would be that Davis would get a lot of information he does not at the moment possess; but I believe it's worth the risk. In fact, he probably would not agree to the whole proposal, which would certainly be a public-relations plus for our team.

My most important point in this letter is my first one: that the proposed McCulloch–'Hughes' conversation is detrimental to our interests and should not take place; and I would be grateful if you would make my position known to everyone concerned, including Mr Heiskell of Time, Inc. *Davis* is really the one who's panicking. Let's not follow suit.

Best regards,
Cliff

At 10:30 a.m. I gave the letter to Shelton's secretary on the 32nd floor. The proposed challenge to Davis, to take a joint lie-detector test, was pure bluff. I had already mentioned the idea to Marty, who had explained that Davis would have to decline the terms since they would breach his theoretical attorney–client privilege with Howard Hughes. One sharp question – 'Is Mr Hughes willing and able to leave Nassau and come to New York?' – and Davis would be forced to invoke the privilege with, 'No comment.' I went back to the 29th floor, feeling cocky, and began to clean up the litter of manuscript and notes.

An hour later Ralph Graves called. 'We're arranging the polygraph over here at one o'clock,' he said.

'What's a polygraph?' I asked.

'A lie-detector test. Fisher called Andy Heiskell and told him your idea. Davis would never agree to it, though. But I think it's great that you volunteered, and we've got a man coming here with the equipment at one o'clock. Can you make it?'

'I think that I'd better talk to Shelton Fisher first,' I said. 'This is all a little sudden.'

I called Ackerman. 'Marty, they're arranging a lie-detector test for me at one o'clock, over at *Time-Life*. They think I volunteered for it.'

'Great idea, kid,' he said. 'That'll really firm up their confidence.'

'I've still got a lot of work to do. I have to catch a plane. I'm not ready. I don't know anything about lie-detector tests.'

'What's there to know? Just tell the truth and you don't have to worry.'

I called Fisher. 'Shelton, what's going on? Graves and Heiskell want me over there at one o'clock for a lie-detector test.'

'Goddamit,' Fisher said, 'those people at *Life* are going too far. What the hell are they horning in for? You're *our*

349

author and this is *our* book. If anyone's going to give you a polygraph it's going to be *us*! I'll call Heiskell.'

He hung up. I sat staring blankly at the wall for a few minutes and then called Graves. 'Ralph, I just spoke to Shelton Fisher. He doesn't want me to go over to *Life* to take a lie-detector test.'

'I know,' Graves said. 'I've got Heiskell on the other wire. Our man's coming over to McGraw-Hill at one-thirty. Good man – one of the best. We'll do it there.'

I called Marty. 'I know,' he said. 'Jehle just called me to tell me about it. I'm coming right over. I'll help them prepare the questions. Don't be nervous.'

'Why should I be nervous?' I hung up and looked at my thumb, wondering why it hurt. I had bitten the skin around the nail down to raw pink flesh during the past five minutes. I sucked the blood as the elevator rose to the 32nd floor. Shelton Fisher and Harold McGraw were waiting for me. Shelton smiled warmly and threw an arm around my shoulder. 'How do you feel, kid?'

'A little confused,' I admitted. 'I have a plane to catch. I have to be at the airport early to ship my wife's paintings.' I found myself making a long speech about Edith's paintings, and how important it was that I be at the airport in time to get them out of Iberia cargo and into the plane. 'If they're not on board with me, it means a divorce.'

'What time does the plane leave?'

'Seven o'clock.'

'Plenty of time,' Harold McGraw said.

'I still have to pack,' I said. 'I haven't packed yet. I haven't packed my clothes. My clothes are back at Marty Ackerman's. I have to pack before I go to the airport.' They looked at me oddly and I had the feeling I was trying too hard to make my point. 'Rush hour traffic . . .' I finished.

'It'll be over in no time,' Fisher said, looking at his

watch. 'Let's go have lunch. I've reserved a private dining room.'

Marty and Faustin Jehle had joined us by the time we had reached the second-floor dining room in the McGraw-Hill Building. The mood was jovial, almost festive. Marty rambled on about his meeting with Chester Davis. 'I'll tell you,' he said for the ninth time, 'that guy's got *balls*.' Shelton blew off steam every now and then about 'those goddam interfering bastards over at *Time-Life*.' Jehle meandered through a discourse on the libel problems involved in Hughes claiming that a well-known actress had stolen his favorite golf ball and had asked him to sodomize her, to which Howard had replied: 'I'd just as soon stick my pecker in a wet loaf of bread.' Harold McGraw sat silently, deep in his grave but always benign thoughts, his face reflecting his emotions like one of the heads carved into the rock at Mt Rushmore.

I had ordered a double Jack Daniels on the rocks and was sipping it slowly. A waitress placed a menu in front of me. I sneaked a look at my watch; it was one o'clock.

I had no appetite at all. 'I'll have the shrimp cocktail to start,' I said. 'Sirloin steak, medium rare. Baked potato, leaf spinach. Strawberry shortcake and coffee later.'

'Any salad, sir?'

'Oh, yes, salad. With Roquefort dressing. After the shrimp cocktail and before the steak.'

'Hey, boy,' Fisher said jovially. 'Ackerman must be starving you over at his place.'

'Spanish habit,' I explained. 'The big meal is always in the middle of the day, before the polygraph.'

Everyone roared with laughter, and even Harold McGraw smiled. I set to work on the shrimp cocktail and then the salad, chewing every leaf of lettuce thoroughly. Halfway through the steak and baked potato I was already feeling slightly nauseous, and I stopped stuffing myself long enough to launch into a long discourse about the art market in New York, and Edith's show two years ago at Selected Artists Galleries, the problems of being a painter, wife, and mother. 'And if I don't have those paintings with me when I get off the plane in Ibiza . . .' I drew a finger meaningfully across my throat, hurting my chewed thumb.

I was in the middle of the strawberry shortcake when Shelton looked at his watch and said, 'Christ! It's a quarter past two. Those people are waiting for us upstairs. This has been a hell of a long lunch,' he said, puzzled.

On the way up in the elevator to the 32nd floor, everyone smiled at me. *Good man*, was the message. *You won't let us down. This will show them.* Yes indeed, I thought, it may do just that. I smiled back, a little palely.

'Gentlemen,' I said, 'there's something I have to tell you before I submit myself to this polygraph and you all look like fools and I am proved a liar. I have never met Howard Hughes in my life. I am the author of the *Autobiography* and Richard Suskind, my researcher, is the co-author. Your money, at this moment, is invested in the name of Hanne Rosenkranz in a numbered account of the Swiss Bank Corporation in Zurich. The portfolio consists principally of IBM, Xerox, Texas Gulf Sulphur, Transamerica, Dome Mines, and Upjohn. We hold no McGraw-Hill stock, for obvious reasons.'

'Did you say something?' Fisher asked me.

I had been muttering to myself through clenched lips. 'Yes, I said I've got to be at the airport by five o'clock. How long does a polygraph usually last?'

'I've never taken one,' Fisher admitted. 'I'll find out.'

Frank McCulloch and Bill Lambert of Time, Inc. were waiting in the anteroom to Harold's office. With them was a short, dark-haired man of about thirty, looking very eager and carrying a large suitcase. He was immediately ushered into the conference room by Shelton and Harold and Bill Lambert. McCulloch drew me to one side. His expression was grim. 'Whose goddam idea was this?' he demanded angrily.

'Well, that's a long story, Frank.'

'Let me tell you,' he rasped, 'I don't like it. What the hell, don't they think Frank McCulloch is a good enough lie detector?'

I suddenly saw his point. He wasn't angry at me. He was hurt. I felt sorry for him and quickly summarized how it had all come to pass. 'It was really my fault,' I apologized. 'Nobody doubts your word, Frank. They know you told the truth. I just sort of maneuvered myself into it. I volunteered.'

'Oh, well, that's all right, then. I was afraid they didn't trust me for some goddam reason.' He had calmed down. 'I guess I'm just getting paranoid.'

'It happens to everybody,' I explained, 'if they hang around Howard Hughes.'

McCulloch was drawn into the other room to talk to the short, dark-haired man I had noticed when I first came into the room. He was Rudy Caputo, a polygraph expert from the Burns Agency. I talked casually with Marty Ackerman and Faustin Jehle while Caputo received his briefing. Then I was ushered into the room.

We were left alone. Caputo sat behind a small mound of papers.

'This is very simple,' he said, 'and there's nothing to worry about.'

'I hope so, because I've got a plane to catch. Did they tell you that?'

He nodded, and then began asking questions. They ranged from the correct spelling of my name to details of my meetings with Howard Hughes. He was precise and pleasant; although at times a little confused. At one point he filled out a standard form of release, which I was to sign, indicating that I was taking the test voluntarily. In the blank space for my name he had printed: *Clifford Michael Holmes*. When I pointed out the mistake

353

he flushed a little and prepared a second form, this time correctly.

I felt that I was about to have a stroke. My heart was already thumping against my chest and I was as thirsty as I had ever been in my life. It's impossible, I realized. I can't pass it, and this is the end. When I asked a question, my own voice seemed to come from a great distance, as though it were floating in some far corner of the room, trying to hide from earshot.

'How soon do you have the results?'

'A preliminary report? Almost right away. There's a written report, of course, but that takes a little time.'

'How does this thing work? Are you allowed to tell me that?'

He had not yet opened his suitcase inside which, I assumed, were his satanic devices.

'It measures all sorts of things. Sweat, rate of respiration, and something like blood pressure – it's called plythesmatic resistance. Has to do with the arteries. It's an old art,' he explained. 'The Chinese started it. Their theory was that a man's mouth goes dry if he's lying. They put rice in his mouth.'

'My mouth is bone dry, and I haven't even said a word.'

I was finished, and I knew it. When it was over and the results were told to the waiting executives, I would tell the truth. What choice would I have? But I had to make one last effort.

Caputo finally opened his suitcase and assembled his gear. A band was wrapped around my arm as though for a blood pressure test. A chain was looped around my chest, then tightened. Two electrodes were wound about the second two fingers of my left hand. The questions, he explained, should be answered by a simple yes or no. I sat in a chair with my back to Caputo. I couldn't see him and I had no idea what he was doing. He just waited in silence – calculated, I assumed, to reduce me to pulp even before we began – while I stared at the wall. With each passing second I could feel my heart pounding and slamming with greater ferocity. Doggedly, in my mind, I began to recite the answers to a little catechism. *I have met Howard Hughes. My name is Clifford Holmes. I have paid all the money to the man I know as Howard Hughes. I was born in Kabul, Afghanistan. I have met Howard Hughes. My name is Clifford Holmes.*

Suddenly, as if on cue, Caputo said: 'Is your name Clifford Irving?'

Instantly I thought *Clifford Holmes* and I replied: 'Yes.' I felt my heart take a heave against my ribs that nearly knocked me out of the chair.

'Have you taken any or all of the $650,000 meant to go to Howard Hughes?'

'No.'

The first heave of my heart had been gentle compared to the one that erupted after that question

'Have you conspired with anyone else to defraud McGraw Hill of any sums of money?'

'No,' I said, and nearly fainted. If I hadn't been strapped to the chair I could have toppled to the floor.

He asked three more questions of a similar nature and then said, 'That's it.'

'Thanks,' I said. Unable to look him in the eye, I staggered from the room. Fisher, McCulloch, Jehle, Lambert, and Marty Ackerman were waiting for me. 'Jesus God,' I whispered to Marty. 'That's inhuman . . .'

A minute later Caputo followed me out of the room. I turned to him at the same time as Jehle, Ackerman, and the others. Caputo shrugged. 'I'm sorry,' he said. 'The results were really inconclusive. There just wasn't enough time. But I'll be sending in a written report.'

'Make sure I get a copy,' I said to Jehle. 'And thanks for the experience. I'm going to run or I'll miss that plane.'

I had to pack and then wait fifteen minutes for a taxi

on Park Avenue. It was rush hour. When I got to Kennedy Airport the Iberia jet had been closed for boarding. I yelled hysterically for five minutes and finally was escorted privately to the 747, where I slumped into my seat like a man lately risen from a hospital bed. My heart was still pounding. I hadn't passed the test. I couldn't have passed it.

For once in this story I must jump ahead, lest the reader be left with any lingering doubts and suffer the horrors of uncertainty as I suffered them. I would inflict that on no man. If there was a written report from Caputo, it was never shown to me by anyone at McGraw-Hill. And the subject of the polygraph, as well as the results, was never again mentioned in my presence.

16

The Swans of the River Limatt

The paintings were not on the plane with me when we landed in Ibiza. They had vanished somewhere enroute. After a dozen telephone calls and cables, they turned up almost a month later in a warehouse in Palma de Mallorca, where we finally retrieved them.

But that was the least of my problems. I had gone through a small hell in New York, but what awaited me in Ibiza was worse. Edith was upset about the missing paintings, but it was easy to see that other things were on her mind. We left the airport and on the way home, thinking I grasped the reason, I said: 'Look, that business of Dick's driving Nina's car to London. *I* told him not to tell you. I knew you'd be angry, but there's no reason to be. He needed a way to get to England and she needed someone to drive her car up there. They made their own arrangements. I had nothing to do with it.'

Edith shrugged it off, which made me all the more wary. When we got home, sitting in the living room, I pulled her onto my lap – but she leaped to her feet, rushed into the bedroom and came out with a thick white packet. She tossed it on the table in front of me. Her eyes were filled with tears, but they were still ablaze with anger and pain.

'You and that bitch,' she said. 'Last May. And when I was in Zurich.'

The packet contained the photographs of Nina that I had taken on the beach at Figueral and had had printed in Beverly Hills. Amid the mess that had accumulated over the summer in the studio, I had never been able to find them. When I had called Edith from the motel in Miami Beach I had asked her to go to the studio and unlock the file cabinet; I had wanted the 'Dear Chester and Bill' letter for Dick. The packet of photographs, with the negatives, had been wedged at the back of the file cabinet, out of sight to myself and to anyone but a woman with a keen sense of smell.

'I knew it,' Edith said, weeping. 'I've always known it. I trusted you and I wanted to believe you, what makes me a fool. *Look at them!*' She grabbed the packet and jammed the photographs in front of my eyes. 'Look at her face! You both lied to me and said it was platonic. Platonic! Naked on the beach, and the look on her face of a woman in love.'

Throwing herself on the couch, she curled into a foetal ball and began to sob.

I tried to protest, to explain, but there was nothing to say. In my heart, since Thanksgiving in Los Angeles, I had known that it was over between Nina and myself, but it was impossible to do anything, after trying to comfort her and being thrust aside, other than shed tears of my own. I was guilty. I had been found out through an absurdity. That the photographs had no meaning to me, that my obsession with Nina was dying and that I was free to give to Edith what she had always given to me, was an irony that offered no comfort.

'I stay with you now,' she said quietly, hours later, after she had calmed down, 'because of the children. But I don't want to go to Zurich. This Hughes thing is no more a joke. You should tell them the truth now – give them back the money.'

'After the book's published,' I said. 'In April, probably.' I convinced her – and myself as well – that I meant it; and she agreed, however reluctantly, to go.

If Edith had been frightened on her previous clandestine trips to Switzerland, she was nearly terrified on the morning of December 28th. But she held her feelings successfully in check. I attributed her nervousness to the problems of the previous week: our failing marriage and Nina. But Edith imagined sinister figures from Intertel, wearing trenchcoats and with their hands stuffed deep in their pockets like spies from an Eric Ambler novel, waiting for her at Zurich Airport or in the marble lobby of the Credit Suisse. A dozen times already, in her mind, she had felt the rough grip of a hand on her elbow and heard the harsh voice say triumphantly: 'Come along, Edith-Helga-Hanne-Sommer-Rosenkranz-Irving-Hughes. The game is up. No, don't try to throw away the wig – *you're caught.*'

Edith was always a child playing an adult game and there was little reality for her in her missions to Zurich. Someone had to go. She had been asked, and she had agreed, like a little girl when the boys decide to steal apples from the orchard and say, 'We need your help. You stand watch.'

'But I am the weak link,' she had said later, long after the game had begun.

We drove to Ibiza airport through the blackness of an early morning drizzle. Edith was a tiny, hurt figure huddled against the door of the Mercedes, twisting the strap of her flight bag round and round in her hands. Her face looked haggard and drawn, the dark circles under the eyes only partially hidden by pancake makeup. She had been sleeping badly for the past two weeks, ever since she had discovered the semi-nude photographs of Nina hidden in the file cabinet. Eugen's death had been another kind of blow. She had loved the tiny monkey too much. We had buried Eugen in a shoebox on land that overlooked the bay of Ibiza.

At the airport parking lot I reached across to open the door for her. I kept my hand there a moment, pinning Edith in the seat. 'I'm positive there's nothing to worry about,' I repeated, 'and if I thought there was, I wouldn't let you go. McGraw-Hill told me the check has cleared. You won't have any problems. But if I'm wrong – if *anything* happens and someone tries to grab you – forget about the money. Save yourself. The money doesn't matter a damn. Throw it up in the air and let them all scramble for it. You just run like hell.'

She didn't answer, only looked at me searchingly with tired, sad eyes. I leaned over to kiss her. She pulled away and my lips just brushed her cheek. 'Do you want some marzipan from Zurich?' she asked.

The flight was bumpy but Edith passed through Zurich customs and immigration without so much as a lifted eyebrow, and at 3:30 that afternoon she was hurrying down to the safe-deposit boxes in the Swiss Bank Corporation's main branch on the Paradeplatz. She removed the H.R. Hughes passport and bank documents from the box. As she stepped out of the bank she ducked to one side, into a stone alcove, quickly put on her spectacles, shoved the corn plasters into her cheeks to make them appear rounder, and tightened the flowered scarf under her chin to distort her voice. She crossed through the traffic of the Paradeplatz to the Credit Suisse.

The teller, a middle-aged woman with graying brown hair pulled back into a bun, recognized her at once. 'Ah, *Frau* Hoogus. How nice to see you again. I hope you had a pleasant journey from Paris.' She escorted Edith behind the teller's cage into a private counting room. 'Your check cleared last week. You intend to withdraw all the money this time as well?'

'I want to keep the account open,' Edith replied, as I had instructed. 'But just the minimum balance.'

The woman left the room, returning with $325,000 in neatly bound bundles of thousand-franc Swiss notes. It was a normal, everyday transaction for a big Swiss bank; the currency of all nations flowed in and out of Zurich with a minimum of questions asked. Edith began stuffing the cash into her airline bag. The teller frowned.

'But, *Frau* Hoogus, you haven't counted it.'

'If I didn't trust the Credit Suisse,' Edith explained, 'I wouldn't bank here.'

'And so much cash. Even to walk across the street with so much is very dangerous.'

Across the street? What did the woman mean? Did the Credit Suisse know about the Rosenkranz account? Was this a subtle warning that Hughes's men were posted outside, mingling unobtrusively with the customers, waiting to catch her *in flagrante?*

'There was a robbery last week in Zurich,' the teller said. 'Imagine! Right here in Zurich.'

Outside in the gathering gloom, she spat out the corn plasters, stuffed the spectacles in her pocket, wiped off her lipstick and loosened her scarf so that she could breathe normally again. With the bag of money clutched under her arm, she recrossed the Paradeplatz to the Swiss Bank Corporation.

A sleek, dapper man in his middle thirties – very Swiss and therefore very correct – greeted her respectfully and led the way into his office on the second floor. As on her previous visits, Edith waded across the thick red carpet and sat down in the hard leather chair beside the desk, facing an original Klee drawing. She unzipped the airline bag and spilled the bundles of francs onto the desk.

'How much have you brought today?' the banker asked.

'I don't know.'

He peered at her uncertainly. 'You don't know?'

'Oh, I didn't count it,' Edith explained. 'Could you do that for me?'

The banker sighed in wonder, flipped an intercom switch, spoke briefly, and a moment later a younger man entered the room and swiftly began counting the banknotes, skimming through them with professional expertise. He spoke into the intercom again, then said to Edith: 'One moment, *Frau* Rosenkranz, while I send for your file.' Edith took out the second list of stocks and bonds that Dick and I had prepared. The banker nodded his solemn approval as he read it. 'You have an excellent and well-informed broker, *Frau* Rosenkranz. A very fine portfolio, if I may be so bold. Your investments are making good profit.'

Edith smiled gratefully. A minute later another young man brought two folders into the room, dropping them on the desk. The senior official frowned. 'I want only *Frau* Rosenkranz's file,' he said.

'But there are two, *mein Herr.*'

The banker flipped back and forth between them, his frown deepening. 'But . . . but . . . I don't understand, *Frau* Rosenkranz. You have two accounts with us now?'

'Do I?' Edith asked.

Fischer waved his assistants from the room. 'Yes, of course. Look, here. Ah . . . yes.' His frown partially cleared. 'You were here three weeks ago with your son, Marcus, to open the trust account. I served you personally. I remember that you . . .' Then he halted.

Edith felt the blood drain from her face. The whole Hughes affair had twisted, turned and gathered momentum from a series of bizarre coincidences that no novelist would have dared to string together in one book. And now, here in the Swiss Bank Corporation, had come the final coincidence – and disaster. Hanne Rosenkranz had apparently gone to Zurich to open a trust account for Marcus, choosing the prestigious Swiss Bank Corporation to handle the details.

The banker looked once again at the two files, then back at Edith, and stammered on. 'Wait . . . no . . . yes . . . wait a moment. It wasn't you, then, who opened this other account . . . there cannot be two Hanne Rosenkranzes with the same address and same birthdate. This is patently impossible. Could she be a relation of some kind?'

'That's it,' Edith said with relief. 'Hanne Rosenkranz is my sister.'

'And you . . .'

'And I am Hanne Rosenkranz's sister, too.'

He looked triumphant. 'Then your name is not even Rosenkranz, since Rosenkranz is her married name.'

'That's true.'

'What *is* your name?'

'I won't tell you,' Edith said petulantly.

The banker made a tent of his fingers and peered across the desk, uncertain of his ground. 'But you used her identification to open this account for yourself.'

'It's so complicated . . .' After glancing behind her to make sure no one could overhear, Edith lowered her voice. 'Family problems . . . I don't want it known that I have this account. My sister Hanne is the only one who knows. She's the only one I trust. If something happens to me, she can take the money out, because she is also Hanne Rosenkranz. Do you understand?'

The banker frowned, trying to concentrate. '*You* must understand,' he said at last, making his decision, 'that I am a very serious man, and knowing that you opened your account with false identification papers, even though they belong to your sister – I cannot keep you as a customer.'

'I understand and respect your decision. Then please give me back the money I just brought in, and please sell all my stocks and bonds, and give me all the cash, and I'll go.'

He coughed delicately. 'But besides being a serious

man,' he explained, 'I am also a serious banker, and I don't want to lose such a good customer as yourself. That,' he said, 'would be a very irresponsible act. Of course, if I let you go, you will take the money to another bank. That would be natural . . . but a pity. I think the best thing is to transfer your account to our branch on Bellevueplatz.' He leaned back, satisfied. 'Would that suit you?'

Edith considered, then said: 'Why not? You're very kind . . .'

He picked up the telephone and dialed his opposite number in the Bellevueplatz branch. Threading his way through an explanation of the circumstances, he neglected to mention that Edith had used her 'sister's' identity card to open the account; he said only that there was 'too much family traffic' in the Paradeplatz branch. Hanging up, he smiled at Edith and said: 'If you hurry you'll have time to fill in the forms and arrange all the details today.'

Thanking him, Edith swiftly left the bank and took a taxi to Bellevueplatz, where another bank official helped her through the formalities of transferring the account. Finally the official cleared his throat. 'I understand,' he said, 'that there are family problems. Naturally I don't wish to inquire into their nature. I do think, however, that it would be wise . . .' he hesitated; Edith waited, beginning to worry again, '. . . to have a code name for the account, which you could use to keep matters more, ah, discreet. Do you have a preference?'

Edith considered 'Helga Hughes,' then decided that might be going too far.

'Erika Schwartz,' she said, giving the name of the cleaning woman in a friend's home in Germany.

That evening, in her room at the Savoy Hotel on the Paradeplatz, Edith sank down on the edge of the bed, too tired even to take off her coat. I had told her, when

364

her business in Zurich was finished, to destroy all the unnecessary bank documents – and, above all, the H.R. Hughes passport. It had served its purpose: the account would never again be used.

Her hands were trembling when she started to rip the inside pages of the passport into little pieces. With a pair of curved toenail scissors from her makeup kit, she began to cut the heavy red plastic cover into strips. It was hard work. A blister formed on her thumb.

When she had finished, she heaped the shreds into an ashtray, struck a match, and held it first to the black-wigged photograph of Helga Renate Hughes. '*Auf wiedersehen*, Helga . . .'

Acrid smoke filled the room. Flakes of burning paper wafted into the air and settled slowly to the floor. There was a heavy pounding on the door, the murmur of voices in the hallway, and a woman cried shrilly, 'Fire! Are you all right in there?'

Edith opened the door. Worried faces peered from doors on both sides of the corridor and the chambermaid stood nervously, holding a bucket of water and sniffing at the smoke.

'It's nothing,' Edith said, ready to weep. 'I was just trying to burn a photograph – a photograph of a man.' She buried her face in her hands. 'I . . . I'm . . .'

The chambermaid clapped her hands together. 'Oh, forgive me! It was the smoke . . .'

A light rain was falling in Zurich. The headlights of passing cars dazzled Edith's eyes, the neon signs blinked blue and red and green. The ball of fear in her stomach made her feel nauseous. In the left-hand pocket of her coat she carried the bundle of shredded papers, some of them charred. She descended a short flight of stone steps beside a bridge until she reached a cobbled path by the edge of the River Limatt.

The Limatt is Zurich's river, famous for its swans. The

lights of burghers' mansions were reflected in dancing yellow and white patterns on the black surface of the water. A wastebasket hung from a low stone wall by the water's edge. Stepping through the gloom, Edith reached into the pocket of her coat. She began to stuff the torn documents into the basket. Half of her task done, she looked up. A man in a trenchcoat, the collar pulled up around his neck, hands buried deep in his pockets, loomed from the mists that twined along the path. It was the man of her forebodings, the man whose hand would tighten on her wrist and whose hard voice would say: 'Come with me . . .'

The man peered at her for a long moment, then walked to the parapet. He reached into his pocket and took out a paper bag. It was filled with chunks of bread, which he tossed one by one into the river. The swans and other waterfowl appeared suddenly out of the darkness, paddling to the floating bread and feeding noisily. The man emptied the bag of bread and left, vanishing toward the bridge.

Edith quickly shoved the rest of the torn papers into the wastebasket. But then: what if the garbage collector is curious when he dumps them out? What if he pieces them together? What if the man in the trenchcoat is more clever than I realize, and is waiting, watching?

A woman with a small boy in tow walked up to the parapet. She lifted the boy to the top of the wall and handed him a bag of bread. 'Hurry up, Hans,' she snapped. 'It's cold. Your father is waiting.'

The boy flung double handfuls of bread into the water. More swans swarmed to the foot of the wall, beating the black water with their wings, churning it to froth. The squawking and honking and cawing of the birds was loud enough to drown the sound of traffic on the boulevard above.

As soon as the woman and child were gone, Edith pulled her bundle of papers from the wastebasket, wincing as her hand encountered bits of wet orange peel and a half-eaten sandwich. The swans honked and swarmed. Edith sighed, understood, then smiled with delight. Moving to the wall, she flung out her arms. The papers and strips of passport fluttered and fell toward the outstretched beaks. The beaks opened wide, gobbling up the passport and bank documents of Helga Renate Hughes. Whatever still floated on the surface of the water was gone in a minute, snapped up greedily by the swans of the River Limatt.

Edith lowered her arms, pirouetted like a ballet dancer, and slowly walked up the stone steps to the boulevard and back to the hotel. In the hotel restaurant, free from fear for the first time in days, she ate smoked salmon and venison, and drank a half bottle of dry white Johannisburger.

Then she went upstairs, fell onto the bed and began to shiver. She drew up the thick eiderdown. When the tremors stopped, even before she had time to take off her clothes, she sank into a deep and dreamless sleep, as though she had been drugged. The lights burned all night in her room.

Part Four

May you live in interesting times.
　　　　　　　　　 – an old Chinese curse

17

Enter Howard Hughes
(or a Reasonable Facsimile)

This time the bundles of Swiss francs, dollars, and Deutschmarks that Edith brought back to Ibiza were dispersed both inside and outside the house. Some went up on the hidden edge of the beam, some were taped to the back of a sliding door to a wardrobe, some I slid into the folds of a heating pad that lay in a box on the bedroom bookshelf. A small stone woodshed stood outside the house. On the first moonless night I pried loose one of the stones, whiter in color than those surrounding it, and shoved the bulk of the cash – some $50,000 worth of various currencies – deep into the wall. I had doublewrapped it in plastic and silver foil to keep out both the damp and any marauding field mice. With a hammer, I tapped the stone solidly – I thought – back into place.

All that remained for me to do was write the introduction to the book. That would run, I reckoned, between 10,000 and 12,000 words. I would let *Life*'s editors excerpt their 5,000-word article from it. The problem in writing the introduction was to make it as richly detailed as possible and yet be skimpy on specifics that might give the Hughes Tool people targets to shoot at. With that in mind, there had been some nervous talk in New York about the possibility *of Life*'s publishing the article after, rather than before, their three 10,000-word excerpts. Whatever the order of publication, I had promised delivery by January 15th.

The weather on Ibiza was wintry and I worked in the studio with both heaters blasting away, trying in vain to combat the cold, wet wind that blew off the sea through the cracks surrounding the balcony doors. My feet were freezing and I took off my shoes, plugged in the heating pad, and placed it under the desk on the tattered old Mexican serape.

It was the home stretch and I vetoed all social activity other than a New Year's Eve party, where I nursed two light gin and tonics throughout the entire evening, and one small dinner party two nights later at home. That same night, Robert Kirsch of *The Los Angeles Times* arrived on Ibiza.

During the day, Barney had come down with a high fever. It was no lower at nine o'clock, when the guests had gathered, so we decided to drive into town for the doctor. It was gloomy and cold, with a light rain falling. Just as I was backing the Mercedes out of the garage the headlights of a taxi blazed into my rearview mirror and it pulled up into the dirt driveway. A bulky, bearded figure stepped out of the taxi, carrying a suitcase. It was Kirsch, and I whooped with pleasure.

'Jump in,' I yelled, 'before you get soaked! I've got to find a doctor and then you can join the party. And stay with us, too. Jesus, it's good to see you. What are you doing here?'

He had flown down from Switzerland. He was still reviewing books for *The Los Angeles Times*, but he wanted a cheap place to live and write his own novels. 'You've been singing the praises of this island for so many goddam years I finally decided to see for myself.'

His wife and daughter would follow, he said, if he found Ibiza to his liking.

'But that's great, Bob. We'll find you a house.'

'And the *Times* is paying for the trip,' he said.

'How the hell did you manage that?'

'Come on . . . don't be naive. They sent me here to interview you. You're on the map, man. And what I want, if you'll agree to it, is to read the Hughes manuscript.'

Kirsch stayed the night with us and we talked the following morning at breakfast. He understood now why I had lied to him that past June in Los Angeles, when I had said I was doing a book on four millionaires. He brushed that aside – but now he wanted the full story. It was more than selfishness on his part, more than the newsman's desire for a scoop. He was a highly respected book reviewer in America, and he felt sure that if he read the material – transcript and manuscript both – he could put the stamp of authenticity on the book and perhaps end the debate that was rising toward manic proportions back in the States. He had known me for ten years and I thought of him as a good friend. He never doubted for a moment – or at least never voiced any doubt to me – that I had met Howard Hughes and interviewed him.

'I can really help you.' He added only one warning: 'But I'll have to call it as I see it. If I *do* have any doubts, I'm going to say so. What I'll offer you in return is my word that I won't leak any of the material to anyone.'

'I take your word for it, Bob,' I said.

It was the most difficult decision I had ever to make concerning the hoax. Kirsch was a self-taught speed reader; he could glance at a page and digest its contents in two seconds, then flip to the next. He could read through both transcript and manuscript in twenty-four hours and remember everything. I was certain that if he read them he would be convinced, as had everyone else up to that point, that the material was not only genuine but sensational. And he would say so in print. He would be the only one outside of McGraw-Hill and *Life* to have read the book. His article would be a coup for him and a plus for me, but I would be using him and conning him, and that made me more than uneasy. What I had done with McGraw-Hill had been necessary; as Dick had pointed out when we began, that was the name of the game. But to bring Bob Kirsch into it was unnecessary. And yet if I refused to show him the material he would have good cause to be suspicious. He was a friend but he was also an honest newsman, and if he smelled a hoax he would say so.

'I'll let you read it,' I said. 'But I've got to get McGraw-Hill's permission for you to write anything about it.'

'Why the hell should they object?'

'Let me call them, Bob.'

I left him reading the manuscript at the house, and went up to the studio to call Beverly Loo in New York. As soon as I announced Kirsch's presence and his mission, she said: 'No! He's a newspaperman first and your friend second. You are *so* goddam naive! He'll leak that material all over *The Los Angeles Times,* and the wire services will pick it up and there goes *Life's* exclusivity to the story. Ralph Graves will be furious.'

That annoyed me and I found myself arguing for Kirsch's proposal even though I had been hunting for a way to reject it. 'He's not interested in how I met Hughes,' I explained. 'He only wants to read the book.'

'And write a review of it? That's the worst thing that he could do! Every other newspaper in the country would be furious. *And don't trust him,'* Beverly repeated.

I reported this to Bob, who shook his head with mild dismay. 'They're crazy,' he said. 'I'm only trying to help you – and them in the bargain. And I'm not going to review the damn book. I'm only commenting on whether or not I think it's authentic.'

A flurry of transatlantic telephone calls followed, and that night Bob wrote a background piece on me and the Ibiza *milieu*, telephoning it in to John Goldman, *The Los Angeles Times* correspondent in New York. The next day, when I went to work at the studio, Robert Stewart called with the request that I had expected but had been dreading. McGraw-Hill was rushing headlong toward March publication, the galley proofs were ready, the Legal Department had made some changes and had dozens of questions – and I had to fly to New York.

'Robert,' I groaned, 'is it a must?'

'We've got to make that printer's deadline and if we airmail the galleys to you we'll be two weeks late.'

'What else is new? How's everyone bearing up?'

'It's quiet,' he said. 'No bomb yet, and Chester Davis seems to have retreated. But we need you here.'

I agreed. 'But on your head be it if Edith sues for divorce.'

When I got back to the house to break the news to her, Bob Kirsch was waiting for me with his piece on the Hughes autobiography. I read it carefully. 'If your publishers object to that,' he said, 'they should have their heads examined.'

'I'll talk to them. Let's just hold up a while on it. It'll be just as good next week as it is now, and I . . . I don't know . . .'

'What's *your* worry?' he asked, puzzled.

'I just don't want to screw things up with McGraw-Hill.' It was a weak argument but I held on to it.

That night, Kirsch telephoned again to John Goldman in New York. When he hung up, he told me that Goldman had heard a rumor that on the following evening, a Friday, Howard Hughes was going to hold his first press conference in fifteen years – by telephone from the Bahamas to seven newsmen in Los Angeles. All reportage would be embargoed until six o'clock on Sunday evening, January 9th. The further rumor went that he was going to deny the authenticity of the autobiography.

'I've got to tell McGraw-Hill,' I said.

'You can't.' Bob shook his head solemnly. 'Goldman gave it to me in confidence and I'm giving it to you the same way.'

'But they've got to know. They're like sitting ducks!'

'What you *can* do,' Bob said, 'is let me release what I've written. The *Times* will sidebar it in print with whatever Hughes has to say. If he stabs you in the back, then at least you've got my story going for you.'

'All right,' I said wearily. 'Go ahead and do it.'

He telephoned his story to Goldman and on Saturday morning – with David Walsh, who had done a new portfolio of Hughes sketches and wanted to deliver them in person to *Life* – I was driven to the airport by Edith and flew off to Barcelona to catch the Iberia jet to New York. It was the last confrontation, and the last chance for the bluff, and I had no idea what I was going to do. All I had was that same dumb faith that it had been all right so far. I had hit the pavement twice already in New York, first with the McCulloch telephone call and then with the lie-detector test, and I had bounced and landed on my feet. I would bounce again – and again, and again if I had to. There was simply no other direction to go.

David and I drove straight from Kennedy Airport in a rented limousine to Marty Ackerman's house in Lakeville, Connecticut. The time change had made us groggy and we dozed on and off as the car sped through the cold winter night, taking an occasional slug from a pint of Scotch that David had bought on the plane.

A few minutes after we reached the house I took

Marty aside. 'I've got the inside word. On Friday night there was a press conference from the Bahamas . . .'

'. . . To seven newspapermen in Los Angeles. I know. McGraw-Hill called me about it. They're already preparing a press release,' Marty said. 'They figure that Hughes is going to deny the autobiography.'

I took a deep breath. 'What are they going to say?'

'They're going to publish. They've got the goods – the contracts, the letter to Harold McGraw, the Osborn report, and the canceled checks. Those checks are like three aces in the hole.'

In five-card stud, I thought. But that was all I needed to know, and on Sunday evening, before dinner, when we gathered in front of the color television set in the living room, I had made up my mind what to do. We had expected to see the first reports on the seven o'clock news, but suddenly in the midst of Mike Wallace's 'Sixty Minutes' news show, there it was: a bleak room in a Los Angeles television studio with seven men sitting eagerly behind a semi-circular table, popping questions at a disembodied voice that came quivering and rasping through a small amplifier.

The key question came quickly, from the UPI correspondent. 'Did you cooperate or did you know a man named Irving who claims to have taped this biography with you?'

'This must go down in history,' the voice replied. 'I only wish I was still in the movie business, because I don't remember any script as wild or as stretching the imagination as this yarn has turned out to be. I'm not talking about the biography itself, because I haven't read it. I don't know what's in it. But this episode is so fantastic that it taxes your imagination to believe that a thing like this could happen. I don't know him. I never saw him. I had never even heard of him until a matter of days ago when this thing first came to my attention.'

'If you recall,' I said to Marty Ackerman, 'the voice

that spoke to Frank McCulloch said exactly the same thing. He'd only heard of Irving "a few days ago." But the McCulloch call was on December 14th – *almost four weeks ago.*'

The voice was hard, and nasal. Whether it was Howard Hughes or not, I had no idea. One of the newsmen, who had not talked to the billionaire in almost twenty years, said: '. . . He hadn't spoken two words and I knew it was Howard Hughes. I'm thoroughly convinced.'

I snorted. Marty looked at me, waiting for The Word.

'That's not him,' I said. 'It's a damn good imitation of what he might have sounded like a few years ago, when he was healthy – but it's not him.'

That was my story, and I would stick to it. A voice without a face to go with it wouldn't turn the trick. *You'll have to come out in the open, Howard. You'll have to show yourself.* And I was betting all my chips that that was the one thing he would – or could – never do.

The executive conferences at McGraw-Hill began on Monday morning and lasted all week. One seemed to bleed into another for me. Most of the men at McGraw-Hill and Time, Inc., whether or not they were willing to state so publicly, believed that the real Howard Hughes had spoken to the world on Sunday night. But it made no difference. They had their book, they had their proofs. They were going ahead with publication. In a quiet, dignified television interview immediately following the Hughes TV circus, Harold McGraw said:

'Despite his denial today, his repudiation today, McGraw-Hill has in its possession a tremendous amount of documentation which in our opinion indicates beyond the shadow of a doubt that this is the authentic autobiography and that we have the authorization to publish it. So that with this documentation and the verification that has been given, we can only wonder:

under what kind of pressure Mr Hughes might have been, if indeed, today, he did repudiate both the document and the author, and say that he's never known Clifford Irving. We can speculate on that, but we do have documentation and we've been in correspondence with Mr Hughes right up until just a month or so ago.'

Marty had to fly to California with his wife on Monday evening. He handed me the keys to his Park Avenue town house, explained the intricacies of the burglar-alarm system, and said: 'Take care of the place for me.'

The house immediately became general headquarters for the battle against Chester Davis. Marty's large, teak-paneled office was the War Room. 'Don't go over there,' Marty warned me, meaning the McGraw-Hill Building. 'The press is waiting to jump on you. Stay inside the house. I'll be back on Friday morning.' He had already made arrangements with Mike Wallace for me to appear on the 'Sixty Minutes' show the following Sunday evening, which meant that the segment had to be taped on Friday. I had argued against making any major public statements, but McGraw-Hill was insistent. 'You can't stay in hiding,' they counseled. 'That looks bad. You've got to speak out – but be damned careful what you say.'

In the meantime I had got hold of a full transcript of the Hughes telephone conference, most of which had been edited out of the television broadcasts. I read it Tuesday morning at breakfast, and immediately called Donald Wilson of *Life*. For the first time I had a genuine doubt that it *had* been Howard Hughes on the telephone.

'Those guys were patsies,' I explained. 'They were set-ups. None of them had spoken to Hughes in twenty years. They were briefed for two hours ahead of time by the Byoir Agency. They asked seven identifying questions and Hughes got five of them wrong.' I reeled off the mistakes he had made. 'But the biggest goofs came later, Don. He said he knew a man named General Harold George, but that George had never worked for him. *But Harold George was the administrative head of Hughes Aircraft for ten years.* How the hell do you explain a lapse of memory like that? And then he was talking about his movies. He said he thought they still stood up pretty well, and that one of them had won some kind of award, although he'd never won an Academy Award, he said. Well, he *did* win an Academy Award. His third film, *Two Arabian Knights*, won the first Academy Award ever presented, around 1928. Don, *you don't forget something like that.* It couldn't have been Hughes. He couldn't have spoken for nearly three solid hours without some long breaks to take oxygen. And he said he had no obvious physical deformities. But he's got a crippled left hand. *It wasn't Hughes.'*

Wilson and the people from McGraw-Hill wanted me to make some preliminary statement before the Mike Wallace show, and on Tuesday I met with three reporters – my cousin, Jim Norman, then with the AP; John Goldman; and Doug Robinson of *The New York Times*. The next morning the headlines shrieked: *AUTHOR: VOICE WASN'T HUGHES.*

Whether or not the world believed me, I didn't know. But I realized – and it was a shattering realization – that whatever the case, they were willing to listen to me.

Wilson called that afternoon. 'Where's the original transcript of the tapes, with Hughes's comments all over it?'

'On Ibiza. I left it with a friend named Gerry Albertini. He's got the only combination safe on the island.'

'We need it. We want the Osborn brothers to go over it, and we want to brush it for fingerprints. We're having a hell of a time finding any of Hughes's fingerprints on any of the letters or contracts. The problem is they've been handled by too many people.'

A few hours later, at Ackerman's, Dick called from Palma. He had been reading *The International Herald-Tribune*. 'You and Hughes have pushed Vietnam off the front page. What's happening? Are you still alive?'

'Barely,' I croaked. 'How would you like to come over here again and hold my hand? And while you're at it, you can pick up the original transcript from Gerry Albertini, the one with Hughes's handwritten comments. Bring it along and *Life* will pay for your trip.'

Dave Maness arrived on Thursday morning to show me the final copy of *Life*'s three 10,000-word excerpts. Our contract required my approval. Maness seemed semi-hysterical – *Life* was rushing to meet its printer's deadline and I was trying to cope with Mike Wallace's production men and the McGraw-Hill people at the same time. At one point I was in the living room talking to Bill Brown, Wallace's producer, who wanted to dismantle the glass doors from a bookshelf in Marty Ackerman's office, where we would be filming.

Maness suddenly threw open the paneled door. His dark eyes popping from behind his glasses, he screamed: 'Will you please get away from those goddam TV people and come in here and *read*?'

That was the atmosphere of the week: a three-ring circus. Robert Stewart had arrived, and after I skimmed through the *Life* excerpts we had a hasty conference in the hallway. 'Robert,' I said, 'they've done the worst editing job I've ever seen. What can we do?' My dismay was genuine; *Life*'s editors had attempted to squeeze as many incidents as possible of the 230,000-word auto-biography into their allotted 30,000 words. It read like a synopsis from a college crib text. 'They've lost the sound of the man's voice,' I complained bitterly. 'They should have taken six or seven excerpts and reprinted them whole. It's a hodgepodge. The reader just won't understand what Hughes is saying.'

Stewart agreed wholeheartedly, and he was equally upset. 'They rushed the job,' he said. 'It could even hurt sales of the book. But it's too late. They've got their deadline to meet and if you tell Maness it's a lousy editing he'll go through the roof.'

That same afternoon the big guns from McGraw-Hill trooped over to Ackerman's house, with Shelton Fisher and Harold McGraw leading the contingent. Time, Inc. was represented by its president, Jim Shepley, and by Don Wilson and Frank McCulloch. The purpose of the meeting was to brief me on what Mike Wallace might ask me and what I was to reply. What struck me immediately was that they all seemed more nervous than I was, at least on the surface. Inside, I knew, my tremors were equal to anything they could muster, even *en bloc*.

'Mike Wallace is tough,' Shepley told me. 'He'll be out to get you. He'll try to cut you up. Why in hell did you pick *him* to talk to, in front of thirteen million people?'

'Because he's the toughest there is,' I said, summoning all my bravado. 'Did you think I'd talk about Howard Hughes to some comedian like Johnny Carson?'

They fired questions at me for over an hour, with McCulloch leading the attack and simulating a bloodthirsty Mike Wallace. When it was over, Shelton Fisher threw a kindly arm around my shoulder. 'Kid, you're great.'

The week of tumult reached its climax on Friday. The CBS television crew arrived at eight o'clock in the morning and began stringing cables in from their trucks on Park Avenue and generally disassembling Marty Ackerman's office and living room. The thick blue carpets were covered with rolls of white canvas which in turn were covered with more cables and mechanical gear than were probably necessary for the Battle of

Atlanta in *Gone With the Wind*. Marty arrived in the mid-morning and took charge. At noon, with the Osborn brothers already waiting impatiently in the study, the telephone rang. It was Dick, calling from the airport. 'I'm on my way. Gerry came with me – he figured it might be fun. I'll be there in an hour.'

Ten minutes before we were due to start taping, the Osborn brothers had finished their preliminary inspection of the transcript. Dick stood nearby, observing. By now my faith was so great, despite the haste with which I had annotated those pages in Pompano Beach, that I had not even the most miniscule doubt as to the outcome. They handed the pages back to me with their blessing. The handwriting was obviously that of Howard Hughes.

Faustin Jehle was watching like a mother hen whose nest of eggs had been invaded by a pair of weasels. He begged the Osborns to treat the pages carefully. 'We've got to run through for fingerprints,' he explained.

'You haven't found *any* yet?' I asked, sounding dismayed.

'Just something that looks like a scar,' one of the Osborns told me. 'Looks like the left palm. Does Hughes have a scar on his left hand?'

Before I could reply, Dick said brightly: '*I've* got one.'

I held back a racking cough and the elder Osborn turned to Dick with a look that struck me as more casual. 'On my right palm,' Dick said. 'I got it playing basketball when I was fifteen.' He extended his hand to Jehle and the Osborns. 'See? Does the print look like that?'

'There goes another theory,' I broke in. 'Dick's handled practically all the letters and he brought the transcript over from Ibiza. But Hughes has a crippled left hand,' I went on hurriedly. 'He holds it cupped like this . . .' and I demonstrated. 'And I can't remember ever seeing the palm. He might press down on a piece of paper with his left hand when he writes, and if he's got a scar there, that's it.' I grabbed Dick's arm. 'Come on,' I said. 'I need your help in the study. They're taking Marty's house apart.'

I shoved him ahead of me into the hall bathroom. *'What the hell is the matter with you? You had to show them your goddam scar? Are you crazy?'*

'Take it easy,' he growled. 'You told them yourself – I've handled all the letters and I even typed up part of the transcript in Pompano Beach.'

'Sure,' I said, 'but they didn't say they found the palm print on the letters or the transcript or the contracts. *What if it was on the envelope of the letter to Harold McGraw?'*

'Oh.' Dick nodded slowly. 'I forgot about that one.'

He looked suddenly so mournful, and I was so concerned with the ordeal about to begin, that my anger evaporated. 'Don't worry,' I said. 'A scar print can't possibly be identifiable. Go downstairs and get a drink – and wish me luck, because in five minutes they're going to shove a goddam camera in my face.'

With the floodlights blotting out all hint of an audience and a microphone draped round my chest under my sweater, I sat in the big easy chair in Marty's study. Mike Wallace leaned forward in the opposite twin chair, smiling at me.

'How do you feel?'

'Fine, Mike.'

'What are those guys in the other room so worried about?' he asked, meaning the publishing contingent.

'They think you're going to chew me up and spit me out.'

'Jesus Christ.' He shook his head, scowling. 'Why should they feel that way?'

'Damned if I know. But go ahead. Fire away.'

The cameras rolled silently and we began to talk about

Howard Hughes and our various meetings. I told the tale of Dick and the organic prune. I answered some questions and ducked others. I had plenty of excuses: my obligations to McGraw-Hill, to *Life*'s exclusivity on the story of our meetings, and to Howard himself, who had enjoined me against giving clues to his true whereabouts. Two hours later I wiped the makeup off my face and found Dick on the stairway leading to the dining room. 'How did it go?' he asked.

'I'm programmed,' I said quietly. 'Push the button and the bullshit flows. I've told those stories and given those answers so many times that I'm beginning to believe they're true.'

On Sunday afternoon, at Mike Wallace's invitation, we watched the Super Bowl in a special screening room at CBS-TV. Betting on the Miami Dolphins, I lost $40 to Dick, Gerry Albertini, and Marty. The 'Sixty Minutes' show followed the ball game. I stared at myself for fifteen minutes. I had never seen a more nakedly insincere man in my life than the Clifford Irving on the twenty-inch screen. Anyone who knew me, I thought, would see I was lying. There wasn't a single natural gesture: the smile was forced, the laughter brittle, and my hands waved clumsily to emphasize every important point. I showed all the honesty of Dick Nixon or Lyndon Johnson on the campaign trail.

The next morning the executives at McGraw-Hill and *Life* telephoned me. 'You were great,' they said. 'You really carried it off. You were casual and you were straightforward. I think we're out of trouble.'

Earlier that week Rosemont had gone to court, seeking a temporary injunction against the book, but no one was particularly worried about that, either. There were such things as prior restraint, free speech, and the First Amendment to the Constitution of the United States. For McGraw-Hill and Time, Inc., everything was all right so far.

For the first time since the hoax had begun, almost exactly a year ago, I felt that events were starting to bypass me. I had become a minor advisor, demoted from commanding general to a lieutenant on the periphery of the battlefield. Two law firms had taken over: White and Case, representing McGraw-Hill, and Cravath, Swaine & Moore, representing Time, Inc., with my own lawyer, Marty Ackerman, standing beside them but cast in the role of junior partner. The change both suited me and worried me. I still had the introduction to finish, and when that was done I intended to head for Ibiza and leave the battle to the legal staffs. But the lawyers' manipulations puzzled me; I had no knowledge of law and I felt estranged and uneasy. Dick, who was staying at the Biltmore with Gerry Albertini, lay around in his hotel room most of the time reading detective novels. Last week's pandemonium had geared down to a mild frenzy. Robert Stewart arrived almost daily with galleys that needed editing, and I was still writing the final pages of the introduction. Feeling starved for sleep, I had come home early and left David Walsh in a restaurant with some friends. He was celebrating a promised one-man show at the Greer Gallery, downing alternate shots of Scotch and Eno's Fruit Salts for his ulcer.

Dick arrived in the morning and a few minutes later Marty cornered us in the hallway. 'No more pussy-footing around with this Chester Davis character,' he said. 'I want both you guys to write out statements of all you know about the whole business.' He turned to me. 'Be specific. Give all the details you can. Break it down into sections – your background and financial position, the payments to Hughes, the checks, and all your meet-ings with him. Take your travel receipts so you get the dates right.'

'What's this for?' I asked.

'This fucking Rosemont shit. We've got to get it thrown out of court.'

He was my lawyer and he knew best. I was too tired and nervous to argue. That day and the next I hammered out a 22-page statement, as detailed as possible, and I handed it to Marty with a certain pride of authorship. He read it carefully.

'What kind of a plane was it that you flew in with this Mexican from Oaxaca to Juchitán?'

'A Cessna 150,' I remembered the model number from some airplane magazine I had read last summer.

'Didn't you once tell me it had four seats?'

'Yeah, I think there was a back seat.'

'Then it couldn't have been a 150.'

'Marty, I think this character Pedro told me it was a 150. But we were speaking Spanish . . . I might have got it wrong.'

'Didn't you write down the identification number of the plane? It would have been lettered on the tail assembly.'

'I didn't look.'

He looked at me curiously. 'And what about the license number of Holmes's car, when he drove you blindfolded to meet Hughes in Florida?'

'That was stupid. I should have written it down.'

He hesitated, then nodded. 'I'll get this typed up and then you can sign it.'

Dick had written a statement about his meeting with Hughes in Palm Springs. Some hours later both documents were typed by Marty's secretary and presented to us to sign. Marty notarized them. Dick and I plodded upstairs.

'You know,' I said, 'those goddam things are affidavits.'

'Which means?'

'I'm not exactly sure. But I think they're sworn statements.'

'I didn't raise my right hand and swear to anything.'

'Neither did I. But we signed them.'

'I think I'm flying back to Spain,' he said. 'Tonight.'

'Me, too. Not tonight, but as soon as I can get the hell out of here.'

Dick had already gone to the airport when I wandered into Marty's second-floor office on Wednesday evening. He sat behind the big executive desk, nervously chewing the eraser end of a pencil. The desk was strewn with notes and memoranda, the debris of the week's chaos. 'Something peculiar's going on,' he said. 'Shelton Fisher called me. They've got some word from Zurich. Apparently . . .' Marty hesitated, seemed to choose his words with care. 'They apparently think that Hughes didn't open that bank account at the Credit Suisse.'

A cold tingle began in my gut. I forced a smile. 'So add one more rumor to the pile.'

'More than a rumor. They seem almost *sure*. Only they're being cagey about it – that's what's peculiar. They want us over there this afternoon to discuss it.'

At three o'clock we gathered in the executive meeting room on the 32nd floor of the McGraw-Hill Building, the same room, I recalled, where the McGraw-Hill executives had leafed through portions of the transcript three months ago, in September. Gathered with me about the round table were Shelton Fisher, Harold McGraw, Faustin Jehle, Frank McCulloch, Ralph Graves, and Marty Ackerman. An hour ago I handed a final draft of the introduction to Robert Stewart on the 20th floor. I was ready to leave New York.

'I wish you wouldn't,' Shelton Fisher said to me politely. 'We're right in the middle of this fight with Rosemont and we need you. Can't you stick around?'

I had walked into the meeting fearing the worst, expecting insinuations, if not accusations. I had already prepared the defense: so what if Hughes hadn't opened

388

the Zurich account personally? Had anyone really expected him to fly to Switzerland? He obviously had a loyal servant to do the job.

But there had been no attack. Where I had expected unsmiling nervousness, I was greeted with warm handshakes and cordiality. 'We're a team,' their attitude seemed to say. 'And we need you,' Harold McGraw echoed aloud.

'Harold, I'll lay it on the line to you. My wife is tired of my being away. There are personal things that enter into this. She wants me back home, and I've got no genuine excuse for not going. I can't fight this lawsuit for you. That's a lawyer's job.'

Shelton Fisher had other things on his mind, and he brought up the question of who had witnessed my meetings with Hughes. He knew of Dick's prune affidavit, and of George Gordon Holmes, and Pedro the Mexican pilot, and Jorge the Puerto Rican go-between. He coughed delicately. 'I've also heard,' he said, 'that Hughes introduced you to Spiro Agnew in Palm Springs.'

'We've checked that out,' Ralph Graves said. 'Agnew was in Palm Springs that weekend.'

'How would it be,' Fisher said thoughtfully, 'if Andy Heiskell and I reached the Vice-President, which I think we could do through some contacts in Washington, and asked him for a confirmation?' He mused for a while, then answered his own question. 'Hell, even if he admitted it privately, he'd never make out an affidavit saying it was true.'

I nodded glumly.

Fisher looked at his watch. I had already had the uneasy feeling that they were waiting for someone else to arrive, and now he confirmed it. 'We've had lawyers in Zurich all week. They should be here by now. There's something goddam funny going on. I don't know how, and I don't know why, but the Credit Suisse gave them some information about that account of Hughes. They don't think it belongs to him. What they said, if you want to know it precisely, was that in their opinion it couldn't belong to Howard Robard Hughes the American industrialist.' The emphasis was on the word *couldn't*.

I frowned. 'Meaning what?'

'Hell,' he drawled. 'I guess it either belongs to a dwarf, a black man, a very young man, or a woman. For some reason I got the idea they think it was a woman.'

Ten minutes later, Oresden Marden of White and Case walked in the door; he had landed at Kennedy Airport just two hours ago and he looked exhausted. He confirmed Shelton Fisher's statement. The account had neither been opened by Howard Hughes nor belonged to Howard Hughes. More than that he didn't know or wouldn't say.

'We left it in the hands of the Zurich district attorney,' Marden said quietly. 'And there's something I think had better be understood by everyone present.' He turned slightly toward me. 'It's out of our hands now. That's the way Swiss law operates. Whatever they turn up, they'll use, and we can't stop them.' He shrugged, as if in apology.

The meeting was about to break up when Harold McGraw stopped me by the door. 'If you can possibly stay . . .'

'I'll call Edith,' I said. 'If she'll come to New York with the kids, I'll stay a week or so. But if she refuses, Harold, I'm going.'

Back at Marty Ackerman's and alone on the fifth floor, I was able to take stock. Stunned by the revelations, yet thrown off guard by the friendliness with which they had been offered me, I had been able to offer no solutions to the questions, direct or implied. I had gone through the afternoon solely on the momentum of the past two weeks. *A dwarf, a black man, a very young man, or a woman.* If that much was known, it wouldn't take long before the dwarf, the black man, and the very young man were eliminated. So it was a woman. But which woman? Would the Credit Suisse dare reveal her identity? What about Swiss bank secrecy? It suddenly seemed to me impossible that they would go further with their revelations, either to McGraw-Hill or the Zurich district attorney. What Swiss law had been broken? Someone had entered the bank with a valid Swiss passport bearing the name of Helga Renate Hughes and had opened an account in that name. The three checks that had passed through the account were legitimate. The Swiss bank can't say any more, I decided. And even if they did, what connection could be established between this unknown Helga Hughes and Edith? A theory could be offered, a theory hopefully incapable of destruction, that a trusted servant of Howard Hughes bearing the passport of Helga Hughes had handled the checks for him and acted as courier, exactly as Edith had done but with rather than without his knowledge. And who would she be? I remembered, in the transcript, how Dick and I had laughingly assigned the name Helga to the woman whom Howard loved in his declining years . . .

There could be no link between Helga and Edith. Of that much I was certain. And suddenly I relaxed. The strain vanished and I felt as if a heavy log that I had been bearing on my shoulders had been removed. Marty was in his office.

'How do you figure this?' he asked me.

'There were three possibilities,' I argued, recapping some of that afternoon's debate at McGraw-Hill. 'Let's consider them all. Let's be unsentimental.' I had hoaxed McGraw-Hill completely; I had met an impostor posing as Hughes; or I had met Hughes, and the Zurich account had been opened by a loyal servant. 'The first one,' I said, 'would mean that I concocted the transcripts, and we know that's an impossibility. Right?' Marty nodded. 'The second one, the impostor theory, has some merit – at least in theory. There might be something planted in that book that could ruin the Hughes empire. But we can't find anything like that in the manuscript. It couldn't have been Maheu, because the impostor rips into Maheu and calls him every name in the book.'

'An impostor could have done it for another motive,' Marty pointed out. 'The money.'

'But think what that would mean. They would have had to dig up an actor who resembled Hughes physically – six-foot-three, 130-odd pounds, 65 years old. He'd have to be indoctrinated for at least a year on the private and public life of Howard Hughes. He'd also have to be a master forger, because the man I met wrote two of the letters in my presence, on Paradise Island last September. He'd have to have at least five or six accomplices. The Mexican airline pilot, the Puerto Rican who met me in San Juan, this guy who calls himself George Gordon Holmes, the man who posed as Agnew in Palm Springs, and two or three men who guarded the bungalow at Pompano Beach. The cost of pulling off a hoax like that would run to two or three hundred thousand dollars. Which means their profit over the course of two years would be about $400,000 – divided five or six ways.'

Marty shook his head. 'It wouldn't make sense. A gang that brilliant wouldn't knock themselves out for peanuts like that.'

'So we're left with only one conclusion. The loyal servant theory. I met Hughes, but someone else – someone he trusted implicitly – opened the account in Zurich for him. Man or a woman . . . doesn't matter. Maybe that person even knows how to sign Hughes's name. It wouldn't be so difficult, I imagine, to learn to forge just a signature. But the letters! No one could forge twenty pages of handwritten letters. Why would they go to all that trouble? So it was Hughes.'

Marty agreed. 'I called Edith,' I said, 'She won't come to New York. She wants me home.'

'You better tell that to Shelton Fisher,' Marty decided. 'Promise him you'll fly right back if they need you. And then get the hell out, fast.'

I called Shelton with my decision. I could feel that he wanted to protest more than he did, but I had made my announcement with no hint that I could be swayed. In the late afternoon, just as I was clearing my desk and getting ready to pack my suitcase, Frank McCulloch arrived with Bill Lambert, *Life*'s Pulitzer Prize-winning investigative reporter. 'We know you're busy,' Frank said, 'and we know you're leaving tonight. We won't take up much of your time – we want to zero in on one thing. The key to the whole mystery is this man George Gordon Holmes. Tell us everything you can remember about him.'

I gave the description again in detail – about 180 pounds, six feet tall, dark hair – adding one or two bits of trivia that I had forgotten. The cigarettes that he chainsmoked, for example, were either Winstons or Marlboros.

'You gave him the manuscript in Los Angeles,' Lambert said. 'Is that correct?'

'Right. Hughes was sick and Holmes called me and arranged a meeting place.'

'Where?'

'A street corner. He told me to drive to a certain place and wait for him. Then this guy walked up, gave me the code word, and took the book from me. That was Holmes.'

'What street corner? Can you remember it?'

I had to hunt quickly in my mind for a likely place. I remembered taking some shirts to a laundry near the corner of Sweetzer and Sunset Boulevard.

'I think it was Sweetzer, just off Sunset.'

Lambert and McCulloch looked at each other sharply. 'Listen,' Frank said, 'we think we know who Holmes is. Your description fits the man perfectly. We've had a hunch all along that confirms it. Do you know a man named John Meier?'

'I know who he is. He worked for Howard in Nevada. Something to do with mining claims or the AEC, I don't really remember.'

'His office,' McCulloch said triumphantly, 'is in Los Angeles, at the corner of Sweetzer and Sunset.'

That evening on the Iberia 747 from New York to Madrid I tried to make sense of it. I had pulled an address out of the hat and it had tied in with a former Hughes aide whose physical description fit the non-existent George Gordon Holmes. Absurdity and coincidence had once again won the day over all the laws of logic and probability. McCulloch and Lambert were hot on the trail, and the trail would lead to nothing. Adding to the lunacy of it, Lambert had thrown a final curve ball at me before the meeting broke up and I ran to catch the plane. He had contacts, he claimed, inside the Hughes organization. They had told him that a letter to Hughes written and airmailed by me to the fictional Holmes c/o General Delivery in Miami – a mid-December letter – written at Shelton Fisher's suggestion and with a carbon copy sent to him – begging Howard to do something about Toolco's denials regarding the autobiography – had been picked up at the Miami post office by someone in the Hughes organization. *Impossible,* I thought – but I only nodded. 'That proves the link,' Lambert said. He and Frank had then asked me to help them set up a trap. At their direction I wrote two brief notes to Howard and put them in the airmail envelopes addressed to George Gordon Holmes, General Delivery, Main Post Office,

Miami, Florida. 'We'll mail them,' Frank explained, 'and then we'll stake out the post office in Miami. Someone will go there eventually to pick them up – Meier, or Holmes, or whoever – and we'll be waiting.'

Dazed as I was, I made one final effort during the flight to Madrid. I had Helga on my mind – the Helga of the Zurich bank account and the Helga of the transcript. If it came to light that the loyal servant who had gone to the Credit Suisse was indeed a woman, I had to keep Edith free from suspicion. Let them believe there was a live Helga still in Howard's life.

Rummaging in my straw basket, I pulled out a pad of yellow lined legal paper. Appropriate, and good for a private chuckle.

Dear Frank (I wrote),

I've been sitting on the plane thinking & thinking about our discussion this afternoon, and playing detective, & a lightbulb has exploded in my brain – triggered by some of your questions, particularly about the room & the house in Florida on the last trip. I'm not sure of the significance; & memory can play tricks especially when you're forcing it as hard as I am now.

But, for whatever it's worth . . .

I remember some more details of the bedroom in which I last saw Hughes. I think I told you there were blinds on the windows. There were also, I believe, flowered curtains – or at least patterned chintz-type curtains. The bedspread, I believe, matched them, or was similar. The furniture was relatively light in both color and appearance, and in good taste but not showy. The easy chair in which I sat was not a big chair, or so I remember it. In other words, what I'm trying to say is: in retrospect it does not strike me as being a *man's* bedroom.

Also: and maybe even more significant – on both

the Dec. 3rd and Dec. 7th meetings, I'm sure that Holmes left the room for several minutes prior to my final departure. On both occasions he came back to get me, lead me into the hallway, blindfolded me, and guided me out of the house. On the second occasion (Dec. 7th), I'm almost positive the car was not in front of the steps where Holmes had originally parked it. I remember his having to guide some distance along gravel or concrete. I got in first; then he got in behind the wheel. He muttered something I didn't catch, *and then shoved the seat back*. The sound is unmistakable. As I've told you, Holmes is about six feet tall. Also, he turned the air-conditioning on full blast (as he always had it), and as it must have been when we originally arrived at the house.

The conclusions, unless I'm really losing my memory or fishing blindly, are obvious. I don't know what significance they have, but I'm zeroing in on this curious hint that the person opening the account in Zurich may have been a woman . . .

I went on a bit further. What good it would do, I didn't know; but one more act would hardly involve me more than I was already involved.

I posted the letter from the Madrid airport. It was a quixotic and fruitless effort.

I was still on the base paths, making a last desperate effort to steal home – but the ball game was over. The crowds had left the stands and I was out there, all alone, and blind. Worse, when I came to bat again, it would be under a new set of rules which none of us had ever dreamed possible.

18

Nightmare in Paradise

The first hint came to me on the flight from Madrid to Ibiza. It came with all the subtlety of a knee to the groin. I was stuffed into a seat with no leg room, overtired and unable to sleep, when a short pleasant-faced man came down the aisle and tapped me on the shoulder.

'Mr Irving?'

'Yes?'

He smiled gratefully. 'I was afraid you wouldn't admit it, and I wasn't even quite sure it was you. I'm Dick Eder of *The New York Times*.'

He dropped into the seat opposite me. Whatever there was to say about the Hughes controversy I had said in New York, and I steered the conversation away from the subject as best I could. I was going home for Rest & Rehabilitation and the last thing I wanted was more speculation or debate about Howard Hughes. 'How come you're going to Ibiza?' I asked.

A mild look of stupefaction crossed Dick Eder's face. He smiled at me as though I were slightly backward. 'Haven't you heard the news?'

'No,' I said, laughing. 'I've sworn off reading the newspapers. I've read so much crap in the last week that I . . .'

'Well, I don't want to alarm you,' he said, 'but you'd

be better off if you were prepared. The Swiss police have identified H.R. Hughes as a woman. They've issued a warrant for her arrest, and have a description. She's evidently a German-speaking blonde in her mid-thirties.'

'*A German-speaking blonde in her mid-thirties?*' Eder nodded. 'That can't be,' I said. 'That's impossible.'

'That description fits your wife. I met her last week on Ibiza.'

'That's why it's impossible. Or something worse than impossible.'

'There's a story,' Eder went on quietly, 'that two arrests have been made here in Spain by the Spanish police.'

'Oh my God . . . Where in Spain?'

'I don't know. It could be a rumor, but it came from a very reliable source. Where's Edith now?'

'Waiting for me at the airport in Ibiza. With my kids.'

'I hope so,' Eder said. 'I really hope so.'

The plane swooped down over the Salinas beach and bumped across the landing strip on Ibiza, coming to a final halt a few hundred yards from the white terminal building. Eder, who had a slight limp, fell far behind me as I strode, half-running, past the stewardess at the wingtip and toward the gate. Halfway there, with my mouth sour with fear, I saw a furry fox coat and two curly blond heads bobbing up and down beside it. Edith grinned at me from the distance. I turned, waved happily at Eder, then charged again toward the gate.

'Not a word to the man on the plane with me,' I said, after I had hugged the kids and drawn Edith to my chest. 'He's a reporter.'

'*One* reporter?' Edith laughed richly. 'What you think is happening here on the island? There is *dozens* of them! They come crawling round the house day and night and in town they come up to me at the Montesol and say,

"What you think of this, Mrs Irving? What you think of that?" I keep telling them, "This man Hughes is crazy. Didn't you know this always?" I have fun with them, but it's ridiculous now. It's a bore.'

'You have no idea how glad I am to see you here,' I said. 'Come on, we're going back to the house and then for a walk in the country.' I was afraid by then that the car, the house, the studio, had all been bugged.

'Don't you want a little sleep?' Edith asked. 'You must be worn out.'

'Later. I've got to talk to you first. Unless this reporter's trying to trap me, Helga's been blown. They think it's you. The Swiss are cracking wide open. And they've described you as a blonde.'

An hour later, after leaving Nedsky and Barney with Rafaela in the sandpit, we parked the Mercedes on a side road overlooking the harbor of Ibiza. It was a gray day with an unsettling damp wind blowing from the south, from North Africa. Edith's confident good mood was on the wane.

'How can they say I was a blonde? I always wore a black wig!'

'I don't know. Maybe the bank teller's confused.'

'No.' Edith trembled a little 'It's – what you call it in English? *Eine Verschwörung* . . . A frame-up! A frame-up, what is the most insane thing in the world could happen!' She started to laugh. 'The Hughes people got to Zurich, to the banks. They're trying to frame me for something not that I didn't do, but that I *did*. It's the last lunatic thing in this whole business!'

'Let's go back to the house. We'll just have to hang on and see what happens next.'

But they were waiting for us back at the *finca:* Eder, Bob Kirsch, a man from *Newsweek*, the UPI correspondent from Madrid, and a young Swiss reporter from one of the Zurich illustrated papers. There was no avoiding them, and it was only the start of the invasion. We were too tired to resist, and Edith broke out a bottle of wine and a pot of coffee, while I collapsed into an easy chair. What made it worthwhile, amid the constant questioning, was the fact that we were receiving far more information than we were giving. Kirsch was there as a loyal friend; he knew nothing and he only wanted to help, to take up some of the strain. The others, including a later arrival – Roger Beardwood of *Time* and then Rudy Chelminski of *Life*'s Paris bureau – were in constant touch with their home offices and fed us the reports and rumors as fast as they came in. Hughes had filed an affidavit in the Rosemont suit, stating once again that he had never met me and never cashed any checks from McGraw-Hill. It was notarized by one of the Mormon inner circle, Howard Eckersley, and bore what appeared to be a complete set of Hughes's fingerprints as purported proof of identification.

But the descriptions of Helga Hughes that flowed in from Zurich had no consistency. Helga was first a 35-year-old blonde, then a 42-year-old brunette, then black-haired in her late twenties, then a blonde again. She had slim, well-manicured hands; later she wore gloves. She spoke German badly, then fluently, then not at all. She weighed 100 pounds; an hour later she miraculously had become 'plump.' Of equal absurdity were the reports from New York. McGraw-Hill had postponed publication of the book, canceled it, and at the same time advanced the date of publication.

It grew wearying after a while and we sent everyone home, except for the Swiss reporter, Rudy Rohr. He was the most knowledgeable about the Zurich situation, and that was what concerned us. Edith spoke to him in German. I was drifting off to sleep in the armchair when she poked me. 'Tell Cliff what you told me,' she instructed Rudy.

He was a pleasant, pink-faced police reporter from

the *Schweizer Illustrierte*. He knew the Zurich police personally and had considerable dealings with them. 'Something funny is happening in Zurich,' he said. 'I can't really explain it. Always the police wait until they have real information before they say anything. But in this case they're talking all the time and contradicting themselves. And there are men in Zurich, Americans, who are trying to put pressure on them. A man named Peloquin. You know him?'

'He's the head of Intertel. That's Hughes's security service.'

'I can't say more,' Rudy concluded, 'except that I don't like what I hear. Let me telephone my colleague in Zurich, and then the police.'

One thought had occurred to me, and it troubled me more than anything else. The more the banking situation in Zurich became public, the deeper the investigators would probe. On her first trip to Zurich, last May, Edith had stayed overnight in a hotel using the name Helga Hughes. On the next four trips – in late May, September, October, and December – she had traveled with the Hanne Rosenkranz *kennkarte*. It had seemed a safe thing to do, granted Swiss bank secrecy. But that secrecy was splitting at the seams. Once the dates of deposits and withdrawals were known – and for all I knew, they were known already – the Swiss police, as a matter of routine, would check hotel registrations. They would come up with a Helga Hughes on the night of May 14th. They would search hotel registries for the other nights and find no Helga Hughes. It was no job to be accomplished in a few hours, but if all the names of all the hotel guests in Zurich on the nights of May 27th, September 28th, October 19th, and December 28th were fed into a computer, one name would appear four times: Hanne Rosenkranz. Edith, in presenting the *kennkarte*, had always registered with the correct address in Germany. Hanne Rosenkranz would be investigated.

And who was she? The wife of Edith Irving's first husband. The next and inexorable step was to check Spanish immigration cards. Leaving Spain each time, Edith had had to fill out an exit card as Hanne Rosenkranz.

She had always said, referring to crossing the borders of Switzerland: 'I am the weak link.' She had been right – not about the border crossings, but about the nights spent in the Zurich hotels. It was a small detail, something we had never considered. And now I saw that it was the one thing that could give us away.

I said nothing to Edith at first. I wanted to hear what Rudy Rohr could find out in Zurich. He drove out to the house just before lunch. He had spoken to his colleague, who had told him that the bank teller in the Credit Suisse had been shown photographs of Edith. At first she had identified Edith as Helga Hughes. A second set of photographs were then shown to her and reportedly she had said: 'Now I'm not so sure.'

'Then I spoke to a man I know at the Zurich police,' Rudy continued. 'They would like you to come voluntarily to Zurich.'

'All right,' Edith said bravely. 'I'll go.'

After Rudy had gone I said: 'No, you won't. Or if you do I'm going with you. But let me call Marty Ackerman first.'

I was as much confused as apprehensive. Some time during that day the *Newsweek* correspondent confided to me that the photographs of Edith had been shown to the bank employees the previous week, on a Tuesday, while I was still in New York. He refused to say how he knew, but his statement wasn't hedged. He *knew*, he said. I called Marty Ackerman in New York late that afternoon, a Sunday, and spelled it out for him.

'Don't let her go to Zurich,' Marty said sharply. 'Come to New York, both of you.'

I balked. 'I just got here.'

'Well, come back. This thing's getting out of hand, and there are some weird twists. I keep calling McGraw-Hill, and they won't even return my calls.'

That night, with Rudy Rohr, we went to a hotel in Ibiza and placed a call to his police contact in Zurich. Rudy spoke first, rapidly, in Schweizerdeutsch, and I couldn't understand a word. Finally he handed the telephone to Edith. She talked for several minutes to a police official named Lack. When she handed the telephone back to Rudy, she was pale.

'I told him I'd come to Zurich,' she said to me, 'but first I had to go to New York with you. He said in that case he was going to put out a warrant for my arrest in half an hour. They won't let me leave Spain.'

'Let's go home,' I said.

I hadn't had a full night's sleep since returning from New York. The world of the hoax seemed to be toppling. For a long time, for almost a year, we had had some very good luck. When it left us, it was not replaced by a vacuum. It was replaced by some very bad luck. Concepts had been thrust at me which I had never considered, with which I was unable to cope. *A warrant for Edith's arrest?* It was as incomprehensible as it was horrifying, and for the first time since I conceived the Hughes autobiography I knew that I had completely lost control of events.

A few days before my arrival in Ibiza, Edith had been approached in a cafe by two Frenchmen who told her: 'We want information. We've got a job to do, and it involves murder. We don't want to do it, but we'll have to if we don't get the information.' She had refused to speak to them, but everywhere she moved now she looked over her shoulder. And early Monday morning I went to my studio and discovered that someone had broken in. The studio had been messy before I left, but now it was ripped apart. If anything was missing or had been planted, I had no way of knowing and no time to investigate. When I got back to the *finca* I found a gaggle of reporters and two television crews from CBS and NBC, flown in from Madrid and Paris. Bob Kirsch and Gerry Albertini were there too, asking us if there was anything they could do to help.

The television crews were clamoring for an interview – the last thing in the world I wanted at that moment. I wanted to get out and nothing more. But what would happen at the airport? I imagined Edith, the kids, and myself stopped at any of three airports – Ibiza, Barcelona, or Madrid – and placed, without the children, on the next plane to Switzerland.

A man named Kaplan headed the NBC television crew. 'Look,' I said to him, 'I'll give you the interview on one condition. We want to leave the island tomorrow morning and fly to New York. Can your camera crew come with us as far as Madrid. If there's any trouble, I want you to film it.'

He thought it over for a few seconds and said: 'It's a deal.'

Gerry Albertini drove into town and bought the air tickets. Sitting outside the *finca* in the chill, windswept morning, Edith and I talked to the TV microphones while the camera silently turned. Afterward, I thanked Bob Kirsch for all his help. I tried to apologize for having drawn him in, but there was no way.

At five o'clock on Tuesday morning we climbed groggily out of bed, packed two suitcases full of clothes and one with books and toys for Nedsky and Barney. We woke them, got them dressed, and at seven o'clock Kaplan and the NBC crew arrived.

At eight o'clock, with a guard of twenty men from the television and newspaper media, we boarded the plane for Barcelona. We waited there and then boarded the Iberia jet to New York. No police stopped us or even questioned us. At Madrid airport the newsmen wished us luck and disembarked. The children, who had been whining and fussing all the way, finally fell asleep an hour after we had taken off from Madrid; and so did I.

Half an hour later I woke suddenly, aware that I had been in the grip of a nightmare, and turned to Edith to say something. But what came from my mouth was only a croak. I tried to speak. I couldn't.

'I've lost my voice,' I whispered.

And I knew why. I knew it immediately. There was simply nothing more that I wanted to say. The fountain-head of all the lies was drying up; something in me was saying, 'No more.'

But there was more. There was one last, desperate effort. I had always been a gambler, not at the gaming tables but in life. Without risk, no battle could be won; whatever the nature of the goal, whatever its greatness or paucity of vision, it could never be attained by letting one's spirit crumble into pudding. I had never in my life been able to cut along the dotted line and feel alive, aware. The whole Hughes affair had been a venture into the unknown, a testing of myself, a constant gauntlet of challenge and response.

I was down to my last chip, but it never occurred to me not to put it on the line, bet it, and roll the dice one more time.

No one had prepared me for what awaited us at Kennedy Airport. Marty Ackerman was there to meet us. A limousine had been hired and we were to be driven straight to his home in Lakeville, Connecticut. 'There are two hundred reporters here,' Marty said. 'Waiting for *you*. They're going to tear you limb from limb if you try to get out of this airport without making a statement.'

'I've lost my voice,' I whispered, bending close to his ear.

'Where's Nedsky?' Edith cried. We had just passed through immigration; I had Barney and a stuffed panda in one arm and my straw basket, overflowing with toys and toilet articles and odd bits of clothing, slung over the other shoulder. I had seen my face in the mirror before we disembarked from the plane; it was gray with fatigue, pouches sagged under my eyes and the capillaries had risen like red spiderwebs to my cheekbones. Nedsky was gone. We chased back and forth from immigration to customs and back again to immigration, and then out to the edge of the runway again. Edith was on the edge of tears. Her son had been kidnaped.

An airport guard found him outside in the cold evening air, watching the luggage carts come rumbling toward the terminal. He was laughing. Edith snatched him up and began to cry.

'Someone take her and the kids to the car,' Marty ordered. 'Come on,' he said to me.

I faced the two hundred newsmen: blinding lights, whirring cameras, howls, and curses – not yet at me. 'Get down, you sonofabitch! . . . You're in my way! . . . Goddammit, look out! . . .' Crammed into the small press room, the gentlemen of the press snarled like wolves and tigers stuffed into the same cage. I had no emotions left other than a mild sense of horror, and gratitude that my family was elsewhere. And I felt that the last strand that linked me to reality was about to snap. I can only remember one question that was fired at me, a question to which I had decided to offer no comment; but I lacked voice and Marty, with whom I hadn't yet spoken, was the only one who could answer.

'*Mr Irving,*' the reporter shouted above the din, '*is your wife Helga Hughes?*'

'Categorically no!' Marty Ackerman shouted back. I wanted to stop him as I had wanted to stop Bob Kirsch on Ibiza, but again there was no way.

We fought our way through the pack, out through the terminal and the gaping crowd, to the limousine. It was a cold January night. Edith and the children were snugly tucked away in the back seat. 'The driver knows the way,' Marty said. 'Don't talk to anyone. Get some sleep. I'll call you tomorrow.'

'Thanks,' I gasped.

We stopped once enroute to buy disposable diapers and then, through the long drive into the snowy darkness of Connecticut, while the children slept and occasionally whimpered, we whispered together in the back seat – trying to think and trying to plan. We felt like refugees in wartime, fleeing the battlefield but with no hope that we could even outdistance the enemy troops. It was ten o'clock at night – 4 a.m. our time – when we reached the house and unloaded the car with the help of Marty's servants. Edith slipped once on the ice outside the front steps. The children were put to bed, crying. During dinner there was a terrible thump, followed by a loud howl, from upstairs. Barney, who had always slept in a crib, had fallen out of bed.

Before morning came he fell out three more times. Edith and I were in bed at midnight, still whispering, as though surrounded by unseen enemies. And we *were* surrounded – I knew it even then, as we lay in the cold darkness and I made our plan. Finally, worn out to the point where we felt we could die from exhaustion, we drifted off to sleep. But we woke constantly during the night, when Barney fell out of bed and other times when there was only silence. And each time we clung to each other, chilled and frightened – looking for warmth, looking for hope. It was a night of true terror.

19

'Arrest Me? For What?'

I called Marty in the morning – a cold, cheerfully blue winter morning. 'I've got to see you,' I said. 'How do I get down to New York?' He gave me instructions and I telephoned to the Lakeville taxi service. At three o'clock that afternoon I kissed Edith and the children goodbye. Both Nedsky and Barney were crying.

The driver was a local man, friendly and full of chatter. 'I know who you are,' he said. 'Name rang a bell immediately.'

'You know the name? How come?'

'Jesus, you can't turn on the TV without hearing about it. I've seen you on that island, whatever its name is, and last night at the airport, too.'

'I guess I forgot to watch,' I whispered. I was still practically voiceless.

'You got two beautiful kids,' he said, and I could do no more than nod, thinking of them back in Lakeville, whimpering. What next? And where?

It was dark when we reached the house on Park Avenue. I still had a set of keys and I let myself in. Marty threw an arm around my shoulder and I said: 'I've got to talk to you. Alone.' Worried that the house might have been bugged, he took me downstairs to the part of the basement that had been converted into a small cinema. I slumped into one of the soft reclining chairs.

'McCulloch and John Goldman have been calling all day,' Marty said. 'They want to come over. They think they've found George Gordon Holmes. They've got photographs and they want . . .'

'Marty!' I cut him off. 'I've got to tell you something. If you throw me out of the house afterwards, I'll understand, because I've abused your hospitality and your trust.' His lips tightened and a worried look came into his eyes. Plucking a pencil from his pocket, he twisted it nervously between his fingers.

'Marty, listen. I wanted to tell you at the airport, but there was no time, and I was scared. Edith is Helga Hughes.'

I threw it at him without frills. He nodded slowly; he said nothing.

The rest of it was the devilishly complicated story that I had concocted on the plane and refined – as much as it was possible to refine a tale out of Irving's *Hughesian Nights* – during the ride to Connecticut and through that sleepless, terrifying night. Hughes had told me in the beginning that no one in his organization was to know he was working with me on his autobiography. But he faced the problem of the checks clearing through one of his bank accounts; he had accountants who went over his books for tax purposes. He had made the proposition to me in March, in Puerto Rico. In April, in Nassau, I had agreed and he had implemented it. Through George Gordon Holmes, he had provided a false Swiss passport for Edith in the name of Helga Hughes. We were to keep the money for him until after the book's publication. Then he would tell me what to do with it. In return for the favor, he was paying me an additional $100,000 above my $100,000 share called for in our contract.

'That's why I told you the loyal servant theory was

the right one,' I finished. 'Because Edith was the loyal servant.'

Marty still twisted the pencil. He put one hand to his face, pinching the skin between his eyes. When he finally looked me in the eye, his skin was as gray as mine had been at the airport.

'You ought to know two things,' he said shakily. 'I've asked the U.S. Postal Inspectors to make an investigation of this whole affair. And you and I have an appointment with Lenny Newman at the District Attorney's office.' He looked at his watch. 'At six o'clock – in half an hour.'

'Call it off,' I blurted. 'I can't go.'

Marty shook his head. 'They'll have your ass in a sling if you don't show up. You've got to go. If you'll take my advice,' Marty said dully, 'you'll tell them everything. Oh, Jesus.'

We arrived at the Criminal Courts Building soon after six o'clock and we were there until just after ten. Leonard Newman, Assistant District Attorney and head of the frauds bureau, was a rough-hewn, gray-haired man in his fifties. Oscar Cohen, another Assistant District Attorney, was small, dapper, alternately friendly and cold-eyed. Three other men of the bureau were there, too, and a detective. 'Tell your story,' Marty instructed me, and I did, in a hoarse whisper that must have been occasionally inaudible. I was sure of only two things: they didn't believe I had laryngitis, and my story made no sense to them. Halfway through, Newman made a brief speech to me.

'If you lie, we'll find out. If you tell the truth now, it will count for you. If you tell half-truths, you'll dig a deeper hole for yourself.'

Oscar Cohen, had a habit of wandering in and out of the room and then suddenly planted himself in front of me, where I sat sagging in a chair. He spoke in a soft, gently insinuating voice. 'It's been my experience,' he said, 'that the more complicated and bizarre a story is, the most apt it is to be a lie.'

When we left the building we were at an impasse. Newman wanted me back in the morning. There was talk of subpoenas, of a grand jury. I understood none of it. 'Listen,' Marty said, hollow-voiced, standing in the dark street, hunting up and down the canyons for a cruising taxi, 'I think they're going to arrest you.'

I grabbed his arm. I had to get close to him so that he could hear my strangled voice. 'Arrest me? *For what*?'

'There's been a fraud committed in New York State. That's for what. Either you defrauded McGraw-Hill of a lot of money, or Hughes has prepetrated a fraud by claiming under oath that he never met you and never got the money, or someone defrauded you by posing as Hughes and taking the money. Whichever it is, it's a crime.'

By the time we reached Marty's house his brother-in-law, a criminal lawyer, had arrived. So had Frank McCulloch and John Goldman. They had been waiting in the living room for two hours. 'You'd better see them,' Marty said.

McCulloch and Goldman jumped up eagerly when I came in, with Marty trailing behind. 'We've got some photographs,' Frank said. 'We think one of these men is George Gordon Holmes.'

The charade had to be played. I leafed through the photographs. I spotted Robert Maheu easily, and one other face looked familiar. It was Gregson Bautzer, a Hughes lawyer.

I dropped the pack of photographs on the table. 'None of them is Holmes.'

McCulloch's face twisted with disappointment. 'Take a good look at this one,' he said, again handing me the picture of a grinning, curly-haired man with slightly pop eyes. 'Are you *sure* that's not Holmes?'

'No way, Frank. I'm positive.'

'That's John Meier. Goddamit!' McCulloch snapped. 'I would have bet a hundred bucks on it.'

'Save your money.' I took a deep breath. 'I've got something to tell both of you, but strictly off the record.'

They nodded agreement and I told them a brief version of the yarn I had already told twice that evening. 'So save your time looking in that direction. Edith is the loyal servant.'

They stared at me, apparently unable to comment. I had only one more thing to say before they left. I knew they were conducting an unofficial joint investigation in order to track down the elusive Holmes as well as verify the meetings between me and Hughes. I had no idea how far they would go, or what resources they had, or what they would turn up, but there was one thing I feared – one thing that had nothing to do with the hoax but everything to do with my life.

'This is off the record, too,' I said. 'I'm asking you as a favor to keep it quiet. You may find out, if you're digging into my Mexican trip, that I wasn't alone. There was a woman with me named Nina van Pallandt. If Edith finds out – ' I shook my head dismally ' – I'm finished.'

The speech had taken some effort, and my voice sounded like gravel rolling down a distant slope. But Frank and John heard, and nodded. I trusted them, which was of course a mistake. They had trusted *me,* and I had repaid them in poor coin. Turnabout was fair play.

Marty and I stayed up until one o'clock, aimlessly debating what to do. 'If you go before a grand jury and you've got something to hide,' he said, nervously, 'then take the Fifth Amendment. If you've only got the truth to tell, tell it.' I had accepted that. I was still unable to tell *him* the whole truth. Had he not been my friend as well as my lawyer, I might have been able to do so; but I would have to confess to more than a hoax and what apparently was a crime – I would have had to confess to duping him personally, involving him and making a fool of him. To me he had never been anything less than loyal. Because I had assumed I could carry out the hoax to the end, and succeed, I hadn't seen that I was paying him back with what could emerge as disloyalty. My introduction to the *Autobiography* had virtually dedicated the book to him. The tribute had been genuine, then; now it seemed a mockery.

He woke me at seven the next morning, buzzing my bedroom on the intercom. We met in the living room. Marty's face was pinched with fatigue. 'I don't think I can help you with this one any more, kid. I'm a civil lawyer and I'm out of my depth. This is a criminal case and you need a criminal lawyer.' Later that day he repeated the statement to the press. To me, he added: 'I've got you one of the best, a guy named Maury Nessen. He'll be here in half an hour.'

It was the last time I would ever see Marty Ackerman. In the turbulence and embarrassment yet to come, his friendship was to vanish and turn to bitterness.

When Nessen arrived I was asked to wait in the study while Marty briefed him. Then I was hauled back to the living room. Maurice Nessen shook my hand. He was a slender, good-looking, trim man with unruly hair flowing to his collar. In a stylish, chalk-striped gray suit with a colorful bow tie, he looked as though he had come straight to Marty's house from graduation exercises at Yale Law School. In fact, he was 45 years old, and he was not strictly a criminal lawyer, but more a litigator of civil cases. Whatever he was, he was my lawyer now. From behind steel-rimmed spectacles his dark eyes seemed to dart in four directions at once.

'Come on,' he said to me. 'Let's go.'

We talked briefly in the taxi on the way to Foley Square, reaching Leonard Newman's office just before ten o'clock. This time the press was waiting. A mob confronted us with cameras, microphones, notepads; television cables stretched like snakes in all directions. 'No comment,' Nessen hissed in my ear.

'I can't *talk*,' I hissed back. We fought our way into the building and the press narrowly missed disaster when a waving microphone collided with a cop's cheekbone. When we had hacked our way to the safety of the lobby, Nessen said: 'I've never seen anything like it.'

The confrontation in the office of the District Attorney lasted for about two hours. He had had no time, Nessen argued, to get more than a few words from his client, and even those words were rarely above a whisper. He came to me where I waited in an outer office.

'They wanted to arrest you,' he said, amazed. 'But they finally agreed not to do it. Now they want me to tell you that if you'll plead guilty, they'll give your wife immunity from prosecution. Just tell me one thing. Are you guilty of a crime?'

'No,' I whispered.

'I've never let an innocent man plead guilty, and I'm damned if I'm going to start now. I'm going to accept a subpoena for you and we're getting the hell out of here.'

He managed it, and an hour later – after confronting the press once more and confirming what they had already guessed, that Edith was the loyal servant – we were sitting in his office at 55th Street just off Third Avenue. I stared at the East River and the wasteland of Long Island City. I heard Nessen's voice only dimly. 'Go back to Lakeville tonight. I'll drive up tomorrow with Harold Weinberger – he's my associate. Get some sleep. Get your story straight. I'm going to ask you a lot of questions and I want a lot of answers. The truth,' he added, almost casually.

Before I left his office I made two telephone calls. I had already strained Marty's hospitality to the limit and I knew that we would have to find somewhere else to stay. That morning a messenger had delivered a letter to me – it was from an old friend, a lawyer named Philip Lorber whom I had first met in Ibiza some sixteen years ago. He had written: 'If you need a place to stay for a while, I have a house in Westport.' I called Phil and as best I could, considering my lack of voice and that I was on the edge of physical collapse, explained the situation.

'You're going to need more than one attorney in this,' he said calmly. 'I'll be in Lakeville tomorrow afternoon by two o'clock.'

The second telephone call was to Edith. 'I'll be back on the night train,' I whispered.

'How did it go?' she asked tremulously.

I was about to say, 'All right so far,' but the words stuck in my already crippled throat.

'We're in trouble,' I said, and let it go at that.

The train jolted and bumped its way through the night toward Lakeville, and I dozed for a few minutes; then woke up in a fright, afraid I would miss the station. At midnight I collapsed into bed, after telling Edith the tale of what had happened in New York.

In the morning she telephoned Rudy Rohr in Zurich, and then Lieutenant Willi Ulrich, who was in charge of the investigation for the Swiss police. She repeated what I had told Leonard Newman: that she was Helga Hughes, and that the money was safe in Switzerland and Spain. Would she come to Zurich? Yes, as soon as the business was finished here in America.

Maury Nessen and Harold Weinberger arrived at noon. Harold was 25, good-looking, bespectacled, with a bushy mustache. Maury wore a duffel coat, an old sweatshirt, and stained blue trousers. Phil Lorber arrived at two o'clock: a grizzled, well-built, grayhaired man of fifty-odd, calm, precise, ready to help in whatever way was possible. I greeted him as an old friend. And then the press arrived an hour later. We had already begun the interrogation when the telephone began to ring and the rapping sounded on both front and back doors.

Marty Ackerman's distressed house servant took me aside. 'I can't keep them at bay, sir. And we have to live here after you've gone.'

'Get rid of them,' I said. 'Please. Tell them to come back in an hour. Then we'll go.'

'To Westport,' Phil ordered. 'Once they've gone we can drive down to my house. You can spend the night there.'

Edith packed hurriedly, dressed Nedsky and Barney, and we piled into the two cars.

I had the feeling of flight, of running away from more than just the reporters who had tracked us down at Ackerman's country house in Lakeville. Again we were refugees. The landscape was gray under a stone-colored sky. Last week's snow had already turned black along the edges of the highway, and lay like patches of fungus on the brown fields among the leafless trees. I sat in the front seat of the Volvo, beside Harold Weinberger. Edith and Maury were in the back with Nedsky and Barney. Maury questioned me without letup, from the moment we left Ackerman's until more than two hours later, when we all pulled up in front of Phil Lorber's place in Westport.

'What did you and Hughes talk about in Mexico?'

'I already told you,' I croaked back angrily.

'I know you did,' Maury said. 'Now tell me again.'

In a barely audible voice I told him once more how I had met Hughes in Oaxaca, how we had flown in Pedro's private plane to Tehuantepec.

'Let's go back a bit. These three letters you received from Hughes. You said they weren't dated, and you stamped them with the date of arrival. Why did you do that?'

'I don't remember.'

416

'Did you stamp them all at the same time or as they arrived?'

'For Christ's sake, Maury, is this important? Can't we get to the meat of it?'

Silence for a moment, then Maury's light, insistent voice once more in my ear. 'Didn't Hughes complain about the secrecy clause in the contract you brought to Puerto Rico?'

'No, he didn't complain about it. He *insisted* on it. I told you that.'

'Quite right. So you did.'

More silence, broken by a kind of sobbing inhalation from Edith. I looked in the rearview mirror. She was under terrible strain. It showed in the dark circles under her eyes, in her forced laughter, in Nedsky's increasing crankiness. I shut my mind to it all and tried to push myself into a kind of trance, to become a vegetable for at least a little while.

But Maury would not let me. He picked at me until I felt myself beginning to bleed as I lied and lied and lied – and knew that I was getting nearer and nearer to the breaking point. I had never noticed before, but now, glancing in the rear-view mirror, I did: Maury had teeth like a shark's, slanted back into his mouth, unusually pointed. I began to hate him. For Christ's sake, why wouldn't he leave me alone?

Blessedly, the trip at last ended. Joan Lorber showed us to our room, and I went right to bed. Maury and Harold continued on to New York. Phil Lorber had followed us down from Ackerman's in his own car. He came to the door and looked in, but Edith put her finger to her lips, indicating that I was asleep. I wasn't, but I couldn't face more questions. A good night's sleep, I thought, and I'll be able to cope with them again.

No way. Next morning Phil came into the bedroom. Edith was dressed but I was still in bed. I must have looked as weary as I felt. The night had been peopled with demons.

'I'm going up to see my son Brian at school,' Phil said. 'It's visiting day. But before I go, I want to tell you that I've been thinking about your story.' He smiled, a little sadly. 'It doesn't hang together. You know, I've known you a long time. I'll give it to you straight.'

'Go ahead, Phil.'

'I think you're full of shit.'

I lay there in stunned silence for a moment, then felt myself crack wide open.

'You're right,' I said. 'It's a hoax.'

The relief of confession was sweet beyond almost anything I had ever known. Phil Lorber had traveled ten miles up the Connecticut Turnpike toward his son's school, then turned the car round to return to the house. 'I just couldn't let you go down there alone,' he said. 'Call it conscience.'

We drove together to the city and dropped Edith and the two children at the Hotel Chelsea. Then Phil and I went to Maury Nessen's office at 55th Street.

'Forget everything I've told you,' I said to Maury, 'and get a good grip on your chair.'

For the next two days and nights, while Maury and Harold Weinberger prodded me with an occasional question, and a confidential secretary took down everything in shorthand, I told the story from beginning to end. I paced back and forth across the pegged pine floor of Maury's office as I spoke hoarsely, gazing distractedly at the East River forty stories below. And as I talked, I saw how absurd the whole scheme was, how Dick and I had conned ourselves again and again. I saw our own gullibility. And yet beyond the naïveté and stupidity, beyond the vulgarity inherent in the amounts of money involved – beyond all this a certain grandeur had rooted itself into the scheme, and I could still spy a reckless and artistic splendor to the way we had carried it out.

Dick had once said to me that it was an act of anarchy. We were showing up the Establishment, he said, in all its corporate myopia, in all its craven worship of the golden calf. I had shrugged off the notion. It was a hoax, a magnificent jape – and maybe, in the end, a profitable one as well. But I recognized now that it was possible I had indeed taken part in an act of anarchy; I had indeed demonstrated, whether consciously or not, but in the most graphic way I could find, a cool contempt for the underpinnings of American society. Carried away by the euphoria of confession, I almost wanted to cry out: 'Sure I did it. And I'm glad I did it. You want me to grovel? I can't. You want me to feel guilty? I don't. *Because I enjoyed every goddam minute of it.*'

But I wasn't sure that was true; and another, more profound guilt nagged at me. That was Edith's involvement, and her constant jeopardy. And beyond that lurked the fangs of revelations yet to come.

Throughout the two days and nights the secretary typed a copy of the confession from her shorthand notes. I began filling in the gaps, amending where I had made mistakes, and trying to dredge from memory all the names and dates. The revised version was typed and at two o'clock one morning we were finished.

'Those notes and that first version have to be destroyed,' Maury said.

I shrugged. 'Tear them up.'

'Those reporters know we're here. They'd go through the garbage to get that first draft of your statement. We'll burn it,' Maury decided.

Even at the end, at a time when the mask of tragedy was being offered me, we were stalked by the comic muse. The notes to be discarded filled an entire wastebasket. Maury, Harold, the secretary, and I carried it into the Men's Room of Nickerson, Kramer, Lowenstein,

Nessen & Kamin. The law firm had thoughtfully provided a stall shower for its partners and associates who sweated through the days and nights on stipulations, affidavits, and briefs. Harold Weinberger poured lighter fluid into the wastebasket and Maury dropped a lighted match. The confession blazed merrily.

'You know,' I said, 'I've had a lot of experience this past year at burning manuscripts. It takes a long time, and it's not easy. You'll see.'

Soon the blaze grew dull. Smoke came first in wisps, then in a thick white cloud, from the stall shower. Harold stumbled from the Men's Room, coughing. In the hallway, the secretary wrinkled up her nose. 'Let me poke it,' I said, but I was driven from the Men's Room within thirty seconds.

I found Maury by the water fountain, his eyes shedding tears behind the glasses.

'Turn on the shower,' he gasped.

Harold, the youngest, blundered through the haze of smoke and found the handle, and the cold water streamed down. It took nearly an hour to reduce everything to charred and soggy pulp. Close to four o'clock in the morning, in the street outside 919 Third Avenue, the job was completed. I dumped the contents through the open grating of a sewer.

'I have a feeling,' Maury said, 'that this is the beginning of a law case I'm not going to forget.'

20

The Baroness Sings Off-Key

I had neither seen nor spoken to anyone from McGraw-Hill since leaving New York in mid-January. The relationship had ended; apparently they realized it as well as I did, despite their public proclamations of 'we're-waiting-to-see-how-this-all-turns-out,' and they made no effort to contact me. I wanted to call Beverly Loo – but what was there to say? The personal apology I had to deliver would also be a confession of guilt; and the moment for that, our lawyers pointed out, had not yet arrived.

At Foley Square in Lower Manhattan, the forces of law and order were convening; the investigation was underway. The United States Attorney of the Southern District of New York and the District Attorney of New York County had elected to pool their investigative resources. 'Which means,' Maury said, 'there's going to be a fight over the body.'

'The body?'

'You, pal.'

We were in his office again and he had just put down the telephone after speaking first to Robert Morvillo, Chief of the Criminal Division of the U. S. Attorney's Office. Pleading that he had not yet had sufficient time to interview his client and learn the facts, Maury had managed a postponement of my subpoena to appear before the two grand juries.

'Let's get down to business.' Maury tilted back in his chair and lit another cigar. 'You're going to have to make restitution to McGraw-Hill, and the sooner the better. The bulk of the money is in Switzerland, in the Hanne Rosenkranz account, and you've told me that there's some of it in Spain. Where in Spain?'

'Here,' I said, reaching into my briefcase for the latest issue of *Time*. *Time* had been following the story with the relentlessness and clearsightedness of Mister Magoo on the track of a stolen flea. I tossed the magazine across the desk to him. It was open to their latest article on the Hughes affair. 'Right there' – and I pointed to a photograph of our house on Ibiza.

'You see that open shed on the right? That one stone that's whiter than the others? There's $50,000 in Swiss francs behind that stone.'

'*In cash!*'

'We left Ibiza in a hell of a hurry. There were reporters all over the place. We had no way to get it out.'

'How much?'

'I never counted it.'

'You,' Maury said, 'are just too goddam much.'

Harry Grigg, with his merry brown eyes and modified Groucho Marx mustache, was President of Interstate Security, Inc., a private detective agency with some 600 employees in New York and New England. When Maury and I told him the problem, Harry's eyes lit up with pleasure. 'This is one I'll handle myself,' he said. 'I'm getting stale behind a desk.'

Harry's job was to fly to Ibiza and extract the cash before someone else – a thief, a reporter, Interpol, or the Spanish police – reached the logical conclusion and did the same thing. The *finca* was completely unguarded except for Rafaela, the maid. I gave Harry a list of the various hiding places, which he committed to memory, and then a handwritten letter of introduction to Rafaela.

'Anything else beside the money? Anything in your studio? Any drugs? Any documents?'

'No,' I said.

He left for Kennedy Airport and 48 hours later the telephone rang in Maury Nessen's office. Maury signaled me to listen on the extension. It was Harry Grigg. 'If anyone can do this job,' Maury had cried, with pixyish delight, 'it's Harry! He's just *great*.'

'I'm at Ibiza airport,' Harry said calmly. 'I've mowed the lawn, I've washed the laundry, and I've got the summer clothes.'

'It must be a bad connection,' Maury replied. 'I didn't quite get that.'

Harry quietly repeated his message. He had mowed the lawn, washed the laundry, and he had the summer clothes.

Sweat popped out on Maury's broad forehead. He cupped his hand over the mouthpiece and hissed at me: 'Did you tell him to get any summer clothes?'

'For Christ's sake – it's *January*.'

'Harry, I think there's some kind of misunderstanding. Cliff said he told you . . .'

'I'll call you back,' Harry said, and immediately hung up.

'I think I'm going to be sick,' Maury said.

'*I* think I'm going to be poor.'

Ten minutes later the telephone rang again. This time it was John Wentworth, the Vice-President of Interstate Security. 'Maury, just before he left there was something he asked me to tell you. There's a code that we set up when I drove him to the airport. It goes like this. What's outside the *finca* is called the summer clothes. What's behind the wardrobe is called . . .'

*　　*　　*

423

The next night Harry arrived back in New York. We had just finished dinner at Maury's apartment. It was the first meal we had eaten at anyone's home since our arrival in New York and the pressures had been building on both Edith and me until I thought we would shatter like glass. That morning, with Maury, I had made my first visit to the U.S. Courthouse at Foley Square to see Robert Morvillo and Jack Tigue, an Assistant U.S. Attorney who had been assigned to the case because of his expertise in Swiss banking practices. Maury had warned me to keep my mouth shut and listen, and I did just that while Morvillo – a chunky, shirt-sleeved man in his late thirties – made a brief speech. 'Morvillo's tough,' Maury had said, 'but straight.' His pitch to me was a simple one. 'If you help us, if you tell the whole truth, you'll stand a better chance. If you don't help us and we have to unravel it ourselves, we'll do it, because we have nothing but time and manpower.' The United States Postal Inspectors, it seemed, had thrown themselves wholeheartedly into the case and were scouring half the Western hemisphere for information. 'Our opinion,' Morvillo said, 'is that you did not meet Howard Hughes. In fact, we're sure of it. And we also have good reason to believe that the story you told, the one in that affidavit in the Rosemont suit, won't hold up. The longer you wait before you talk, the worse it will be for you.'

Maury and I had a good idea what they were talking about, but that evening, at his house, we had no heart to go deeper into it. We sat with his three children for a while in front of the television set, watching a hockey game.

A few minutes before we were ready to leave, Maury received a telephone call. He drew me into another room. 'That was from a reporter,' he said. 'They know about Nina.'

I felt the first twist of the knife and asked: 'How much do they know?'

'That she was with you in Mexico last February. They've been hunting for her the last few days. They've found her in the Bahamas.'

'They'll think she's visiting Howard Hughes.' I tried to make light of it, but the going was hard. 'Has she talked to anybody?'

'I couldn't find out.'

'She won't,' I said. 'I know her. She'll tell them to go stuff it, or she'll just say "No comment."'

But *I* had to talk, because I knew that whether or not Nina did, the story of the Mexican trip and our meeting in California would come to light now. I had to talk to Edith. That night at two o'clock in the morning, in our room at the Chelsea Hotel, I told her that I had not been alone in Oaxaca and Beverly Hills.

Edith cried herself to sleep.

Whatever our private sense of desolation, the mundane world existed and threatened, and each challenge had to be met with a response. Dick was still in Palma – alone, uninformed, and vulnerable. I had called him from Connecticut the day I had made the decision to tell the truth to Maury. 'Don't,' he begged, and I had to say, over and over, 'I know what I'm doing. Trust me. I'm only talking to lawyers, not the police.'

Since then the Postal Inspectors had been to his home in Palma, threatening him with a subpoena and suggesting extradition. When they vanished, the reporters appeared. Dick locked the door and sat down to sweat it out.

'But why does he need a lawyer of his own?' I asked Maury. We were in his office once more, on the morning after my confession to Edith. I was exhausted; I had slept fitfully all night, drifting in and out of nightmares. 'Dick and I are a team. We went into this – ' the word 'crime' stuck in my throat like a bone – 'this hoax, together. We trust each other. Why can't you represent us both?'

'Because there's what's called a conflict of interest.' Maury sighed and stuck a panatella in his mouth. 'Usually, where there are two or more people involved in a crime, you get a rush to the courthouse. They're practically beating on the door to get in.' He hesitated. 'If I could arrange it, for example, what would you say to you and Edith going down to the U.S. Attorney's office and confessing? I mean, if in return for it, you'd get immunity.'

'Immunity from prosecution?'

'That's right. Anything's possible. The only thing is it would mean that Dick would go to prison, probably for five years.'

'You know damn well I wouldn't do it.'

'Quite right. You probably wouldn't. But that's what Dick will be offered – immunity in return for a full confession. His attorney would be less than ethical if he didn't explain the opportunity. I couldn't make him that offer myself – that would mean betraying the trust of my clients, of you and Edith. That's why Dick needs separate counsel.' For the first time, Maury's slight smile faded. 'You know Suskind. I don't. Now you tell me – would *he* make a deal like that if it's offered to him?'

'No, he wouldn't do it, either. Not Dick.'

'I'm glad you're so sure. In the same set of circumstances, I've seen brother turn against brother.'

'Not Dick,' I repeated. 'He *couldn't* do something like that. Even forgetting me for a minute, he'd be throwing Edith to the wolves.'

But inside I was shaken, all the warmth and security of my feelings about Dick suddenly cast into shadow by Maury's words.

Pinpoints of doubt still pricked me when I called Dick later that morning and told him that Maury had arranged for two lawyers, Merton Sarnoff and Fred

426

Boyden, to represent him, and that Boyden would be flying to Mallorca the next day – and probably bring him back to New York.

'One thing more,' I said. 'You have my word that I won't do anything here in New York without talking to you first. So . . .' I hesitated. 'Don't *you* do anything, Dick, without letting me know.'

The U.S. Postal Inspectors and a team of reporters from *The Los Angeles Times*, including John Goldman, had tracked Nina to the Bahamas. Our first knowledge of this came directly from John Marshall, who telephoned Maury on the evening of February 2nd. The conversation was transcribed verbatim by a secretary at our end of the line. Federal authorities, Marshall related, had come to see them at Treasure Cay. 'We didn't refuse to see them,' he explained, 'because I saw no useful purpose in not answering the questions. I had already read the Irving affidavit. Nina is shattered and doesn't want to talk to him . . . Nina said she went to Mexico with Irving and Irving told her that he was going to Mexico to see Howard Hughes, who he was writing an autobiography about. Irving claims he met Hughes. Nina has not corroborated,' he emphasized. 'At no time, to her knowledge, did he meet anybody at all. She told the FBI that as far as she knew he did not take a plane trip.'

Maury said nothing.

'Nina is ultimately respectable,' Marshall went on. 'She comes from a good family. It's sad that it's got out that she has had an affair with him. She has to set the record straight. I've told Nina that under no circumstances must she tell anything but the truth. She's agreed to go to the United States. She must clear her name. Her image is the height of respectability. I would like you to tell Clifford from me and Nina that he must take the consequences. *I*, as Nina's manager, must insist that she tell the truth. He showed very little love for Nina in involving her. *I* see no justification for her protecting him.'

He pontificated in this vein for a while and then Maury broke in to ask: 'Are you with the Henry Fords?' We had had a hint of that already and it was later corroborated by Frank McCulloch, who told John Wentworth that he had tracked Nina from London to Bermuda in the Fords's company. But Marshall neatly ducked the question.

'We're with the Guinesses and Rootes people in the Bahamas.'

'I'm sorry we didn't reach you,' Maury said.

'Give Clifford a message from Nina and I.'

Maury laughed. 'What kind of an Englishman are you? You mean *me*.'

'No,' Marshall replied, missing the point. 'Nina and I. We're extremely sorry and we hope that whatever he's involved in, he'll sort it out. I can't allow Nina to protect him in any way if it will damage her reputation.'

He hung up and Maury turned to me with a sad but still slightly devilish glint in his eye.

'So much for your faith in Nina, pal. If she's told that much, she'll tell everything.'

For a while I couldn't answer. Nina knew the details of the hoax. She had always said to me: 'Be careful, darling.' And yet, knowing what it would mean for me and Edith and Dick, she had not hesitated to tell anyone who would listen that I couldn't possibly have met Howard Hughes in Mexico.

'I don't understand it,' I said, feeling a little numbed.

But in the days to come it became clear to anyone who was neither blind nor deaf, including me, what it was all about. John Marshall and his budding superstar were ready to grant any kind of interview to any member of the media. Nina blushed and said, 'It's all so ridiculous.' Then she went on, quoted in a dozen newspapers: 'I am flabbergasted. I can't understand the whole thing . . . Quite honestly, you know, I didn't know very much about Howard Hughes until I read about him . . . I would see Clifford again. I am loyal to my friends. And I would love to hear the truth from him . . . It seems I've been deceived by a man who seemed to have everything – he was gentle, nice, amusing, and highly intelligent . . . I only pray to God that he will have an acceptable explanation that will justify his actions . . . It's been a harrowing experience for me, and I have come back to the United States to do what I know in my conscience I must do – tell the truth.'

It might all have been viewed as a machine-gun barrage of misquotations, except that in the midst of it an article appeared in the London *Sunday Mirror*, reprinted in *The New York Post*. It was written by Nina. It remains one of the most amazing peripheral documents in the Hughes affair, rivaling in a minor way both my affidavit and the *Autobiography* itself. In part, she wrote: 'It's all getting a little bit like James Bond. The events of the past four days have been in a world of sheer fantasy. All I keep hearing are two names. One is Howard Hughes, the eccentric millionaire I've never met in my life. The other is Clifford Irving, the name of a man I have loved and an author I still believe has pulled off the literary coup of the century.

'It was seven-and-a-half years ago in Ibiza when we found ourselves in a small beach party together. Clifford – I'd read several of his books and knew him by reputation – was in the party and we discovered we both lived on the island. I was then living with my husband, Frederik, and our children. Ibiza is a small island and it has lots of social life and it wasn't long before I was bumping into Clifford at cocktail parties and other functions. He became a family friend. It wasn't until last year that our friendship developed into any kind of relationship.'

She then described the Mexican trip, repeating that I could not have met Howard Hughes, and went on: 'Last November, Clifford and I met again in Los Angeles. I picked him up at the airport and he was all aglow over his manuscript on Howard Hughes. Clifford had sworn me to secrecy about the whole thing. At the house we borrowed from a friend I cooked some steaks for Clifford and my manager, John Marshall, and over dinner Clifford told us of the strange meetings he had with Howard Hughes.

'It all seemed so fantastic, and Clifford showed us the original letter he had received from Hughes granting him the rights to the biography.

'It looked perfectly genuine. Apparently he had known Clifford over a number of years and trusted and respected him . . .'

A few days later, Nina and Marshall arrived in New York to testify before the two grand juries. The interviews continued nonstop, this time at the St Regis Hotel and along Fifth Avenue in the February sunshine. NBC, CBS, and ABC were on hand, and dates were booked with the Mike Douglas Show, David Frost, Johnny Carson, and Dick Cavett.

Marshall capped it all by stating: 'No singing until after the grand jury. This isn't a circus, you know. We're here for serious business, to help the authorities get at the truth.' Possibly unsure that his audience had got the point, he added: 'Look, you understand, we're not here for the publicity.'

I watched some of the performances on television. This was a woman I had loved and trusted. I had held back nothing from her; I had told her everything. Edith was already facing the threat of extradition to Switzerland by the District Attorney's office in Zurich. Edith was a woman whose loyalty had no limits. The carelessness with which I had plunged into the Hughes caper had placed her in the worst jeopardy, and it brought no relief to know that if I had understood the consequences to her and my children I would never have taken the first shaky step that long year ago in Ibiza. With steadfast dedication I had hurt her and lied to her, and all for a woman who had betrayed me – lightheartedly, smiling.

I felt slightly sick. And more than that, ashamed.

Two days prior to her appearance before the grand jury Maury had managed to contact her attorney, Richard Russell. We had known that ultimately I would have to tell the full and true story under oath, and I said to Maury: 'You've got to stop her from perjuring herself.' Maury said to Russell: 'For your client's sake, she should tell the truth, the whole truth, and nothing but the truth – and my client will do the same.'

Before the Federal grand jury, Nina told her oft-repeated tale that I could not possibly have met Howard Hughes in Mexico. She denied, under oath, any prior knowledge on her part that the autobiography may have been a hoax.

When it finally came time to confess everything to the U.S. Attorneys and the New York District Attorney, Leonard Newman came to the subject of the Baroness van Pallandt. 'Did she ever know it was a hoax?'

I had no way of knowing what Nina had told the grand juries. 'Yes,' I said.

'When did you tell her?'

'At the beginning,' I said. 'In Mexico. In February, last year.'

'Would you be willing to take a lie detector test and say that?' Newman asked sharply.

I knew then that Nina had lied. 'Yes,' I said, 'I'll take a test.'

'You're sure you're not saying this just to get some kind of revenge?'

'Revenge?' I smiled sadly. 'No, Lenny. I'm saying it because I promised to tell you the whole truth.'

A week later both the Federal and State grand juries called Nina before them, to give her the opportunity to recant. The alternative was a perjury charge which I would have faced had I lied and had she told the truth the first time. She was informed beforehand what was involved, that the truth was now out in the open, and she confessed that she had known from the beginning that it was a hoax; she wept openly in the elevator in the U.S. Courthouse and before the Federal grand jury. A witness said: 'It was an Oscar-winning performance.'

For Nina the tears were apparently a brief interlude, and despite her admission to the grand juries that she had lied, the public charade continued. On April 18th, she appeared on television on the Mike Douglas Show. After letting her sing an appropriate ballad called 'Try to Remember,' Douglas began to chat with her. This was the dialogue:

DOUGLAS: You have a very nice manager . . . he's very British though, isn't he?
NINA: Yes, he is.
DOUGLAS: He's a good manager, isn't he?
NINA: He's super. He really protects me and looks after me and has helped me through a lot of things which I really couldn't have managed without him.
DOUGLAS: Did you feel at any time that this whole thing was a fraud? Did you sense that in the beginning at all?
NINA: No. Not really until Mr Hughes himself denied it in the interview he did by telephone. You remember?

One day, shortly before that, I had been talking with Bob Morvillo in his office at Foley Square. 'Tell me something,' he suddenly said. 'If you know the answer. Why do you think, at the beginning, that she went seventy-five per cent of the way toward crucifying you, but she wouldn't go a hundred per cent?'

'I suppose she was trying to protect me,' I answered.

Morvillo's look was brief – first a flash of puzzlement and wonder, then of pity. 'Protect *you*?' he said.

And then he chuckled softly, and we moved on to other business.

21

High Stake Poker at Foley Square

Dick, with Fred Boyden, the attorney we had dispatched to Spain, landed at Kennedy Airport on the evening of February 7th. Dick still had no real idea of the furor the Hughes Affair was causing throughout the country. He had been visited by reporters from the wire services and magazines, and teams of cameramen from the television networks. But compared to the hordes that descended upon Edith and me every time we poked our noses out of the Chelsea Hotel, he was living in all the blissful isolation of an anchorite.

That came to an end within minutes after he landed. With policemen on either side of him, with Boyden clutching his arm and warning him to answer 'No comment' to any and all questions, he left the International Arrivals Building and plunged into a blaze of popping flashbulbs, shouting reporters, and television cameramen stumbling backward over cables that looped in all directions. The late edition of *The New York Post* ran a photograph of him on the front page. He looked like a boar at bay, lip curled back in a tooth-revealing snarl, eyes wild and frightened – about as far removed from his usual gentle self as I could imagine.

Mert Sarnoff spirited Dick off to the Chelsea Hotel, where we had reserved a room for him a few doors down the hallway from us, and an hour later they joined me in Maury's office. I took Dick by the elbow, hauling him into an adjoining conference room. Maury's warnings about the mad scramble for the courthouse door had never left my mind.

'Welcome to panicsville.' I gave him a friendly slap on the shoulder. 'Did Boyden spell it out for you?'

Dick laughed weakly. 'Yeah,' he said. 'But don't look so worried. I couldn't have done it to you – not even if Edith wasn't involved. We're a united front. We'll sink or swim together.'

I shook his hand, and said: 'Come on and meet Maury. We've got a lot of talking to do.'

That evening, in concert with the five lawyers, we mapped out our general strategy. We would have to make a deal and we knew it. To plead 'not guilty' would almost certainly mean a long and costly trial, with only a slim chance of winning. We knew that Nina's testimony, in the long run, might hurt us but could never convict us; Maury's cross-examination of her on the witness stand would eventually force her to admit that she had known all along it was a hoax. That admission would destroy her credibility before both judge and jury. Our case was threatened by Edith's involvement with the Swiss banks in Zurich and by my mistake in the affidavit, where I had sworn that George Gordon Holmes had picked me up at the airport on the day of my arrival in Miami on December 2nd, taken me to see an ailing Hughes, and then driven me to the Newport Beach Motel. The rental contract for my car at Miami Airport had been time-stamped and so had my arrival time at the motel. What I had claimed to have done in two hours could only have been done in five.

'And even if we win in court,' I said, 'what happens to Edith? Can the Swiss still extradite her?'

'Probably,' Maury declared.

'Then it makes no sense. Let's bargain.'

The concept of plea-bargaining – the early revelation of the truth without trial in return for a lighter sentence – is at the root of the American judicial system. Without it, both the courts and prisons would be jammed to overflowing and the system itself would collapse like an overburdened donkey. Both the U.S. Attorneys and the New York District Attorney had already made the overtures to us; it only remained to make the best possible arrangement.

Our primary aim, we decided, was to keep Edith out of prison. She was the least guilty of the three of us, and we had Nedsky and Barney to worry about – if both of us drew sentences, they would be parentless. Next, we would try to keep Dick's sentence to a minimum. He was my co-conspirator, my collaborator, but I was to be acknowledged as the mastermind who had so success-fully sold the scheme to McGraw-Hill and *Life*. From the beginning there was no doubt that the sharpest edge of the judicial knife would fall on my neck. I accepted it with few qualms. I had never realized I was committing a crime – I had thought of it as a hoax. The money had always been there for restitution; the concepts of mail fraud and grand larceny were foreign to me and I had never dreamed of the possible penalties – but the feeling of guilt was still there. My heart was sore, rubbed raw with the knowledge that I had drawn Edith into some-thing she had never understood. That was the deeper guilt. For that, in all ways, I suffered, and had to take the consequences.

That same evening the newspapers broke the story of my trip to St Croix with Anne Baxter, whom the press immediately dubbed 'Scuba Annie' in the same light-hearted way they had called Nina 'the Danish pastry.' It made titillating reading – for everyone but Edith. We were in Maury's office, and she plucked the newspaper from my hand as soon as she saw the expression on my face. I had spotted Annie's photograph. Edith ran through the hall to Harold Weinberger's office, and I followed her. She turned on me like a cornered cat.

'Nina wasn't enough,' she cried. 'You had to make a fool of me again. You make me sick. All these papers,' she said, 'I save! To show to your sons when they're grown – so they know what kind of man their father was and why I left him.'

'It meant nothing,' I said, and the words sounded as hollow as they must have sounded to the millions of men who had spoken them before.

'To you,' Edith shot back. 'Because you never knew how much I loved you. You did what you pleased, while I waited for you and worried about you. But if it wasn't one, it had to be another . . .'

Tears and screams intermingled; it was too much catastrophe for her to absorb and the fury, the hurt, had to find an outlet and a victim. She swept Harold's desk clean of papers and litter, seized a china jar of pencils and hurled it at the wall. As it shattered, and as I moved forward to stop her, she turned on me and swung. A clenched fist, a lucky blow – it caught me on the neck, below my left ear, on a nerve – and I fell like a stunned buffalo to the floor of Harold's office.

If I had expected Edith to fall on her knees beside me and wail her sorrow, I would have waited forever. A minute later, when I managed to climb to my feet and drop into Harold's desk chair, she was gone. I laid my head in shaking hands and waited for the pain to go away.

That night I walked through the streets of the city, alone, more miserable than I had ever been in my life.

Toward the end of the week we made our arrangements with Bob Morvillo and Lenny Newman. I would tell them everything and plead guilty before both a Federal and a State court. Dick would be named only as a co-conspirator in the Federal court and would plead guilty to the State. No promises would be made to me by the government; the sentence would be entirely in the hands of the judge. Morvillo would make no recommendation. If I received two years' or more imprisonment in the Federal court, Dick would get a maximum of one year from the State. If I received less than two years, Dick's maximum would be six months. Edith, whom both prosecutors realized had been no more than a courier and a loyal wife, would be granted immunity from prosecution. Morvillo and Jack Tigue volunteered to fly to Switzerland to plead with the Swiss prosecutor, Peter Veleff, the Zurich District Attorney, on Edith's behalf. There was to be no double jeopardy in the United States and Switzerland. That, as far as I was concerned, was the key and the *sine qua non* to the deal. Edith had to go free.

Morvillo and Tigue took off from Kennedy Airport on a Thursday night, flying Sabena Airlines to Brussels, where they were picked up by a U. S. Postal Inspector. From there they flew to Zurich. Early Friday afternoon they met with Veleff and Lieutenant Willi Ulrich of the Zurich police.

Late that night, Bob Morvillo telephoned Maury from Switzerland. 'I had a hell of a time,' he said, 'but it's okay.'

Veleff, he explained, had been horrified at the idea of plea-bargaining in general, and also at the American concept of the Fifth Amendment, which gave a man the right not to testify against himself or to make a statement which might tend to incriminate him. 'However, he thought our pitch was strong and inherently reasonable,' Morvillo said, 'and he had no objection – but he had no power to ignore the fact that a crime had been committed.' He could not let Edith go free if she were simply given immunity from prosecution in America.

Disturbed at the reaction, Morvillo persuaded Veleff to take him to see the Attorney-General of the Canton of

Zurich, Doctor Luty. 'Then I came up with the idea,' Morvillo related, 'of charging Edith with conspiracy. If we included all the Swiss charges in a single conspiracy charge before the Federal court, it might get round the problem. Luty got the point and thought it was a good idea. He agreed that if we charged either of the Irvings with anything, the Swiss wouldn't proceed with their charges. In fact, he agreed to put a stop to the extradition proceedings.

But Veleff, the prosecutor, was unenthusiastic about the arrangements, and the following morning a second meeting was held. 'We re-stated the proposition,' Morvillo explained, 'and Veleff agreed to go along with the deal.'

Our relief and gratitude were short-lived. The promise of freedom for Edith lasted less than a week, by which time we had committed ourselves to confession. Bob Morvillo and Jack Tigue had done their best; their actions had been not merely self-serving but humane. On Monday morning, however, the newspapers bannered the story on page one: *SWISS OK DEAL ON IRVING'S WIFE*. The story in *The New York Daily News* went on: 'Swiss and United States authorities have made a secret deal to drop charges against Clifford Irving's wife, provided author Irving cooperates with investigators and that "someone goes to jail" . . .' The other New York newspapers trumpeted the alleged deal with equal certainty and disregard for the consequences.

How the story leaked to the press, no one knows or will admit. But the damage was done. Apparently deciding that dignity was more precious than either justice or a firmly given commitment, the Swiss authorities wrote to Robert Morvillo. 'They've simply reneged,' he told Maury. 'They take the position they had made no deal.'

Later the Swiss authorities claimed that it had all been a misunderstanding. 'But there was no possible misunderstanding,' Morvillo said flatly. 'We had an interpreter with us, and Jack Tigue speaks German. It was repeated three or four times on two separate occasions. I wouldn't have left Zurich if it was vague or ambiguous in the slightest. They just reneged.'

We sat in the anteroom of Morvillo's office for hour after hour while Nessen, Sarnoff, and Lorber hassled back and forth with Morvillo, Tigue, Newman, a sprinkling of postal inspectors, and other government and state attorneys. We could hear the voices but not the words – except when the tone grew acerbic or loud with rage, when Morvillo's cutting tenor came through the door like a knife, underscored by a bass rumble from Sarnoff, speaking around his ever-present pipe, and by placating noises from Phil Lorber's slightly deeper tenor.

I felt like a kid who had been caught playing hooky and was waiting to see the principal. Dick and I made feeble attempts to chat with the two secretaries in the anteroom. Once, after a particularly virulent outburst of angry voices, Phil came out shaking his head. 'That Maury,' he whispered. 'Playing brinkmanship like Kennedy with Khrushchev! I wouldn't have the balls.'

Periodically Sarnoff would come out to confer with Dick and Maury with me. Then they would return to Morvillo's inner office and the poker game would go on. The stakes were our freedom – in effect, our lives.

Buried as we were in the rotted hold of a sinking ship, there was still time for humor. 'It's either laugh or cry,' I said to Dick. 'I don't give a damn what the press thinks. They want me to beat my breast and grovel in public, but I can't do it. I didn't kill anybody or rape a ten-year-old girl. They're big boys over at McGraw-Hill and *Life*.' I remembered the lie-detector test and the mysterious absence of the promised final written report. A moment in time arrives, I decided, when the victim's willingness may lead him, consciously or otherwise, across the thin dividing line between gullibility and culpability.

By then *Time* had dropped President Nixon from the cover of their February 21st issue and substituted a portrait of me – which even my own children couldn't recognize as their father – naming me *Con Man of the Year*. Among other things I was accused of being in debt to Carlo Gambino of the Mafia, wife-beating, drug-taking, and heavy drinking; and if they had known I had a pet mongrel dog back in Ibiza, bestiality might have been included in the list of my sins. *Time* had Dick rushing to the U.S. Attorney and 'in exchange for immunity from prosecution . . . willing to testify that contrary to his earlier affidavit, he had never seen Hughes.' Equally fictional was *Time*'s report on my reaction to Frank McCulloch's informing me that 'we've got the Phelan manuscript . . . and we're going to lay it down alongside your manuscript in the morning and read them together.'

Jim Phelan was the writer who had ghosted the first version of Noah Dietrich's book, which Stanley Meyer had so affably given to us. Phelan arrived in New York and the manuscript was compared with *The Autobiography of Howard Hughes*. The similarities were obvious, but *Time*'s editors worked dutifully and doggedly, eliminating every possible difference between the two versions, in order to make it appear that passages had been plagiarized. At the same time Phelan was telephoning night and day to the Chelsea Hotel, desperately trying to reach me. Calls from the press had become so burdensome that we had asked the switchboard to put them through to a friend, James Sherwood, a writer also living in the Chelsea. Sherwood acted as a buffer between us and the outside world, and this produced one of the minor ironies of the whole affair. Our voices were similar and I was often in Sherwood's apartment; half the time when Phelan thought he was talking to Sherwood, he was actually talking to me, pretending to be Sherwood.

Sherwood and I often took notes and Phelan once said: 'Cliff stole my property? Bullshit! I never thought it was any good myself. It wasn't worth stealing – but Cliff dressed it up and made it look pretty good . . . There I was, up on top of McGraw-Hill, and all seven vice-presidents opposite me, stuffed shirts hanging onto their precious book they wouldn't let me see . . . Here's this sunshine kid coming from his island to the big city, and fighting for his life, and this old gumshoe who earned a salary all his life is living it up . . . This whole fraud caper really boils down to one generation against another.'

Later, in an article commissioned by *Esquire*, but which that magazine finally decided not to print, Sherwood wrote:

'. . . A voice on our telephone came through with desperate loneliness. He identified himself as Jim Phelan, being featured in the *Time* cover story. Jim's was a halting style of phone conversation. His voice was whiskey-hardened. Its tone was garden-path gravel. Every syllable crunched. Said Phelan: "I want Cliff to know I'm Inspector Javert and he is Jean Valjean . . . I've gone down in the sewers after him, and I've found the truth . . . He's written a very great book on Hughes. My book was so bad I never wanted to sign it, and no one wanted to give me a dime for it until Cliff came along. Now I've made $60,000, thanks to Cliff . . . I can tell you this. I know the truth, and I can turn around on a dime and support Cliff, only *Time* paid me more than a dime. If I stand up to support Cliff, I'll never live to sit down. I'm 59 years old, and *Time* has too much invested in my story . . . Cliff Irving has been knifed by some of the great corporations of this country, because he's shown them the truth . . ."'

After his trip to Zurich, Bob Morvillo returned to New York and flew on from there to Barbados for a week's vacation with his wife. In Barbados he picked up *Time* and read the story, which quoted him as saying, in a warning to Maury Nessen: 'All right, but Irving should know that we'll break his balls before the grand jury if he says he met with Hughes.' Morvillo had never said anything faintly resembling those words, and he had never spoken to a *Time* reporter. He flew into a mild rage and handed the article to his wife. She read it and said: 'This man Irving must be a horrible person.'

Morvillo laughed. 'I just finished telling you that everything they said about me and the U.S. Attorney's office was a lie. What makes you think the rest of the garbage they write is true?'

It was a good summing up, but it also occurred to us that *Time* might be launching an advance smokescreen to obscure any possible revelations concerning their sister publication, *Life*. It was already known that we had had access to the version of Noah Dietrich's autobiography written by Jim Phelan, but no one as yet had revealed that our principal mine of information was the secret files of *Time-Life* itself. Apparently no one in the publishers' ranks intended to reveal it, either. Ralph Graves, *Life*'s Managing Editor, who with Dave Maness had given me access to the files that past June, wrote an extraordinary editorial in the February 25th issue of *Life*. 'Close parallels,' he said, 'have been discovered between Irving's book and an unpublished manuscript by James Phelan based on talks with Noah Dietrich (*Time*, Feb. 21), but much remains unaccounted for and much remains to be learned about Irving's sources and how he got them. Both *Life* and McGraw-Hill intend to continue their investigations . . .'

'For Christ's sake,' I said to Dick, astonished. 'They know where I got the material. *From them!*'

Dick shook his head sadly at what he considered my naïveté. 'You forget, *amigo*, there's no con game without a mark, a sucker. And more often than not, the mark

443

makes it all work because *he* thinks he's going to make a killing. He usually shuts up at the end and you don't hear a peep out of him – unless, of course, it gets down to the wire and he knows someone else is going to blow the whistle. Remember W. C. Fields's classic statement. It's the last word on hoaxes: "You can't cheat an honest man."'

'Come on. What are you trying to give me? The people at McGraw-Hill and *Life* are honorable men.'

'So was Brutus, and *I'm* not trying to give you anything. The judge is going to give it to you, schmuck – right between the eyes.' Dick guffawed.

'That reminds me,' I said seriously, 'what do you say when he peers down at you and pronounces sentence? Can you protest? Or do you just say: "Thank you, Your Honor . . ."?'

'You don't say anything.' Dick's laughter trailed off, too. 'You just faint.' He managed a weak smile – 'But don't worry about hurting yourself on the floor of the courtroom. If you fall in the right direction, you'll land on me.'

Harold McGraw had finally announced, 'We've been taken,' and McGraw-Hill was later to return to *Life* the monies received for serialization rights.

Until the day we pleaded guilty, Dick and I practically lived in Maury Nessen's office. Dick awoke at six, waited for the 23rd Street Automat to open so that he could eat his usual substantial breakfast, and then walked briskly up to 55th Street and Third Avenue – a jaunt which, he said, 'starts the day off right. And from then on it's downhill all the way.' I fumbled awake around nine, had a sleepwalker's breakfast of coffee and cake, and reached Maury's about an hour later. We would immediately begin the round of question and answer, speculation and maneuvering which would keep us occupied seven days a week, often till midnight or even later, until the middle of March. Maury was on the telephone almost daily to Morvillo, Tigue, and Newman.

When Maury was not fencing with the prosecutors, he and Mert Sarnoff and Phil Lorber were putting Dick, Edith, and me through our paces, preparing us for our appearances before the grand jury and also for the private sessions of *mea culpa* with the U. S. Attorneys and the District Attorney. Time and again during those preparations, Dick was reduced to stuttering, helpless silence.

'All right,' Mert Sarnoff would say to him, pinpointing a date or an event, 'don't tell me what you thought. Listen to the question! I want to know: *what did you say to him, and what did he say to you?'* – and Dick would attempt to reconstruct our conversations in Palma at the quayside, in our bungalow in Pompano Beach, in Palm Springs, getting the dates confused, forgetting when we had been where, and almost totally unable to remember the whereabouts of the $750,000 we had received from McGraw-Hill. I couldn't understand what was wrong: it wasn't like Dick to fall apart this way, and all of us – the attorneys and myself – began to worry that he would collapse before the grand jury and seriously compromise our intent to tell the truth. And then I suddenly understood what the problem was, what was making him hunch down in his chair and edge nervously around the simplest questions: he was conscience-stricken at the thought of laying so much of the blame on me. I took him to one side – it was nearly two o'clock in the morning and we had been talking non-stop since early that afternoon. I said: 'Listen, old buddy, words like "stool pigeon" and "squealer" don't apply in this situation. We've got a story to tell and I've been elected the bad guy.'

'Yeah,' Dick said, wearily. 'And I'm the dupe, with two hundred grand stashed away in Zurich and another fifteen in stocks with Merrill Lynch.'

'If it's any comfort to you, you're going to wind up a pauper.'

I was referring to the fact that efforts toward restitution had begun a few days after my arrival in New York. On my behalf, Maury had told both the U.S. Attorney's office and McGraw-Hill that I was willing and able to return the full amount of money they had given me over the course of the year: $750,000. Those efforts, however, were frustrated almost immediately by three parties: the Swiss government, the U.S. Internal Revenue Service, and McGraw-Hill itself. The Swiss had instantly frozen not only the Hanne Rosenkranz account, but Edith's long-standing account with the Union Bank of Switzerland in Winterthur.

The Winterthur account contained only $5,000 of the 'Hughes' money (a repayment by me of an old debt to Edith, dating from the time we bought our house in Ibiza), but the Swiss apparently made no distinctions: they were out to put a lock on everything and anything, including Edith's inheritance from her family. The IRS had frozen all our bank and brokerage accounts in the United States, and demanded $500,000 as income tax on the $750,000 'earned' in 1971, despite my announcement that it was to be returned to McGraw-Hill. McGraw-Hill, in turn, had triply complicated the financial picture by refusing, through their lawyers, to take a position on restitution of the money until after our plea of guilty. They would not want the world to think we were forgiven our heinous crime.

'So stop the soul-searching,' I said to Dick. 'If you don't think society knows how to take revenge on *zhlubs* like us who make the Establishment look like dummies, you're just kidding yourself. And the worst is yet to come.'

As soon as Dick realized that he was hanging with me on the edge of a vat of boiling oil, he became his old self again – not quite as cheerful as before, but at

446

least a reasonable facsimile – and the rehearsal for cross-examination began to make progress.

One reason we spent so much time in Maury's office – aside from the need to get the facts straight before our grand jury appearances – was because the alternatives had become so unpalatable. In the street, in restaurants, or even in the Chelsea Hotel, we were treated like celebrities. A celebrity, I soon realized, is a form of social freak: prey to every chance passer-by, a foreigner to the joys of anonymity and therefore deprived of all peace and privacy, and liable to be misquoted if he asks for the time of day. Vanity may be tickled the first time, or even the tenth time, but by the hundredth time it becomes a weariness of the flesh. On two occasions, however, it did give me a good chuckle. One morning in the Automat on 23rd Street and Seventh Avenue a short, tired-looking, middle-aged man in a windbreaker came up to me and said, 'Mr Oiving, I want ya to know the woiking people are behind ya.' A few nights later, at midnight, returning to the hotel after walking the babysitter home, a drunk planted himself squarely in my path. 'I wanna tell you something,' he said, 'cause I know who you are.' He looked red-eyed and dangerous, and when he jabbed a stubby finger at my chest I thought we were in for some trouble.

'Okay,' I said, warily.

'Don't give back a penny of it, kid,' he whispered.

I could see that we made good copy for the media, but after a while that made no sense to me, either, unless my invariable reply of 'No comment' simply whetted the newsmen's appetite for something more substantial. Were we heroes? Anti-heroes? It puzzled me. Had we been truly *successful*, we might have felt like heroes – although the world would never have known. But we had failed. In the repressed, middle-class world of America, where so few men try to do anything other than cut along the dotted line, could the failure itself of a bold and lunatic scheme be the image of ultimate success? Whatever the answer, it would have to be beside the point. I knew what we had done: we had created a fictional autobiography, tried to perpetrate a hoax, and had been caught. I was still the man I had always been. Some five or six years ago, in another book, I had written: 'Men wear masks on which they carve portraits of what they would like to be or think they ought to be. Opportunity, like fortune, does not change a man – it unmasks him. What is under the mask may surprise you; as it often surprises the man. But it was there before.'

In Maury's office we could be ourselves: our crime was known to the last jot and tittle. We were not specimens, objects of curiosity: we were people about whom one might say, 'There but for the Grace of God . . .' Maury soon became more than our lawyer; he became our friend. Such was his confidence in us that he provided us with a key to the office so that we could come in and work at any hour of the night. We had valuable documents, too, that needed a secure resting place; and after the first week we were given the combination to the firm's safe. I was touched.

'Think of it,' I said to Dick. 'They gave me the combination to the safe. Don't they know I'm "Con Man of the Year"?'

Dick brought me back to earth. 'That just proves it,' he said, shaking my hand.

By contrast the world outside the office was an obstacle course and a jungle – and nowhere more so than in the Chelsea Hotel. There, in our two-bedroom suite on the fourth floor, Edith and I nightly created our private version of hell. Recriminations, tears, apologies, more recriminations, with the children yelling and crying, and Dick fleeing back to the less painful isolation of his own room; sometimes until three or four o'clock in the morning, Edith poured forth her anguish from wounds I had inflicted and which my mere appearance reopened; hour after hour I begged, I entreated, I pleaded, I apologized.

But it had to be borne, because what she bore was worse. I could only, in retrospect, see Edith as a victim – a victim of her love for me, her trust, and her own naïveté. I had asked her to travel to Zurich for me as a courier and she finally agreed, and the reason for that agreement – which she gave to me now in New York for the first time – was an astonishing one. But I knew her, and I knew it was true. 'I guessed about you and Nina,' she said. 'I knew it wasn't really over. I thought this would bring us closer together, what we needed. And I thought, what makes me sick now to realize how dumb it was of me, that if you did this thing it would keep you so busy you'd stay out of trouble.' By trouble, of course, she meant only one thing: Nina.

The Zurich bank and police officials had already stated their absurd conviction that Edith was probably the mastermind behind the whole scheme, because of her 'sophisticated knowledge of Swiss banking procedures.' Even *The New York Times* dug up a quote from 'a friend, Mrs Christine Geiser,' who supposedly said: 'If this Hughes thing is true, it was Edith who was the active person. Clifford may have thought of it as you would think of a plot for a book, but she is the one who all at once says, "Come, let's try it." She does what she likes, like a child of 4. She has no inhibitions.' Neither Edith nor I had ever known a woman named Christine Geiser.

Edith had trusted me and I had failed her and betrayed her in every way possible. She faced charges in Switzerland as well as America, and it looked as though the Swiss were out for blood as well as the pound of flesh: their banks – their *raison d'être* as a nation, since the cuckoo clock had gone out of fashion – had been embarrassed and might even be accused, by a jury made up of other than Swiss bankers, as culpable. The sense of guilt I felt regarding the fate of her and the children cut deeper into my heart than any guilt I would have to plead before the court. My guilt before the law was clear and the limits of punishment were equally clear. But the limits of punishment and the method of payment for having placed Edith in such jeopardy, for having damaged her pride as a woman, and for the precarious future I might have created for two small boys – these punishments and penalties had no boundaries.

I had hit the pavement at last, but there was more wreckage than just my bones.

In early March we gathered in Bob Morvillo's office to tell the tale. I went first, reciting the facts through a session that lasted nearly seven hours. Bob Morvillo leaned back in his chair and fired the first question.

'Have you ever met Howard Hughes?'

'No,' I said.

From then on it was a dreary session. There were only two moments when the prosecutors appeared to doubt me. The first was when Lenny Newman asked if Nina had ever known that it was a hoax. The second came when I was asked the identity of the forger. Jack Tigue had already suspected it was me, and I had given handwriting samples to the Federal grand jury; even an unprofessional eye could see that there was a natural similarity between my handwriting and that of Howard Hughes. Back in late January, when the U.S. Attorney's office had first decided on a joint investigation with the New York District Attorney, the prime suspect for the forger had been Elmyr de Hory, my ex-friend who had been the protagonist of *Fake!* and the premier art faker of the century. The government investigators cast a wide net. According to Robert Morvillo, they also contemplated the theory that I had had an accomplice inside either McGraw-Hill or Time, Inc. But they simplified matters with the decision that in the long run I had the key which could unlock the entire mystery, and so all efforts were concentrated to induce me to come in and tell the story.

Lenny Newman still seemed slightly skeptical that I was the forger. After all, as Dick had remarked a year ago in January, forgery was a profession. You just didn't pick up a pen and a single sample letter and write eighteen pages of script that received the unequivocating stamp of authenticity from two famous handwriting analysis firms. Newman looked at me, frowning.

'How long did it take you to write that nine-page letter from Hughes to Harold McGraw?'

'Not very long. Maybe an hour. Maybe less.'

'Our handwriting expert says that would be practically impossible. How many drafts did you make?'

'Just one.'

Newman raised an eyebrow. 'Would you mind?'

'No, what the hell. Give me a pad of lined paper.'

Chuck Clayman, Newman's assistant, provided me with a pad of lined paper.

'Just a letter to yourself,' Newman said. 'Sign it "Howard R. Hughes."'

Resting the pad on my knee, I knocked out a brief note once again giving me Howard's permission to offer his autobiography to McGraw-Hill. Newman blinked twice, then showed it to Clayman. 'I'd like one, too,' Jack Tigue said. 'I want to show it to our expert in Washington.'

I wrote another letter. Tigue clucked his tongue and handed it to Henry Putzel III, the youngest of the Assistant U.S. Attorneys. Putzel later framed it and hung it on the wall of his office in the United States Courthouse building at Foley Square. Close to six o'clock, nearing the end of the long interrogation, we came to the incident of the purported Howard Hughes telephone call to the seven newsmen. 'Why the hell didn't you say it *was* Hughes calling?' Jack Tigue asked me. 'That might have given you a better chance.'

'It just never occurred to me,' I said.

'Didn't you recognize the voice?' Henry Putzel asked, puzzled.

On that note, with all of us laughing and Putzel looking slightly red in the face but taking the *faux pas* with his usual good humor, we all shook hands and decided to call it a day.

We had one more session, this time with Dick and I together, to go through the transcript and indicate our sources for each anecdote, each bit of information.

'We got that from the *Time-Life* file,' Dick or I would say. 'That was in the Dietrich manuscript, but in a different form.' 'That's out of the whole cloth – pure bullshit.' This last response was the one most frequently heard, and invariably invoked Morvillo's high-pitched peal of laughter, and amused head-shaking from Tigue and Putzel.

Toward the end of the session, Tigue said to me: 'What I don't understand is why you treated John Meier so kindly – calling him "a nice kind of dope."'

'That wasn't John Meier,' I said. 'That was Johnny Meyer, Hughes's publicity man during the war.'

'No,' Tigue said, 'it was Meier. I haven't got those pages here, but I'm sure of it. I read it.'

'But I *wrote* it. You're wrong, Jack.'

Tigue's lips set in a tight smile. 'Not a chance. It was John Meier, the guy who's running for Senator in Nevada.'

'I'll bet you a year.'

Maury gasped and Morvillo jerked upright in his seat. 'I'll check it in Maury's office,' I said. 'I've got a copy there.'

I was right, and I called Tigue and read him the passage. 'But I can understand why you were confused,'

I said, 'so I won't hold you to the full year off the sentence. I'll settle for six months.'

There was a moment of embarrassed silence; then Tigue said lightly: 'If it was in my power, Cliff, you'd have it.'

After that we went before the Federal and State grand juries to repeat the tale, this time under oath. The long, disheartening hours of *mea culpa* were finally enlivened when it came time for the Federal grand jury to dismiss Edith from the room. Edith had finished the recital of her various trips to Zurich; there was little else she knew or could tell. Jack Tigue directed the foreman of the jury to dismiss her, and the foreman said: 'You're excused, Mrs Hughes.'

22

Guilty, Your Honor

Indictment day: Thursday, March 9th – one day before McGraw-Hill had scheduled official publication of *The Autobiography of Howard Hughes* – opened with howls from Barney, whines from Nedsky, and with me burrowing deeper into the bedclothes in an effort to avoid facing what had to be faced.

Maury and Phil were to pick us up at nine-thirty and take us down to the Federal Courthouse, where we would hear a portmanteau charge which included Conspiracy to Defraud, Forgery, the Use of Forged Instruments, Using the Mails to Defraud, and Perjury. At nine o'clock, as I was somnolently munching pound cake and sipping coffee, Dick came in. He was wearing what he called his 'courthouse suit' – a black single-breasted worsted, with a white shirt and black knit tie. It also happened to be his only suit.

'I've got the answer to the question.'

'What question?' I muttered.

'You asked me last night how to keep your nails trimmed in prison, when they won't let you have a nailfile.'

'Yeah. How?'

'Claw the walls.' He burst into loud laughter, which

454

lasted until he stuffed a chunk of pound cake into his mouth with trembling fingers.

Edith said, '*Merde.*' I winced; and the babysitter looked at Dick as if he had lost his mind: which in a sense he had.

Dick was not named in the Federal indictment, except as a co-conspirator. He set out on foot for Sarnoff's office on 41st Street; from there they would take a cab to the State Courthouse, where we would join them and where all of us – Dick, Edith, and myself – would plead guilty to Grand Larceny, Conspiracy, and a variety of other charges. In this way the demand 'for a body' by State and Federal authorities would be satisfied; although, since Dick outweighed me by about seventy pounds, New York State was getting more for its money.

Before Judge John M. Cannella of the Southern District of New York, Edith and I were officially indicted, which was the prelude to formal arraignment. Edith, in fact, had already been arrested two weeks previously, based on the Swiss warrant for extradition. Bail had been fixed at $250,000 and her physical presence was limited to New York and Connecticut. 'If you go more than halfway across the George Washington Bridge,' Maury had tried to explain to her, 'you're out of the jurisdiction and you forfeit the bail.' But the reality of this failed to permeate Edith's mind and she was never able to understand how she was under arrest when she could trek with Nedsky and Barney every morning to the corner grocery store and spend her afternoons in the Chelsea Hotel, painting. Not that she believed herself to be free, for the Chelsea and New York City itself were for her a prison without bars.

As soon as the courtroom formalities had finished, I was led down to what seemed to be the dungeon of the building, fingerprinted, and photographed in color with a Polaroid camera. My bail was fixed at $100,000. Our appearance in the State Court before Judge Joseph

455

Martinis was much the same as in the Federal Court. Dragging a train of reporters and cameramen behind us, we were escorted by detectives to the Fifth Precinct House on Elizabeth Street to be booked. The newsmen poured into the precinct house on our heels and immediately began setting up lights and cameras as though it was a Hollywood soundstage. We were then led into a back room from which the press was barred.

The room had all the charm you might expect in one of New York's oldest precinct houses – peeling yellow-green walls, scarred furniture, posters of wanted men tacked up on a cork bulletin board.

A detective brought in some papers for us to sign. 'You're allowed to make one phone call,' he said. 'If you don't want to make it, sign these waivers.' Edith and I both signed, but Dick hesitated. 'Is it all right if I call my wife? She's expecting it.'

'Sure, go ahead,' the detective said.

'Well, she's in Spain,' Dick said.

'Gee, I don't know. Spain . . .' The detective scratched his chin. 'I'll have to find out about that.'

'Never mind,' Dick said. 'I'll call her later.'

We were taken out into the turmoil. We stood at the rail facing the desk, jammed in on all sides by lawyers, detectives, uniformed patrolmen, and about fifty reporters, a dozen of whom jabbed microphones in our direction. The microphones also lay across the huge desk before which we stood. They seemed to be silently pleading with us to say something – *anything*. I whispered to Mert Sarnoff, who was standing at my right shoulder: 'It's a fucking circus.' This appeared in the daily press as: 'Irving turned to his attorney and whispered, "You're standing on my foot."' Of such stuff is history fashioned.

'Where to now?' I said.

'To be photographed and fingerprinted again,' Phil explained.

456

'You know,' Dick said, 'by the time they get through with you, they make you feel like a criminal.'

After three sets of fingerprints were taken of each of us in the Criminal Courts Building, there was another inexplicable delay. Detectives popped in and out, and once Leonard Newman of the D.A.'s office appeared. All seemed worried and I asked Maury what the problem was.

'They've got to take the mug shots soon, before the photographer closes up shop.'

'What happens if he closes up?'

'What happens is that you and Edith and Dick spend the night in The Tombs – in jail.'

It came home to me in full strength: *I was going to jail.* It gave me a sick feeling in the pit of my stomach – and the feeling did not go away as we crossed the street and entered The Tombs.

Down iron stairs; past brownish-yellow tiled walls; iron bars; a green corridor whose walls were covered with graffiti. 'You should see this place after night court,' said the detective at my side. 'Packed end to end with whores and pimps, drunks puking on each other. You guys are getting the VIP treatment.'

Edith was first to be photographed. As the assistant hung the number under her chin and turned her face to the left, Dick pointed to a large 500-pound scale standing against the wall.

'Who the hell could weigh five hundred pounds?' he asked.

I had my revenge then for his remark about clawing the walls in prison to keep your nails trimmed. 'Your cellmate at Riker's Island,' I said. 'The one who sleeps in the upper bunk. They've got him all picked out for you. He hates Jews, he's queer, and he farts all night.'

An article appeared in that day's *New York Daily News* speculating that if we were convicted of all the counts with which we were charged, I could get something over a hundred years. Dick said: 'Well, I'll take my twenty-five percent, as always. That way you'll only have to do seventy-five years in Danbury or Allanwood. If you eat your vitamins regularly and take plenty of exercise and fresh air, you'll still be in good shape when you get out – and you'll only be a hundred and fifteen years old. I'll . . .' he broke off, unable to go on, and tears filled his eyes. 'Oh, God,' I heard him murmur.

On Monday, March 13th, we pleaded guilty in both the Federal and State courts. That evening the manager of the El Quixote Restaurant, next door to the Chelsea, where we had occasionally dined during the past weeks when we were sick of TV dinners and the confinement of the hotel room, left a bottle of Spanish white Rioja wine outside the door to my room. We put it on ice and drank it at midnight. The taste reminded us instantly of Ibiza: the hot windswept summers at the Salinas, the rainy autumns, the cold winter nights when we had sat by the fire with the children while Eugen munched fresh-cut apple in her cage, the springs when the almond blossoms lay like snow across the green fields and my boat was hauled up on the slip at the Club Naútico to be ready for the first sunny breeze of May. It was far away – too far away. What price idiocy? My reputation as a writer was crippled; I was known as a liar and a con man; I had achieved – and hardly by design – not fame but notoriety. I owed, with Dick and Edith, well over $1.5 million to McGraw-Hill, the IRS, and our lawyers.

The year of the hoax seemed a strangely dim memory. In what lifetime had it happened? In whose lifetime? And why? The children were asleep, Nedsky moving about restlessly in his bed, Barney rocking in his crib. Edith finished the last of the wine and began to cry softly, and there was no way to comfort her.

I walked Dick back to his room at the end of the hall. We were three months away from a prison sentence –

three months that would certainly be a form of purgatory. Living with that threat hanging over our heads would be like living with an amputated arm or leg. The phantom ache of my missing freedom already nagged at me, like the phantom ache of the missing limb. Freedom – that most elusive and abused of abstractions – had suddenly become as palpable as the lump in my throat when I contemplated what we had done in the past and what awaited us in the future.

'Sorry,' I said to Dick, in the hallway.

He understood. 'Don't be a damn fool,' he said. 'You didn't con *me*. I knew what I was getting into . . . I think. And I take the responsibility for my own actions.'

'Knowing what you know now, would you do it again?'

He was silent for a long moment. 'It was an interesting experience,' he said, 'but I could have done without it. And you? Would you do it again?'

'Never. I've lost too much.' Then I managed a slight smile. 'But I had a crazy idea this morning, standing there in court. Listen to this. When we get out of jail and I finish my novel, we go down to Argentina. We take a trip back into the jungle, or the pampas, and one day . . .'

'I'm ahead of you,' Dick said, his red-rimmed eyes already sparkling. 'I had the same idea. We meet this very old man, white-haired with a little white mustache, and we get to drinking, and become friendly, and he says, "Ah! You're the men who wrote the autobiography of my old friend Howard. I am getting very old, Clifford, and *ach du lieber*, it is time I, too, finally told the true story of my life." And you say: "Well, Adolf . . ."'

We both tried to laugh; but it was difficult.

On the morning of June 16, 1972, before United States District Judge John M. Cannella of the Southern District of New York, Clifford Irving was sentenced to two-and-a-half years' imprisonment. He spent seventeen months in three federal prisons, including two stays in solitary confinement, before he was paroled and released on February 14, 1974.

Judge Joseph Martinis of New York State sentenced Richard Suskind to six months' imprisonment, and with time off for good behavior he served a total of five months.

Edith Irving received from Judge Cannella a sentence of two years, all but two months of which were suspended; she served those two months in Nassau County Jail, near New York City. Swiss charges against her were not dropped, as previously promised, and in March 1973, despite the prosecutor's recommendation that she not be incarcerated, a Swiss tribunal in Zurich sentenced her to two years' imprisonment. On May 5, 1974, she was finally paroled and released.

Howard Hughes died on April 5, 1976, in a Lear jet en route from Acapulco, Mexico to Houston, Texas.

The Autobiography of Howard Hughes, by Clifford Irving and Richard Suskind, has never been published.

Q AND A – THE HOAX,
Clifford Irving

1) How do you feel that your time in prison has changed you?
I learned to eat a meal with a spoon. I learned to cook a stolen steak on a roll of burning toilet paper. I learned how to live with and like black men. I learned to distrust government officials and men in uniform even more so than before. I doubt that the experience changed my nature – it just brought out some of the hard edges in me. It was a time to develop survival techniques, and I did. I grew tougher. And, paradoxically, perhaps more compassionate.

2) The events leading up to *The Hoax* seemed to be peppered with strange coincidences – looking back do you feel to an extent that you were pawns of fate?
I don't believe in coincidence and I don't believe in fate other than as a device for Greek dramatists. The events happened because we made them happen. I felt godlike during this period. In retrospect, that's ridiculous . . . but no less true for being ridiculous.

461

3) When writing *The Hoax* did you find it hard putting voices to the people you have loved or known well and retelling their participation in your scam without hurting them?

Not at all, because if I love someone and write about them, the love shows clearly. And, if I told the truth, and I did, it couldn't possibly hurt anyone, since the truth – as best we can imagine it – is always liberating.

4) Do you feel it is important for a book such as yours to be given a wider audience by translating it into a film?

It will be amusing for moviegoers and readers to compare the book to the movie. In my view the book and the movie have practically nothing in common, so there is no genuine 'translation'. Nevertheless, if somehow the movie encourages intelligent people to read this edition of *The Hoax* and also to read my new novel, *I Remember Amnesia* and the *Autobiography of Howard Hughes*, arguably, at present, the most famous unpublished book of the 20th century, as well as other good novels of mine, I'll be delighted. But my ego is not inflated enough to think that that's 'important'.

5) Before embarking on the hoax you spoke of 'deliberately projecting an air of contentment' that in reality you felt you hadn't yet attained. Have you found that contentment now?

Yes, for the most part I've found it. I'm happily mated to a beautiful, caring, witty Australian woman who is also a superb cook, and for an old dog my health is good. I live half the year on a beach in Mexico and the rest in the snow-capped mountains of Colorado – terrestrial heavens. I know how to live extremely well without being rich and without the curse of ambition riding my back. I work hard. I love to write and paint and eat good food with my friends and sleep on a big firm bed and do yoga and hike on grass and swim in cool clear water.

I did say 'for the most part'. That's because I don't choose to incur the wrath of the gods, and also because until I find out whether time really exists and whether there is any more to human existence than perception and attitude, I will not be truly, fully, totally content. I'll always feel prodded to expand my limited knowledge. And I don't mind that at all.

A SELECTED LIST OF FINE WRITING
AVAILABLE FROM CORGI AND BLACK SWAN

THE PRICES SHOWN BELOW WERE CORRECT AT THE TIME OF GOING TO PRESS. HOWEVER TRANSWORLD PUBLISHERS RESERVE THE RIGHT TO SHOW NEW RETAIL PRICES ON COVERS WHICH MAY DIFFER FROM THOSE PREVIOUSLY ADVERTISED IN THE TEXT OR ELSEWHERE.

All Transworld titles are available by post from:
Bookpost, PO Box 29, Douglas, Isle of Man IM99 1BQ
Credit cards accepted. Please telephone +44(0)1624 836000, fax +44(0)1624 837033,
Internet http://www.bookpost.co.uk or
e-mail: bookshop@enterprise.net for details.
Free postage and packing in the UK.
Overseas customers allow £2 per book (paperbacks) and £3 per book (hardback).